ROMANIA

VERSUS

THE UNITED STATES

THE INSTITUTE FOR THE STUDY OF DIPLOMACY,
an integral part of the Georgetown University School
of Foreign Service, concentrates on increasing
knowledge of the dynamics of diplomacy and its pivotal
role in international peacemaking. The Institute's
programs of research, publications, and public affairs
draw upon scholars and practitioners for insights useful
in the study and conduct of international relations.

ROMANIA

VERSUS

THE UNITED STATES

Diplomacy of the Absurd,
1985–1989

ROGER KIRK & MIRCEA RACEANU

An Institute for the Study of Diplomacy Book

St. Martin's Press
New York

First published in the United States of America 1994

Printed in the United States of America

ISBN 0-312-12059-1

Library of Congress Cataloging-in-Publication Data

Kirk, Roger
    Romania versus the United States : diplomacy of the absurd,
  1985-1989 / Roger Kirk and Mircea Raceanu.
      p. cm.
    "An Institute for the Study of Diplomacy book."
    Includes bibliographical references and index.
    ISBN 0-312-12059-1
    1. United States—Foreign relations—Romania. 2. Romania—Foreign
  relations—United States. I. Raceanu, Mircea. II. Title.
  E183.8.R8K56 1994
  327.730498'09'048—dc20   93-44702
                                                                    CIP

Interior Design by Digital Type & Design

To those who gave their lives

in December 1989

for freedom in Romania

Contents

APPENDICES

Preface

In November 1985 Roger Kirk assumed his appointment as U.S. ambassador to Romania, where he served until July 1989. As a career officer in the Foreign Service of the United States, he had also served, among other postings, in the U.S. embassy in Moscow, as ambassador to Somalia, and as ambassador to the United Nations organizations in Vienna.

Mircea Raceanu was a Romanian career diplomat who had been deeply involved since 1959 in U.S.–Romanian relations, at both the Romanian Foreign Ministry in Bucharest and the Romanian embassy in Washington. He was the ministry's leading expert on the United States. During most of the period covered in this book, he was acting deputy director of the Romanian Foreign Ministry's Americas directorate and head of the department of U.S. and Canadian affairs within the directorate. Raceanu's mother and stepfather were early members of the Romanian Communist Party and had known the Romanian leaders, including President Nicolae Ceauşescu, for many years.

In January 1989, the Romanian authorities arrested Raceanu and accused him of being an American spy. On July 21, 1989, a military court convicted him and condemned him to death, but Ceauşescu's downfall in December 1989 led to Raceanu's release from prison. His open criticism of the post-Ceauşescu government, particularly at a May 1, 1990, rally at University Square in downtown Bucharest, earned him the enmity of the Romanian authorities. After two attempts on his life, he considered it wise to leave Romania for the United States with his family in the early summer of 1990.

ON SOURCES

We, the authors—sometimes one, sometimes both of us—took part in virtually all of the events and meetings we describe in this book. Where we were not eyewitnesses, we identify the participants who told us at the time what took place. We drew extensively on this personal experience in writing the book.

In addition, Kirk had full access to the classified State Department files on the period of his ambassadorship and to all communications between the embassy in Bucharest and the Department of State during that time.

These are the primary written source materials for the book. Although they remain classified for the most part, Kirk was able to obtain declassification of key letters to the Romanians from the U.S. president and secretary of state as well as President Ceauşescu's letters to Reagan in reply. The texts of these letters are in the appendices to this work, as are two key public statements.

We have also drawn on our notes and personal letters written at the time of the events described and on relevant public papers, congressional documents, books, and periodicals published in both countries. We footnote these in the text when we draw from them a specific quote, fact, or judgment.

ACKNOWLEDGEMENTS

We would like to express our appreciation to the Department of State for access to files, search and copying assistance, and classification review of the manuscript. We would also like to thank the Institute for the Study of Diplomacy (ISD) of the Georgetown University School of Foreign Service, as well as the United States Institute of Peace, for their support of this project. We owe particular gratitude to Margery Boichel Thompson, ISD's director of publications, for her editorial advice and support, as well as to Professor Dinu Giurescu, New York Times correspondent David Binder, and Dr. Ernest Latham for their review and comments. The views in the study are, of course, our own and do not represent those of the Department of State or of any other person or institution.

Prologue

We authors were the two chief actors on opposite sides of the U.S.-Romanian dialogue in Bucharest from mid-1985 to mid-l989, the last years of Nicolae Ceauşescu's dictatorship. In this book we explore, from our respective vantage points in Bucharest, the attempts of the United States and Romanian governments to communicate with each other—and to influence each other's behavior—during a period in which relations between the two countries deteriorated markedly. We also reflect more generally on problems that arise in relations between very different and hostile states.

In this case, we examine the diplomatic initiatives each government took, the motivations behind them, and what they were intended to achieve. Because we were working on different sides of the table, we can also describe how one government's initiative was perceived by the other, often very differently from its intended effect. The structure of the book, however, is essentially chronological. Though its focus is on the bilateral relationship, we also describe the internal situation in Romania and general East European developments as they affected the dialogue between the United States and Romania.

The first chapter gives a brief survey of U.S.-Romanian relations before mid-1985, touching very lightly on the historical background and giving more detail as the time of the main events approaches. The next chapters carry the story through the U.S. high-level attempts, in 1985 and 1986, to convince the Romanian leadership that the "special relationship" between the two countries was under threat due to Romania's human rights situation. Our story then moves from the increasing U.S. emphasis on human rights and the resulting U.S. alienation from Romania in 1987 to the February 1988 Romanian renunciation of most-favored-nation tariff treatment (MFN), the very symbol of the special U.S.-Romanian relationship.

We explore in some detail Ceauşescu's apparent belief that the United States needed Romania so badly that it would grant him MFN status without the conditions mandated by U.S. law. We chronicle his attempts to persuade the United States of this and the American effort to convince him this was impossible, on legal as well as political grounds.

We then describe the deterioration in U.S.-Romanian relations. As repression in Romania intensified, reform was spreading in the Soviet

Union and Eastern Europe, leaving Ceauşescu a virtual international pariah by the middle of 1989.

We do not seek to reach a judgment on the effectiveness of U.S. policy during the 1980s, in part because it is too soon after the fact and in part because we would like to leave that to the reader. We ourselves, it is only fair to say, are divided as to whether it was wise for the United States to have maintained its relationship with Romania for so long into the Ceauşescu regime and in particular for it to have extended MFN status to Romania until 1988.

Raceanu considers that except for U.S. assistance to Yugoslavia, U.S. support of the Ceauşescu regime in Romania, including its granting of MFN, was America's worst political and economic investment in the countries of Eastern Europe. Ceauşescu's independence in foreign policy, which was the basis for granting MFN, did not cause a rupture within the Soviet bloc, nor was it accompanied by internal reforms in Romania. By the late 1980s, in fact, Romania found itself not only isolated internationally but also suffering, under Ceauşescu's dictatorship, the most oppressive and inhuman regime in its corner of the world.

Kirk, on the other hand, feels that the benefits the United States gained from MFN—the continuing emigration to the United States of 2,000 to 3,000 Romanians a year, the resolution of individual cases of imprisonment and persecution, and some tempering of Ceauşescu's interference with the practice of non-Orthodox religions—were worth the benefits Ceauşescu derived from Romania's MFN status.

The reader is invited to reach his or her own judgment after perusing the evidence in our book.

Our final chapter reviews the lessons to be learned about communication between hostile governments, especially when one government is authoritarian and the other is not. It is our hope that this account will be useful as primary source material and shed light on the history and politics of U.S.-Romanian relations during the period.

NOTE: Because both of us were players in the story, we abandon the first person plural for the third person singular when writing of our own roles in the chapters that follow.

▼ 1 ▼

Setting the Stage

Romania was the darling of the United States among the communist Warsaw Pact members for almost twenty years, from the mid-1960s to the early 1980s. By 1989, it had sunk to last place among those countries in U.S. eyes. The reasons for this change included increased repression in Romania, reform in the Soviet Union and Eastern Europe, and shifting priorities in the U.S. approach to the relationship. Fundamental misunderstandings and failures of communication also played a role. A brief recapitulation of the history of U.S.-Romanian relations in the period before mid-1985 will help set the stage for the events described in succeeding chapters.

The United States established consular and then diplomatic relations with Romania soon after that country came out from under Turkish rule in the 1860s. Bilateral discussions in the period before World War II focused largely on commercial questions. As a harbinger of things to come, however, they also covered U.S. concern over Romania's treatment of its minority populations, especially its Jewish minority, and Romanian apprehension over manpower losses caused by emigration to the United States.

Romania allied itself with Nazi Germany in November 1940 and declared war on the United States on December 12, 1941. It contributed forces to the German effort against the Soviet Union but formally switched to the Allied side in August 1944. Soviet forces occupied Romania shortly afterward, facilitating the early formation of a communist-front government. The United States reestablished diplomatic ties with Bucharest in 1947 but treated Romania as a typical Soviet satellite. Relations in the 1940s and 1950s remained sparse and cold.

The thoroughly communist Romanian government, while recognizing that it owed its accession to office, and indeed its retention of power, to the Soviet Union, nevertheless resented Soviet domination. So, too, did the Romanian people. Because their language is Latin-based, not Slavic, they considered themselves a Latin nation and resented being dominated by Russians and Russian communism.

Romania has had a long history of difficulty with its big neighbor. In 1812, Tsarist Russia annexed Bessarabia, a traditional part of the Romanian lands. Romania recovered Bessarabia in the post–World War I peace settlement, but the Soviet Union regained it in 1940 and kept it after World War II. In 1940, the Soviet Union also gained Bukovina, a strip of traditionally Romanian territory that Romania had recovered from Austria by the Treaty of St. Germain in 1919.

Soviet forces occupied Romania in 1944 and stayed for more than a decade. The Soviets behaved particularly badly during the "liberation" phase, raping, shooting, and stealing anything they could move, thus reinforcing the low opinion Romanians already had of Russians. Following World War II, the Soviets demanded and received extensive reparations from Romania on the grounds that Romania had been allied with Germany during most of the war.

In the 1940s and early 1950s, Romania's communist leaders, like most of their counterparts in Eastern Europe, subordinated national interests to those of the Soviet Union. After Stalin's death in 1953, however, and especially after Khrushchev's 1956 denunciation of Stalin and his ways, the Romanian communist leaders took a variety of quiet measures to reduce Soviet control of Romanian life. In 1958 they finally succeeded in obtaining the withdrawal of Soviet troops from Romania, in good part because Moscow had full confidence in the Romanian leaders' willingness and ability to keep their regime communist. Indeed, Romania remained very much a communist state and a part of the Soviet bloc after the troop withdrawal, although it began to show increasingly public signs of eagerness for good relations and trade with the West.

In March 1960 the United States and Romania signed an accord settling their mutual financial claims resulting from nationalization of Americans' property by the postwar communist regime. In December the two countries signed an agreement on cultural and technical exchanges. The major breakthrough in relations came in the spring of 1964 (before Nicolae Ceauşescu's rise to power in the mid-1960s). A plenum of the Central Committee of the Romanian Communist Party in April 1964 publicly affirmed Romania's determination to be an independent socialist state and declared Romania's neutrality in the bitter Sino-Soviet dispute. The Central Committee's statement also affirmed Romania's eagerness to trade with all states, no matter what their social system.[1]

Washington warmly welcomed the Central Committee's statements. Subsequent U.S.-Romanian discussions resulted in agreement, inter alia, to raise diplomatic relations to the ambassadorial level, to simplify U.S. issuance of licenses for the export of certain classes of products to Romania, and to permit the extension of short-term credits to Romania through the U.S. Export-Import Bank. Perhaps most important, the discussions signaled the desire of both sides to put their relations on a new and friendlier footing, one that contrasted with U.S. relations with most other East European countries at the time.[2] American preoccupation with the Vietnam War slowed the development of U.S.-Romanian relations in the years immediately following, even though Romania served as a channel between Washington and Hanoi in 1965–1967 and President Lyndon Johnson himself received Romanian prime minister Ion Gheorghe Maurer in June 1967.

Relations between the United States and Romania took a qualitative leap forward after the accession of Richard Nixon to the U.S. presidency in 1969. Indeed the Nixon and Ford terms, 1969 to 1977, mark the period of closest bilateral relations. Several Romanian actions in the 1967–1968 period laid the foundation for this. Romania demonstrated its independence from Moscow in a way very pleasing to the United States by establishing diplomatic relations with West Germany in early 1967 and by refusing to break diplomatic relations with Israel in the aftermath of the Arab-Israeli war later that year (in contrast to Romania's Warsaw Pact allies).

In March 1967, in a move that was perhaps his most important from the point of view of subsequent relations with the Nixon administration, Ceaușescu organized a first-class protocol reception in Bucharest for ex-Vice President Nixon, then at a low ebb in his fortunes in the United States. Romania's attitude toward Nixon's trip was in marked contrast to that of the Soviets, who treated him as a private citizen, and of the Poles, who refused him entry. Nixon never forgot Ceaușescu's gesture.

In August 1968, Ceaușescu refused to join other Warsaw Pact nations in invading Czechoslovakia. In the days before the invasion, he demonstratively visited Prague and signed a treaty of friendship, cooperation, and mutual assistance with the Czechs. When the invasion took place, he publicly and forcefully condemned it and announced the immediate mobilization of his people to defend against any similar action against his country. Furthermore, he had the Romanian parliament pass a law stating that the Warsaw Pact could not hold ground-force maneuvers on Romanian soil without the express permission of the parliament. No such maneuvers took place for the remainder of Ceauşescu's regime, a fact the U.S. government noted and applauded. In the months following the invasion of Czechoslovakia, Ceauşescu allowed some relaxation of internal controls, thereby gaining a considerable measure of support in popular and intellectual circles in Romania and abroad.

A series of top-level visits between Bucharest and Washington after Nixon's accession to the presidency in 1969 symbolized the new relationship. President Nixon visited Bucharest in August 1969 and received Ceauşescu in the United States in 1970 and 1973. During the 1973 meeting, the two presidents signed a joint statement that called for development of relations on the basis of equality, respect for sovereignty, independence, noninterference in domestic affairs, juridical equality, mutual advantage, and refraining from the threat or use of force.[3] In later years, Ceauşescu constantly cited these principles when he rejected U.S. human rights complaints as "interference" in Romania's internal affairs. President Ford welcomed Ceauşescu in June 1975 and visited Romania in August of that year. The respective secretaries of state, ministers of foreign affairs, and several other cabinet members visited each other's capitals virtually every year during the Nixon-Ford presidencies.

Much of the relationship consisted only of public displays of friendship, but there was some substance in it as well. The Romanian government had, for example, been useful to the Nixon administration as a confidential channel between Washington and Beijing in the period just before Henry Kissinger's 1969 visit to China. The two countries signed numerous economic and cultural agreements. Romania joined such international institutions as the General Agreement on Tariffs and Trade (GATT), the International Monetary Fund (IMF), and the World Bank (IBRD), and was widely welcomed in the West as the maverick of the Warsaw Pact.

U.S.-Romanian trade increased to somewhat over $400 million by 1974, but its growth was handicapped by Romania's lack of most-favored-nation tariff treatment (MFN).[4] U.S. extension of MFN status to Romania, first granted in 1975, was to become the symbol of the special relationship between the two countries and the most important substantive concession to Romania by the Nixon and Ford administrations.

Most-favored-nation trade status provides that the tariffs a country levies on imports of another nation's goods will be no more onerous than those it levies against imports from other nations. The United States traditionally grants most-favored-nation treatment to virtually all of its trading partners, and other nations do the same. However, the United States had withdrawn MFN status from Romania and other communist-dominated countries in June 1951.

It was only in early 1975 that Congress, in passing the Trade Act of 1974, finally permitted the president to extend MFN to communist countries. Section 402 of this act, referred to as the Jackson-Vanik amendment, prohibited extension of MFN to any nonmarket-economy country, such as Romania, that denied its citizens the right or opportunity to emigrate, or imposed more than a nominal tax or charge on doing so.

Section 402 also provided, however, that the president could waive this provision if he found that such a waiver would "substantially promote the objectives of freedom of emigration" and if he had received "assurances that the emigration practices of that country would henceforth lead substantially to the achievement of the objectives of freedom of emigration." The initial 18-month waiver could be renewed for 12-month periods by the president, but either house of Congress could reverse the presidential determination by passing a resolution of disapproval within 90 days of being informed of his decision.[5] This annual determination process was to be a key factor in U.S.-Romanian relations in the 1980s.

The sponsors of the trade act and the Jackson-Vanik amendment had in mind the Soviet Union primarily, but Romania moved quickly to take advantage of the legislation's provisions. After prolonged negotiations, the United States and Romania agreed on a formula whereby Ceauşescu gave an oral "assurance" to President Ford that he would abide by his 1973 joint statement with President Nixon to the effect that both countries would "contribute to the solution of humanitarian problems on the basis of mutual confidence and goodwill."[6] The U.S. side accepted this indirect reference as the "assurance" on freedom of emigration called for by the Jackson-Vanik amendment, and Ford made the necessary "determination" to that effect. The fact that the 1975 agreement mutually extending MFN contained no written Romanian commitment on emigration was one basis (albeit a specious one) for Ceauşescu's assertion in later years that there were "no conditions" on MFN for Romania.

Congress approved the entire Romanian trade package in late July 1975, and the new MFN duties went into effect on January 3, 1976. Partly as a result of these lower duties, Romania's exports to the United States nearly doubled, from $133 million to $233 million, between 1975 and 1977. By 1985 they totaled over $900 million. MFN status also made Romania eligible for credits from the U.S. Export-Import Bank.[7]

The value of MFN was as much symbolic as practical, however. It put Romania—together, at various times, with Poland, China, and Hungary—in a special class of communist states with regard to relations with the United States. As the flow of high-level visits between the two countries slackened after the late 1970s, MFN became the primary symbol of the "special relationship" Romania enjoyed with Washington, which President Ceauşescu valued highly.

Largely for this reason, the annual renewal of MFN became the U.S. administration's principal tool for influencing Romanian behavior. The Jackson-Vanik amendment specifically tied MFN to emigration, and the United States used this fact to persuade Romania to grant emigration permission to over 180,000 persons from 1975 to 1988, when Romania's MFN status terminated.[8] By that time, the United States had begun increasingly tying extension of MFN to Romanian action on other human rights issues of particular U.S. concern, including religious freedoms, release of imprisoned dissidents, and even the economic deprivation of the Romanian people.

The Trade Act of 1974 also opened the way for the U.S. administration to extend the generalized system of tariff preferences for developing countries (GSP) to those communist countries that were members of the International Monetary Fund and the General Agreement on Tariffs and Trade, that were not controlled by international communism, and that enjoyed MFN status. The GSP made it legal for the United States to levy lower tariffs on certain types of imports from developing countries.

Romania fell within the definition of a developing country for these purposes. The U.S. government decided Romania's independence from Moscow was sufficient to qualify as a country not controlled by international communism. Romania was also a party to GATT and to the IMF. Once Romania received MFN, therefore, it became eligible for GSP, and the United States gave it such status for a period of ten years starting January 1, 1976.[9]

While the relationship between the United States and Romania was basically good during the Nixon-Ford years, it was not without its frictions. Ceauşescu's modest internal liberalization of the late 1960s was short-lived, and continuing human rights abuses aroused indignation in some congressional circles.

With the coming of the Carter administration in 1977, Romania was concerned that human rights would take a more prominent part in U.S. foreign policy and feared that the United States would be reluctant to support a government grossly violating such rights. Ceauşescu therefore sent a personal envoy to Washington early on to assure the new U.S. president that Romania shared his concern over human rights. Carter and his advisers welcomed the envoy's assurances that Romania would increase emigration to the United States in family reunification cases. They also valued Romania's relative independence from Moscow.

Carter thus continued the "special relationship" with Romania, and each year recommended extending MFN. In 1978 trade between the two countries topped $600 million. Carter received Ceauşescu for a state visit in April 1978, and other high-level U.S.-Romanian visits continued to occur, albeit at a somewhat reduced rate from the intense pace of the Nixon-Ford administrations. Relations received another boost when Ceauşescu's representative at the United Nations failed to join his Warsaw Pact colleagues in voting against the January 1980 U.N. resolution condemning the Soviet invasion of Afghanistan the previous month.[10]

Since the December 1989 revolution, reports have come out to the effect that Romania was covertly selling Soviet military equipment to the United States and that the Ceauşescu family was directly involved. Neither Kirk nor Raceanu had any personal knowledge of these alleged sales, which were reportedly concentrated in the late 1970s, before Kirk's appointment as ambassador. In a possibly related development, an American businessman of Czech origin whom Raceanu received in the early 1980s at the request of the Ministry of Foreign Trade told Raceanu he had for years been involved in arms deals with Romania. Raceanu never received any reactions to his written report on the conversation.

The Romanians welcomed the accession of Ronald Reagan to the White House in 1981. The real progress in U.S.-Romanian relations had come under Republican presidents, and the Romanians thought Reagan would give less emphasis to human rights than had Carter. Relations between the two countries, in fact, went relatively well during the early years of the Reagan administration.

Congress, however, began showing increasing concern over human rights and emigration issues. Although it did not veto Reagan's renewals of MFN in 1981 and 1982, it heard considerable testimony about Romania's human rights violations, particularly offenses against Protestants and dissident Romanian Orthodox clergy and discrimination against the Hungarian minority (some 1.5 to 2 million of Romania's total population of some 23 million).

A major problem arose when Romania announced in October 1982 that it would require emigrants to pay the Romanian state a sum in hard currency equivalent to the cost of their higher education.[11] This decree was in direct violation of the sections of the Jackson-Vanik amendment that denied MFN to any country that imposed more than a nominal charge or tax on emigrants.

After months of quiet but fruitless negotiations, Reagan announced in March 1983 that he would terminate Romania's MFN status and other benefits as of June 30, 1983, if the education tax remained in effect on that date.[12] After two more months of intensive discussions, the Romanian government agreed not to impose the tax, even though it would keep the decree on the books. The agreement was finalized during Foreign Minister Ştefan Andrei's visit to Washington in late May.

On June 1, 1983, Reagan and Ceauşescu exchanged confidential letters on the subject. Ceauşescu stated that he would not apply the tax, a commitment he kept until the end of his rule. Reagan reiterated his support for Ceauşescu's policy of independence, said he would extend MFN once again, and promised that the United States would examine the possibility of providing MFN to Romania on a multiyear basis.

Mircea Raceanu took part in these negotiations and in drafting the Romanian letter to Reagan. He also accompanied Foreign Minister Andrei on his trip to Washington. Upon Raceanu's arrival in Bucharest a few days after Andrei's return, the minister told him U.S. officials were insisting that Romania show goodwill by issuing some emigration permissions before June 3, when the White House was scheduled to send the president's favorable determination on MFN renewal to Congress. Andrei was to see Ceauşescu on the subject that afternoon and asked Raceanu to select several names for Ceauşescu's approval from the lists of those who had applied for emigration.

Realizing that there would not be enough time for Andrei to have the names checked with the Securitate (the regime's security forces) before his meeting with Ceauşescu, Raceanu decided to include in the list of about 20 families the names of a close friend and his family, whose emigration the Securitate had consistently blocked. He at first thought to put his friend's family toward the end of the list, so as not to draw attention to them, but then decided to put them near the top in case Ceauşescu did not approve the entire list. Indeed, when Andrei presented the list to Ceauşescu, the dictator drew a line below the first few families, saying, "That is enough to prove our goodwill to the Americans." As it happened, the line was just below Raceanu's friend's family, and they soon went off to America. Such is the way human fate was determined in the Ceauşescu dictatorship.

Reagan announced another year's extension of MFN for Romania on June 3, 1983, and Congress did not overrule his decision.[13] Romania's ballooning foreign debt, however, now added another irritant to relations with the United States. By 1982 this debt had exceeded $11 billion, and the IMF was giving Ceauşescu a lot of advice on how to cope with it and get his economy moving.

Ceauşescu insisted he would take care of the problem himself and proceeded to initiate a debt reduction program. His approach eventually succeeded in eliminating the debt, but at the cost of substantially lowering the Romanian population's standard of living through draconian limits on imports, including fuel, and the export of scarce foodstuffs. The suffering of the population under this program was an issue U.S. representatives would later raise with the Romanians. In the early years of the decade, however, the fall in U.S. exports to Romania and the growing imbalance in U.S.-Romanian trade were the principal U.S. complaints with the debt reduction program.

The Reagan administration signaled its continuing interest in the special relationship with Romania, and with the liberalizing regime in Hungary, by sending Vice President George Bush to visit the two countries in September 1983. The visit to Romania went well, even though Bush took the occasion to raise U.S. concerns on a variety of human rights issues.

In a speech in Vienna on September 21, 1983, Bush articulated the U.S. administration's approach to Eastern Europe. The administration, he said, would "differentiate" among the countries of Eastern Europe on the basis of the extent to which "countries pursue autonomous foreign policies, independent of Moscow's direction" and "to what degree they foster domestic liberalization—politically, economically, and in their respect for human rights." He added, in a passage Ceauşescu frequently cited, that the United States would "engage in closer political, economic, and cultural relations with those countries such as Hungary and Romania which assert greater openness or independence."[14]

It was clear the United States had singled out Romania on the basis of the independence of its foreign policy and Hungary on the basis of its openness. This policy of "differentiation" on two possible grounds was to guide the Reagan administration's approach to Eastern Europe for the next several years. It was what kept Romania in U.S. favor, despite internal repression, until Mikhail Gorbachev's changes in Soviet foreign policy and his loosening of Soviet control over the East

European countries made irrelevant the "independence" basis for differentiation.

Reagan recommended another year's extension of MFN for Romania in June 1984, and there was no move in Congress to deny it.[15] One reason was that Ceauşescu was enjoying much favorable publicity in the United States from his decision to send a team to participate in the 1984 Summer Olympics in Los Angeles while the Soviet Union and its other Warsaw Pact allies were boycotting the games. Another was Ceauşescu's release from prison of Father Gheorghe Calciu, a dissident Orthodox priest whose 1979 arrest had been the subject of congressional testimony in 1981 and a matter of continuing congressional and international concern ever since.

In spite of these positive signs, the U.S.-Romanian relationship began to sour in the second half of 1984. A year later it was in sufficiently bad shape to lead Reagan, Bush, and Secretary of State George Shultz to warn the Romanian leadership that they must take some action to meet U.S. human rights concerns if they were to preserve the special relationship with the United States. Furthermore, Ceauşescu was displaying heightened suspicion that U.S. criticism reflected a desire to weaken or even overthrow his regime, the U.S. trade balance with Romania was deteriorating, and reform was beginning to take shape in some other East European countries and in the Soviet Union.

Ceauşescu had long since abandoned the tentative liberalization of the late 1960s and was moving to mold Romania into his vision of a socialist society. This involved removing the remaining vestiges of private initiative and enterprise, increasing state control over all aspects of life, and remaking the Romanians into a homogeneous, socialist people. In part as a means to accomplish this, and in part as an end in itself, Ceauşescu increasingly concentrated power in his own hands and asserted his independence of any other influence, inside or outside the country. He tolerated no criticism and demanded more and more public and private adulation. He would not be deterred from his chosen course by the wishes of the population or the hardships it imposed upon them. If they would not follow his lead voluntarily, he would compel them to do so.

Ceauşescu's policy entailed extensive violation of what the West considered human rights. There was no freedom to criticize the regime or even to voice a personal opinion. The Securitate used a network of informers, rumored to include as many as one out of every three Romanians, to ferret out and censure any deviation.

The Securitate had carte blanche from Ceauşescu to preempt any threats to his power. It exercised extensive surveillance of private citizens—monitoring their contacts with foreigners, screening their mail, tapping their telephones, and in some cases breaking into their homes or offices. Romanians who owned typewriters had to provide the authorities with a sample of its type so the police could trace the producer of a subversive document through the typeface. The state encouraged children to report on their parents, brothers on their sisters. It subjected persons suspected of disloyalty to varied forms of harassment, including physical violence, arrest, and imprisonment. No one, not even those close to Ceauşescu and his family, felt secure in the company of others.

The atmosphere of paranoia grew as the state's control tightened and Ceauşescu became ever more imperious. He accumulated more and more offices for himself and for his family. In addition to being president of Romania, general secretary of the Romanian Communist Party, and supreme commander of the armed forces, Ceauşescu headed the Defense Council, the Supreme Council for Economic and Social Development, and the National Council of Working People. His wife, Elena, was a first deputy prime minister and a member of the five-to-seven person bureau of the party's top-level Political Executive Committee. She chaired the Party and State Cadres Commission responsible for the placement of high-level personnel and headed the councils dealing with culture, education, science, and technology.

Ceauşescu appointed other family members to critical party and government positions. He elevated his playboy son, Nicu Ceauşescu, to alternate member of the Political Executive Committee. He made one brother, Ilie Ceauşescu, deputy minister of defense and chief of the Higher Political Council of the army and appointed another, also named Nicolae Ceauşescu, as head of personnel in the Securitate under the name of Nicolae Calin. Ceauşescu's nepotism favored many other members of his family and was indeed unrivaled in Eastern Europe.

At the same time, the physical conditions of Romanian life became increasingly grim. The inefficiencies of state industry and the moves to squeeze out the remaining private marketing and farming operations worsened the people's economic situation. Lines to buy food became longer, and more goods disappeared from the stores altogether. Heat and electricity were short and would become more so. Pay dropped as managers withheld wages in retaliation for underfulfillment of impossibly high, centrally planned quotas. Many people lost their dwellings to an "urban reconstruction" program, which emphasized the erection of imposing buildings for government offices and modest, standardized living quarters for the population.

Ethnic minorities lost many opportunities to enjoy their own culture or to go to schools that taught in their own language. Though attendance at the Romanian Orthodox Church was possible, it was not advisable for anyone wishing to make a career in state service, which included most professional activity. Adherence to any other faith was even more suspect, and the practice of other than the fourteen authorized religions (Orthodox, Catholic, Muslim, Jewish, and several major Protestant denominations) was illegal and sometimes punished.

The authorities frowned on contact with foreigners. Even when they authorized it, they viewed it with suspicion, and many Romanians simply avoided it altogether to obviate the possibility of raising questions about their loyalty. Thus when Raceanu in the mid-1980s asked Emilian Manciur, head of the Foreign Ministry's culture and press section, why he never accepted invitations to the American embassy or to the American library, Mancur said he was "not so stupid as to walk barefoot on fire" by exposing himself at such functions to detailed Securitate observation and analysis of his behavior.

Meanwhile, the state bombarded the people with propaganda about how wonderful their life was and required them to come out to cheer Ceauşescu and his wife wherever the royal couple went. Ceauşescu's personality cult became more and more extreme, with continual praise for himself and his wife in all the media and obligatory ceremonies honoring and thanking them for all they had done for Romania. The media described Ceauşescu as the "guarantor" of the nation's independence and progress and a "visionary architect of the nation's future" whose "genial thought" was the source of all Romania's accomplishments.

These phenomena had been evident in Romania for some time. In the second half of the 1980s, however, they got worse, and the outside world, especially the United States, began to pay more attention to them. Western correspondents frequently wrote analytical or "human interest" stories about the economic deprivation of the Romanian people and their lack of freedom, both of which were increasingly apparent to any visitor as the 1980s progressed. The restrictions on religion, particularly on the fundamentalist Protestant faiths, were offensive to religious groups in the United States with influence in the Reagan administration. A vocal Hungarian community in the United States criticized the increasing discrimination against their fellow ethnics in Romania. Western preservationists were concerned at the toll urban reconstruction was taking on historic civic and religious buildings. The increasingly overweening Ceauşescu personality cult disgusted everyone.

As a result, congressional criticism of conditions in Romania built up in volume and force until it became a serious inhibition on the administration's freedom to pursue a "special relationship" with Romania. These increasing human rights concerns within the U.S. Congress and among the public played an important role in altering U.S. policy toward Romania and figured more and more prominently in official U.S. discussions with the Romanians.

Support for Romania within the U.S. business community was also dwindling. Because of the Romanian debt reduction program, imports from the United States fell drastically (from $720 million in 1980 to $246 million in 1984 and $207 million in 1985).[16] Increased internal Romanian police controls made doing business in that country more difficult. United States exporters became less interested in Romania as an actual and potential market. Lobbying by American businessmen for MFN for Romania lost much of its force in the mid-1980s, and the increasing U.S. trade deficit with Romania became a source of contention between the two countries. At the same time, Ceauşescu's need to acquire raw materials without spending hard currency led to a marked increase in his trade with the Soviet Union, worrying those in the United States who believed this would compromise his ability to pursue a relatively independent foreign policy.

Ceauşescu, as noted above, had looked for a marked improvement of relations with the passing of the Carter "human rights" administration and the coming to power of the Republicans, with whom he had had such luck in the 1970s. As succeeding pages will show, he was quite disappointed that the Reagan administration did not follow the path of its Republican predecessors. Eventually, he came to believe that Reagan was out to overthrow him for ideological reasons. Ceauşescu began to view U.S. human rights demands as part of a plot to undermine his entire regime and was thus increasingly reluctant to accommodate these demands. This stance only intensified the frustrations of Congress and the administration and further soured the relationship between the two nations.

The first stirrings of reform in Eastern Europe and the Soviet Union in the mid-1980s contrasted markedly with the trend in Romania. Ceauşescu viewed these reforms with great suspicion from the start and grew increasingly critical of them, at first privately and then publicly. By the late 1980s he was the most outspoken critic of Gorbachev's *perestroika* and *glasnost* campaigns.

As reform progressed in his neighborhood, Ceauşescu looked more and more out of place. Much of the East European old guard showed a readiness to compromise with the new generation of politicians, those willing to accommodate rising desires for democracy and a market economy; but Ceauşescu hung on to his old ideas. His differences from his Warsaw Pact allies became negative instead of positive in U.S. eyes and began to work not for him, but against him.

These factors were not as clear in 1984 and early 1985 as they later became, but there were definite warnings of trouble ahead. In late 1984 the Reagan administration, noting that the law governing the extension of tariff concessions to developing countries under the Generalized System of Preferences would expire in January 1987, asked Congress to renew this authority for another ten years. Congress did so, but added, over the administration's objections, a provision making the extension of GSP to any country contingent upon that country's granting "internationally recognized worker rights," including the rights of association and collective bargaining.[17] This was to lead to Romania's loss of GSP in 1987.

The heightened suspicion about the United States in high Romanian circles was leading to a steady reduction in the number of Romanian scholars going to the United States under existing bilateral exchange programs. Trips of this kind required the approval of Ceauşescu's wife, Elena, as chairperson of the National Committee for Science and Technology and first deputy prime minister responsible, inter alia, for the Ministry of Education. She deeply suspected U.S. intentions and feared the possible subversive effect of contact between Romanians and Americans. As the years went on, she was to work systematically, and largely successfully, for the reduction of all such exchanges.

In the middle of May 1985 U.S. ambassador to Bucharest David B. Funderburk completed his tour in Romania and departed. In a long interview in the *Washington Post* on May 15, he strongly criticized Ceauşescu and what he saw as the U.S. government's unduly friendly policy toward him. Coming from someone who had been the U.S. representative in Bucharest for over three years, his views influenced Congress and the public. The Romanian government was furious at Funderburk and gave instructions to its embassy to do all it could to discredit him and refute his allegations.[18]

On the other hand, Senator Robert Dole of Kansas, the Republican leader in the Senate, had a relatively successful visit to Romania at the end of May 1985. Senator Dole's wife, Elizabeth, who was serving at that time as U.S. secretary of transportation, accompanied her husband. Although the American side made it clear that Mrs. Dole was traveling in her private capacity of spouse and not as a cabinet member, Ceauşescu's office instructed the Ministry of Transportation to make a number of official appointments for her and told the Romanian press to include her name and title prominently in their reportage of the visit. Behind this lay Ceauşescu's conviction that any member of the cabinet, as a person appointed by and presumably close to the president, was far more important than a mere member of Congress, even one in Dole's position, and he wanted to honor such a person and be sure that Romanian and world public opinion noted her presence in Bucharest.

Ceauşescu personally assured Senator Dole that Romania wanted good relations and increased trade with the United States. In response to Dole's request, Ceauşescu said he would allow Father Gheorghe Calciu, the dissident Orthodox priest who had been released from prison in 1984, and Dorin Tudoran, a prominent dissident writer, to emigrate to the United States. Shortly after Dole's visit, Ceauşescu instructed the Romanian authorities to prepare the formalities to permit the two to leave, although he withheld final approval for their departure until later that summer.

Ceauşescu liked if at all possible to avoid the appearance of having given in to pressure, even when he had in fact done so. He was much more likely to make good on a concession some time after being asked than to act on the spot. As a result of the relatively forthcoming Romanian position Dole encountered, however, he gave a fairly upbeat report on his visit to his congressional colleagues in early July, a report that proved helpful to Romania in the Senate hearings on MFN later that month.[19]

Meanwhile, in early July 1985, Representatives Tony Hall of Ohio, Christopher Smith of New Jersey, and Frank Wolf of Virginia visited Romania to look into the state of human rights and religious freedoms in that country. They met with Protestant clergy, other religious figures, and numerous Romanian officials, but not with Ceauşescu. Although it had been the practice over the years for congressional delegations to have an audience with Ceauşescu, the Romanian bureaucracy recommended that he not receive the group in view of what the officials described as the delegation members' critical attitude toward Romania and their contacts with dissident and "anti-social" elements. Ceauşescu concurred and had Foreign Minister Andrei receive the group in his stead.

Andrei countered the group's arguments in some detail but assured them that he would consider their points and relay their concerns to Ceauşescu. In fact, however, the ministry's written report to Ceauşescu, drafted by Raceanu's department as instructed, played down the congressmen's criticisms and highlighted their more favorable, or merely polite, comments.

Ceauşescu also received misleading reports on the Romanian public's response to the congressional visit. Raceanu, who accompanied the delegation on its travels, learned of this firsthand. By telephone he reported to State Secretary for Foreign Affairs Aurel Duma in Bucharest that in Oradea, in western Romania, over 2,000 people had participated in a Baptist religious ceremony attended by the delegation. As Duma later told Raceanu, Ceauşescu launched into a tirade when Duma told him this news. He declared Duma ignorant of the facts and insisted that only a much smaller number had been present at the service. Clearly he had received a report from the Securitate minimizing the size of the crowd in an effort to downplay the importance of religion to a population the Securitate was supposed to control.

The congressional delegation, after returning to the United States, publicly criticized the situation in Romania.[20] Their account added considerable fuel to congressional and public doubts about President Reagan's policy of friendly relations with Romania and his June renewal of Romania's MFN privileges for another year.

State Department Counselor Edward Derwinski had visited Bucharest in June 1985 to discuss various problems that troubled the administration and that might cause difficulties later in congressional hearings that would consider whether to countermand the president's decision. Both President Ceauşescu and Foreign Minister Andrei received Derwinski. They knew he had been a member of Congress for many years, still had many friends on Capitol Hill, and was now a senior State Department official, comparable in rank to the assistant secretary in charge of all of Europe.

Derwinski raised religious and human rights problems and asked about the apparent discrimination against the Hungarian minority in Romania. The Romanians' replies to Derwinski on these points were polite but without concrete commitments. Derwinski did make progress, however, on the difficult situation facing Romanians who had received their government's permission to emigrate to the United States but were still awaiting U.S. permission.

The condition of these potential emigrants was indeed unfortunate. They normally lost their jobs, and usually their Romanian citizenship, as soon as they received their emigration passport from the Romanian authorities. As access to housing generally derived from a person's place of work, loss of job often meant loss of housing as well. These individuals also lost the right to purchase rationed food such as sugar and cooking oil, they became ineligible for state medical care, and their children could no longer go to school.

Between 2,000 and 3,000 persons were in this situation at any one time during the 1980s. Most had to wait several weeks or months for U.S. permission to immigrate, and some were ineligible under U.S. regulations, with no apparent prospects of getting to America.

Derwinski suggested that U.S. and Romanian officials work together to correct this situation, and the Romanians agreed. Negotiations between the two sides soon began and later that summer concluded with an agreement. The Romanians would give an individual they had decided to allow to emigrate a "notification" to that effect. This would have no effect on the individual's work or civil status, except that those in "sensitive" positions might have to move to comparable nonsensitive work. Armed with this notification, the individual could apply for an immigration visa at the U.S. embassy, which would inform the applicant when it eventually received authority to issue the visa. Only then would the individual obtain the actual emigration passport, with its consequent effect on employment, living quarters, and the like. Just as soon as the individual had completed these formalities and was ready to leave, the U.S. embassy would issue the visa.

The U.S. side wanted this agreement on emigration procedures in writing. The Romanians insisted that it remain only an oral understanding. To formalize it, they said, would create a precedent for their relations with other countries. A more important reason was that they did not want to record formally that they had modified their internal procedures to accommodate an outside power. The agreement worked reasonably well, but the U.S. desire to have it in writing was a subject of fruitless bilateral discussion for months to come.

Derwinski was the administration witness at the Senate hearings on MFN on July 23, 1985. On that occasion he was able to tell the senators that the emigration procedures problem was on the way to resolution. He was also able to say that the Calciu family, who had received permission to emigrate to the United States, would be leaving Romania shortly.[21] Ceauşescu, as noted above, had made a commitment to Senator Dole on this case in late May but had delayed giving final permission for Calciu's departure. Just before the Senate hearings began, the Romanian embassy in Washington sent a telegram to the Foreign Ministry in Bucharest saying that a large number of senators had indicated that they would oppose MFN renewal if the Romanians continued to hold Calciu. The embassy urged the ministry to take action before the hearings opened.

Ceauşescu now agreed to Calciu's emigration and gave instructions that his decision should be implemented at once. In their haste to carry out Ceauşescu's order, the Securitate, at Raceanu's request, even guided Calciu to the American embassy to get his immigration visa. The Romanian government was anxious, however, that Ceauşescu's action should appear to be a friendly gesture to Senator Dole and the administration, not a response to pressure from "hostile" elements in the Congress. The Foreign Ministry therefore instructed their embassy in Washington to give the news directly to Dole and Derwinski, emphasizing that the decision was a follow-up to Dole's conversation with the Romanian chief of state.

While the Senate hearings revealed progress on emigration, the issue linked to MFN by the Jackson-Vanik amendment, they also highlighted deep congressional concern over human rights in Romania and a growing tendency to link MFN to broader human rights issues. Thus some 19 senators sent a letter to Ceauşescu after the hearings expressing their concern over the human rights situation in Romania and stating that this raised questions in their minds about the desirability of MFN.[22] This identification of Romania's MFN with the whole gamut of human rights in that country was later to intensify, transforming the MFN dialogue in Congress and between the two governments into a general human rights discussion.

These developments in late 1984 and early 1985 set the stage for the deterioration of U.S.-Romanian relations in the ensuing four years.

▼2▼

The Cast of Characters and the First Act 1985

R oger Kirk's entry into the U.S.-Romanian dialogue came when he sat in on the meeting of Secretary of State George Shultz and Romanian Foreign Minister Ştefan Andrei during the 1985 United Nations General Assembly (UNGA) session in New York. It had been the custom for several years for the U.S. secretary of state to meet with the Romanian foreign minister at the UNGA as a mark of Romania's special place among East European nations and of its willingness to vote differently from the Soviet Union at the United Nations.

The meeting took place on September 26 in the offices of the U.S. delegation, down the street from the U.N. headquarters building. The secretary of state met with many foreign ministers during his few days in New York at the beginning of the UN General Assembly session each fall, and the U.S. delegation staff had worked out a standard procedure for funneling foreign visitors in and out on a tight schedule. In the lobby, a delegation officer met Andrei and his party, consisting of Raceanu and the Romanian ambassadors to the United States and the United Nations, and escorted them to a meeting room in the U.S. delegation suite. Assistant Secretary of State for European Affairs Rozanne Ridgway, Kirk, and a State Department note-taker joined them there.

Foreign Minister Andrei—a tall, rather imposing figure with a high forehead and lively but somewhat crafty eyes—struck Kirk in this first encounter as intelligent, confident, and smooth. Kirk's subsequent meetings with Andrei basically bore out this first impression, although Kirk was disappointed by Andrei's determined parroting of the Ceauşescu line even when Andrei surely knew it was absurd.

Secretary of State Shultz, accompanied by Assistant Secretary of State for Public Affairs Bernard Kalb, came into the meeting room a few moments after Andrei. Shultz and Andrei greeted each other warmly.

The two had met often and respected each other, though they represented two very different regimes.

Shultz, whose schedule was tight as always, quickly launched into his opening presentation. He spoke of U.S. concern regarding the treatment of ethnic minorities in Romania, the Romanian Protestants' need for Bibles, and U.S. interest in emigration permission for the wife and son of Napoleon Fodor, the former head of the Romanian commercial office in New York who had defected to the United States in 1982. Shultz said he wanted to help maintain the bilateral relationship but that progress on human rights issues was fundamental because these issues affected Romania's image in the United States.

The Fodor case was a sore point between the two governments and would remain so until Ceauşescu's downfall. After Fodor's defection in 1982, his wife had returned to Romania to bring Fodor's son to the United States, but the Romanian authorities refused to allow them to leave. Fodor's work in New York had won him many friends in the U.S. business community and in Congress, and he and they had been active since then in calling attention to the case.

The Romanians refused to budge. Their intransigence sprang from Ceauşescu himself, who had thought highly of Fodor and had personally selected him for the New York job in 1971. During Ceauşescu's visits to the United States, he always consulted Fodor on economic and trade matters. In Ceauşescu's eyes, therefore, Fodor's defection was a personal insult as well as a betrayal of the Romanian state.

Andrei responded initially in general terms to Shultz's presentation, emphasizing Romania's dedication to its independence and its rejection of any interference in its internal affairs. He said the United States should exercise restraint in its approach so as not to jeopardize the entire structure of the U.S.-Romanian relationship. Then, moving to the attack, Andrei expressed his surprise and displeasure at comments on Romania's treatment of its Hungarian minority made by the head of the U.S. delegation at a meeting of the Conference on Security and Cooperation in Europe (CSCE) in Ottawa a short while before.

Andrei then noted disapprovingly that some people in the United States were talking about the desirability of changing Romania's borders. While he did not specifically say so, he was referring to calls for returning to Hungary the region of Transylvania, in the northwestern part of Romania, which had a substantial ethnic Hungarian minority. Farfetched as border changes seemed in those days of Cold War immobility, the Romanian government was in fact very sensitive on this point.

Shultz replied that it was perfectly proper for U.S. representatives to talk about the rights and treatment of ethnic minorities, but he assured Andrei that the U.S. government accepted current European borders. The 30-minute meeting then turned to a brief discussion of world affairs, in which Shultz solicited Andrei's views on the international implications of Mikhail Gorbachev's accession to power. Andrei's response was not particularly enlightening, but he was pleased at being asked, a result that was one purpose of the question. The United States considered Andrei a useful interlocutor.

A construction engineer by training, Ştefan Andrei had played an important role in U.S.-Romanian relations for many years, both as foreign minister since 1978 and as head of the Central Committee Department for International Affairs for many years before that. Shortly after his 1985 U.S. visit he left the Foreign Ministry, but he remained interested in U.S.-Romanian relations and resumed his active involvement in those relations in October 1987, when he became deputy prime minister with responsibility for foreign trade.

Raceanu, who worked with Andrei for many years, notes that Andrei had an unusually quick mind. His thoughts ran faster than his words, and he would often leave a sentence half-finished when going on to the next one—making life exceedingly difficult for his interpreter (usually Raceanu). Similarly, Andrei grasped what others were saying before they had finished expressing their thought. He had an ability to get to the heart of a problem and focus on it, leaving less important aspects to his subordinates. He was willing to take initiatives and make decisions within the strict limits set by Ceauşescu. Although he himself had much experience, he did not hesitate to seek advice from experts and often took it. At the same time, he found it very hard to fire an incompetent. Raceanu found him an easy man to work for, one who took good care of his subordinates in the Byzantine atmosphere of the Ceauşescu court.

Andrei's principal weakness was his eagerness to maintain his position near the top of the Romanian hierarchy. Convinced that the socialist regime was the best for Romania and that Ceauşescu would remain at the head of it for the foreseeable future, Andrei identified himself and his own career with the dictator and continued to seek Ceauşescu's favor and do his bidding until the very end. Andrei enjoyed the good life and liked to receive presents. His reddish face and slightly dissipated look betrayed a fondness for fine drink and pretty women that limited his prospects for the highest posts in the Romanian hierarchy, as did the antipathy between Andrei's flamboyant actress-wife and the dowdy Elena Ceaușescu.

Andrei was a positive factor in the U.S.-Romanian relationship—or as much as he could be within the limits set by Ceaușescu's policies. He had a personal interest in the success of the U.S.-Romanian relationship, both because of his long association with it and because he seemed genuinely to believe it to be in his country's interest. He also knew how important the relationship was to Ceaușescu and therefore how useful his expertise was. During Andrei's period as foreign minister, he used to joke with American officials whom he met that he, not Raceanu, was the desk officer directly responsible for relations with the United States. Andrei's long familiarity with the United States gave him a relatively sophisticated, if far from perfect, insight—certainly better than that of most other Romanians—into the problems Romania faced within the American body politic. He had some sense as to how the American system worked, though even he did not really understand such matters as the limitations on the power of a U.S. president.

Despite his deference to Ceaușescu, Andrei was willing to speak more frankly to the dictator than were most other Romanian leaders. In the 1980s, in fact, Andrei probably represented the best Romanian channel for getting a U.S. message to Ceaușescu. Because of the importance he attached to the relationship with the United States and his willingness to take steps to further it, Andrei was the best person to approach to get action on a problem if it lay within his power to take such action.

At the same time, he suffered from the same limitations as all of Ceaușescu's advisers: total dependence on the favor of the First Family, the Securitate's suspicions about everyone's trustworthiness, the intrigues of peers jealous of his power and position, and the distorted picture of Romania and the world provided by the reports he and the rest of the leadership received from their subordinates. As late as the spring of 1988, Andrei was astonished when Raceanu told him that the United States was fed up with Ceaușescu.

Andrei made no effort to distance himself from the dictator, however, neither then nor even in November 1989, when Ceaușescu accused him of being simultaneously pro-Soviet and close to France. Andrei would pay for this continuing subservience to Ceaușescu: he was arrested after the tyrant's fall in December 1989, tried, and sentenced to 14 years' imprisonment. (He was released in 1993 and pardoned in March 1994.)[23]

After the September 1985 meeting with Shultz, Andrei told Raceanu he was surprised that Shultz had led off with human rights and had adopted such an "aggressive" tone on the subject. This was in fact the first time that Shultz had begun a conversation with Andrei by raising the subject of human rights. Andrei understood it as an early signal of the growing role of human rights in the U.S.-Romanian relationship and of how this could overshadow other issues.

That Romania was still accorded special treatment by the United States, however, was demonstrated when Vice President George Bush received Andrei at the White House on September 30, 1985. Except for Soviet Foreign Minister Eduard Shevardnadze, none of the other Warsaw Pact foreign ministers attending the U.N. General Assembly were so honored. Andrei had asked Ceauşescu if he should seek this meeting, and Ceauşescu had instructed him to make every effort to do so. The State Department told the Romanian embassy in Washington that the vice president would receive Andrei but that he could spare only five to seven minutes. Andrei was not at all troubled when Raceanu informed him of this. "Even thirty seconds would be enough to be photographed at the White House with the American vice president," he said.

Andrei's reaction illustrates a fundamental point in Ceauşescu's approach to Romania's relations with the United States. The mere fact that a meeting took place meant more to Ceauşescu than its substance. He was much more interested in public signs of a "special relationship" with the United States and of U.S. "approval" of his regime than he was in the actual content of relations. That is why Andrei knew 30 seconds would be enough to please his boss.

Time and again the U.S. side found the Romanians pressing hard for high-visibility meetings and then having no real business to transact at them. Moreover, even when the United States set up a meeting to give a tough message to the Romanians on human rights or other matters, the meeting was interpreted by the Romanian side as evidence that the "special relationship" was in good shape, regardless of what the United States actually said at the meeting itself. What the United States often meant as a warning of trouble, Ceauşescu took as a sign of approval.

At the September 1985 White House meeting with Vice President Bush, Andrei was accompanied by Raceanu and Romanian ambassador to Washington Nicolae Gavrilescu. Bush's national security adviser, Donald Gregg, Assistant Secretary Rozanne Ridgway, Paula Dobriansky, the National Security Council staff member for Eastern Europe, and Kirk accompanied the vice president. A few minutes after the two groups had assembled in a sitting room in the White House West Wing, they were ushered into the vice president's office. Bush stood at the door to greet Andrei, whom he had met on several previous occasions. The office was a light and cheerful room, the furniture comfortable and fresh. The atmosphere was pleasant and friendly as all sat down in what seemed more like a living room than an office; but the conversation quickly turned serious.

Andrei led off with an assessment that relations between the two countries were going well but could be better. He mentioned Romania's desire for licenses for high-technology exports from the United States and for exchanges of high-level messages and visits.

For his part Bush stated that although the United States would not intervene in Romania's internal affairs, it held deeply felt views on human rights. Human rights were important to the United States, he said, and the Romanians should do whatever they could to respond to U.S. concerns. Bush then referred to the growing feeling in Congress about religious and human rights in Romania. He noted the increasing congressional tendency to link most-favored-nation tariff treatment for Romania to Romanian performance on human rights in general, not just to emigration, despite the fact that the relevant legislation, the Jackson-Vanik amendment, mentioned only emigration. The United States wanted relations to move forward, but this would require action from the Romanian government.

In reply, Andrei stressed the need for the United States to respect Romania's independence. He argued that if Romania opened the door to U.S. demands in the name of "certain principles," it might have to open the door to demands from other nations in the name of Marxist-Leninist principles, demands that could threaten Romania's independence. Romanian leaders often used the argument that concessions to the United States might create a precedent for concessions to the Soviet Union. This in part represented a genuine Romanian concern. The Soviets had reproached them more than once, especially in the 1970s, for turning down proposals from Moscow that the Romanians then accepted from Washington, such as holding bilateral consultations on international affairs.

The Romanian argument also reflected Ceauşescu's almost obsessive desire to be able to do exactly as he wished in Romania without having to heed any foreign advice, whether from officials, bankers, or private individuals. Ceauşescu was constantly asserting, whether relevant to the occasion or not, the need to resist "interference from all quarters." He and his associates argued that acceding to such "interference" would threaten the independence and territorial integrity of Romania. Ceauşescu's comments to his own associates indicated his real fear that concessions on human rights and democratic reforms, even minor ones, could threaten his own position, and even the communist regime. This fear colored his judgments on all reform proposals and was one of the factors that made him so reluctant to grant even seemingly small human rights concessions.

Andrei was clearly troubled by his September 30 conversation with Bush. Normally he sent only a brief, nonsubstantive report on his conversations with Americans, reserving the details for a report he would present in person to Ceauşescu. He knew that any telegram to Ceauşescu, even a personal one, would be read by the Securitate. He would not want to expose the details of his conversations to them, preferring to enhance his own position by maintaining his personal role as Ceauşescu's principal source of information on the U.S. relationship. He also preferred to be able to judge, while actually talking to Ceauşescu, just how frank he could be in relaying what the Americans said.

On this occasion, however, Andrei instructed Raceanu to prepare a detailed telegraphic report on the conversation and to include the vice president's references to human rights matters and his reflections on the future of U.S.-Romanian relations. Andrei asked Raceanu to give particular emphasis to a comment from the vice president that Andrei recalled as "The U.S. is ready to do its part if Romania will do hers."

Raceanu concluded that Andrei wanted to send a detailed message because he sensed a change in the American attitude toward Romania and wanted to be on record as having warned of it. Andrei clearly felt that U.S. policy would in the future be greatly influenced by Romanian internal developments and in particular by Romanian responsiveness to U.S. human rights concerns. At the same time, Andrei was convinced that Ceauşescu would not agree to liberalize any of his internal policies. Anticipating a deterioration of the U.S.-Romanian relationship and wishing to avoid being accused of not having warned Ceauşescu of the danger signals, Andrei wanted a full account of the vice president's warnings to be in the official written record.

The only falsification in the report was a statement that Bush had warm words for Ceauşescu and had asked Andrei to convey his greetings and best wishes to him. The need to include sentiments of this kind in the report of any conversation with a foreign leader had become an unwritten rule that even Andrei could not violate, despite the fact that the vice president had said no such thing.

Ceauşescu and his associates took the fact that Vice President Bush had received Andrei, a mere foreign minister, as proof that relations between the two countries were excellent and that the United States continued to hold Romania in high esteem. The news the following month that Secretary Shultz would visit Romania in late 1985 reinforced this feeling. In this atmosphere, Romania's decision makers paid little attention to the danger signals relayed in Andrei's telegram, if they credited them at all.

The executive branch was not the only part of the U.S. government that was sending warning signals. Romania's standing in Congress, long shaky, was deteriorating even further. On October 22, 1985, almost four months after their visit, Representatives Tony Hall, Christopher Smith, and Frank Wolf introduced a resolution (H.R. 3599) proposing a six-month suspension of MFN for Romania. They had observed no improvement in the Romanian government's policies on human rights and religious freedom and had seen for themselves the harmful effects of those policies. And they had received no reply to their follow-up letter to Ceauşescu of July 16 or to their telegram of September 12.

The purpose of the resolution, as defined by Representative Hall, was to put Romania "on probation" by suspending MFN for six months and by making restoration of MFN contingent upon a determination by the administration that Romania had made sufficient progress on religious freedom and human rights during that period.[24] Senators Paul Trible of Virginia and William Armstrong of Colorado introduced an identical bill in the Senate (S.R. 1818) on November 1.[25]

Also on November 1, the Senate passed an amendment to the State Department appropriations bill, stating that "the sense of the Senate" was to condemn the Romanian government for the "barbaric and repugnant" repression of its people. The amendment called on the United States to take an active role in restoring human and religious rights to the Romanian people and asked the president to consider human rights violations in deciding whether to extend MFN to Romania in the future.[26]

Even though this was the first time since MFN was granted in 1975 that such a critical motion had passed, the Romanian government did not give it much attention. The amendment came too late to affect prolongation of MFN for the 1985–1986 period and was initiated by legislators the Romanian government believed had long been hostile to Romania. The Romanians attached more importance to the announcement on

November 14 that Secretary George Shultz would visit Romania, an announcement they viewed as showing their good standing with the U.S. government.

On November 11, a few days before Raceanu's return to Bucharest from his temporary duty with the embassy in Washington, Ilie Vaduva replaced Ştefan Andrei as foreign minister. No reason for the shift was announced, but in Raceanu's view several factors played a part. Andrei had been foreign minister for over seven years and had earned the envy of a number of those closest to Ceauşescu. Ceauşescu himself was certainly not pleased that Andrei's prestige abroad seemed to be increasing as his own was falling, a point illustrated by the sour expression Andrei told Raceanu he saw on Ceauşescu's face when Foreign Minister Andrei Gromyko of the Soviet Union told Ceauşescu at a Warsaw Pact summit in Sofia in May 1985 that Andrei was "the most popular foreign minister of all his Warsaw Pact colleagues."

Finally, Andrei's relations with Elena Ceauşescu were not good, in part because of her jealousy of Andrei's attractive wife. Raceanu often heard Andrei tell his friends that relations between his wife and Elena Ceauşescu were so "good" that "if his wife were driving a car and Elena were riding in a train, they would still collide." According to Andrei, Elena told a late October meeting of the policymaking Political Executive Committee of the party that Andrei had traveled around enough. Noting that Andrei was an engineer by training, she said he should spend some time at home and become familiar with Romania's economic problems.

At that same October meeting, the Political Executive Committee decided to remove Andrei from the Foreign Ministry and nominate him as party secretary for the economy at the next Central Committee plenum in mid-November. His removal was a loss to the U.S.-Romanian relationship.

Andrei's replacement as foreign minister, Ilie Vaduva, had extensive Romanian academic training as an economist. He had been a professor at the Romanian Academy of Economic Studies in Bucharest since the early 1970s and the academy's president from 1980 until the Ceauşescus named him foreign minister. Vaduva had little background in foreign affairs, although for a brief period he was head of the Romanian interparliamentary group that handled relations with the parliaments of other nations.

The job of foreign minister clearly overwhelmed him. Officials of the ministry quoted an old Romanian saying: "His hat [the job] is bigger than his head." Phone calls from Ceauşescu reduced him to such a state of nervousness that Raceanu had seen him perspire visibly, stutter into the phone, forget completely what Ceauşescu had asked him to do, and turn to Raceanu to guess what it might have been.

In Kirk's opinion, Vaduva's external appearance betrayed his inner self. A man of medium height, he appeared shorter than he was and had about him a soft, squishy look and the anxious air of one who wants to please but is not sure if he is succeeding. Kirk never extracted a single meaningful, substantive comment from Vaduva. It was always "You have already heard the President's [Ceauşescu's] views on this matter" or "I cannot comment now but we will discuss this later."

Vaduva seemed pleasant enough to Kirk, but Raceanu notes that Vaduva's insecurity caused him to lash out at his subordinates in difficult moments. Vaduva's main preoccupation as foreign minister was to stay out of trouble with his patrons, Elena and Nicolae Ceauşescu, to whom he owed his sudden elevation. In Raceanu's view, Vaduva was afraid even to think thoughts the Ceauşescus might not have thought, much less to express them or act on them. As Vaduva had little knowledge of foreign affairs and only infrequent access to the Ceauşescus, he was not sure what the Ceauşescus wanted and hesitated to make any decision for fear of being wrong. When he did make a decision, his primary concern was how his action would look to his peers and to the Ceauşescus, not the merits of the decision itself.

Vaduva was not a negative influence on Romanian policy toward the United States; he had no policy line at all. His extreme reluctance to reach a decision made it difficult to get action out of the ministry, however, and his refusal to pass any information to the Ceauşescus that he thought might displease them made effective communication between the U.S. and Romanian governments, imperfect under the best of circumstances, even more difficult.

The unfortunate consequences of Vaduva's appointment became apparent to Raceanu during his initial call on the new minister in mid-November. Vaduva had visited Washington for half a day in September 1985 as head of the Romanian interparliamentary group, a protocol visit he and an interpreter spent with Capitol Hill supporters of MFN for Romania. Thus when Raceanu outlined his concerns in November about the deteriorating U.S.-Romanian relationship, Vaduva noted that his impressions from his own trip led him to doubt Raceanu's pessimistic assessment of the U.S.-Romanian relationship. Raceanu therefore prepared a written note for the minister and for his deputy, Aurel Duma. Duma was a genuine party activist, tough, unprincipled, and utterly convinced of the superiority of the socialist system. Narrow-minded and simplistic, he was not capable of going beyond standard party jargon. He was different from some in that he actually believed the party line and expounded upon it at great length, not only from duty but also from conviction. He had no conception of conditions in a democratic society and no particular desire to know them. He approached relations with the United States on an ideological basis and viewed U.S. insistence on human, religious, and minority rights as gross interference in Romania's internal affairs.

Duma's views were important, for he had established excellent relations with the Ceauşescu family in the early 1960s when he was head of the State Council for Physical Education and Sport. He was an alternate member of the party's top-level Political Executive Committee from 1969 until 1970, when Ceauşescu sent him as ambassador to China. When Duma returned to Bucharest in 1974, he worked closely with the Ceauşescus as party secretary in charge of the Central Committee section responsible for, inter alia, party administration and Ceauşescu's secretariat.

In 1980 Duma rose to second-in-command in the Foreign Ministry and remained in this position, under four foreign ministers, until Ceauşescu's fall in December 1989. In this capacity he had the title of "minister state secretary for foreign affairs" and was a member of the cabinet. He did not succeed Andrei as foreign minister in 1985 primarily because he was already over 65 (normal Foreign Ministry retirement age was 62) and was not well (in 1984 he had been hospitalized for nearly six months for a colon problem).

Duma had little respect for the profession of diplomacy. He believed that a member of the Foreign Ministry should be a loyal party activist above all and that any faithful party member could do a diplomatic job. He was very hard on his subordinates and they feared him, partly because he had excellent relations with the Securitate and, indeed, was the principal liaison between it and the ministry. In this capacity he did much to advance the Securitate's interest in influencing the ministry's staffing and monitoring its operations.

Kirk found Duma unhelpful, unpleasant to deal with, and uninformed about the United States, almost the caricature of a *nomenklatura* member. Stocky, coarse, and often rude, he liked to tell crude sexist jokes at diplomatic dinners, even when women were present, and seemed to have no sensitivity toward his audience. He loved to receive gifts, especially Cuban cigars, which he smoked at all times of the day. Whenever he summoned Kirk, it was clear that the interview would be about something unpleasant, for Duma normally dealt with the American embassy only when he had something to complain about.

In Raceanu's mid-November report to Vaduva and Duma on U.S.-Romanian relations, he outlined U.S. human rights concerns. He predicted that failure to address them would lead to a further deterioration in the relationship and would even cause Romania to risk losing its most-favored-nation status in 1986. Duma returned without comment both his own copy of the report and the copy intended for Vaduva. Raceanu thinks Duma had read much more optimistic embassy and Securitate accounts of the U.S. view of Romania and in any case did not want to send bad news upward, especially if there was a chance it might reach Ceauşescu himself.

To the best of Raceanu's knowledge, this was the only memorandum of its kind written in the ministry during the 1985–1989 period. No one wanted to write or read, much less pass on to Ceauşescu, anything suggesting that there was a problem with the United States or that implied a need to adopt more flexible positions on human rights. As far as Raceanu could find out—and he had excellent sources in Ceauşescu's office—the Securitate reports from Washington were no more frank than those of the Foreign Ministry, despite the Securitate's theoretical obligation to give Ceauşescu the unvarnished truth. Indeed, the Securitate spent much of its time reporting how successful it had been in spreading positive reports about Romania, placing articles favorable to the Ceauşescus in the American media, and working through individual Americans, especially businesspeople interested in trading with Romania, to influence Congress. Thus Ceauşescu had little information on the true feelings in the U.S. administration and Congress about his regime, except what he received directly from American visitors.

The U.S. embassy and State Department at least partially suspected that this was the case, even though they did not realize the extent of Ceauşescu's isolation. They therefore believed it important to pass U.S. views to him directly, and they encouraged visitors, especially those trusted by Ceauşescu, to meet with the dictator and to be frank with him.

Although this was useful, most people accorded the courtesy of being received by the chief of state hesitated to give him unpleasant news, in the view of Kirk, who often accompanied such visitors. Private individuals found it somewhat embarrassing, even impolite, to do so, especially when they knew that their frankness would not be appreciated. Even

Americans with official roles usually liked to be liked and were inclined to fear, with some reason, that too aggressive a presentation would offend rather than convince. All visitors, official or unofficial, were inclined at a minimum to coat their messages with the sympathetic phrases to which a man like Ceauşescu would ascribe more importance than to the less pleasant message itself. The result was that some visitors were so polite that they gave a totally misleading impression. The direct channel to a ruler is important, but it is no substitute for a continuing flow of accurate information from his or her own sources.

Kirk's basic mission in Romania, as explained to him before his late November 1985 departure for Bucharest, was twofold. He was to engage the Romanian government in as broad a dialogue on international affairs as possible and seek to increase contacts with all levels of Romanian society. At the same time, however, he was to make clear to the Romanian government that continuation of the special U.S.-Romanian relationship was dependent on at least some Romanian action to meet the human rights concerns of the U.S. Congress and even of the Reagan administration.

Developments earlier in November, before Kirk reached Bucharest, illustrated this duality in U.S. policy toward Romania. Ambassador Warren Zimmerman, then a deputy to the head of the U.S. delegation to the nuclear and space arms talks with the Soviets, went to Bucharest twice that November, first to brief the Romanians on the U.S.-Soviet disarmament talks and then to report on the recent Reagan-Gorbachev summit. Although Zimmerman's first trip, on November 12, coincided with Vaduva's first day in office, Vaduva took the time to receive him. Later that day one of Romania's leading figures, Ion Coman, party secretary responsible for defense and for the Securitate and a member of the Political Executive Committee, attended U.S. chargé Henry Clarke's dinner for Zimmerman. The Romanians expressed keen appreciation to Zimmerman for his visit and told him that their Soviet allies had made no such effort to brief them on the talks.

Such U.S. briefings flattered Ceauşescu. He cited them to the Soviets and others as an indication that the United States listened to him and "consulted" him. This treatment led him to echo some U.S. positions in his public statements—withdrawal of intermediate-range nuclear missiles from Europe, for instance—both as a sop to the United States and as a demonstration that he could perform a bridging function between the two great powers. Thus, on November 13, after praising the Soviet disarmament position in a speech to the Romanian Central Committee plenum, Ceauşescu added that "some of the proposals by the United States similarly constitute an appropriate basis for making it possible for the two superpowers to reach a mutually acceptable agreement."[27]

This kind of language from a Warsaw Pact member was highly unusual. The U.S. government considered it useful testimony to the reasonableness of the U.S. position. The United States was also intrigued, if not wholly convinced, by a later Romanian assertion to Zimmerman that the Romanians had succeeded, at a meeting of Warsaw Pact leaders a few days after the Zimmerman conversation, in softening the pact's public criticism of the U.S. disarmament proposals. In the context of 1985 this was rare and, in U.S. eyes, welcome independence on the part of a Warsaw Pact member. Even if it did not change the substance of the Soviet disarmament position, it was a small crack in what otherwise appeared to be a monolithic facade on foreign policy. The United States wanted to encourage these small beginnings both for their own sake and in the hopes they might lead to something more significant.

On Zimmerman's second trip, on November 22, this time as presidential envoy, Ceauşescu himself spent nearly an hour with him. One interesting aspect of their conversation was that it was the last between Ceauşescu and an official of the U.S. executive branch that was devoted solely to foreign affairs. Thereafter, no matter what the principal subject of the discussion might be, the United States side would raise the issue of human rights in Romania.

The circumstances of the November 22 meeting were illustrative of Ceauşescu's power and his method of operation. Ceauşescu was tied up with Polish president Wojciech Jaruzelski until it was almost time for Zimmerman's departure on the Romanian airline. Zimmerman noted the time problem when Romanian officials summoned him for his presidential audience, but the protocol officer told him not to worry about that. When the interview ended, over half an hour after the plane's scheduled departure time, the Romanians sped Zimmerman directly to the tarmac. The airplane, with the other passengers already aboard, sat waiting in the afternoon sunshine. As he prepared to board, the airport's commanding officer noted to a nearby American, "Ah, I see the fog has lifted. The airplane can now take off." In his Romania, Ceauşescu could even determine the weather.

Meanwhile, the United States was seeking through a variety of channels to convince the Romanians that they needed to take action on human rights issues. State Department Counselor Edward Derwinski told the Romanian ambassador in early November that without some positive developments in the field of human rights and emigration, the administration would have a very difficult time defending MFN renewal the following summer.

Kirk's first contact with Ceauşescu came on November 29, when Kirk presented his official credentials to the dictator in a ceremony that marked the formal beginning of Kirk's ambassadorial assignment in Bucharest. This formal event, like most of Kirk's 20-plus meetings with Ceauşescu, took place at Communist Party Central Committee headquarters, a grandiose, columned edifice across a square from the old royal palace. As for all such meetings, Foreign Ministry protocol officers met Kirk at a mutually agreed place in plenty of time to assure that the party would arrive by car at the front door of the Central Committee building three to four minutes before the meeting time. (In winter, when visitors would have coats to take off, arrival was two to three minutes earlier.) The protocol officers did not use a siren to force their way through the relatively light traffic; when necessary, they waved a red-and-white stick out their car window and shouted.

The cortege drove up to the main door of the building, passing by guards patrolling in front of a half-enclosed courtyard into which no one but Ceauşescu's visitors were allowed to enter. As the car doors opened, so did the big bronze door of the building, and an ample figure, always the same man, stood at the threshold to welcome the visitors, while someone else took any coats they might have. (In 1990, fully eight months after the revolution of December 1989 had toppled Ceauşescu, Kirk was somewhat startled to be greeted by this very same doorman upon entering the Romanian Parliament building. Obviously noting the surprised look on Kirk's face, the man shrugged and said, "We all have to live somehow, don't we?")

On these occasions a presidential protocol officer then escorted Kirk and his party, a few top embassy officers, up a long flight of marble stairs. The protocol officer glanced at his watch to be sure the time was exactly at the agreed hour and then asked the party to wait a moment while he told Ceauşescu they were present. About a minute later, an aide opened a door leading directly into Ceauşescu's reception room and the visitors entered. In the three and a half years Kirk was in Bucharest, he never had to wait more than two minutes after the appointed time to enter into Ceauşescu's presence, nor did Ceauşescu ever postpone or delay a meeting once the time for it had been fixed. On the other hand, the Romanians would not set the time for any meeting with Ceauşescu until a few hours before it was to take place.

Ceauşescu's reception room was a cavernous, high-ceilinged affair, with tall windows along one side looking out on a large open square and the former royal palace beyond. Gray, rather hard, upholstered sofas and chairs lined this and the other long side of the rectangular room, with little tables in front of them with chocolate candies and a kind of grapefruit juice. Ceauşescu often drank the juice, but Kirk never saw him take a candy. Kirk regularly did so; the candy was quite good—better, certainly, than the sickly sweet juice.

Visitors entered through a door that faced the windows on the square. At the far end, to the right as they entered, stood two large armchairs separated from the rest of the furniture by a good ten feet. A few Romanian landscape paintings hung on the walls, but the overall impression was of a large, empty space with a few chairs. Kirk could not help but reflect on the contrast with Bush's pleasant and cheerful office, where he had been with Andrei two months before.

Ceauşescu stood in the middle of the room to greet his visitors, while 10 to 20 representatives of the press took photographs. After a handshake and a few polite words, Ceauşescu motioned his visitor to the big armchair nearest the window and sat in the other himself. Those in attendance arranged themselves in the chairs along the two sides of the room, the foreigners under the windows and the Romanians on the other side. Ceauşescu's note-taker sat at a table some distance behind the dictator. After a few more pictures, Ceauşescu waved the press away. There were no questions from the press; indeed, in Kirk's experience the media representatives never uttered a word. As the press left, Ceauşescu's interpreter drew up a chair between the president and his visitor, and the substantive discussion began. This scenario never varied for such meetings, though Kirk noted that toward the end of his service in Bucharest he got only juice; no candies came out unless there was a visitor from the United States with him.

Kirk was somewhat nervous and preoccupied in his first meeting with Ceauşescu, but he remembers being struck by what an unprepossessing physical figure the man was. Short (under five feet, six inches) and graying, with a somewhat pinched face, he had a slight stutter or tic that interrupted his speech, particularly when he was under strain. His motions were generally quick and sharp and his eyes lively. He sometimes adopted a pleasant expression when talking with Kirk or an American visitor, but it did not seem to come naturally to him. Ceauşescu's cold stare when angry was famous within the Romanian hierarchy.

Kirk's initial impression was reinforced at many more such meetings as well as by observing Ceauşescu at various ceremonies, at speeches to Parliament and other bodies, and at occasional large receptions. Kirk never saw him at any informal occasion or small, friendly dinner, nor did any of Kirk's diplomatic colleagues.

Nicolae Ceauşescu was born on January 26, 1918, to a drunken father, Andruţa Ceauşescu, and a patient, long-suffering mother, Alexandra, in the village of Scorniceşti, some 90 miles northwest of Bucharest. Here the awkward, stuttering farm boy went through the first years of elementary school without distinction. At age 11, he was apprenticed to a shoemaker in Bucharest who had married Ceauşescu's sister, Niculina. Ceauşescu lived with the family and must have been somewhat of a trial to them, as he was apparently a rowdy boy who would fly into a rage when offended and who was often involved in street brawls of one sort or another.[28]

Ceauşescu joined the tiny Young Communists' League in 1933 at the age of 15. He served two prison terms for his communist activities, from 1936 to 1938 and from 1940 to 1944. It was in prison that he grew to know a number of Communist Party leaders, including his future patron, Gheorghe Gheorghiu-Dej, whom the young Ceauşescu served as personal assistant and virtual valet during his 1940–1944 prison term. Ceauşescu participated actively in Communist Party activity as it resumed after the liberation of Romania in 1944. He became a member of the party's Central Committee in 1945. Dropped from the committee in 1947 along with a number of others to make room for the communists' new Social Democratic allies, he was reelected in 1952 and remained on the committee for the rest of his life.

Ceauşescu obtained a high-school-equivalency certificate by attending night classes, which were arranged for leading party members in the 1940s. In 1948 Gheorghiu-Dej put him in charge of political indoctrination of the army, a job carrying the rank of major general. In this capacity Ceauşescu spent eight months at the Frunze Military Academy in Moscow, an experience that strengthened his Marxism but confirmed his dislike for Russians.[29]

Raceanu's mother, Ileana, knew the Ceauşescus well in the 1940s. She herself had been active in the tiny Communist Party from the late 1920s and even gave birth to Mircea in prison in 1935, while she was being detained for her communist activities. Mircea's father, Andrei Bernat, was shot by the Nazis in the spring of 1944 while in prison for communist activities. His mother subsequently married Grigore Raceanu, who had joined the party in the early 1930s.

A friend who had shared a small house with the Ceauşescus in their early years, right after World War II, told Raceanu that Ceauşescu was known in those days as the "stuttering shoemaker" and that most of the other communists held him in contempt as an uneducated bootlicker. He was useful, however, because he was hard-working, discreet, and willing to carry out any command. Then and later he was temperate in food and drink. He refrained from the womanizing that characterized some of his colleagues and, as time went on, would sometimes remove high officials for such conduct.

Ceauşescu was briefly deputy minister of agriculture in 1950 and then moved to deputy minister of defense.[30] In 1955 he received the key post of member of the political bureau of the party's Central Committee, with particular responsibility for organization and personnel, and used this to build a strong power base. His emergence as first secretary of the party after Gheorghiu-Dej's death in 1965, however, was attributable in part to the belief of older party leaders that they could control Ceauşescu. He maneuvered brilliantly in the next few years and succeeded in cementing his supremacy over his rivals. He made himself head of state in 1967 and assumed the title of President of the Republic in 1974.

As Ceauşescu grew more powerful, he lost the diffidence of the humble errand boy and began to assert his authority over those around him. He worked hard, with partial success, to reduce his stutter, and took lessons in projecting a commanding presence. By 1985, when Kirk first met him, Ceauşescu was supremely confident, even arrogant. Accustomed to power, he exercised it with ruthlessness and determination in every field of human activity. Although he had no particular charm or charisma, he was able, even without mass killings or wholesale arrests, to inspire fear and obedience in those around him and indeed in virtually an entire nation.

He had a peasant's shrewdness and mistrust of others, impressive native intelligence, an excellent memory, and a good head for detail. He was a master at controlling and manipulating others. He was vengeful, suspicious, and without scruples in pursuit of his ends. As his power grew, he became more impatient with subordinates, humiliating them and often threatening to fire them on the spot. He did not like being contradicted, and he would not long keep around him those who disagreed with him or ventured their own opinions.

Unfortunately for the Romanian people, Ceauşescu had a very clear sense of where he wanted to take Romania. His goals sprang from a primitive conception of communism, one that emerged from Stalin's popular interpretations of Lenin rather than from the philosophical arguments of Marx or even from the writings of Lenin himself. Lacking extensive formal education, he derived most of his knowledge of and faith in communism from his association with Romania's early communists in the prewar and wartime underground communist movement.

Ceauşescu appeared to retain to the end of his life his simplistic faith in some of communism's more extreme aims. All available evidence suggests, for example, that he actually believed he could create a new socialist man, freed from the shackles of capitalism and the vestiges of the oppressive past. Temporary sacrifice was the price his people had to pay, but he believed that establishing true communism was worth the price and apparently assumed that most of the population believed so as well. He railed against any form of capitalism at a time when almost all his fellow communists in the Soviet Union and Eastern Europe were recognizing that some capitalist-type incentives were essential to get their economies moving. The remarkable thing is that he kept stating these beliefs not only when communists in the Soviet Union and Eastern Europe were modifying them, but even at the end, when he himself was on trial for his life.

Ceauşescu's speeches were long, dull, and uninspired until he touched upon one of his favorite subjects, such as independence from foreigners, the drive to create communism in Romania, or the evils of capitalism. Then he would depart from his prepared text. His voice would rise, his hands pump, and his eyes shine with conviction. He aroused little genuine enthusiasm in his audience, but their orchestrated chants in response left him looking pleased and proud. As will emerge in later pages, he seemed genuinely to believe that his programs were a success, that his people supported him, and, until the last year or two of his regime, that the international community, including the U.S. government, valued him highly.

Ceauşescu put great store by the counsel of his wife of many years, Elena, who had become the second most powerful person in Romania by 1980. Elena Petrescu's official birth date was January 7, 1919, but most Romanians believed she was born a year or so earlier, making her slightly older than her husband. A quiet village girl from a fairly well-to-do peasant family, she did poorly at school and left at age 14 when asked to repeat a grade. A couple of years later she moved to Bucharest to live with her brother and sister-in-law.

Elena met Ceauşescu through her attendance at party affairs with her communist sister-in-law. After a courtship interrupted by Ceauşescu's prison terms, the two married in 1946.[31] They remained devoted to each other for the rest of their lives.

In their early years together, Elena Petrescu Ceauşescu was a retiring, diffident housewife for whom the other party wives had real contempt. She was a person of few talents, little intellect, and a primitive understanding of the world around her. Her husband urged her, indeed almost compelled her, according to Raceanu's mother, to start studying again and to work hard at it. Elena Ceauşescu attended chemistry classes in 1955 and 1956, started as a researcher at the Bucharest Chemical Research Institute in 1960, and became the institute's director in 1965, having in the meantime been awarded a doctorate in chemical engineering.[32] She was even made a member of the Romanian Academy of Sciences in 1974 and its president in the 1980s. She never, however, publicly displayed even a rudimentary knowledge of chemistry, and it was clear that it was Ceauşescu's position that had led to her advancement. Nevertheless, she seemed genuinely to believe in later years that her titles made her a scientist. Thus, even during her trial in December 1989 just before her execution, she replied to a judge who asked who wrote her books, "Such impudence! I am a member and chairwoman of the Academy of Science. You cannot talk to me in such a way."[33]

Elena Ceauşescu's rapid promotion in the party started only after her husband became general secretary in 1965. She was elected a member of the party Central Committee in 1972 and became a full member of the top-level Political Executive Committee in 1973. In 1979, she became head of the Party and State Cadres Commission, a position that gave her immense power over all party and state personnel appointments. That year she also took over leadership of the National Council of Science and Technology, and in 1980 she was made first deputy prime minister, with responsibility for culture, education, science, and technology.

While Elena Ceauşescu acquired power and academic titles, she never lost the narrow-minded, primitive outlook of her rural youth, and she never acquired wisdom or judgment to compensate for her lack of intelligence. She did lose her early diffidence, however, and became a trial to all those around her because of her demanding nature, towering rages, and appetite for flattery.

Her tastes were crude. She has been accused of having the Securitate plant hidden cameras in the bedrooms of high Romanian officials to watch the resultant films of their lovemaking. The authors cannot vouch for this, but a friend told Raceanu that the Securitate had ordered a photographer close to him to develop a clandestine film of the Ceauşescu's son Valentin making love to a female friend in his apartment. The photographer was convinced that the Securitate wanted the film developed in her top-quality studio so it would be good enough for Elena Ceauşescu's viewing. This was speculation, but the Securitate would never have dared place a hidden camera in Valentin's apartment except on the explicit instruction of Nicolae or Elena Ceauşescu, and it is quite possible that the film was developed for her entertainment.

Elena Ceauşescu also acquired a taste for expensive jewelry, furs, and shoes. An inventory of the Ceauşescu residence after the 1989 revolution revealed a large quantity of luxury items, including full-length mink coats and glamorous jewels. During the Ceauşescus' 1970 visit to New York, Raceanu spent many hours going from furrier to furrier to arrange a showing in Mrs. Ceauşescu's suite. As the Ceauşescus' scheduler during their December 1973 visit to Washington, he had to arrange a time for an embassy third secretary to bring to her suite a large selection of jewelry from W. Bell & Co., the discount house, for her consideration.[34]

Mrs. Ceauşescu was deeply suspicious of the United States. She had acquired an absolute faith in rudimentary communism and viewed the United States as the evil archenemy of Romania's communist regime. The wealth and power of the United States obviously impressed her during her visits, however, and she felt considerable inferiority in the face of both American power and the glamour and sophistication of the American women she met.

Elena Ceauşescu was determined to reduce America's influence over her husband and her people. She consistently sought to reduce academic exchanges with Americans, all of which required her approval in her capacity as first deputy prime minister in charge of science. As a result of her policies the number of Romanian lecturers in the United States under the Fulbright program fell from 38 in 1979 to 2 in 1988. She discouraged cultural and scientific contacts with other Western countries as well. It is Raceanu's view that her isolation of Romanian intellectual life from the West constituted her greatest crime against the Romanian people.

Raceanu had personal experience with Mrs. Ceauşescu's attitude toward educational exchanges with the United States. In 1984 he accompanied Charles Wick, then director of the United States Information Agency, when Wick called on First Deputy Prime Minister Gheorghe Oprea. Wick complained that the Romanian side had not sent as many educators and researchers to the United States as stipulated by the cultural agreement between the two countries.

After Wick's departure, as Oprea was preparing to see Elena Ceauşescu in her adjoining office, Raceanu suggested he raise with her the question of sending more academics to the United States, as called for by the U.S.-Romanian cultural agreement. When Oprea returned 20 minutes later, he told Raceanu that she had responded to his suggestion by saying that the number should be reduced, not increased. When Raceanu asked the basis for her position, Oprea said, "Comrade Elena Ceauşescu is of the opinion that the Americans are only interested in recruiting Romanian scholars to work against us. That is why they are urging us to send more Romanians to visit the United States."

As time went on, the two Ceauşescus became increasingly detached from the reality of what was happening in their country and in the world. They grew virtually paranoid in their reaction to criticism and in searching for the motives that might have inspired it. Ceauşescu inflicted more and more hardship on the population in the name of his grandiose schemes and his personal glory. The Romanian people, Ceauşescu often said in the final years of his rule, were lucky to have him as their leader, for someone like him was born only once in 500 years. For this, at least, it is true that the Romanians would be grateful.

All this background was not in evidence on the occasion of Kirk's presentation of credentials to Ceauşescu on November 29, 1985, but it was clear that all the Romanians in the room, including the media representatives, were most respectful, even frightened, of the dictator. As was customary for credentials ceremonies, the media representatives remained while Kirk, still standing in the middle of the room, handed his written letters of credence to Ceauşescu and read a brief formal statement. Ceauşescu then replied equally briefly before dismissing the press and motioning Kirk to the usual armchair for a brief talk.

Ceauşescu seemed to Kirk to be making a real effort to appear agreeable on this occasion. Raceanu points out that the Romanians were in fact pleased that the new U.S. ambassador in Bucharest was a career diplomat. They considered the appointment of a career officer to be a sign of the high importance the United States administration attached to relations with Romania. They also felt that a career ambassador would faithfully reflect what they believed was the U.S. administration's favorable view of Romania. This fact, plus a desire to start off on the right foot with a new ambassador, may have accounted for Ceauşescu's relative amiability.

Once Kirk and Ceauşescu were seated, the president briefly discussed his desire to see more progress in the disarmament talks between the United States and the Soviet Union and in wider arms control forums. On this occasion and on many thereafter, Ceauşescu stressed the utility of including some of the smaller countries in disarmament negotiations and hinted that Romania would be a good candidate for such a role. Then he turned to another favorite subject, U.S.-Romanian trade, and asked for a more forthcoming U.S. attitude on licensing exports of technology to Romania.

The licensing question was a continuing refrain in Romanian presentations to U.S. officials. The Romanian position was that U.S. refusal to license the export of many types of technology to Romania was a prime factor blocking U.S. exports to that country and a vast expansion of U.S.-Romanian trade in general. Yet the few license cases pending during this period were not of major commercial or technological importance. Furthermore, when U.S. officials asked just what additional technology the Romanians wanted, they typically failed to come up with any specifics.

It appeared to the U.S. side that the Romanians, including Ceauşescu, were using the licensing issue as an excuse for the gross imbalance in U.S.-Romanian trade (3 to 1 or 4 to 1 in Romania's favor) and that they valued favorable treatment primarily as a matter of prestige. Some have argued that the Romanians wanted to obtain technology they could pass on to the Soviets, but it seems likely that the Romanians would have been more specific in their requests if they were really fronting for the Soviets.

In his brief reply to Ceauşescu's presentation, Kirk spoke of his instructions from Washington to develop a broad dialogue with the Romanian government and of his obligation to reflect his country's concerns for human rights and its interest in the welfare of human beings everywhere. Ceauşescu listened without comment. The Romanian protocol officer had told Kirk that Ceauşescu would signal the end of the interview by reaching for his glass of champagne or fiddling with his jacket button. After the talk had gone on for some 20 minutes Ceauşescu reached for his champagne glass. As Kirk ventured two more concluding sentences, Ceauşescu was already fiddling impatiently with his jacket button. He clearly was a man who wanted his signals to be obeyed at once.

When Kirk left Ceauşescu's office, the chief of protocol told him that the length of the talk was a great honor; none of the more than 100 presentations the protocol chief had attended had lasted so long. The embassy duly reported this to Washington, only to discover later that this was a standard line; Kirk met at least a dozen ambassadors to whom the chief of protocol had said the same thing. It was an early lesson in Romanian officials' penchant for telling foreigners what they thought they wanted to hear, even at the expense of the truth.

Kirk was able to meet with several Romanian officials in his first few weeks in Bucharest, including Foreign Minister Ilie Vaduva, former foreign minister Ştefan Andrei, and Party Secretary for Military and Security Affairs Ion Coman. To all of them he said his instructions were to broaden the dialogue between the United States and Romania on international issues and to convey accurately the concerns in the United States about human rights in Romania and the effect these might have on the relationship. He mentioned a few specific issues, including the provision of Bibles for the Protestant communities, the recognition of additional Protestant denominations, and the need for a written agreement on emigration procedures. His interlocutors stressed the Romanian desire for good relations with the United States on the basis of non-interference in internal affairs and gave little speeches about Romania's tradition of independence since the days they fought the Romans in the first century after Christ.

This theme of independence was one that all Romanians from Ceauşescu on down stressed at length with every American visitor. They usually started by citing a comment by Greek historian Herodotus to the effect that the Geto-Dacians (the forerunners of modern Romanians) were "the bravest as well as the most just of all the Thracian tribes."[35] They then described the Dacian kingdom in the first centuries B.C. and A.D. and its valiant struggle against the Romans. It is interesting that Romanian historiography laid great stress on this point, while deriving immense pride (and the country's name) from the fact most of the country then became part of the Roman Empire and remained so for some 150 years.

The Romanians would next point out that Romania had preserved its Latin heritage in spite of the barbarian invasions and that Romania, even today, was a "Latin island in a sea of Slavs." (Kirk used to tell visitors that they would hear that phrase in the first half hour of their introductory talk with Ceauşescu or any high Foreign Ministry official; he was seldom proven wrong.) The Romanians would remind the visitor that Romania had never been occupied by the Turks but had only paid tribute to them (and had its rulers chosen by them). The history lesson concluded with the statement that Romania was upholding its tradition of independence vis-à-vis "our neighbors" at considerable cost and that it would not give it up to anyone (including, by implication, the United States).

The retelling of this history was in part simple aping of one of Ceauşescu's pet themes and in part laying a historical groundwork for the rejection of U.S. human rights demands. But it also reflected a genuine national pride, historically accurate or not, on the part of many Romanians, including Ceauşescu himself. Sophisticated Americans tailored their presentations on human rights to accommodate this spirit of independence by disavowing any intention to interfere in Romania's internal affairs, while the Romanian side would characterize, and to some extent actually consider, any unwelcome comment as constituting just such interference. It was one more block to communication between the two governments.

Kirk made his most detailed presentation of Washington's concerns to Deputy Foreign Minister Maria Groza, a tall, graceful woman of well-groomed, almost elegant appearance, whose welcoming manner charmed visitors while her obvious knowledge inspired their respect. Her responsibilities included the Western Hemisphere, cultural affairs, and the press. Groza was the daughter of Petru Groza, a left-leaning Romanian lawyer who had headed a communist-dominated government from March 1945 until 1947 and was then president of Romania until 1958.

Maria Groza had accompanied her father on many of his travels and served as his secretary during much of his period in office. Born in 1920, she was a graduate of the Romanian Academy of Economic Studies. Active in national and international women's organizations from a young age, she became a secretary of the Romanian National Council of Women in 1958 and its vice chairperson in 1965. That same year she became vice chairperson of the Grand National Assembly (Romania's parliament), a post she held for the next ten years. During this time she often served on the Romanian delegation to the United Nations General Assembly in New York, and in 1971 was chairperson of the General Assembly's Social, Humanitarian, and Cultural Committee. Following her service as deputy chairperson of the Grand National Assembly's Constitutional and Judicial Committee from 1975 to 1980, Ceauşescu personally appointed her, in January 1980, to the position of deputy minister of foreign affairs, her position when Kirk came to Bucharest in 1985.

Groza was more sophisticated and considerate than most of her colleagues. While she faithfully echoed the official line, she had some understanding of the real situation and was able to resolve a number of problems, especially those regarding cultural exchanges and family reunification. She was not a strong-willed individual, however, and she did not want to do anything that might jeopardize her job in the Foreign Ministry. She was unmarried and without children, and her job was her major interest. She was not a particularly influential voice, even in the councils of the Foreign Ministry, especially after Ştefan Andrei, who had great confidence in her, left the post of minister in late 1985. She made a favorable impression on most foreigners, however, and some American visitors even urged Ceauşescu to give her more responsibility or send her as a special envoy to the United States.

She listened to Kirk's presentation on December 4, as on many later occasions, with patience and courtesy, but made no commitments to take action. Much of Kirk's interaction with Groza on this occasion, and indeed his principal preoccupation during the first three weeks of his mission, concerned the preparations for Secretary of State Shultz's December 15 visit to Romania.

▼ 3 ▼

Shultz Tackles Ceauşescu Directly 1985

In the fall of 1985 Secretary George Shultz indicated his willingness to make a brief visit to Eastern Europe in connection with his December trip to the annual NATO foreign ministers' meeting. He wished to visit those East European countries that stood out from their neighbors. Yugoslavia was clearly a prime candidate because of its position outside the Soviet bloc. Hungary was the other initial choice, in recognition of its move toward greater internal liberalization and economic reform. The U.S. policy of differentiation also reserved special treatment for signs of independence in foreign policy, however; and in that regard Romania was clearly best qualified among the East European countries.

The State Department's European bureau therefore recommended that Shultz include Bucharest in his itinerary, despite Ceauşescu's low marks on human rights. A visit would not only recognize Romania's relative independence in foreign policy; it would also give Shultz the chance to tell Ceauşescu directly that his harsh internal regime was hurting his relations with the United States. Shultz agreed, but he stipulated that he would not spend the night in Bucharest, given his distaste for Ceauşescu and all he had heard about conditions in the Romanian capital. Shultz also insisted that the visit to Romania be arranged around his other official commitments, leaving Sunday, December 15, as the only available day.

The first indication the Romanian government received about Shultz's decision to visit Bucharest came in an early November meeting between Raceanu and officials of the State Department's Office of East European and Yugoslav Affairs, who told Raceanu they had "good news and bad news" for him. The good news was that Shultz had decided to include Romania in his East European trip. The bad news was that the visit would last only six hours and would have to be on Sunday, December 15. As the visit was added to an already planned trip, any effort by the Romanian government to change the date or duration of the visit could result in its being canceled altogether. They wanted Raceanu to know this before the U.S. embassy in Bucharest formally approached the Romanian government on the matter.

Raceanu immediately telegraphed this news to Bucharest. The idea of a Sunday visit troubled the Romanian bureaucracy, who knew that Ceauşescu did not like to receive foreign visitors during weekends. But when Ceauşescu learned of the U.S. proposal, he approved it immediately. He was "too aware of the importance of the visit" to risk its postponement or cancellation, according to Ştefan Andrei, who was himself delighted that Shultz was coming. From the tenor of his September 26 conversation with Shultz in New York, Andrei had wrongly concluded that any such gesture by the United States was highly unlikely.

When U.S. chargé Henry Clarke informed the Foreign Ministry the next day about the proposed visit, he was surprised to receive immediate agreement to both the visit and the date. Normally he would have been told that the ministry official had to consult a higher authority and then subjected to haggling over the inconvenience of Sunday, the short duration of the visit, and so forth.

In this instance, informal communication between these two hostile governments avoided a potential problem. Such success depended, however, on the existence of midlevel officials prepared to deal honestly and informally with each other. Raceanu had to know and trust his interlocutors enough to realize that the message they were passing was an accurate one, not just a product of bureaucratic eagerness to carry out Shultz's precise wishes. He needed to take their comments as an effort to be helpful, not as an ultimatum. Then there had to be someone on the Romanian side with access to Ceauşescu who was willing to tell him of the importance of accepting the unpalatable American conditions and who knew how to do so without offending him. Ştefan Andrei was such a person; his successors as foreign minister over the next four years were not. Indeed, such people are rare in authoritarian societies, increasingly so as the Supreme Leader becomes ever more intolerant and self-important.

Ceauşescu's willingness to accommodate Shultz's schedule sprang from his eagerness for such a visit, particularly in the context of growing criticism of his regime in the U.S. Congress and in the American and West European press. Having the U.S. secretary of state come to see him would enhance his image as a world statesman and underline once again what he saw as Romania's special relationship with the United States.

It supported his belief in high-level dialogue as the best way to promote relations between countries, as well as his desire to maintain or improve relations with the United States, notwithstanding the internal policies he was unwilling to change.

Once the date of the visit was set, the two sides went to work on the schedule. In addition to meetings with the foreign minister and with non-official individuals of particular significance, it is U.S. practice that secretaries of state meet with the presidents and prime ministers of the countries they visit. Any foreign leader is supposed to be honored to receive the U.S. secretary of state, despite the difference in rank. Although difficult to accomplish in the course of a six-hour visit, the U.S. side thus proposed meetings with Ceauşescu, Prime Minister Constantin Dascalescu, Foreign Minister Ilie Vaduva, former foreign minister Andrei, and Romania's chief rabbi, Moses Rosen, a person with a considerable reputation in the American Jewish community.

A major problem, however, was that it was discomfiting for Romanian high officials to talk with a visitor just before or after Ceauşescu did, especially if the conversation was to cover the same subjects. Ceauşescu would give the definitive word on the topic, and there was little that other officials dared add. Their offices were thoroughly bugged by the Securitate, and any comment differing from the line Ceauşescu took could mean trouble. They could, of course, discuss specifics within their area of responsibility, but a conversation between the secretary of state and the prime minister, for example, was likely to be at the same level of generality as with Ceauşescu. The prime minister could not go beyond what Ceauşescu said and would be highly embarrassed if anything he said were different from the boss's line.

Thus a meeting with the prime minister in addition to the president would be a waste of time, especially because in Ceauşescu's Romania the foreign and defense ministers reported directly to Ceauşescu and not to the prime minister. Furthermore, American visitors generally had not asked to talk with the prime minister; insistence on doing so could irritate Ceauşescu and lead him to question U.S. motives.

Raceanu, knowing all this well, urged the United States to drop its request to see Dascalescu. When U.S. officials seemed reluctant to do so, he told them quite frankly that to pursue the matter would risk spoiling the whole visit. The embassy in Bucharest urged Washington to accept

Raceanu's advice. The State Department finally agreed not to press for a Dascalescu meeting, as the idea had originated from the general principle of seeing prime ministers and not from any particular interest in Dascalescu himself.

It was different in the case of former foreign minister Andrei. In addition to Secretary Shultz's personal friendship with him, the United States considered him one of the few people with access to Ceauşescu who would pass him a relatively tough message from Shultz about the effect Ceauşescu's human rights policies were having in the United States and the significance of this for future U.S.-Romanian relations. The embassy pressed hard for a meeting, but Ceauşescu refused to permit one on the advice of Ion Stoian, the Central Committee secretary for international affairs, and Tudor Postelnicu, chairman of the Department of State Security (the Securitate).

The motivations of the two men were part personal, part ideological. Andrei was their rival for influence with Ceauşescu, and they wanted to deny him the personal prestige of a meeting with Shultz. Knowing that Andrei derived some influence with Ceauşescu from his knowledge of U.S. affairs, they wished to reduce his value as a channel to the dictator. They also favored a tougher line toward the United States than did Andrei and feared that Andrei's presentation of the U.S. position might persuade Ceauşescu once again to make concessions on issues of concern to the United States to preserve MFN. The U.S. side was unaware of the details of this internal byplay but finally yielded to the wishes of the Romanians, as Shultz's hosts and in light of the difficulty of squeezing the Andrei meeting into Shultz's tight schedule. A U.S. attempt to have the Romanians include Andrei in their luncheon for Shultz was similarly unsuccessful.

The proposed meeting with Chief Rabbi Rosen fell victim to time constraints, and the embassy never even raised it officially with the Romanian government. This meant that Shultz would have substantive discussions only with Ceauşescu and his new and ineffective foreign minister, Ilie Vaduva. The secretary would not be able to present his case to other Romanians who might have reinforced his message with Ceauşescu.

Shultz, as usual, was traveling with senior State Department and National Security Council (NSC) officials, some of whom had important roles in U.S.-Romanian relations. Since only two of these officials, State Department Counselor Edward Derwinski and Assistant Secretary of State for European Affairs Rozanne Ridgway, would attend the Ceauşescu meeting, the embassy suggested to the Romanians that it would be useful for the others to discuss bilateral issues in more detail at the Foreign Ministry while the Ceauşescu meeting was in progress. The Romanians agreed that Deputy Foreign Minister Maria Groza and her associates would meet with the visiting officials during this time.

The final issue on the schedule, one discussed almost exclusively within the Romanian side, was whether Ceauşescu would host the luncheon for Shultz. He had done this for two previous secretaries of state, Henry Kissinger in 1974 and Alexander Haig in 1982, and Raceanu was hopeful that he would do so again.

Ceauşescu's decision on the lunch was obtained in the usual manner for such matters in Romania. No one dared ask him if he would host a lunch for a mere foreign minister, so the ministry presented him a draft schedule listing Foreign Minister Vaduva as the host. The ministry interpreted Ceauşescu's failure to volunteer to host the lunch himself as his decision not to do so. Ceauşescu may well have made a conscious decision not to host Shultz, as he probably suspected that Shultz's message was not going to be as pleasant as those of his predecessors; but his subordinates did not even raise the question with him.

While the two sides thus reached agreement on the date and program of the visit, they had markedly different objectives in mind for it. The papers the State Department prepared for Shultz noted that his visit would once again emphasize to Ceauşescu and whoever would succeed him (the 67-year-old Ceauşescu had been ill that summer) that the United States still valued Romania's relative independence in foreign policy and would not welcome any change in this orientation. However, it wished to engage the Ceauşescu government in a broader foreign policy dialogue as one way of encouraging Romanian independence from the Soviet Union, and the briefing materials urged Shultz to emphasize to Ceauşescu that he had instructed Kirk to launch such a dialogue. They also said that Shultz should urge Romania to continue to vote against anti-U.S. resolutions in the United Nations and should encourage it to look to the West, not to the East, for trade. All this was in fact compatible with Romania's aims.

The briefing papers further advised Shultz, however, to use the visit to express U.S. concern over Romanian human rights practices and to raise a number of specific issues: the need for written confirmation of that summer's oral agreement on Romanian treatment of would-be emigrants; permission for the importation of Bibles for the country's Protestants; authority for a number of smaller Protestant denominations such as the Nazarenes to practice their religion legally; and emigration permission for the family of Romanian defector Napoleon Fodor. A principal purpose of the whole visit, the paper pointed out, was to make Ceauşescu aware that his human rights violations threatened the entire relationship between the two countries.

The Romanian side, for their part, saw the visit primarily as a counter to the growing criticism of the Ceauşescu regime in the United States and Europe and a reinforcement of Ceauşescu's prestige. The very fact that Shultz was coming to Bucharest at all achieved these overall Romanian objectives. It also fitted neatly with Ceauşescu's concept of relations between countries as primarily a matter of personal contacts between their leaders.

The visit would also achieve further specific Romanian objectives. One was to obtain reiteration of U.S. support for Romania's policy of independence. Another was to reinforce the "special relationship" between Romania and the United States by agreeing in principle to increase visits by high-level governmental, parliamentary, and business figures. Drawing the United States closer to Romania had recently assumed new importance in the Romanian mind, because the first signs had appeared that Gorbachev's reformist approach might bring the Soviet Union and the United States closer together, and Ceauşescu wanted to be the United States' best friend in the Warsaw Pact.

Ceauşescu would also welcome the opportunity to rebut current criticism in the United States about his human rights and religious policies. In expounding his views, he could combat in advance any adverse comments that Shultz might hear in Budapest, his next stop, about Romania's treatment of its Hungarian minority. Ceauşescu would also use his contact with the U.S. secretary of state, as he had used similar visits in the past, to enhance his own importance and that of his country in the eyes of his Warsaw Pact and Third World partners. Finally, the visit would give impetus to U.S.-Romanian commercial ties, including Romania's most-favored-nation status.

Ceauşescu's briefing papers, unlike Shultz's, did not suggest what points the Romanian president might make; that would have been presumptuous. They merely noted the issues and assumed that Ceauşescu would know what he wanted to say. A separate set for Vaduva, as a new foreign minister, went into considerably more detail and spelled out what he might say in response to each point the U.S. side might raise. As one of the members of the ministry's Americas section said, "We have to put the words in old man Vaduva's mouth."

The Foreign Ministry was not the only government department sending briefing materials to Ceauşescu. His office also received papers from the Ministry of Foreign Trade, the Department of Religious Affairs, and the Securitate, as well as from a number of economic ministries that had business with U.S. firms. The material from the Securitate, for example, included information on economic and commercial dealings with the United States, some of which went through firms and organizations controlled by the Securitate; on emigration to the United States and to other countries, including cases of special interest to the American side (such as Fodor); and on human, religious, and minority rights cases that had received publicity abroad. A team from the Central Committee staff reviewed the material sent to Ceauşescu's office, dropped the less important items, and checked everything for accuracy and suitability. They then reproduced the briefing papers in large type for Ceauşescu to read more easily.

As it turned out, Ceauşescu did not consult his briefing materials during his talk with Shultz or even bring them with him to the meeting. This is one of the paradoxes of modern diplomatic life. Larger and larger staffs prepare more and more material for busy ministers who have less and less time to read it. Some pay no attention to it at all. Most will read the summary and glance through other parts. Some will study it carefully; a few will even read aloud from it during their meetings. This is partly a matter of individual style and partly of the time available and the individual's familiarity with the issues.

Ceauşescu, despite his vanity and experience, did normally review the material sent to him and usually appeared familiar with even the details of the issues raised with him by the U.S. side. While he did not normally bring his briefing material into the room, he would on occasion ask an aide to fetch it from his desk so he could cite a particular statistic or American statement. He did not, however, do this during his meeting with Shultz, but seemed to Kirk to be well versed, as was Shultz, both in the basic U.S.-Romanian issues and in the general international problems they discussed.

The most important U.S. preparation for the visit was a letter from Ronald Reagan to Ceauşescu. Shultz handed the signed copy to Ceauşescu when he met with him on December 15, although the State Department had instructed Kirk to give an advance copy to the Romanians on December 8. The purpose was to give Ceauşescu, who had much more respect for presidents than for foreign ministers, advance word that the problems in the relationship were serious and that the Romanians needed to do something about them.

The letter stated Reagan's desire to broaden and enhance the U.S.-Romanian relationship but expressed uneasiness at the stresses that had appeared in it. The letter called for a further serious effort to break the momentum of these stresses. While indicating respect for Romania's sovereignty, it mentioned a number of specific issues touching on Romania's internal affairs: the lack of a written agreement on emigration procedures, the importation of Bibles, administrative discrimination against religious groups not recognized by the Romanians, and emigration permission for Fodor's family. Neither the Foreign Ministry nor Ceauşescu's office made any comment on the letter, nor did the letter persuade Ceauşescu to take a conciliatory line with Shultz.[36]

As the day of the visit approached, communication about the details of the schedule, briefings, and protocol intensified. As always, Washington was particularly concerned about the secretary's security. The inability of an advance U.S. security team to land in Bucharest because of fog and the absence of precise details on such matters as the schedule and the motorcade route troubled the U.S. security people greatly. The U.S. embassy assured Washington that one thing they did not have to worry about was security. Bucharest was always under very tight police control, and the Romanians would provide any distinguished visitor total security, no matter what the inconvenience to the population.

Sure enough, when the visit took place, the streets down which Shultz traveled were totally cleared of other traffic, and omnipresent security personnel held the public away from whatever area Shultz was in. The U.S. security people were delighted and gave the impression that they wished they could do the same in Washington.

Shultz arrived on schedule. He found a "gloomy city that seemed to have lain unimproved since the 1920s except for the unfinished and ugly high-rise buildings that were sprinkled about, the twisted rods of their structural beams sticking out, making them seem more like bombed-out buildings than ones still under construction."[37] He went immediately to meet with Foreign Minister Vaduva, to whom he expressed his wish for a constructive visit. The United States, he said, valued Romania's unique position in the Warsaw Pact and would like to enhance U.S.-Romanian cooperation in fields such as counterterrorism. But, there were problems in the relationship.

Shultz handed Vaduva a letter from House Minority Leader Robert Michel of Illinois that Shultz said illustrated some of the current problems in the U.S.-Romanian relationship. The letter addressed the issues of importation of Bibles, the destruction of churches in the course of urban reconstruction, and permission for religious groups not officially recognized, such as the Nazarenes (to which Michel belonged), to practice their religion in Romania. Shultz said the United States had respect for Romania's views on independence and sovereignty, but these human rights issues were affecting relations between the two countries.

Vaduva made no substantive response whatsoever. He uttered a few meaningless pleasantries and then excused himself to brief Ceaușescu for his meeting with Shultz. Vaduva was new at the job and timid by nature, but his conduct certainly underlined the inhibition of Romanian officials (even ministers) in talking to visitors who were also to meet with Ceaușescu. It is even doubtful that Vaduva's briefing included many of Michel's or Shultz's critical points, as Vaduva did not want to give Ceaușescu bad news and he may have hoped that Shultz would omit such unpleasant items in his meeting with the chief of state.

Shultz's meeting with Ceaușescu, immediately after the Vaduva meeting, lasted nearly three hours. It followed the same format as Kirk's previously described meeting with Ceaușescu: arrival at Central Committee headquarters in time for the meeting to begin at the agreed hour, a standing greeting by Ceaușescu, photographs, and then to the armchairs.

It was Ceaușescu's practice to let his foreign visitor speak first, and Kirk always recommended that visitors make all their points in this first presentation; once Ceaușescu started to speak, the visitor might not get another chance. Even if the visitor spoke for 15 or 20 minutes, Kirk noted, Ceaușescu would remember, without taking notes, all the visitor's major points, and respond to them one by one. His memory was indeed good, and this meeting proved no exception.

Shultz started his presentation by declaring the U.S.-Romanian relationship on the whole worthwhile but in some respects at a difficult moment. There was great concern in the United States about certain Romanian policies. He mentioned the issues he had raised with Vaduva in summarizing the Michel letter. He also referred to the U.S. desire to put into writing the oral agreement on emigration procedures reached with State Department Counselor Derwinski that summer. Finally, he pointed out that the refusal to allow the Fodor family to emigrate had attracted considerable unfavorable attention in the United States. Schultz noted that satisfying the U.S. concerns on these points would not require a change in Romanian laws or involve interference in Romania's internal affairs.

Ceaușescu took a wholly uncompromising line: No more Bibles were needed, and freedom of religion was greater in Romania than in most other countries, with the government even paying priests' salaries. Written emigration procedures were not necessary, and anyone who violated Romanian laws (i.e., the individuals for whom the United States was requesting release from jail or emigration permission) would be punished. He emphatically reasserted Romania's dedication to independence and gave an impassioned rejection of anyone's right to interfere in Romania's internal affairs. The U.S.-Romanian relationship "could be better," he said, and he called on the United States to help through such measures as relaxing restrictions on the export of U.S. products to Romania.

Shultz then suggested that the bilateral matters the two men had discussed should be pursued in the two capitals through diplomatic channels. He would name Ambassador Kirk in Romania and Counselor Derwinski in Washington as the American interlocutors. Ceauşescu agreed to the suggestion and said Vaduva or his deputy would represent the Romanian side in Bucharest, and Ambassador Gavrilescu would do so in Washington. Ceauşescu said it would be important to keep these matters out of the press, however. (He did not wish to be party to any public hint of differences between Romania and the United States.)

This proposed arrangement, although agreed to by both Shultz and Ceauşescu, never amounted to anything at all. There was not a single meeting in either Bucharest or Washington that could legitimately be called a follow-up exchange. The U.S. side made repeated demarches in both Bucharest and Washington on the issues raised by Shultz but never succeeded in initiating a genuine diplomatic dialogue.

In retrospect, the failure of this diplomatic channel was not surprising, although the arrangement seemed a natural and sensible one from the American point of view. In U.S. dealings with other countries, when the political leaders have agreed that the problems between them should be resolved, they often give lower officials the task of defining the issues and developing ways to accommodate or reach a compromise over opposing points of view. These officials work out the problems and present the results to their superiors for approval and resolution of the remaining differences. It is a technique used often in diplomatic discourse.

But in regimes like Ceauşescu's, the Supreme Leader is the only person who can determine negotiating positions. Individuals lower in the hierarchy, even ministers, cannot explore compromises. They can only repeat the hard line. If there are complex questions to be dealt with, as in arms control negotiations, talks can be useful in clarifying issues even in the absence of any agreement. But when the issues are relatively clear, as in the U.S.-Romanian case, such talks are of little use; indeed, they can serve to solidify disagreements rather than resolve them.

Shultz and Ceauşescu also discussed the world scene during their December 15 meeting. Shultz began by stating that President Reagan would welcome Ceauşescu's views on Gorbachev and the general international situation. An extensive exchange ensued, with Ceauşescu expressing some differences with Soviet policy but offering no substantially new information or penetrating insights.

The talk did clear up one misunderstanding, though. Shultz had recently made a public statement to the effect that it was "unnatural" for Europe to be divided by the Berlin Wall. Ceauşescu had apparently interpreted this as meaning that the United States wanted changes in European borders. Romania had gained Transylvania from Hungary in 1918, but Hitler and Mussolini had forced Romania to cede part of it back to Hungary in 1940. After World War II, Romania had recovered the territory, but the possibility of losing some or all of it again was an enduring Romanian concern. Ceauşescu therefore took the occasion to state that "many" were concerned that the United States wished to change borders in Europe.

When Shultz assured him that the United States desired no border changes, Ceauşescu was obviously pleased. He asked if Shultz would say that publicly, and Shultz agreed to do so. It was clearly no accident that a Romanian "correspondent," looking very much like a government official, asked Shultz at his press conference in Bucharest later that day about his view on Europe's borders. The Romanian press duly reported Shultz's response.[38]

While Shultz, Kirk, Derwinski, and Ridgway were meeting with Ceauşescu, other leading members of Shultz's party—led by Peter Rodman, director of the State Department Policy Planning Staff, Mark Palmer, deputy assistant secretary of state for European affairs, and NSC staff member Paula Dobriansky—met with a Romanian team consisting of Deputy Foreign Minister Maria Groza, Acting Director of Western Hemisphere Affairs Ion Beşteliu, Acting Deputy Director Mircea Raceanu, and others. This meeting, which brought together many of the leading officials concerned with U.S.-Romanian relations, was a good deal more tense and detailed than Shultz's talk with Ceauşescu.

Palmer stated that the U.S.-Romanian situation was deteriorating. He had never seen a worse atmosphere in U.S.-Romanian relations in the four years he had been dealing with Eastern Europe. Dobriansky added that Romanian human rights issues were of concern to President Reagan. There had been no progress on them in recent years. The U.S. officials then reviewed the principal issues. They mentioned a number of individual human rights and emigration cases that the United States wanted to see resolved and attempted to hammer home the real difficulties in the U.S.-Romanian relationship. Raceanu and Groza came out of the meeting convinced that something had to be done if the relationship was to be preserved.

In a well-functioning and open ministry, signals from the lower level can be very useful in alerting the top leadership that a situation is more serious than the language of ministers and presidents would suggest. This did not happen in this case. Vaduva received a written report of the Groza meeting, but he did not ask Raceanu to forward it to Ceauşescu, as was the normal practice. Raceanu was convinced that Vaduva never gave Ceauşescu even an oral indication of the tough tenor of the Groza meeting: He would not have wanted to make such a report to Ceauşescu, especially when the latter had already received the American message directly from a more authoritative source, the U.S. secretary of state. Vaduva himself probably felt the officials' stark presentation exaggerated the seriousness of the situation, given Secretary Shultz's more moderate language.

Vaduva's luncheon in Shultz's honor followed immediately after the Ceauşescu meeting. It took place in the "Rhapsodia" room, on the top floor of the Intercontinental Hotel in Bucharest, a remnant of the 1970s when Ceauşescu's reputation in the United States was high and it seemed as if Romania might be able to attract large numbers of American tourists. Despite its name, the Rhapsodia was dark and drab, its folkloric decor faded and slightly soiled. Although most of the guests had been waiting for over an hour and a half for those attending the long Ceauşescu-Shultz meeting to arrive, all had been careful not to drink much. They knew that the Securitate microphones would pick up their remarks, at least at the table.

Diplomatic lunches and dinners can be the occasion for an informal and very useful exchange of views on the issues discussed earlier or on matters deemed too delicate to be brought up in formal talks. At this lunch, however, neither was possible. Not only was Vaduva not one to elaborate or embellish on what Ceauşescu had said, but he and Shultz sat on opposite sides of the table. At least half a dozen people in addition to their interpreters would hear anything they did say to each other. Furthermore, the Romanians, as was their custom, arranged for music and a folk dance demonstration during lunch. This was a nice gesture, and interesting for the guests who had not seen it before, but it effectively precluded almost any conversation.

Toasts at diplomatic meals are often important statements of policy, and Shultz's and Vaduva's staffs had worked hard on texts for their bosses to use. When Vaduva rose to make his toast, however, he said that he merely wanted to express his pleasure in hosting Shultz but would make no further comment, as he could add nothing to the authoritative exposition of Romania's position just given to Secretary Shultz by President Ceauşescu himself.

Shultz, in reply, thanked his host for the many courtesies shown his party and referred briefly to his conversation with Ceauşescu, saying it had been frank, detailed, and worthwhile and had covered areas on which they agreed as well as areas on which they did not agree. Even these few words conveyed a signal to the Romanian officials present, as they constituted an unusually downbeat description of a conversation with Ceauşescu. No one was ever supposed to confess to disagreement with the Supreme Leader.

After lunch and a visit to the American embassy to offer some words of encouragement to the staff, Shultz returned to the Hotel Intercontinental to hold his press conference, the final item on his program. Those present were representatives of the Romanian press, newspeople traveling with Shultz, and the few foreign correspondents in Bucharest at the time. Shultz said he had agreed with Ceauşescu that relations between the two countries "could be better." He noted that he and Ceauşescu had identified areas in which they were in agreement, others where their points of view differed, and some where more effort was called for. They had discussed why relations were not better and what could be done in this regard, and had set up some procedures that the secretary hoped would help resolve what differences there were.[39]

The Romanian press reported Shultz's statement that there was disagreement between himself and Ceauşescu, a most unusual public admission and a sign to readers that all was not well in the U.S.-Romanian relationship. This impression was heightened when Ceauşescu added some tough, extemporaneous words on the importance of noninterference in internal affairs in a speech he gave to a Plenum of Working People the next day. The American embassy, in its report to Washington, characterized the situation as "flashing yellow," with Ceauşescu's nationalism aroused.

Overall, however, the Romanian side interpreted and portrayed the Shultz visit as a renewed recognition by the United States of Romania's policy of independence and as a further sign of the existence of a "special relationship" between the two countries. The Romanian media's treatment of the visit stressed these points, citing the Ceauşescu-Shultz meeting and Shultz's statement that one of the purposes of his trip was to "pay his respects" to many of the foreign policy positions Romania had taken.[40] Vaduva and Aurel Duma told Raceanu that Ceauşescu was very pleased with the visit, and Vaduva congratulated the Americas Department on its good work in making the visit a success. This was one of only a few times this happened during Raceanu's many years at the ministry. It indicated to him that Ceauşescu felt the visit had gone well, as Vaduva would not have dared to congratulate anyone on something involving Ceauşescu without the dictator's direction.

In his briefing for top Foreign Ministry officials, Vaduva characterized the visit as another "success" for Romania's foreign policy and an American "recognition" of Ceauşescu's important international role. When discussing the problems raised by Shultz, Vaduva gave no specifics, noting only that Shultz had raised "a few problems" that revealed his unfamiliarity with Romanian realities and that "The Comrade" (Ceauşescu) had given appropriate responses. As was usual in Vaduva's handling of Ceauşescu's meetings, he gave no other, more detailed, briefing, nor did he circulate a written record of the conversation.

The Foreign Ministry's Americas Department got some additional information through personal contact between Raceanu and Ceauşescu's interpreter, Gheorghe Petricu, but this was strictly informal and unauthorized. When Andrei had been foreign minister, he used to give the department some details on Ceauşescu's meetings, but Vaduva was not a man to pass on what Ceauşescu might consider private remarks. Thus on this occasion, as on many others, Kirk and his staff were the ones to tell their Romanian counterparts what Ceauşescu had said at his meetings with the American visitors.

The phenomenon of unreported or partially reported presidential conversations, not unknown in the U.S. government at times, complicates diplomats' work immensely. Because policy direction flows from the top down, it is hard for diplomats to function if they know a subject has been discussed by their president but do not know what position he or she took. This is especially true in a regime such as Ceauşescu's, where the greatest sin is to be at variance with the boss, and where officials know that their office meetings are taped by the security forces. The result is that officials are reluctant to commit themselves in any way and are driven to repeating hackneyed lines rather than commenting meaningfully on the points raised. It is a serious obstacle to the kind of informal diplomatic interchange that can identify and often resolve problems before they become major issues.

In the case of the Shultz visit, the misleading private and public Romanian accounts of Shultz's discussion with Ceauşescu meant that most of Romanian officialdom, as well as the Romanian public, took the visit as a sign that all was well in U.S.-Romanian relations, instead of as a warning that Romania needed to take action to reverse a deterioration in those relations. For Shultz and his party, Ceauşescu's rigidity, the uselessness of the talks with the foreign minister, and the party's fleeting glimpses of the gloomy Romanian capital constituted a depressing experience. What started out as a trip to accentuate the positive—by recognizing Romania's relative foreign policy independence while conveying U.S. concerns on human rights—became a dash of cold water, convincing the U.S. participants that relations would deteriorate further unless talks through diplomatic channels revealed more flexibility on the Romanian side. Other than granting emigration permission to a few of the persons mentioned by the U.S. side in the meeting with Groza, however, such flexibility was not forthcoming, and relations worsened.

The first sign of Romanian intransigence was Ceauşescu's January 7, 1986, reply to the letter President Reagan had sent him in connection with Shultz's visit. After commenting on a number of international issues, Ceauşescu complained that "certain circles" were trying to interfere in Romania's internal affairs by making U.S.-Romanian economic relations (a reference to MFN) conditional upon Romania's meeting U.S. human rights concerns.

He then proceeded to reject the specific points raised in Reagan's letter. He said that U.S. human rights complaints were artificially created by special groups, that written procedures on emigration were unnecessary, that the state of religion in Romania was admirable, and that no imported Bibles were needed. In short, the letter gave no hint of any flexibility whatsoever.[41] It remained to be seen if the diplomats could do any better.

Kirk tried out the diplomatic channel immediately upon his return to Bucharest from Christmas leave. His first meeting was with Ion Stoian, Communist Party secretary for international affairs. Tall, thin, and red-haired, Stoian was an important figure. Besides his party secretary post, he was an alternate member of the party's top-level Political Executive

Committee. He had served as head of the Romanian party academy in the late 1960s, and in the mid-1970s became party boss of the county of Constanta, which contained Romania's chief port and the principal seaside resorts for the party elite. In the late 1970s he was made ambassador to Albania, and in 1984 party secretary for international affairs.

Stoian was a typical party activist, whose view of the world was shaped by his conviction of the superiority of the socialist system and unquestioning loyalty to the Ceauşescu family. He never understood the way a democracy worked and consistently favored a tough line toward the United States. He was aggressive and rude toward his subordinates, often threatening them with dismissal if he found fault with their actions or statements. Tried after the December 1989 revolution, he was sentenced to 14 years in prison, released in 1993, and pardoned in March 1994. [42]

Stoian opened his January 14, 1986, meeting with Kirk by stating that the "success" of the Shultz visit "opened new possibilities" for Kirk to have a broad dialogue with the Romanian government. To Stoian's annoyance, Kirk then went through the list of U.S. human rights concerns. Stoian rejected all these complaints, noting that the United States was making "too much noise" on emigration, especially as the United States could not find employment for 20 million (*sic*) of its own citizens and had a huge trade deficit with Japan. The U.S. complaints about religion in Romania arose from America's lack of understanding of Romanian culture; the Romanian government tolerated religion and even paid salaries to the priests. Stoian concluded by suggesting that the United States should extend MFN to Romania on a multiyear, not on an annual, basis.

It was clear from Stoian's remarks that he had no grasp of the essence of U.S. human rights concerns or of the threat they posed to the U.S.-Romanian relationship. Kirk, hoping a visit to America might help open Stoian's eyes, invited him to come to the United States. Stoian thanked Kirk without making any commitment. According to comments to Raceanu by Ceauşescu's interpreter, Gheorghe Petricu, whom Stoian promised to take with him if he went, Stoian at first liked the idea of a visit. Upon reflection, however, he found the prospect of having to argue about human rights with the Americans very distasteful and therefore never responded to Kirk's invitation.

Kirk's next effort was with Vaduva. In a meeting with him on January 18, Kirk recalled that President Ceauşescu and Secretary Shultz had assigned Vaduva and Kirk to discuss problems between the two countries to see if solutions could be found. He said that Romania's friends were disturbed by the atmosphere currently surrounding Romanian-American relations. The mood in Washington was not favorable to Romania. Even the Metro buses there were carrying large posters saying "Romania cries for freedom." Kirk then reviewed the outstanding American concerns in detail.

In an effort to deflect the Romanian contention that his remarks constituted interference in internal affairs, he made a point of saying that in raising these issues he did not question Romania's right to decide its own internal policies. He felt it his duty, however, to keep Romania informed of the concerns in the United States so that the Romanian government could take them into account in determining its policies. Kirk repeated this line in many subsequent conversations.

Vaduva responded briefly, noting that President Ceauşescu had covered these issues in his conversation with Shultz. Vaduva said he had little to add but would be prepared to discuss Kirk's points in more detail later on and looked forward to an early meeting to do so.

Afterward, Raceanu, who had been present at the meeting with Kirk, told Vaduva that Kirk's formulation constituted a new element. In recognizing that decisions on the human rights matters he raised were within Romanian jurisdiction Kirk had countered, at least rhetorically, Romania's argument that raising these concerns constituted interference in its internal affairs. At the same time, Kirk's approach meant that Romania, not the United States, would be responsible if failure to remove these concerns resulted in U.S. actions against Romania. Raceanu urged Vaduva to call this new element to Ceauşescu's attention.

There is no evidence that Vaduva did so, nor did he ever follow up on his promise to go into these issues with Kirk in more detail. Although Kirk himself raised these matters with Vaduva on many subsequent occasions, Vaduva never engaged in a substantive discussion of them.

The high-level U.S.-Romanian contacts in the fall of 1985—Foreign Minister Andrei's meetings with Shultz and Bush, Shultz's meeting with Ceauşescu, and the exchange of letters between Presidents Reagan and Ceauşescu—turned out to be some of the last in the series of contacts at this level that had taken place between Romania and the United States over many years. These latest contacts constituted a top-level American warning to the Romanians that the "special relationship" was in serious trouble and that Romanian moves in the human rights field were essential to preserve it. Romanian policymakers, starting with Ceauşescu, simply did not get the message.

The principal cause of this failure of communication was that Ceauşescu could not imagine the United States dropping its "special relationship" with him and viewed Shultz's presence in Romania as proof of this. He therefore saw no reason to grant the U.S. requests, which he felt could undermine his independence and even threaten his regime.

Other, more mundane factors contributed to the lack of understanding. One was Foreign Minister Vaduva's decision to leave the leading role in dealing with Ceauşescu on U.S. matters to party secretary Stoian and Securitate chief Postelnicu. Those who knew Vaduva believed unanimously that his action did not reflect a personal antipathy toward the United States but rather his fear that any association with the United States could hurt him in the eyes of Elena Ceauşescu, his principal protector. To a cautious man like Vaduva, this made it important to avoid any association with U.S. affairs wherever possible.

Having Postelnicu and Stoian as Ceauşescu's principal advisers on relations with the United States was unfortunate, for Postelnicu was as hostile to the United States as was Stoian. This was perhaps to be expected from one who, like Postelnicu, had been head of the Securitate for five years; but Postelnicu's hostility also derived from his inherently suspicious and unscrupulous nature, which led him to expect the worst of everyone.

Postelnicu was not a nice man. Council of State Vice President Manea Manescu, in an interview published in the newspaper *Romania Libera* in January 1990, described Postelnicu as Mrs. Ceauşescu's confidant— a man who informed her about everyone, "including us"—and called him "a born criminal."[43] Postelnicu's formal education was rudimentary (he acknowledged at his trial after the revolution in 1989 that he had left school after the sixth grade). He had proved himself useful to the Ceauşescus by covering up a serious automobile accident caused by their ne'er-do-well son Nicu in the 1970s. He was rewarded for that and for his continuing loyalty by a series of promotions, leading eventually to his becoming, in 1984, an alternate member of the Political Executive Committee and, in 1987, interior minister, a job he held until Ceauşescu's downfall. Postelnicu was tried in February 1990 and sentenced to life imprisonment.[44]

Stoian and Postelnicu resented U.S. human rights demands. They disagreed with their content and considered them gross interference in Romania's internal affairs. To accede, they felt, would be a sign of weakness. They believed that the United States was advancing these views to destabilize the Ceauşescu regime and feared that granting the U.S. requests might actually achieve this purpose. Finally, they disliked the United States and had no sense of the broader utility of Romania's relationship with Washington. They seldom reported U.S. concerns to Ceauşescu and slanted their presentations when they did. Their role adversely affected U.S.-Romanian relations to a significant degree.

The incompetence of the Romanian ambassador in Washington, Nicolae Gavrilescu, and the confidence the Romanian leadership and Ceauşescu personally placed in him constituted another problem. Ceauşescu had appointed Gavrilescu ambassador to Washington in April 1985 in the belief that he was a close friend of Vice President Bush. The background of this belief was as follows.

When Bush came to Bucharest as vice president in September 1983, he asked that the guest list for one of the functions in his honor include both Gavrilescu, who had been Romanian ambassador in Beijing during Bush's service there, and Corneliu Bogdan, whom Bush had known as Romanian ambassador in Washington in the 1970s. Bogdan was an outstanding diplomat who had been named by *Newsweek* in 1972 as one of the five most active ambassadors in Washington at the time. Bogdan fell into disgrace in 1982, however, when his younger daughter asked to emigrate to the United States, as her older sister had already done. The ministry's briefing paper for Ceauşescu in 1983 therefore did not mention Bush's inclusion of Bogdan; it stated only that Bush had requested the inclusion of Gavrilescu, then minister of tourism. Ceauşescu thus concluded that there was a close personal relationship between the two men.

Raceanu learned later at the State Department that Bush had first asked State to have only Bogdan added to the guest list. Upon being advised that naming only Bogdan might heighten Bogdan's problems with Ceauşescu, Bush had added Gavrilescu. There had never been much of a personal relationship between the two; in fact, the only time Bush ever received Gavrilescu in Washington was when Gavrilescu accompanied Andrei to the vice president's office in September 1985.

Unaware of the background of Bush's 1983 request to see Gavrilescu, and a great believer in the importance of top-level friendships in relations among states, Ceauşescu thus sent "Bush's friend" as ambassador to Washington and kept him there even after hearing privately from a number of Americans outside of government that Gavrilescu was a disaster.

Unfortunately for U.S.-Romanian relations, Gavrilescu spoke poor English and had no feel for the U.S. system. His clumsy demarches to the executive and legislative branches often worsened matters rather than improved them. He had little understanding of U.S. policy concerns and no desire to trouble his boss with unpleasant news about them. As a protégé of Elena Ceauşescu, he wanted to avoid any appearance of special pleading for the United States for fear of offending his patron. The information Ceauşescu obtained from his ambassador in Washington on U.S. matters therefore reinforced the misleading reports he was receiving from his advisers at home.

A final complication in U.S.-Romanian relations was that the heads of many Romanian government ministries and departments dealing with areas of U.S. interest (educational and scientific exchanges, religion, emigration, and security) had a negative attitude toward U.S. concerns or felt that doing anything to meet those concerns would endanger their personal bureaucratic future. They were aware of Elena Ceauşescu's growing influence and knew she would resent any concessions to the United States. They wished to avoid offending her in any way.

Although this negative attitude went against President Ceauşescu's general policy of maintaining good relations with the United States, these officials knew that the president also wanted to minimize exchanges between the two societies, even while publicly encouraging top-level visits. They thus felt reasonably safe dragging their feet on lower-level exchanges. The result was a continuing decline in the already small numbers of Americans accepted by the Romanians as part of an academic exchange or as Fulbright scholars and the virtual cessation of travel to the United States by Romanian scholars. When coupled with the political and economic restrictions on the import of Western publications, this left the Romanian scientific and educational communities almost totally isolated from the West.

All these factors set the stage for Romanian intransigence on the bilateral issues the United States considered important. The effort of the United States to break through this intransigence and the eventual failure of this effort became the basic themes of the succeeding months and years.

▼4▼

Human Rights Take Center Stage
1986

The early weeks of 1986 were marked by renewed visits to Bucharest by prominent American Jewish leaders. They were attempting to persuade Ceaușescu of the seriousness of the congressional situation vis-à-vis Romania and the need for some gestures on his part to meet American concerns. The first was Rabbi Arthur Schneier, head of the Appeal of Conscience Foundation and a frequent visitor to Romania, whom Ceaușescu greatly respected for his world prestige and ecumenical approach.

On February 12, with Roger Kirk present, Rabbi Schneier spent almost two and a half hours telling Ceaușescu about the clouds on the horizon of U.S.-Romanian relations. Schneier suggested sending an envoy to the United States to present Romania's case to the administration and to Congress. The envoy should be knowledgeable about the issues, should speak English, and could usefully be a woman. (He was, in fact, describing Deputy Foreign Minister Maria Groza without specifically naming her.) Ceaușescu, however, gave no ground on any of these points.

Schneier was followed in quick succession by Alfred Moses, an American Jewish leader with a long-standing interest in Romania, and by Jack Spitzer, honorary chairman of B'nai B'rith. Accompanied by Kirk, they joined together on February 17 for a meeting with Ilie Vaduva and later met with Ceaușescu, with whom they raised the familiar problems. Ceaușescu responded that there could be no interference in Romania's internal affairs; if that was the price of MFN, MFN was not worth it. The emigration issue was already resolved, he asserted, more Bibles were not needed, and additional denominations would not be recognized.

In an attempt at a counterattack, Ceaușescu challenged his interlocutors to say how many copies of Marx's works there were in the

United States. He was certain that the U.S. government severely limited their number and did not credit his visitors' explanation that their number would depend solely on the demand for them. Spitzer replied to Ceauşescu's long discourse by urging him to demonstrate flexibility and cooperation on the significant problems he and Moses had raised.

Moses took advantage of the interview to inform Ceauşescu about a project to have a Romanian Jewish youth choir sing in the U.S. Capitol at the annual Holocaust commemoration in May 1986 and tour the United States afterwards. This would call prominent public attention to Romania's tolerant policy toward the religious and cultural life of its Jewish community, probably the most lenient policy of any country in the Soviet bloc at the time. Moses asked if the Romanian national airline, TAROM, could provide the choir's transportation to the United States. When Ceauşescu noted that TAROM was an independent agency, Moses rejoined that he was sure Ceauşescu's encouragement would help TAROM reach a decision, a remark that brought forth a chuckle from the dictator.

When Moses returned to the issue later in the conversation, Ceauşescu said he "saw no problem" in TAROM's providing the transportation, a comment that the Americans (and the Romanians) in the room took as a promise that TAROM would do so. Provision of the funds and travel permission were not forthcoming, however, and the trip by the choir was thus put on ice. The following year Moses pressed the Romanians hard to permit the choir to travel and to provide transportation. Officials of the Romanian Department of Religious Affairs informed Chief Rabbi Moses Rosen in April that the government would give the choir travel permission but that the U.S. sponsors would have to pay the transportation costs.

▼ ▼ ▼

Moses Rosen was one of the more remarkable figures in Ceauşescu's Romania. He had good access to Ceauşescu, at least until 1985–86, and used it to gain concessions for his coreligionists. As he was more willing than most Romanians to tell Ceauşescu about American human rights concerns, the United States used him as a conduit to the dictator.

A rabbi since 1938 and chief rabbi since 1948, Rosen had been able to achieve privileges for the Romanian Jewish community unequaled by other religious groups in Romania or by Jews elsewhere in Eastern Europe, accomplishing what President Chaim Herzog of Israel characterized in a letter to Rosen as an "almost impossible mission."[45] Perhaps the most important privilege gained for Romanian Jews was their ability to emigrate relatively freely, a fact that had reduced the Romanian Jewish community to less than 30,000 members, mostly elderly, by 1985.

The Jews who remained received special privileges as well. They were the only religious group permitted to conduct formal religious education for their young and to run hostels for their old, financed largely by U.S. funds. The community had published a Hebrew-language newspaper, *Revista Cultului Mozaic,* since 1957 and had a Yiddish-language theater and a choir whose uniforms incorporated the blue and white of the Israeli flag. When Kirk attended a Hanukkah service at the main synagogue in Bucharest in December 1985, the new Israeli ambassador, Yosef Govrin, was next to him. Govrin, who had just come from heading the East European division in the Israeli Foreign Ministry and who had served in Moscow in the 1960s, shook his head when the choir appeared. "I can't believe this," he kept saying as the choir sang traditional Jewish songs in Hebrew, Yiddish, and Romanian.

The favored position of the Jews, especially concerning emigration, was well known in Romania, leading some Romanians to "rediscover" their Jewishness and others to seek it. Rosen kept a sign in his office: "No conversions accepted. Argument is useless."

Rosen's chief asset in achieving this success was the interest of the U.S. Jewish community in the welfare of their coreligionists in Romania and their willingness to use their influence in Washington to promote good relations with Romania on the condition that favorable treatment of their Romanian brethren continued. Another asset was Rosen's consummate skill at operating within the Romanian system and his willingness to be useful to Ceauşescu, by lobbying for Romania in the United States and by issuing public statements of gratitude for Ceauşescu's Jewish policy even while pushing Ceauşescu for additional concessions.

Rosen's maneuverings and his self-importance—he was addressed as "His Eminence" in the Jewish community, drove about in a chauffeured, if very old, Mercedes sedan, and, like other major religious leaders in Romania, was a member of parliament—earned him the enmity, even contempt, of some observers inside and outside Romania. Others considered his service to Ceauşescu a betrayal of his honor and even of his faith. Kirk and Raceanu, however, believe that Rosen was sincere in trying to help his people and that a more uncompromising position on his part would have been less effective. Throughout Kirk's three and a half years as ambassador he kept close contact with Rosen and never failed to enjoy a discussion with the rabbi, a portly, white-bearded individual with a puckish sense of humor and a keen insight into the workings of the Romanian society and government.

The Romanian government's reluctance to fund the youth choir's travel to the United States was typical of the small-mindedness of the Romanian leadership and showed an abysmal lack of understanding of the situation in the United States. To fund the travel would have cost the government virtually nothing, as the airline was state-financed and in any case usually had empty seats on the New York flight.

The government's refusal greatly annoyed some of America's most prominent Jewish leaders, people whose understanding and support the Romanian government badly needed. In addition, the Romanian government was jeopardizing an invaluable public relations opportunity in the United States, one they could not buy for hundreds of thousands of dollars. The choir, a group of enthusiastic and attractive youngsters dressed in the colors of the Israeli flag, was a unique phenomenon among the Iron Curtain countries and was potentially Ceauşescu's greatest propaganda asset. When the choir finally went to the United States in 1987, with travel paid by the American Jewish community, it made a fine impression and probably led many Americans to believe, incorrectly, that things were not so bad in Romania.

Ion Cumpanaşu, head of the government's Department of Religious Affairs, told Raceanu privately in April 1987 that Elena Ceauşescu had vetoed the idea of paying for the transport. According to Cumpanaşu, she had said to him, "The American Jews are rich; they have lots of money and so they can pay for the transport expenses as well as for the costs of the choir in the United States. The Romanian side will not pay anything for this."

It may well be that Ceauşescu's wife was the decisive factor in his canceling the 1986 commitment. Cancellation accorded with her views; she had a definite anti-Semitic streak and only a minimal understanding of the outside world, and few other people could reverse a Ceauşescu decision. Elena Ceauşescu would not have been alone in her attitude, however. Many Romanian leaders would have hesitated to see Romania represented by a Jewish choir, and few would have understood the impact such a group could have had in the United States.

When Rosen was informed of the government's decision not to pay the travel costs, he sought an audience with Foreign Minister Ioan Totu to complain that President Ceauşescu himself had promised the Americans that Romania would pay. Totu refused to meet him, but detailed Raceanu to tell Rosen that there was no chance the Romanian government would cover the transatlantic travel. When Raceanu went to Rosen's office to deliver the message a few days later, the rabbi said, "But Ceauşescu promised!" When Raceanu replied that the situation was "not President Ceauşescu's fault," Rosen interrupted him, pointing toward the telephone next to his chair as a signal that the Securitate recorded all conversations in the office.

His warning came too late, however, to stop Raceanu from saying, "The trouble comes from office number two" (that is, Elena Ceauşescu). The conversation then turned to other matters. After the two men had finished their talk and were walking down the hall from Rosen's office, Rosen said he didn't know what "that woman" had against the Jewish community, that she seemed to encourage anti-Semitic elements, and that she sought to influence her husband in that direction. Raceanu, after looking around to be sure they were alone, agreed with Rosen, adding that the leaders of the American Jewish community should be made aware of that fact.

Rosen's warning about being overheard in his office was well advised. After Raceanu's arrest in 1989, his interrogators cited his 1987 conversation with Rosen as an example of his revealing information about the views of the country's leaders to unauthorized persons. This careful Securitate recordkeeping and the very fact that the Securitate had installed microphones in the office of a prominent religious leader, an individual well known abroad and a member of parliament, were typical of the situation in Romania at the time. The Securitate kept particularly close tabs on prominent persons: government and party leaders, provincial heads, religious and media chiefs, anyone with authority. All conversations with such persons had to be conducted with regard for the Securitate microphones as well as for the individuals in the room.

While this Securitate bugging was annoying for a foreigner, it was a crucial consideration for the Romanians. They had to weigh every word for its effect on the Securitate and how it would appear in Securitate reports to the leadership. Logic, originality, expressions of agreement or understanding, even politeness, all took second place. It was therefore virtually impossible for any Romanian official to deviate from the party-line script.

This constituted one of the most serious obstacles to effective communication and negotiation. As shown in the case of Raceanu and Rosen, it made the walk down the hall to the door often the most important part of a conversation. At that point the Romanian could say a few private words to the foreign visitor or diplomat that might indicate areas of flexibility or the true reasons behind the Romanian position. The Romanian could do this, however, only if certain that the foreign interlocutor would guard the privacy of the comment and not repeat it in rooms where Securitate microphones would record it.

Many diplomatic theorists have commented on the importance of maintaining privacy during the course of negotiations and on the inhibitions placed on negotiators by the prospect of possible public disclosure of their positions. Having everything recorded by the security services is also inhibiting, but especially so to the negotiator whose security services are doing the recording. The problem is compounded by the atmosphere of mistrust that usually accompanies such surveillance, and by the fact that the negotiator's comments will be viewed from a suspicious, often xenophobic angle by his country's security officers, who usually lack an appreciation for the issues or for the subtleties of diplomatic interchange. These circumstances account for many of the seemingly ridiculous party-line statements made by diplomats who obviously know better. It complicates and sometimes blocks negotiations, even if the other individual in the discussion makes allowances for it.

The U.S. administration soon had several occasions to air its view of Romania publicly. In February 1986, President Reagan sent Congress an interim report on the status of religion in Romania and, shortly afterward, a more comprehensive description of the human rights situation in Romania as part of the State Department's annual report on human rights practices worldwide. The 1986 human rights report (on developments in 1985) was noticeably harsher than the previous year's, reflecting the deterioration of conditions in Romania, the lack of any dramatic positive event (such as Romania's participation in the 1984 Olympics), and the added importance the executive branch was giving to Romanian human rights abuses.[46]

On February 26, at Senate hearings on Romanian MFN status, administration witnesses from the State and Commerce departments and the Office of the U.S. Trade Representative argued that MFN was justified by Romania's performance on emigration (the only specific criterion in the Jackson-Vanik amendment), by its relative independence in foreign policy, and because of the leverage MFN gave the United States to achieve concessions on human rights cases. These witnesses, however, also noted and criticized the many human rights violations in Romania and described the dilemma they presented for U.S. policy.

Thus Assistant Secretary of State Rozanne Ridgway's statement, read by her deputy Mark Palmer, noted that "we have used our MFN leverage to secure a distinct improvement in Romanian emigration performance" and that the annual MFN review process had enabled the United States to highlight and resolve some individual human rights cases. It acknowledged, however, that "the process is tiring and frustrating and we and you in the Congress share disappointment and outrage."

In conclusion, the Ridgway statement noted that "our relations with Romania confront us with tough choices. On the one side, we have national security interests and our ability positively to affect the lives of individuals who need our support. On the other side, we have a sense that our engagement brings us into association with a repressive regime that neither shares nor responds to the high principles of human rights which are so important to us." The executive branch made it clear in its testimony that the administration's position on MFN would depend on Romania's meeting U.S. concerns.[47]

This was considerably tougher language than the administration had used in previous testimony, although it was mild compared to the words used by congressional and nongovernmental critics of Romania in their testimony before the committee. On March 27 Senator Larry Pressler, who had chaired the February hearings, joined Senator Richard Lugar to introduce a nonbinding Sense of the Senate resolution asking the Department of State to call the attention of the Romanian government to the need for improvements in human rights and religious freedom before the congressional debates on MFN in June.[48]

The Romanian embassy in Washington reported to Bucharest on these public documents and statements, and the Romanian leadership read these reports with concern. In fact, these reports had considerably more impact on the leadership than did Secretary Shultz's presentation to Ceauşescu or even President Reagan's December letter. As noted, Ceauşescu and his associates were so pleased with the fact of Shultz's visit—which they took as a sign of the special importance the United States attached to Romania—that they discounted, if they even heard, the critical words Shultz and Reagan addressed to them. Had the U.S. side realized this, it might have relied in following years more on public statements and less on high-level government envoys to get the message across to the Romanians.

The Romanians did not conclude from the statements and hearings that the entire U.S.-Romanian relationship was at risk, merely that a tactical problem existed in getting MFN through the renewal process. The basic reason for this misapprehension was Ceauşescu's inability to see that the overall U.S. attitude toward Romania was beginning to change and that this was bringing a worsening of relations. Ceauşescu still believed that his policy of independence would prevent the U.S. government from giving up its special relationship with Romania. He was convinced that the criticism of Romania in the United States came basically from groups hostile to Romania, such as Hungarians who wanted to return Transylvania to Hungary, and that these groups had been able to influence a small number of senators and representatives who, he felt, were responsible for his problems in the Congress.

The ministry's reports to Ceauşescu most frequently singled out the following as hostile to Romania: Senators William Armstrong of Colorado, Christopher Dodd of Connecticut, Jesse Helms of North Carolina, Steven Symms of Idaho, and Paul Trible of Virginia, and Representatives Philip Crane and John Porter of Illinois, Robert Dornan and Tom Lantos of California, Tony Hall of Ohio, Richard Schulze of Pennsylvania, Mark Siljander of Michigan, Christopher Smith of New Jersey, and Frank Wolf of Virginia. Ceauşescu believed that the adoption of minimal measures would be enough to blunt the arguments of this group and thus assure renewal of MFN. He therefore ordered a number of steps to this end.

First, Ceauşescu personally instructed Ioan Totu and Ion Cumpanaşu to prepare a white paper refuting the State Department's interim report on religion in Romania. The resulting document had two columns. The left column listed the points in the State Department's report, while the right, prepared with the help of the Orthodox patriarchate, gave a refutation that was in part factual, in part fabricated. There was no indication in the version sent to Ceauşescu as to which of the material was accurate and which was false.

Ceauşescu instructed the Department of Religious Affairs to produce foreign-language brochures on freedom of religion in Romania for distribution abroad by Romania's diplomatic missions, especially in the NATO countries. The United States received special attention: the Romanian embassy in Washington was to send copies to every senator and representative. In addition, Ceauşescu sent delegations of religious leaders to the United States to explain the favorable situation of religion in Romania, particularly to members of Congress. Such delegations went to the United States several times over the next four years. They usually included prominent representatives of the Orthodox, Jewish, and Protestant denominations, with the senior Orthodox representative (Metropolitan Plamadeala of Sibiu on two or three occasions) as principal spokesman. Sometimes Orthodox or Jewish leaders went alone, but Ceaușescu never trusted the Protestant leaders to go by themselves, for fear they might make statements damaging to him if left to their own devices.

As for the State Department's human rights report, Ceaușescu told Ilie Vaduva that the ministry should make official demarches to the United States in Bucharest and Washington, stating that the U.S. report was based on "dubious" and "ill-intentioned" sources, gave a distorted picture of the situation in Romania, and represented gross interference in the internal affairs of the country. Ceaușescu also told the ministry to say that no one had given the United States the right to arrogate to itself the position of judge over other countries.

These moves of the Romanian government to improve its image represented a substantial effort and some expenditure of very scarce hard currency, but the government's expectations were far too high. The printed material and brochures the Romanians handed out had very little impact in the United States, as they were widely, and correctly, regarded as pure propaganda. The U.S. embassy in Bucharest was completely unaware that the document on religion in Romania had had such high-level attention in the Romanian hierarchy and regarded it as just another propaganda sheet. The embassy forwarded its copy to Washington by mail, not telegram, with the notation that a brief inspection had shown it to be not only misleading, but positively false in many respects and that the embassy did not intend to devote resources to checking it out in detail.

Kirk and his colleagues rejected the Romanian criticism of the State Department's human rights report without even awaiting instructions from Washington. They told the Romanians the report was based on information from private individuals and organizations as well as from the government, the procedure followed for the reports on every country. The Department of State took the same basic line in discussions with the Romanian embassy. The annual human rights report always brought complaints from many countries, and protestations from a regime like Ceaușescu's had minimal impact in Washington.

The Romanian religious delegations were colorful, and moderately well received in Washington, but Ceaușescu's reputation was already bad enough in congressional and governmental circles to make most Americans who saw the delegations discount heavily what they had to say. The media showed no great interest, and they, too, were sufficiently hostile to Ceauşescu not to want to give space to what they considered to be propaganda. The one emissary who did have an impact was Rabbi Rosen. Rosen's argument that preservation of MFN was essential to the continuing welfare of the Romanian Jewish community weighed heavily with administration and congressional circles.

The information Ceauşescu received on these activities of course emphasized their positive impact. The reports sent to him included every favorable or conciliatory phrase that appeared in the U.S. media while omitting critical comments. If Romanian agents succeeded in placing favorable material, sometimes even for money, in some obscure paper or television station, the Romanian embassy or Securitate immediately forwarded the text to Bucharest. The Romanian press, totally under state control, then reprinted such articles and the television carried reports on them, leaving the impression with the Romanian public and even in official circles that U.S. media were highly supportive of Romania and Ceauşescu.

Romanian diplomatic reports on the trips of the religious delegations emphasized the enthusiastic receptions accorded them and the great impact of their presentations. The delegation leaders, of course, always stated that their trips had been a great success. The foreign minister duly reported this to Ceauşescu, who in any case felt that the mere presence of these imposing religious figures, with their dramatic flowing beards and long robes, would persuade the Americans that religion was flourishing in Romania. As for the diplomatic demarches, Vaduva's reports on them to Ceauşescu detailed what the Romanians had said but gave only brief mention to the American counterarguments.

Ceauşescu did take some small concrete steps to meet U.S. concerns, principally in the field of emigration, the area tied by law to MFN. He gave instructions to increase approvals of applications for emigration to the United States, Israel, and West Germany so that by June 3, the date by which President Reagan would have to send his report on MFN to Congress, the number of approvals for 1986 would be higher than that for the comparable period in 1985. This would demonstrate that emigration from Romania was increasing, as called for by the Jackson-Vanik amendment.

The Romanian government in fact issued 1,489 emigration approvals for persons qualified to enter the United States in the three-month period between April and June 1986 (over half as many as had been approved for the entire year of 1985, even though, as it developed, considerably more Romanians actually left Romania for the United States in 1985 than in 1986). The Romanians also released from prison Constantin Sfatcu and Dorel Catarama, two of the individuals whose cases Americans had raised, and allowed them and a few other individuals mentioned by American visitors to emigrate to the United States later in the summer.

The history of this period shows the results the United States was getting from MFN and the strenuous efforts needed to realize them. It took official envoys, visits by prominent private Americans, public statements, and congressional outrage to convince Ceauşescu that he had to make some gestures to preserve MFN and keep the special relationship with the United States. He finally responded with a propaganda effort, an increase in emigration permissions, and favorable action on a few individual cases. These and a slight increase in U.S. exports constituted the concrete benefit of MFN to the United States in 1986.

The debate within the administration and in Congress over the annual renewal of MFN was increasingly turning on a single issue: whether these benefits outweighed the appearance of favoring Ceauşescu's oppressive regime. Ceauşescu, for his part, weighed whether maintenance of MFN as an economic benefit and a symbol of the special relationship with the United States was worth the price of listening to American complaints about his internal policies and making occasional concessions on emigration and human rights cases. The problem between the two governments was compounded by the fact the Americans believed that the concessions they requested were minor, while Ceauşescu was convinced that such concessions could be threatening to his regime and might even be part of an American conspiracy to undermine it.

Ceauşescu's apprehensions about American intentions toward his government were reinforced by his misconceptions about the nature and origin of occasional public demonstrations outside Romanian installations in the United States. The prospect of such demonstrations always called forth energetic and high-level protests to U.S. officials in Washington and Bucharest. The Romanians demanded that the U.S. government prevent the demonstrations and threatened that, if the demonstrations took place, the Romanian government would have difficulty preventing its population from expressing its indignation by demonstrating outside the

U.S. embassy in Bucharest. Such demonstrations in Bucharest never actually materialized, probably because the Romanian government was not anxious to encourage its population to express its feelings in the street, even under governmental supervision.

Kirk had difficulty understanding why the Romanians made such an issue out of what were in every case peaceful demonstrations and did not usually involve large numbers of people. It is now clear that the Romanian leadership, from Ceauşescu down, could not conceive that such demonstrations could take place without the connivance, indeed the encouragement, of the U.S. government. Nor could they imagine that the demonstrators could be other than people who had some special reason to be hostile to Romania; thus they concluded that the demonstrators were mostly Hungarians who wanted Transylvania, gained by Romania at the end of World War I, transferred back to Hungary. Any demonstration outside a Romanian installation in the United States appeared to the Romanian leadership to be a U.S. government–encouraged threat to Romania's territorial integrity.

In March 1986, the Romanians received word of a planned demonstration outside the Romanian mission to the United Nations in New York. They called in U.S. chargé Henry Clarke in Bucharest (Kirk was out of town) and protested vigorously, and State Secretary Aurel Duma followed up with Kirk when the latter returned to Bucharest a few days later. The Romanian ambassador in Washington made a similar demarche at the State Department.

A very small demonstration did take place in front of the Romanian mission in New York, and some of the demonstrators did indeed call for the return of Transylvania to Hungary. The Romanians were officially indignant, and U.S. officials again had to explain that this did not mean the U.S. government was "against" Romania or in favor of a transfer of territory from Romania to Hungary. Most Romanian officials, including Ceauşescu, were unconvinced.

Another source of misunderstanding was the ever-present desire of Ceauşescu's subordinates to flatter him and to find opportunities for him to shine on the world stage, whether through high-level meetings, presidential greetings, or diplomatic initiatives. The U.S.-Libyan crisis of April 1986 was the occasion for an example of this. The U.S. bombing of Tripoli that month had damaged the Romanian embassy and wounded some of its employees. Ceauşescu summoned Kirk on April 15 to deliver a firm but measured protest and to state that Romania was ready to help achieve a negotiated settlement between the United States and Libya.

A few days later Foreign Minister Vaduva summoned Raceanu to his office. There Raceanu found virtually the entire top command of the ministry in a state of high excitement, caused by a report of a conversation the previous day between Nuel Pazdral, the U.S. embassy political counselor, and an unnamed ministry official. According to this report, Pazdral had said that the United States was ready to negotiate with the Libyans. This was different from the public U.S. position, and Vaduva and his colleagues saw it as an opening for Ceauşescu, who had good relations with Muammar Qadhafi, to serve as a channel between the two countries. Vaduva and his colleagues were on the verge of sending a memorandum to Ceauşescu recommending that he approach the Americans and Libyans on the point. They had summoned Raceanu because they thought, mistakenly, that he was the individual with whom the U.S. political counselor had spoken and they wanted to scold him for not telling them sooner of this marvelous opportunity for their president.

Raceanu told them that, although he had in fact met Pazdral the previous day, the political counselor's meeting to which they were referring had been with another ministry official. Raceanu also said he felt there had been some misunderstanding. He found it hard to believe that the United States had changed its position so soon after the bombing of Tripoli or that the United States would have made that change known through this particular channel. He urged Vaduva to allow him to check with the American embassy before approaching Ceauşescu. Vaduva's colleagues argued strongly against this, saying this was a golden opportunity to seize at once. They obviously wanted the kudos for opening an opportunity for Ceauşescu to figure prominently on the world stage. Nevertheless, Vaduva, ever a cautious man, authorized Raceanu to check with the U.S. embassy.

When Raceanu called Pazdral, the counselor said that when he had talked about Libya at the ministry he had been recounting the history of a U.S.-Libyan encounter several years before and that he had no information to indicate that the United States was ready to negotiate at the current moment. When Raceanu reported this to the foreign minister, the latter scrapped any approach to Ceauşescu. Vaduva called in his chief of staff and in Raceanu's presence gave instructions to pass the word that he would allow no one to make a fool of him in Ceauşescu's eyes and that anyone who did so would be fired from the ministry.

During this period Kirk decided to try out a technique that would convey the U.S. message to the Foreign Ministry in a setting more informal than the ministry while fostering a more personal relationship between embassy officers and ministry officials. He therefore told Raceanu in March that he would like to invite four or five members of the ministry, led by Ion Beşteliu, acting director for the Americas, to an informal luncheon at Kirk's residence with Kirk and three or four members of the embassy staff. The purpose, he said, was to provide the opportunity for a detailed but informal review of the bilateral issues under discussion between the embassy and the ministry and to get to know each other better. The Romanians agreed, after checking with their superiors, and the lunch took place in late March.

Kirk continued to hold such lunches five or six times a year throughout his stay in Romania. The U.S. side treated them as useful but rather casual affairs, with each embassy officer bringing up what he or she thought most important and with only minimal coordination beforehand as to what topics to cover. The Romanians, on the other hand, planned their strategy with some care, agreeing carefully on the points to be raised and the line to be taken. After a drink and some mingling before being seated, there would normally be just one general conversation at the table, with Kirk and Beşteliu or Raceanu taking the lead and their staffs chiming in as necessary. Separate conversations would resume after lunch, with the whole affair taking a little over two hours.

Kirk was never sure these lunches had any significant impact other than to foster better personal relations among the officers concerned, despite the fact that the conversation was usually more friendly, specific, and detailed than on more formal occasions. Raceanu, however, considered useful such direct exposure of ministry officials to U.S. concerns as enunciated by Kirk and his staff. The Americas directorate regularly sent a written report on these meetings to the foreign minister and to Aurel Duma, as well as to Maria Groza as deputy foreign minister with supervisory responsibility over the Americas directorate. The report would often recommend that the ministry seek action on some of the U.S. complaints, and this did happen on occasion. Raceanu usually tried to include one of the Securitate members of the Americas directorate in the group so that he would also hear the Americans directly and report accordingly through his channels. Thus these bimonthly luncheons were probably worthwhile, though they were no substitute for an informal relationship at the deputy minister level or a focused series of meetings to clarify or resolve particularly knotty issues.

According to Raceanu, Beşteliu hated to go to these lunches. As the senior Romanian official present, he knew he would be expected to take a leading role in the discussion, which would cover all the issues between the United States and Romania. Furthermore, the Securitate microphones, which could be expected to be placed throughout Kirk's residence, even in the garden, would record the exchange, and the Securitate would doubtless review Beşteliu's every word for orthodoxy. Beşteliu did go, but he tried to keep his comments at the lunch brief and anodyne and asked Raceanu to take the floor whenever possible.

Beşteliu was a tall, soft-spoken individual who had been acting director of the Americas directorate since 1982 and remained so until early 1989. Beşteliu was "acting" director for these seven years because after 1980 Elena Ceauşescu had to approve all appointments to posts of director or deputy director in Romanian ministries. As no foreign minister—Andrei, Vaduva, or Ioan Totu, Vaduva's successor—knew what she might do, they preferred to avoid the problem by leaving subordinates with the "acting" title. Raceanu was "acting" deputy director under Beşteliu for seven years for the same reason. Another reason for the "acting" status was that all directors and deputy directors in the ministry were supposed to be Securitate officers. Beşteliu and Raceanu were not, though of course they had to cooperate with the Securitate when asked.

Beşteliu was a graduate of the Academy of Economic Studies and joined the Foreign Ministry in 1963 at the age of 34. Former foreign minister Ştefan Andrei, a distant relative, had arranged Beşteliu's appointment as counselor at the Romanian embassy in Washington in 1973 and as deputy director in 1980, and later acting director, of the Americas directorate, which dealt with Romanian relations with Canada, the United States, and Latin America.

Beşteliu was a quiet survivor. His basic aim was to stay in his position with a minimum of work or responsibility. He was quite content to let Raceanu deal with the time-consuming and sensitive subject of U.S.-Romanian relations. He kept as low a profile on U.S. affairs as he could and had little impact on the course of U.S.-Romanian relations.

When Raceanu was arrested as an "American spy" in 1989, Beşteliu was one of the first to denounce him for betraying the country and the party and to call for his execution.[49] Despite the fact he had worked closely with the accused for so many years, Beşteliu escaped with a transfer to another directorate of the ministry with the same salary. In 1990 the post-Ceauşescu government appointed Beşteliu ambassador to Lebanon.

The remainder of the spring and summer of 1986 witnessed repeated American efforts to make progress on human rights in Romania. Several American visitors, official and nonofficial, came to Bucharest. Most repeated the familiar message: the special U.S.-Romanian relationship was in trouble and the Romanians had to take action on human rights cases of particular interest to the administration and Congress if they were to retain MFN.

One such visitor was American businessman Milton Rosenthal, U.S. chairman of the U.S.-Romanian Joint Economic Council, a body composed of American businesspeople trading with Romania and Romanian trade officials dealing with the United States. The council met annually, alternating between Romania and the United States, and Rosenthal had thus been in Bucharest often. Ceauşescu, who knew Rosenthal well from these visits, received him on April 29.

Afterward, Rosenthal told Kirk and Raceanu that he had spoken to Ceauşescu about congressional concerns regarding the religious situation in Romania, including the importing of Bibles, the operation of unrecognized religious groups, and the demolition of churches. Ceauşescu showed no flexibility on any of these issues and characterized them as interference in Romania's internal affairs. As Rosenthal later told Congress, Ceauşescu even said at one point during the interview: "Look out the window. What do you see out there? It is a church, and, if you go around this town, you will find more churches than you will find anywhere else."[50] Kirk himself had heard Ceauşescu use this line with more than one visitor; it made Kirk nervous, as Ceauşescu seemed to show some resentment at the church that spoiled his view. Kirk feared that Ceauşescu might well order the demolition of the offending building some day, but the church, Biserica Creţulescu, was still standing when Ceauşescu fell.

Symbolizing the state of the complex U.S.-Romanian intergovernmental relationship was the early April visit of Ambassador Maynard Glitman, chief U.S. negotiator at the intermediate nuclear force reduction negotiations with the Soviets. His visit was intended as another in the series of U.S.-Romanian consultations on international affairs, deemed particularly valuable in this case as a demonstration of and encouragement for Romania's relative independence within the Warsaw Pact.

After Glitman concluded his remarks at his meeting with Ceauşescu on April 11, Kirk, making clear he was speaking under instructions, said that continuation of MFN was in serious jeopardy unless Romania acted rapidly on the human rights issues of concern to the United States. U.S.-Romanian relations were entering a serious crisis. The State

Department recommendation to the president on extension of MFN was due within a month, and unless something changed there was serious doubt as to what the department would recommend. Ceauşescu responded that this was an inappropriate comment, indeed an inadmissible attempt to interfere in Romania's internal affairs. The 1975 trade agreement was reciprocal, with no conditions attached.

Ceauşescu seemed truly annoyed, and Rabbi Rosen informed Kirk later that Deputy Foreign Minister Groza had told him that Ceauşescu was "very upset" at Kirk's comments. This was probably due not only to their unwelcome content but to the fact that they were made by a mere ambassador (albeit one speaking under instructions) and that they came in the course of a meeting set up to discuss other, more congenial subjects. Despite this dispute, the Romanian media portrayed the Glitman visit as further proof of Ceauşescu's important international role and the closeness of U.S.-Romanian ties; they did not even acknowledge that bilateral matters came up.

World affairs continued to be the subject of consultation between U.S. and Romanian representatives, and Kirk and members of his staff went periodically to the Foreign Ministry to exchange views and brief them on U.S. positions. Romania, indeed Ceauşescu himself, had played useful roles on some international questions in the past. Ceauşescu, for example, had been helpful in connection with the U.S. opening to China in 1969 and with the visit to Israel of President Anwar Sadat of Egypt in 1977. Ceauşescu remained practically the only chief of state in the world to enjoy good relations, indeed formal diplomatic ties, with both Israel and the PLO.

His public statements on international affairs occasionally differed from those of his Warsaw Pact colleagues, including Soviet spokesmen, as did some of his country's votes in the United Nations. Thus on the 10 "key" 1985 United Nations votes tabulated by the U.S. State Department, Romania voted against the United States on 3, with the United States on 3, and abstained or was absent on 4. The Soviet Union and its more faithful allies voted against the United States on 9. In addition, Romania voted in favor of only 4 out of 11 resolutions that condemned the United States by name. The Soviet Union and the other Warsaw Pact members voted in favor of all 11.[51]

These votes aside, Romania's value to the United States in international affairs was declining in this period, in part because of Ceauşescu's worsening international reputation and increasing unacceptability as a serious interlocutor, but also because the United States was opening its own channels to former pariahs such as China and even the PLO. In addition, Gorbachev was moving toward a more open and accommodating Soviet foreign policy. With the Soviets withdrawing from Afghanistan and moving toward fruitful talks with the United States on matters such as Angola and the Middle East, there was less need for an intermediary and less distinctiveness in Ceauşescu's position within the Warsaw Pact.

Nevertheless, the differences between Ceauşescu's behavior and that of his Warsaw Pact colleagues still intrigued the United States. Five days after the Chernobyl nuclear disaster, for example, Ceauşescu instructed his ministers to request that a U.S. team come to Romania to monitor the amount of radiation Romania had received, as the Soviets had given the Romanians very little useful information about the nature of the radiation leaks or their effect. The U.S. team arrived within five days of the request and received full access to Romanian monitoring installations. Its conclusion, based on on-site observations, was that the radiation levels were not medically significant.

Although Ceauşescu never mentioned publicly that he had asked the Americans to come, he did make several statements deploring the effects of Chernobyl and stressing the need for rigorous safety precautions at such installations. Although such independent initiatives seem trivial in the atmosphere of the 1990s, they were highly unusual for a Warsaw Pact member in 1986. They represented the extent (and the limits) of Ceauşescu's "independence" in foreign affairs at that time and attracted attention in Washington.

Kirk returned to Washington in early May to participate in the Department of State debates on its recommendation to the president on MFN extension. It is always useful for an ambassador to be present when the State Department is formulating and acting on crucial recommendations concerning policy toward the ambassador's country of assignment. This is the best way to help shape the options presented to the decision makers and to influence the decision itself—much better than sending telegrams and analyses that may go unread. But it can happen only if the ambassador can both learn when the critical time in the decision process will come and get to Washington during that time. It is worth considerable personal inconvenience to do so.

In Washington, Kirk found that opinion within the State Department was divided on extension of MFN. The draft of the State Department options paper presented three alternatives: oppose MFN renewal; renew MFN; or suspend MFN for six months with renewal dependent on progress on human rights issues. Suspension thus appeared to be the moderate option. But suspension, as Department of Commerce representatives had testified to Congress in February, would really amount to termination. It would disrupt trade and break commercial ties. Even if the suspension were only temporary, many businesspeople would hesitate to resume their activities, as they would fear another possible suspension.[52]

Furthermore, given the predictably angry Romanian reaction to MFN suspension, the chances of Romania's making sufficient progress on human rights to justify resumption of MFN six months later were virtually nil. If that was the result the administration sought, it would be much cleaner simply to terminate MFN. Another problem, as Kirk pointed out, was that the paper's renewal option, stated in its unconditional form, looked distinctly weak in the light of developments over the past year.

To deal with these problems the office covering East European affairs rewrote the options paper. The drafters added to the renewal option a stipulation that the president would accompany his recommendation for renewal with a letter to Congress critical of Romania's human rights record and with another confidential letter to Ceauşescu warning that he expected improvements in the human rights field and that such improvements would be necessary to get MFN through Congress.

Kirk attended the meeting with Assistant Secretary Rozanne Ridgway to select the option the European bureau would recommend to Shultz. Ridgway said the essential point was that MFN was saving human lives by ensuring some emigration from Romania and freeing some individuals from Ceauşescu's jails. The proponents of suspension made their case, but the humanitarian argument carried the day. Interestingly, there was little attention given to Romania's policy of independence, one of the principal reasons for treating Romania favorably in the past.

A little later John Mroz, head of the Institute for East-West Security Studies, told the Romanians during a visit to Bucharest that there had been serious division within the National Security Council as to whether to recommend that President Reagan grant MFN once again. The Romanians had great respect for Mroz. They knew he had served at State and the NSC and credited him with being one of the few Americans with access to Yasir Arafat, a leader with whom Ceauşescu was on good terms. Furthermore, Mroz had organized a well-attended seminar on East-West relations in Romania in 1982, and Ceauşescu had received him and been impressed by him at that time.

It was Mroz's comment that finally convinced the Foreign Ministry that Romania had real problems in the U.S. executive branch and not just in Congress. Several American officials, including Assistant Secretary Ridgway publicly, had already made clear that the executive branch was seriously weighing whether to grant MFN. The Romanians, however, often preferred to use an indirect rather than a direct channel to convey a message, particularly one they thought the recipient might not like. They assumed the United States would do the same. In their enthusiasm over high-level visits, they disregarded the direct approaches the United States made on such occasions, but did pay attention to what they felt was a quiet, indirect signal from the U.S. government. Whether this was a Balkan, or a communist, or just a Romanian trait, it appeared often in the relationship. It made communication difficult for the normally straightforward Americans and resulted in a number of missed signals on both sides.

President Reagan did in fact grant Romania the usual 12-month extension of MFN on June 3, 1986. In his message to Congress on the subject, he noted that his decision had "been taken with difficulty, following careful deliberation within the administration." He pointed out Romania's responsiveness to U.S. concerns about emigration and cited the high rate of "recent" emigration approvals (April and May). He was "disappointed," he said, by Romania's "very limited response" to U.S. concern about human rights and religious issues but felt that MFN would enable the United States to "have an impact on human rights concerns and to help strengthen the extent of religious observance in Romania." He listed a number of specific U.S. human rights concerns and said that he was instructing the secretary of state to "press our concerns" in these areas and to report back to him and to Congress every six months.[53]

The president also sent a private letter to Ceaușescu. It was an unusually tough message to a supposedly friendly chief of state. The letter stated that Reagan had decided to recommend MFN "after considerable deliberation, which revealed strong congressional opposition and reservations within my own administration. This was a difficult decision for me." The Romanians took this phraseology as confirmation of Mroz's point to them about divisions within the NSC on MFN for Romania and proof that his comment had been a signal from the administration.

Reagan's letter then said that his decision would not be easy to defend. He noted "heartfelt concerns" in the United States regarding religious freedom, which he personally shared and presumed were neither "artificial or unfounded." He went on to state, "Your government's unwillingness to accommodate these concerns has placed at risk our policy, which benefits Romania substantially."[54] Ceauşescu, not surprisingly, was not at all pleased, and gave instructions that there should be no reply.

Administration witnesses defended extension of MFN at hearings of the House and Senate subcommittees on trade in June and August. State Department Counselor Edward Derwinski said bluntly, "We have no other effective means of influence over developments in Romania." The administration witnesses were able to report Romanian agreement to print several thousand Protestant Bibles, the release of several political prisoners as part of a widespread amnesty announced June 2, and receipt of emigration permission by several persons who had been the subject of congressional and administration approaches to the Romanians.[55]

At the same time, they had to note failure in a number of other areas. Two in particular were troublesome. There had been reports that a historic "Spanish" synagogue in Bucharest would fall victim to "urban renewal." Spokespersons for the American Jewish community and the U.S., Israeli, and Spanish governments had expressed concern over this possibility in talks with the Romanian government and with Ceauşescu himself. As recently as June, Groza had assured the U.S. embassy, on Vaduva's explicit instructions, that the synagogue would not be demolished. Nevertheless, demolition began on July 1, 1986, and was completed at top speed.

Destruction of the synagogue angered the governments concerned and the American Jewish community, whose influence with Congress Ceauşescu needed badly. Then Ceauşescu further damaged his cause by demolishing the principal Seventh-Day Adventist church in Bucharest in the last days of July despite the protests of much of the congregation and the U.S. embassy.

Most of the nonadministration witnesses at the summer congressional hearings on MFN condemned Romania in harsh terms; only a few supported MFN as a means of pressure or an aid to trade. The "independence" argument rarely surfaced, although Ridgway advanced it with some force in the August hearing, saying this independence "still exists and distinguishes Romania from all other Warsaw Pact countries," a statement the Romanian government noted and welcomed.[56]

Despite the criticism of Romania at the hearings, Congress took no action on MFN extension for Romania in the 90 days available to it after June 3, except for a procedural vote in the House that the opponents of MFN lost, 216 to 190.[57] Thus MFN was extended for another year. The U.S. administration, however, continued to struggle with the ambivalence of its relationship with Romania in the months to come.

▼5▼

Whitehead Tries to Make a New Start
1986

E very U.S. ambassador has a set of goals and objectives worked out between the ambassador and the Department of State in the first few months of the ambassador's tenure. These are formalized in a letter from the secretary of state to that ambassador. Secretary Shultz's letter to Kirk, despatched in April 1986, described current U.S. priorities for relations with Romania.

The top priority was promotion of emigration and human rights, followed by encouragement of Romanian divergence from the Soviet Union. This reversed the priorities of the preceding decade and, given Romania's bad human rights performance, made a further deterioration in U.S.-Romanian relations highly likely. Somewhat inconsistently, other goals for Kirk were to preserve or increase the proportion of Romania's trade going to member countries of the Organization for Economic Cooperation and Development (48 percent was with countries outside the Soviet bloc in 1985), to renew and broaden the U.S.-Romanian dialogue, to increase U.S.-Romanian military-to-military contacts, and to achieve more balanced trade between Romania and the United States by increasing U.S. exports to Romania.

Romania's priorities for relations with the United States, although not as formally developed, were clear to those serving in the Foreign Ministry. The top priorities were to promote a high-level dialogue, preferably through publicized meetings between leading figures of the two governments; to preserve Romania's MFN status; to elicit official U.S. statements supporting Romania's policy of independence; to intensify intergovernmental and interparliamentary contacts; to hold periodic consultations on international affairs; and to maintain economic benefits such as Romania's eligibility for low tariffs under the U.S. Generalized

System of Preferences program, access to investment guarantees under the Overseas Private Investment Corporation (OPIC), and eligibility for U.S. Export-Import Bank loans.

The differences between the U.S. and Romanian goals set the stage for some of the difficulties between the two countries over the next three years. The U.S. embassy sought to achieve all the aims set for it, keeping the relative priorities among them in mind. Washington pursued the same agenda, and with new vigor, with the assignment of special responsibility for Eastern Europe to Deputy Secretary of State John Whitehead, Shultz's immediate subordinate. Whitehead's visit to Bucharest in mid-November 1986 represented the U.S. administration's last major attempt to get the relationship on a more positive footing. The Romanians, meanwhile, drummed away at their theme of high-level meetings. Their resistance to and resentment of U.S. "interference" in their internal affairs continued unabated.

The Romanians made their position clear during an early July 1986 visit by Senator Larry Pressler of South Dakota. When he met with Ceauşescu on July 10, the senator raised the need for Bibles, the willingness of Americans to provide funds for that purpose, and their concern over the demolition of churches and freedom of operation for unrecognized religious groups. Ceauşescu replied that these were internal matters and that so-called religious "problems" in Romania were in any case only inventions of "ill-intentioned" persons. He even attempted to defend his position on Bibles by claiming that the United States would not allow foreign currency into the United States to print communist literature, an assertion that Kirk and Pressler denied.

In his report to Congress on the trip, Senator Pressler said that Ceauşescu's reply to the generous offer to expedite the printing of Bibles surprised him. He came away with the impression that Ceauşescu felt those who wanted to print Bibles were "using it as an excuse to oppose his regime."[58]

In the summer of 1986, the foreign policy aspect of the U.S.-Romanian relationship took temporary prominence with the August visit to Bucharest of Vernon Walters, U.S. ambassador to the United Nations, a well-known figure and cabinet member. Walters had come to exchange views with the Romanians on U.N. matters. Although Romania's votes on some U.N. matters of special interest to the United States were more aligned with U.S. views than were the votes of other Warsaw Pact members, it seemed somewhat surprising to Kirk that Walters himself would visit Romania, given the poor reputation of the Ceauşescu regime.

Kirk thought he might have found part of the answer when he learned that Walters, who had traveled all over the world, had never been to Romania. Furthermore, Walters had a passion for subways and was eager to see the newly opened Bucharest metro. As soon as the Romanians learned this, they arranged a special metro train for Walters and let him drive it. In best dictatorial fashion, normal use of the metro was suspended well before the time the Walters train was to operate lest it be delayed by any other traffic. The crowds of people Kirk saw waiting for the metro during Walters's rush-hour trip were vivid testimony to the regime's lack of consideration for its population.

Walters led off his two and a quarter hours with Ceauşescu on August 14 by expressing "on behalf of President Reagan and Secretary Shultz" U.S. respect for the independent position Romania had taken on many occasions and the U.S. desire for closer relations with Romania. Walters said Reagan wished to establish a broad dialogue at a high level to discuss common problems. He mentioned a number of bilateral issues and then reviewed the international situation, noting particularly those points on the U.N. agenda to which the United States attached special importance and on which it appreciated Romania's past position or hoped for future support.

Ceauşescu expressed his gratitude for the message from the president and the secretary of state. He said he attached "great importance" to Romania's relationship with the United States based on "mutual respect" and "noninterference in internal affairs." There had been "no problems" in U.S.-Romanian bilateral relations until the granting of MFN. He did not want Romania's internal affairs to be the subject of U.S. congressional discussion. There should be no difficulty on Bibles, as the Orthodox Church had agreed to print as many as needed. As for the destruction of the synagogue and the Seventh-Day Adventist church, Ceauşescu visited the Bucharest reconstruction sites almost daily, and "no one" there had ever complained to him about the demolition of old buildings. He did not see why the United States was making an issue of it.

Kirk, hearing Ceauşescu make this comment, wondered what kind of fools he imagined Walters and Kirk to be. It was quite true that Ceauşescu visited the reconstruction sites almost daily, but he did so surrounded by officials, aides, and security guards. Occasionally "spontaneous demonstrators" were trucked to the spot to applaud the dictator, but the general public was kept many yards away. Anyone who tried to complain to Ceauşescu would have been arrested on the spot, as would those who had allowed the individual to get that close to the president.

Ceauşescu should have known that there was real opposition to his urban reconstruction program, however. When he met with some 60 historians in May 1980, for example, the Romanian historian Dinu Giurescu and a few others had argued that Romania's architectural heritage should be preserved for economic, cultural, and historic reasons. Romanian historians and architects had addressed a number of petitions and memoranda to the Central Committee on the matter since that time, and it had been the subject of a good deal of international comment.

Ceauşescu may, nevertheless, have meant his remark to be at least partly serious. Those around him praised all his actions and said they were wildly popular. The public demonstrations he saw were all supportive. He probably felt that opposition to the demolitions was minor, as well as misguided. Finally, he himself firmly believed that he was doing the right thing, one of the traits that made him so dangerous. Thus he probably considered his remark to Walters to be basically sound in its implications, as well as a good debating point.

A similar event occurred in Kirk's presence in February 1988, when Ceauşescu told Whitehead that the Romanian legislature's unanimous votes in favor of his programs were proof of their popularity. If they were not popular, Ceauşescu said, the legislators would have voted against them. This comment seemed absurd when applied to a group of "parliamentarians" who applauded Ceauşescu on cue with rhythmic chants at least 20 times during each speech, who owed their positions to his favor or that of his officials, and whose very freedom would be at risk if they expressed themselves any other way. Yet Ceauşescu seemed really to believe that he had genuine support in parliament, as borne out in part by his statement at his trial, after his arrest in 1989, that he would "answer any question, but only before the Grand National Assembly and the representatives of the working class."[59]

An incident in May 1987 provides another example of Ceauşescu's ignorance of the true situation in his own country. At that time, several leading officers of a Canadian nuclear energy firm that was helping to construct Romania's first nuclear power reactor visited Romania. According to Ceauşescu's interpreter, when the Canadians said that the reactor's first unit would not be ready until 1990 or 1991, Ceauşescu, visibly surprised, asked if the interpreter was sure he had translated correctly. Ceauşescu said he had understood the first unit would be ready in 13 months, by June

1988. When the interpreter said he was sure that is what the Canadians had said, Ceauşescu asked them to repeat it because he felt sure they had misspoken. The Canadians reaffirmed that the earliest the first unit could be ready with maximum priority from the Romanian side was 1990, and it would more probably not be ready until 1991.

Ceauşescu made no further comment but asked First Deputy Prime Minister Gheorghe Oprea and Deputy Prime Minister Ion Dinca, who were responsible for the reactor construction project and who were present at the meeting, to stay after the Canadians left. He apparently scolded them unmercifully as they attempted to explain the discrepancy and to assure him that the reactor would be ready sooner than the Canadians had said. One of Raceanu's associates served as the interpreter for the Canadians' subsequent meeting with Oprea and Dinca. He told Raceanu the two Romanians had sharply criticized the Canadians for mentioning the date to Ceauşescu, saying that they should not bring up such matters with the president.

Ceauşescu's misconceptions about the mood of his people and the actual situation in his country led him to consider U.S. protestations misguided and out of place. He first thought they were due to misinformation and the machinations of persons hostile to Romania, but gradually found more sinister explanations, eventually concluding that they were part of a plot to get rid of his regime and perhaps dismember the country. Ceauşescu's government had long used the argument that Romania was surrounded by enemies as a way of solidifying and justifying its tight control over the population, but in the second half of the 1980s Ceauşescu actually began to believe it.

As time went on he became increasingly suspicious, even paranoid, about foreign plots to overthrow his regime. Thus, in the course of the Romanian party congress in November 1989, Ceauşescu virtually accused Bush and Gorbachev of planning to connive together against true socialists at their forthcoming December summit in Malta.[60] Even during his trial on December 25, 1989, Ceauşescu steadfastly maintained that the Romanian people supported him and that "foreign agents" had helped organize the antiregime demonstrations that triggered the revolution, which he characterized as a "putsch."[61] This frame of mind was, of course, a major obstacle to communication with Ceauşescu and one that badly distorted his view of the basic U.S. position.

In his August 14, 1986, talk with Walters on foreign affairs, Ceauşescu reiterated his long-standing differences with the Soviets and added a couple of new ones. He said Romania would not accept missiles on its soil and implied that Romania had successfully resisted Soviet pressure to accept such missiles. He may have spoken the truth in this case, as Romanian territory constituted a noticeable gap in the ring of Soviet-manned SA-5 anti-aircraft missile sites around the Soviet bloc. Ceauşescu also said that he favored a unilateral 5 percent reduction in military expenditures by the members of NATO and the Warsaw Pact (a proposal he later publicized, urged unsuccessfully on his Warsaw Pact allies, and then carried out unilaterally for Romania at the end of 1986).

The Romanian papers the next day, August 15, carried an official Romanian press agency communiqué, stating that Walters had thanked Ceauşescu for the opportunity to meet with him and had expressed President Reagan's "special appreciation for the policy of independence and peace which is firmly promoted by President Nicolae Ceauşescu." It added, "The questions discussed during the talks regarding the evolution of bilateral relations emphasized both countries' desire to develop Romanian-American cooperation further on the basis of completely equal rights, respect for national independence and sovereignty, noninterference in domestic affairs and mutual advantage." The communiqué then reported on the discussion on international matters, summarizing Ceauşescu's comments on a variety of topics. Romanian radio and television gave prominent coverage to the visit, conveying the impression that there was close cooperation between the two countries in the international field.[62]

This was typical of how the Romanian press handled Ceauşescu's meetings with Americans. The coverage was officially inspired, indeed officially dictated. It included anything flattering the visitor had to say to Ceauşescu, especially greetings from another head of state (there was usually no reference to greetings from lower officials, such as Secretary Shultz, as they were inferior to Ceauşescu in rank). It virtually always stated that relations should be based on the principles of noninterference, and so on. It made no mention of difficulties in bilateral relations and certainly no mention of any criticism of Ceauşescu's policies. It focused mainly on world affairs, reporting largely Ceauşescu's comments on them. The public image was that the foreigner had praised Ceauşescu, had talked about bilateral relations while agreeing that Ceauşescu's internal policies were his affair, and had listened respectfully to his views on international matters.

This lack of sound information on the Romanian side was a continuing handicap to U.S. efforts to convey the notion that the bilateral relationship was in trouble because of Ceauşescu's repressive policies and required urgent Romanian action to improve it. The appearance was rather that the two countries had friendly relations and were close collaborators in international affairs.

Throughout this period the Romanian government strove to be a significant foreign affairs player in U.S. eyes. Thus after Yasir Arafat's appearance as the featured official guest at Romania's 23 August national holiday, Ceauşescu instructed his foreign minister to tell Kirk that Arafat had informed the Romanians he was ready to make a public statement indicating new willingness to talk to the Israelis in the context of an international conference. The minister also told Kirk that the Romanians stood ready to convey any comments from the United States to Arafat.

When Kirk reported this, the State Department expressed little interest, telling Kirk to make no response unless the Romanians raised the subject again, in which case he was to say merely that the Romanian report would be reviewed with great care. The department authorized him to add, however, "We value the unique role President Ceauşescu is able to play and hope we can continue our dialogue on Middle East issues." Washington clearly did not want to close any doors, even one as dubious as Ceauşescu.

The Romanians never pursued the point. This was typical of Romanian behavior. On other occasions as well they hinted at the possibility of some major foreign policy breakthrough to induce the United States to use Ceauşescu as a channel. If the United States did not take the bait right away, there was no follow-through, strongly suggesting that there had been little if anything to the Romanians' "special information" in the first place.

Ceauşescu continued to air his differences with Moscow on arms control questions. In October 1986, he publicly opposed making U.S. abandonment of its Strategic Defense Initiative a precondition to East-West agreement on intermediate-range nuclear missiles, rejecting the linkage Moscow was insisting upon. He pushed his proposal for unilateral 5 percent reductions in military expenditures, equipment, and manpower at a Warsaw Pact foreign ministers meeting in Bucharest in mid-October, even though his Warsaw Pact colleagues did not agree with it. He made an independent suggestion for breaking the deadlock in the Mutual and Balanced Force Reduction talks in Vienna.

When Soviet Foreign Minister Eduard Shevardnadze visited Bucharest in October, Ceauşescu had the Romanian press omit the part of Shevardnadze's press conference that contained criticism of the United States. He later claimed to American interlocutors that he was responsible for keeping criticism of SDI out of the bilateral Soviet-Romanian communiqué issued at the conclusion of Shevardnadze's visit.

A few days later Ceauşescu's minister of defense, General Vasile Milea, paid an official visit to the United States (from October 25 to October 31), the first time a defense minister from a Warsaw Pact state had done so. The U.S. military treated him well, as they did all official guests. He visited West Point and was impressed by the beauty of the place and the smartness of the cadets on parade. He met with the Joint Chiefs of Staff in the "tank," their special meeting room in the Pentagon. He observed U.S. army field maneuvers and a firing demonstration. He even had his picture taken in an American tank in the field.

It was clear Milea was delighted with the visit when Kirk talked with him about it after his return. He spoke with feeling about the wealth of the United States as well as the hospitality accorded him. The Romanians considered Milea's visit to the United States a great success. They tried for the next three years to persuade the chairman of the U.S. Joint Chiefs of Staff, Admiral William Crowe, to visit Romania, but his schedule was full in 1987, and U.S.-Romanian relations had soured sufficiently by 1988 to rule out such a visit. General Milea was still in office at the time of the 1989 revolution, and paid with his life on December 22, 1989—either suicide (the official version) or possibly execution—for his refusal to give his troops the order to fire upon demonstrators in Bucharest.[63]

Ceauşescu sought international prestige in other ways and in fact had a virtual obsession about securing a place in history as a major international figure. As one way to achieve this, he mobilized the entire Romanian information apparatus, as well as the resources of all ministries with foreign contacts, to secure publication of favorable articles and the text of his speeches in prestigious foreign newspapers and journals. The Securitate for years spent substantial amounts of hard currency to place articles and interviews in the foreign press.

The result of this activity was the publication of some 50 books and over 1,000 articles on Ceauşescu and his wife in various countries, especially in the developing world. Sometimes these were in the form of paid advertisements, subsequently reported as news stories in the Romanian media. The themes the Romanian government sought to place in the foreign press consisted of the intellectual brilliance of the two Ceauşescus, their successes in creating a modern Romanian state that was a model for developing countries, and President Ceauşescu's major role in promoting international peace and cooperation, furthering disarmament, and resolving regional conflicts.

This propaganda effort occasionally backfired. Thus the U.S. embassy in Rome reported that on March 1, 1988, the Italian paper *Il Messagero* carried a half-page advertisement extolling the scientific accomplishments of Elena Ceauşescu. It was signed by two Italian scientists, one identified as a faculty member of the University of Bologna and the other with the Academia Tiberium. The following day another paper, *La Republica,* reported that the University of Bologna denied that the first scientist was a faculty member, while a third paper, *Corriere della Sera,* reported that the Academia Tiberium said it knew nothing of the second. Those reports, plus the word that the advertisement had cost the Romanians $11,000, caused great amusement in Italy at the Ceauşescus' expense.

An important part of the Romanian public relations effort was arranging interviews of Ceauşescu by correspondents of leading print media. This was not an easy task. While Ceauşescu welcomed a free discussion with a correspondent, he wanted complete control over what was published. He therefore insisted upon some quite specific conditions. The questions had to be submitted in advance in writing, their final form arrived at through discussions between the Foreign Ministry press section and the interviewer. Ceauşescu would reply to these questions in writing. The interviewer had to guarantee that Ceauşescu's written answers would be printed in full, without change. The written exchange, rather than the actual discussion with the journalist, had to form the basis of the journalist's report. The result of these conditions was, of course, that it was virtually impossible to set up a Ceauşescu interview with a prominent Western publication.

Nevertheless, *New York Times* correspondent David Binder, who had visited Romania often over the years, decided to try. Negotiations over the questions and conditions lasted seven months. The Romanian embassy in Washington finally reported to the Romanian government that all conditions were agreed and that it had obtained an assurance from the *Times*'s Washington bureau that the interview would appear in full.

Binder went to Bucharest in late September, and Ceauşescu received him on October 8, 1986. The Romanian press and television reported that Ceauşescu had received the "head" of the Washington bureau of the *New York Times*. When Binder told the Foreign Ministry press official with whom he was dealing that he had made it clear that he was an assistant news editor, not the head of the Washington office, the official replied, "President Ceauşescu does not speak to deputies or assistants."

The *New York Times* did not publish the interview in full. What it did publish was an article by Binder summarizing the interview and describing the harm Ceauşescu's cult of personality was causing in Romania.[64] This provoked a violent reaction in Bucharest. Foreign Minister Ioan Totu and Constantin Mitea, head of the party Central Committee's press department, instructed the Romanian ambassador in Washington to make a firm approach to the leadership of the *New York Times* protesting publication of an article "disrespectful to Romania and the Romanian head of state" and insisting that the *Times* publish the entire interview, in accordance with the "assurances" it had given the Romanian embassy. The *Times* denied it had given any such assurances, and the Romanian ambassador's demarche had no effect. The U.S. embassy in Bucharest shrugged off a parallel approach from the Foreign Ministry by citing the freedom of the American press.

The result of this incident was not only that Binder went back on Romania's list of undesirable persons (he first went on the list in 1966, apparently for writing that Ceauşescu was at that time little known in the Romanian countryside), but also that the Romanians further tightened the conditions for foreign interviews. Ceauşescu, for his part, avoided the American press thereafter. Requests for interviews from U.S. publications, even from *Time* and *Newsweek,* remained unanswered or were met with so many conditions, restrictions, and review rights that the interviewers eventually gave up the quest.

It is doubtful that Ceauşescu could have obtained favorable treatment from any responsible American journal by 1986, but he certainly cut himself off from such an outlet for his side of the story by his wholly unrealistic concept of the operation of major Western media. The absurdity of the Romanian conditions for interviews, or even for entry visas for American correspondents, and the refusal of visas to those whose previous stories displeased the Romanian government helped assure Romania highly unfavorable press in the United States. The U.S. embassy often made this argument to the Foreign Ministry when urging them to grant a visa to some journalist, almost always without success.

In fact there was little to write about in Romania that was favorable to Ceauşescu and much to criticize. Conditions of life for the population were abominable and getting worse. Cuts in the electricity supply had already begun in October 1985; one 40-watt bulb was the limit for each residential room. Television broadcasts lasted only two hours a day and devoted fully half of that to reportage on Ceauşescu and the accomplishments of his rule. Shops were dimly lit, and restaurants closed at 9:00 P.M. The Bucharest authorities removed the bulbs from every other street light on the main arteries, and many side streets had no light at all. Only the routes Ceauşescu might travel and his urban reconstruction work sites were brightly lit. The pressure of natural gas, the source of heat and cooking fuel for most of Romania's cities, was already so low that it was hard to get a strong enough flame on the stove to boil water. The official "norm" for residential heat was 50 degrees Fahrenheit, and offices were not much warmer.

Food was in short supply. While the Romanians were not starving, obtaining food took time and effort, and assuring a varied, nutritious diet was a real challenge. Meat was almost impossible to obtain over the counter. Eggs appeared only sporadically, as did cheese. Milk was available only in the early morning. Sugar and cooking oil were rationed, but not always to be found even with a ration coupon. The coffee for sale was severely adulterated, and even that was in ever shorter supply. Bread was available, though rationed outside of Bucharest. In winter, vegetables and fruits were usually limited to poor cabbage, carrots, and apples. More were available in season, but foreign imports, such as citrus fruits, simply did not appear.

Ceauşescu's response was to criticize the Romanian people for eating too much. He had the Romanian parliament promulgate a "scientific diet" that included less food, especially less meat. One of the main authors of this scientific diet, Dr. Iulian Mincu, was appointed Minister of Health in October 1992.

The continual propaganda extolling the "Golden Era" of the Ceauşescus and praising their extraordinary talents formed a nauseating contrast to bleak reality. And all this took place, in Bucharest and in many other cities, against a background of constant demolition of residential and business areas to make way for urban reconstruction, a project that never seemed to finish. The construction dust and noise, day and night, hung over Romanian cities like a dark cloud of gloom.

The regime was a mean-spirited one. The embassy learned of an unpublished edict, enacted in mid-December 1986, that prohibited the cutting of trees just in time to stop the supply of Christmas trees. Pork and beef, always in short supply and available only through "informal" channels, disappeared almost entirely in the period before Christmas, when they were needed to make the traditional Christmas sausage, only to reappear too late for Christmas day (which was declared a normal workday). The embassy was told there was even an early December edict postponing the start of the winter school vacation until December 27, an edict that was mysteriously revoked a few days later, after many families had canceled their Christmas vacation plans.

Restrictions on contact with foreigners were ever tighter. The government issued a secret decree, number 408, in late December 1985. It required Romanians to obtain official permission before meeting foreigners and afterward to report what had been said to their superiors, who in turn could inform the Securitate. It restricted foreign visitors in all state establishments to so-called protocol rooms, which were amply equipped with devices for recording conversations. Raceanu observed concrete evidence of this when he visited a protocol room on the third floor of the Foreign Ministry the day after an earthquake in mid-March 1987. The quake had damaged the room's walls, and microphones were hanging out of several of the cracks.

Decree 408 also forbade foreigners access to the working areas of industrial enterprises. It stipulated that the heads of the protocol sections of all state establishments and the chiefs of staff of all ministers must be members of the Securitate. Romanian employees of foreign embassies and firms could not have contracts valid longer than one year, with renewal subject to Securitate approval.

An interesting thing about the decree was that only those responsible for enforcing it were allowed to read it; the ordinary citizen was not allowed to see it, although many had to sign a piece of paper agreeing to abide by it. Enforcement of the decree, and of other restrictions on contact with foreigners, grew tighter and tighter as 1986 wore on, exerting a negative effect on contacts of all kinds, including commercial and scientific contacts of potentially significant benefit to Romania.[65]

Two major industrial establishments that Kirk was able to visit during a trip he made in November 1986 to Slatina and Craiova in southern Romania pointed up both the tremendous efforts required by Ceauşescu's industrialization policy and how misguided it was. In Slatina, Kirk went to one of the largest aluminum-smelting plants in Europe, with a capacity of 250,000 tons, a huge establishment built at great cost. The manager, a man of about 50 who had been with the plant since its inception 21 years before, seemed dynamic, intelligent, and knowledgeable. He took the party through one of the main halls where aluminum was being smelted. The atmosphere was dense with chemical vapors and steam from the pools of material in the process of electrolysis. The pools had no covers or guardrails, and a misstep would plunge a visitor or worker into molten metal.

The manager said there was a plan to put a protective dome over each pool, but he mentioned no time frame and the visitors did not have the impression that this would happen soon, if at all. He explained that workers spent only six hours on a shift and could retire at age 55 after 30 years of service. They were given a special meal before each shift and a liter of milk and carbonated beverages to drink during it to counteract the vapors they inhaled. The manager advised the Americans to wash thoroughly and have a large cognac after their visit, which they did.

The most depressing aspect of this visit was that there was no prospect that the smelter, located in an energy-poor country, could refine aluminum economically, and indeed much of its product lay unsold nearby. The effort and expense to build the plant and the risks taken in running it were of little use to the economy, and the plant's high energy consumption (as high as 10 percent of Romania's total electrical energy use) actually made the plant a net economic loss for Romania. Ceauşescu, however, felt every modern country should have an aluminum smelter, and where better to put it than in the capital of the county where he was born, a fact marked by huge portraits of an idealized President and Mrs. Ceauşescu mounted atop Slatina's highest hill and visible from every part of the city.

In Craiova, Kirk's party visited an automobile assembly plant constructed as a joint venture with Citroën of France. The plant was clean and well laid out, with modern machinery, even robots, from all over the world; but it was startlingly empty. The manager, an impressive 45-year-old, told his American visitors that the plant's capacity was 150,000 vehicles a year, but it was currently producing only 30,000. The assembly line was moving at one-quarter of its projected speed.

Citroën had virtually abandoned the venture because of problems of quality control, energy and parts supply, and bureaucratic interference. Later, Citroën officials expressed surprise that Chrysler, which was impressed by the plant and, at the time of Kirk's visit, was weighing whether to replace Citroën, took so long to decide not to sign up. This expensive modern plant, one of the best industrial facilities in Romania, remained largely idle for the rest of Ceauşescu's rule.

During this same trip, it is only fair to say, Kirk's party experienced much that was touching and beautiful. The party enjoyed VIP treatment from the local authorities, gracious hospitality from everyone, and a warm welcome from heads of museums, hotels, churches, and monasteries throughout the area. The Orthodox metropolitan of Craiova offered a wonderful six-course dinner, with a rendition of church music by his staff. Romanians have a rich cultural heritage and traditional warmth, which made it doubly tragic to see them so oppressed by communism and Ceauşescu.

The U.S. administration made one more determined effort to put relations on a better footing, despite its repugnance at the regime's treatment of its people. This endeavor was directed not so much at Romania in particular as at all of Eastern Europe. For years the Department of State had accorded low priority to Eastern Europe. The assistant secretary for European affairs had to cover the Soviet Union, all the countries of Western Europe, and Canada, in addition to Eastern Europe, which paled in importance by comparison. Even the deputy assistant secretary responsible for Eastern Europe was also responsible for the Soviet Union. With a few exceptions, Soviet rather than East European affairs attracted the ablest officers interested in the Soviet bloc, and U.S. ambassadors in East European capitals were often Soviet specialists getting their first ambassadorial opportunities at the expense of the East European experts.

At the same time, the deputy secretary of state traditionally suffered from a lack of specific supervisory responsibility, serving rather as an amorphous "second-in-command" to the secretary, who was increasingly able to use modern communications to conduct foreign affairs from anywhere in the world. Secretaries of state therefore began to ask the deputy secretary to assume responsibility for a particular subject matter, preferably one that was important but would not otherwise receive sufficient high-level attention.

Eastern Europe in the mid-1980s fit this description nicely. With the winds of reform starting to blow in Eastern Europe as well as in the Soviet Union, it seemed that there might be new opportunities for U.S. initiatives. Furthermore, the assistant secretary for Europe had her hands particularly full with the changing Soviet Union, the moves toward West European integration, the question of Quebec's separatism, and the U.S.-Canadian free trade negotiations.

In the late summer of 1986, Secretary George Shultz thus gave Deputy Secretary John Whitehead a special mandate to follow East European affairs and see what possibilities the changing world situation opened up there. Whitehead "had strong credentials in the Republican party," according to Shultz, and "took on his new assignment with enthusiasm and flair."[66] Whitehead was, in fact, determined to see if there was some way he could put U.S. relations with Eastern Europe on a new and more constructive footing.

There was a significant change in personnel on the Romanian side as well during that summer. The very morning in August on which Vaduva had talked with Kirk about the alleged breakthrough in the prospect for Middle East negotiations, Ceauşescu summoned Vaduva and told him, to Vaduva's complete surprise, that he was to move to the Ministry of Foreign Trade. The public announcement came an hour or so later. According to Manea Manescu, who had participated in the Political Executive Committee meeting that ratified Ceauşescu's changes, Ceauşescu had mentioned that Vaduva "had not understood very much about foreign affairs." Vaduva was, in fact, almost wholly ineffective, as well as being a difficult boss, and most in the ministry and the diplomatic corps welcomed his departure.

Vaduva's replacement was Ioan Totu, a highly trained economist with a much more impressive résumé and better grounding in international affairs than his predecessor. A strong, square-set individual, he was forceful, dynamic, and direct. Before coming to the Foreign Ministry he had borne major governmental responsibilities, including the post of chief of Ceauşescu's cabinet in the early 1980s. From 1983 to 1986 he was deputy prime minister with responsibility for finance, the banking system, and religious affairs, as well as Romania's representative to the Council on Mutual Economic Assistance, the economic coordination organization for the Soviet bloc. In 1984 he became an alternate member of the party's top-level Political Executive Committee. The ministry personnel welcomed Totu's appointment, feeling it would add to the ministry's influence.

Totu was intelligent, patient with his subordinates, a good administrator, and much more self-confident than Vaduva. He would not simply parrot the party line but would try to make it more credible by presenting it in his own words, in a well-organized and systematic fashion. The fact that he firmly believed in the superiority of the socialist system added to the force of his presentation, though it diminished his ability to appreciate the U.S. point of view.

Totu remained loyal to his beliefs to the end. He left the Foreign Ministry in September 1989 to become head of the State Planning Committee and became a full member of the Political Executive Committee in November of that year. After the revolution in December 1989, Totu was arrested and tried together with other members of the committee. During the trial he was one of the most vocal defenders of the former regime. At one point he declared, "I would like to live, even if I have to eat dirt, in order to be able to sit in judgment on those who are in power today." As it happened, however, he committed suicide by hanging himself at his home on April 21, 1992, one day after being sentenced to 16 years' imprisonment. He left a note saying he "could no longer endure the humiliation, suffering, and injustice."[67]

Kirk's assessment of Totu after their first meeting was that Totu "knew that Ceauşescu was boss" and would not go beyond his instructions. At the same time, Totu seemed capable of growing in office and of understanding the subtleties of the U.S.-Romanian relationship. In fact, however, Totu had a negative effect on the ministry and on the U.S.-Romanian relationship. Despite his background and vigor, the ministry's overall influence continued the decline begun under Vaduva, resulting in its increasing marginalization in foreign-policy decision making.

Totu made a particular effort to distance the Foreign Ministry from U.S.-Romanian relations. He said the ministry should not intervene in matters having to do with the United States that were within the primary competence of another ministry (such as foreign trade or culture). He cut down to a minimum the participation of Foreign Ministry personnel in events involving the U.S. embassy or American visitors.

Like Vaduva, Totu sought to avoid getting personally involved in Romanian-American relations. When he did participate, he took an aggressive, ideological approach rather than a pragmatic one. He carried the notions of "independence," "reciprocity," and "noninterference in internal affairs" to an extreme, in part because of his own convictions, but also because he believed that the more powerful his foreign interlocutor, the more aggressive he himself should be. He also knew a tough line with the United States would please his prime patron, Elena Ceauşescu, who was considerably more hostile to the United States than was her husband.

All this was not apparent to the U.S. embassy, or to the Foreign Ministry, at the time of Totu's appointment, however, and the embassy thus recommended that Secretary Shultz and Vice President Bush meet with Totu when he went to New York for the U.N. General Assembly in September, just as they had met with Foreign Minister Andrei the preceding year. The Department of State replied that the vice president was too busy with the midterm political campaign and that the secretary's schedule was full. It noted that Deputy Secretary Whitehead had been given special responsibilities for Eastern Europe and would be happy to meet with Totu.

The lack of an appointment for the Romanian foreign minister with the secretary of state during their mutual attendance at the U.N. General Assembly broke a tradition of several years' standing. It caused especially deep offense in the Romanian hierarchy, given the importance Ceauşescu attached to the outward symbols of Romania's "special relationship" with the United States. Totu personally was very upset, fearing that his failure to have a formal meeting with Shultz would diminish his standing with Ceauşescu.

As it turned out, Shultz was able, under the urging of the State Department's European bureau, to find some 15 minutes to spend with Totu in New York during the UNGA session, but this brief interview was not enough to assuage Totu's dissatisfaction. It had been too impromptu and too short to remove his feeling and that of the Romanian hierarchy that Romania had been downgraded, especially as Shultz had maintained the tradition of holding a formally scheduled meeting with the foreign minister of Yugoslavia, the only other East European country normally so honored by the secretary of state. When Totu returned to Bucharest, he gave instructions that appointments for U.S. officials should be on a "strictly reciprocal" basis, a line he tried to follow thereafter.

Totu had a longer conversation in New York with Deputy Secretary Whitehead, who declared human rights the most serious underlying difficulty between the two countries. The U.S. ability to be responsive to Romania depended, he said, on Romanian responsiveness to these U.S. concerns. Totu stated that human rights, which he defined as the right to such things as employment and education, were an "absolute priority" for the government of Romania.

Totu's comment foreshadowed an increasingly prominent theme in Romanian responses to U.S. complaints about human rights, namely that Romania guaranteed rights neglected in the United States. These were rights to employment, education, health care, "life" (not sending their people into battle), and even religion (the Romanian government paid priests' salaries). If the Americans countered that they felt individual human rights, such as freedom of speech, worship, and assembly, were the fundamental issue, the Romanians would state that they disagreed and that the United States should not attempt to force its concept of human rights upon them.

To some extent this was only a debating point, but it also seemed to represent some degree of genuine conviction, especially on the part of convinced Marxists like Ceauşescu and Totu. American dismissal of the Romanian line of argument fed the suspicion of Ceauşescu and others that the United States had some ulterior motive when it claimed to be interested in "human rights" in Romania, a suspicion that continued to grow over the next three years.

Whitehead decided to make a trip to all the countries of Eastern Europe in November 1986 in pursuance of his new responsibilities. He told the Romanian ambassador shortly before the trip began that his aim was to get acquainted with the area and its leading personalities, to reduce or eliminate points of friction, and to search out opportunities for building bilateral relations.

Whitehead indeed brought to Eastern Europe specific suggestions that he hoped would move relations forward. On November 14 he enunciated these in meetings with Totu and Ceauşescu in Bucharest, after presenting greetings from Reagan and Shultz and explaining his commission by Shultz to follow East European affairs.

Whitehead told Totu and Ceauşescu that he wanted to intensify America's relationship with Romania and had three suggestions for doing so. First, he proposed semiannual meetings at the deputy secretary, assistant secretary, or deputy assistant secretary level to discuss international affairs, focusing on one geographic region at a time. Second, he suggested early confidential consultations at the "operational level" on how to deal with terrorism worldwide. Third, he proposed a renewed effort to increase mutual trade and to promote American investment in Romania. Such investment, he said, had played an important role in many countries around the world, and he was sure there were good possibilities in Romania if both sides worked to promote it.

Trade between the United States and Romania was, in fact, the largest in Eastern Europe. Romanian exports to the United States totaled $950 million in 1985 and $754 million in 1986. U.S. exports to Romania were $207 million in 1985 and $251 million in 1986.[68] United States firms had signed contracts worth over $115 million at the Bucharest Trade Fair the month before Whitehead arrived. Prospective deals for the sale of new

Boeing aircraft to the Romanian national airline and additional General Electric generators for Romania's nuclear power plant appeared imminent (but were delayed, with the deals still not concluded by the time of Ceauşescu's fall in 1989). Actual American investment in Romania was minimal, however, confined largely to one modest joint venture involving manufacture of computer drives in cooperation with the U.S. computer giant Control Data.

Continuing payment and contract disputes troubled commercial relations, as did Romanian reluctance to allow American business representatives to visit Romanian plants. Equally troubling was the government's control over Romanian employees of American firms in Romania. These difficulties became even more severe under the previously described Decree 408 of late 1985 on top of the regime's growing obsession with secrecy and its endeavor to hide Romania's worsening economic situation from foreign eyes.

The Romanians for their part continually complained that U.S. quotas on imports and restrictions on the export of technology were major obstacles to trade. U.S. quotas on steel and textiles, for example, were in fact somewhat of a handicap to Romanian exports in these fields, but they did not materially reduce overall trade figures. U.S. restrictions on the export of technology were of more symbolic than practical significance for U.S.-Romanian trade, given Romania's hard currency shortage and limited ability to use such technology.

After Whitehead discussed with Totu and Ceauşescu his ideas on ways to move the U.S.-Romanian relationship forward, he turned to the subject of human rights, stressing that their importance to the United States was fundamental, arising out of the history of America from the time of the arrival of the first European settlers. The United States respected the sovereignty of other countries, but it felt strongly about human rights. It raised them in its dealings with all nations while recognizing that they often involved a country's internal affairs.

Whitehead reviewed several specific U.S. concerns about Romania, including emigration, Bibles, church buildings for the Seventh-Day Adventists and Baptists, and individual hardship cases. He specifically mentioned Ion Ruţa, whom the police had arrested for embezzlement and sentenced to seven years in prison shortly after his wife elected not to return to Romania from a business trip to the United States. Whitehead told Ceauşescu that these matters were important to the United States and could be resolved at no real cost to the Romanian government. They should be the subject of discussions between the two sides leading to solutions.

Romanian press accounts of the meeting were brief and relatively unin-formative but noted prominently that the deputy secretary had con-veyed "warm greetings" to Ceauşescu from President Reagan.[69] The Romanians had achieved their principal objective by the simple fact that Whitehead came and was received by Ceauşescu. They therefore gave little importance to the content of that discussion.

The Romanian hierarchy, starting with Ceauşescu himself, had still not grasped that the state of U.S.-Romanian relations had changed funda-mentally since the harmonious period of the 1970s or that they had to pay attention to what U.S. spokespersons were saying. Despite all they had heard from these U.S. representatives, they refused to recognize that the official attitude of the United States had changed and that this change required adjustments on the Romanian part if the relationship was to be preserved. Ceauşescu in particular felt that the basic U.S. policy was still the one initiated by President Nixon. He could not yet admit to himself that the Reagan administration was gradually veering onto a different course.

Ceauşescu told Whitehead that he welcomed the suggestion of regu-lar consultation on foreign affairs but believed that the working-level talks the United States had proposed should be supplemented from time to time by meetings at the ministerial or chief-of-state level. He expressed the hope that President Reagan would visit Bucharest. He and Totu agreed to talks on terrorism but noted the distinction between terrorism and the struggle for national liberation. Ceauşescu said that the way to increase trade was for the United States to extend MFN on a multiyear basis, remove quotas, and liberalize licensing of technology exports. He would welcome more joint ventures, as long as they were in conformity with Romanian law (which required majority Romanian ownership and severely restricted the transfer of profits outside of Romania).

In responding to Whitehead's presentation on human rights, Ceauşescu expounded on his version of such rights and how Romania guaranteed them. He also pointed out that Romania, unlike the United States, was not a country of immigration; Romanians were proud that their people had been in place for millennia, and they wanted them to stay there. He would, however, allow some emigration, especially for family reunification, on a case-by-case basis. He knew "by chance" of the problems of the Seventh-Day Adventist church in Bucharest and the Baptist church in Oradea and said there should be no problem in finding replacements for the "two rooms" those congregations had lost. Baptist Bibles had been printed in Romania in the past (in 1921) and could be printed again.

Ruţa was a "criminal," Ceauşescu said, but he would look into Ruţa's case "if he concerns you so much." He could not help wondering why the United States was so interested in this individual, who deserved to be in jail. Whitehead responded that as a chief of state, Ceauşescu would have to decide for himself whether it was better to keep a man in jail or to have good relations with the United States. Ceauşescu rejoined that, in principle, if good relations with the United States depended on matters like that, he would have to reconsider those relations.

Totu was more combative. He said Romania did not like to have its internal affairs discussed in connection with MFN. If that continued, the United States should not be surprised if Romania renounced MFN. "People of ill will" toward Romania were exploiting the MFN process in the United States. He also complained about the criticism of Romania's human rights record in statements by Representative Steny Hoyer, one of the U.S. representatives at the CSCE meeting in Vienna. He noted that the United States had its own problems, such as unemployment, people sleeping in the streets, and a poor educational system.

In addition to governmental contacts, Whitehead's schedule in Bucharest included meetings with nongovernmental individuals in an endeavor to obtain a more balanced picture of the situation. Kirk hosted a reception for leaders of several religious denominations at which Whitehead reported that he had given great emphasis to religious questions in his conversation with Ceauşescu. The embassy also organized a lunch at a local restaurant with several Romanians outside of government.

Because the luncheon was contrary to the government's practice of limiting visitors to approved contacts (who would spout only the official line), Romanian officialdom viewed it with great irritation and suspicion. They repeatedly tried to get the U.S. side to cancel it, and they successfully discouraged several of the Romanian invitees from attending.

Three individuals did attend, however, all persons who had been close to the regime but were now somewhat out of favor. Two of them, Silviu Brucan (a former minister to the United States and then ambassador to the United Nations) and Mihnea Gheorghiu (an early member of the Communist Party and a leading communist intellectual through the years), had been close associates of Ceauşescu in the early years of the dictator's rule and still enjoyed a certain freedom of dissent due to their prominent communist past. The third, Alexandru Duţu, was editor of the *Revue des Etudes Sud-est Européennes,* published by the Romanian Institute of Southeast European Studies. The Romanian government had begun to view him with some suspicion and had recently refused him a passport to travel abroad.

The negative government reaction to this U.S. effort to have Whitehead meet nongovernmental individuals, even ones with ties to the Romanian leadership, illustrates the two governments' basic difference of approach to relations among countries. U.S. practice has been to promote relations at all levels of government, indeed of society. It has put heavy emphasis on frequent and open exchange, cultural and scientific programs, and contacts among persons in widely different fields. The U.S. government has taken a particularly active role in promoting unofficial and semiofficial contacts in the case of authoritarian regimes such as Romania, where private, independent channels for such contacts are shut off. In such cases the United States has been particularly anxious to have its officials see persons outside of government, even semiofficial ones like the Romanians invited to meet Whitehead.

The Romanian leadership's approach at that time, on the other hand, was to evaluate relations with other countries in terms of the contribution these relations made to the prestige and power of the Romanian government. Actions serving this end, such as high-level visits, public demonstrations of a "special" relationship, and especially MFN status, were of value. Lower-level or unofficial contacts were not. Indeed, Ceauşescu and his associates feared that unofficial or even semiofficial contacts might undermine their regime. Whitehead's proposals for increased working-level contacts, while making excellent sense from the U.S. point of view, did not have great appeal to the Romanian leadership. They were willing to go along with such contacts in the area of international affairs, but their real desire, as stated by Ceauşescu, was to move even these to the highest level of government for the symbolism this would entail. The Romanians had no interest in setting up working-level meetings to seek solutions to bilateral problems; they knew their officials at such meetings could decide nothing and they feared the discussion might put dangerous ideas in those officials' heads. Therefore Whitehead's suggestion of such meetings proved to be no more fruitful than Shultz's proposal for a special Kirk–foreign minister channel had been the year before.

Another reason for the failure of this idea was Totu's own opposition to such meetings. This was illustrated by the fact that although the party high command had given approval for a trip to the United States by Maria Groza in early 1987 as a follow-up to Whitehead's proposal, Totu did not tell anyone about the approval until Groza had left the ministry in May

1987. At that point he sent the written approval to Raceanu with the notation "for the file."

Even though one or two intergovernmental meetings did take place in the wake of Whitehead's visit, they did nothing to change the basic relationship between the two countries. Furthermore, Whitehead's generally upbeat presentation was soon overshadowed by a U.S. move the Romanians would interpret as a highly unfriendly political act.

▼ 6 ▼

Frictions Mount
1987

The year 1987 opened with a basic misunderstanding by the Romanian government about why it lost its preferential status under the Generalized System of Preferences, the program that gives developing countries tariff advantages for some of their exports to the United States. Romania was one of the countries so favored.

In 1984, over the objections of the administration, Congress had renewed the program with an amendment stating that to be eligible for the program a country must have taken or be taking steps to grant "internationally recognized worker rights." This amendment gave the president until January 1987 to complete a review of all recipients' practices to ensure conformity with the new requirement.[70] In connection with that review, the AFL-CIO in June 1985 submitted a complaint asserting that Romania had not taken, and was not taking, such steps. The Romanian government presented its rebuttal that August, and there the matter rested until the summer of 1986.

With the January 1987 deadline approaching, the Office of the U.S. Trade Representative raised the question of Romania's continuing eligibility under the amendment. Worker rights in Romania were certainly meager and did not include the right to form free labor associations or to engage in collective bargaining, two key "internationally recognized" worker rights from the U.S. point of view. The issue was whether the president could say that Romania was "taking steps" toward according such rights. Washington instructed the U.S. embassy in Bucharest to bring this problem to the attention of the Romanian government and to note the deadline for the presidential determination. In late September 1986 the Ministry of Labor responded that in Romania the workers' collectives themselves owned the factories. The workers thus did not need the kind of rights mentioned by the United States, which should take into account how Romania's situation differed from its own.

The U.S. embassy in Bucharest forwarded the Romanian reply with a recommendation that Washington grant Romania an exemption from the new requirement on economic grounds, as allowed for in the legislation. The embassy cited as arguments the fact that Romania was a leading market for U.S. goods in Eastern Europe (over $200 million worth per year). There were also prospects of deals worth tens of millions of dollars in aircraft and large turbines, which the Romanian reaction to withdrawal of GSP would probably jeopardize. The embassy and the State Department also argued that the Romanians would take withdrawal of GSP as a political act contrary to the U.S. policy, so recently articulated in Bucharest by Deputy Secretary John Whitehead, of keeping lines open to Romania. Nevertheless, the interagency committee reviewing the matter recommended withdrawal of GSP from Romania. The State Department's arguments, whatever their political merit, were not sufficient to overcome the reality of Romanian behavior and the requirements of law.

When the embassy informed the Romanian Foreign Ministry in early December of the impending decision, to be announced in January, the reaction was as predicted. Ministry officials warned Kirk's deputy, Henry Clarke, that the "highest levels" of the Romanian government would view the move as a "political decision" that could only damage U.S.-Romanian relations. Deputy Minister Maria Groza reinforced the point with Kirk on December 11, saying the decision would have political effects that would strengthen the hand of the many Romanian officials who opposed good U.S.-Romanian relations.

Raceanu notes that Groza's assertion, while appearing to Kirk largely a device to pressure the United States, also reflected the fact that a growing number of the Romanian hierarchy actively favored adopting a tougher line with the United States. Among these were Elena Ceaușescu, Prime Minister Constantin Dascalescu, Emil Bobu (the second most powerful man in the party hierarchy), First Deputy Prime Minister Gheorghe Oprea, Deputy Prime Ministers Ion Dinca and Barbu Petrescu, Party Secretary for International Affairs Ion Stoian, Interior Minister Tudor Postelnicu, Securitate head Iulian Vlad, and Foreign Minister Ioan Totu. The Romanians for the most part dismissed the embassy's counterargument that the decision of the administration was merely the natural consequence of the January 1987 deadline in the law enacted by Congress in 1984.

On January 2, 1987, President Reagan announced his determination that Romania and Nicaragua would lose GSP beneficiary status under the terms of the 1984 congressional amendment.[71] In mid-January, upon returning to the Foreign Ministry from leave, Raceanu was surprised to see a joint memorandum that the Ministry of Foreign Affairs and the Ministry of Foreign Trade had sent to Ceauşescu playing down the implications of GSP withdrawal. The memo estimated that only some $7 million of Romanian exports would be lost, although actual 1985 U.S. imports from Romania covered by the GSP program totaled $134.7 million.[72] The memo further asserted that the U.S. decision was not yet final and suggested taking a variety of measures to reverse it.

When Raceanu criticized the memo for belittling the economic impact of losing GSP, his colleagues told him that higher-ups in the ministry had dictated its basic approach; he later learned that the figures in the memo had come from the Securitate. Raceanu ascribed this approach to the universal knowledge of Ceauşescu's aversion to bad news and of the penalties sometimes inflicted upon those who gave it to him. Thus all parties, including the Securitate, would rather give him a misleading picture than an unpleasant one, often leading him to act on the basis of distorted information.

Ceauşescu accepted the ministries' recommendations for measures to reverse the U.S. decision. On January 10 Foreign Minister Totu, under instructions from Ceauşescu, summoned Chargé Henry Clarke and gave him a formal note "for the attention of President Reagan". It characterized the U.S. action as essentially a political decision based on misjudgments about the situation in Romania and an act inconsistent with the pledges of Secretary Shultz and Deputy Secretary Whitehead that the United States desired closer political cooperation with Romania. The note called the U.S. action discriminatory and said bilateral relations would suffer. A letter from the minister of foreign trade to Secretary of Commerce Malcolm Baldrige and a demarche by Ambassador Gavrilescu in Washington expressed similar sentiments.

It was clear the Romanians were taking the U.S. withdrawal of GSP as an important political signal, although this was not Washington's intention. The State Department therefore took the unusual step of sending a letter from Secretary Shultz to Foreign Minister Totu, which was duly delivered to the ministry by the U.S. embassy in Bucharest. In his letter, dated January 23, Shultz said he wanted "to ensure that there is no misunderstanding as to the motivation behind" withdrawal of GSP. He continued: "The action we took in response to a mandate from the Congress does not imply that the United States no longer seeks to improve and expand our bilateral relations. On the contrary, I want to reaffirm that my government values its relationship with Romania and stands ready to work cooperatively with you to the fullest extent possible." After detailing some efforts the United States was making to this end, he added a cautionary note: "There are a number of outstanding problems, particularly the decline in emigration in 1986, which could place MFN in jeopardy. I would urge that your government focus on these concerns in the months ahead."[73]

The Romanians did not respond to this letter, but continued to criticize the withdrawal of GSP in talks with Americans over the next few months. They did not, however, seem to make a major issue of it.

Ceauşescu, meanwhile, was showing no signs of relenting in his internal policies. His wife, Elena, was becoming ever more prominent, and her influence showed in tightened restrictions on intellectuals, including their contacts with foreigners. Speeches by Ceauşescu as early as January 1987 had condemned reformist ideas; in what was clearly a jibe at Gorbachev's reforms, he asserted that a true socialist society could not accept even small-scale capitalism. People who said this was the time to "relax" were wrong, Ceauşescu said. The struggle to build genuine socialism should proceed with renewed vigor. As if to give force to his words, private cars were banned from Bucharest's roads as of January 30, and supplies of food in the markets diminished further.

On January 30, harshly criticizing various failures in the economy, Ceauşescu called for a major effort to reduce Romania's foreign debt.[74] Paying off Romania's foreign debt was in fact becoming an obsession with Ceauşescu, one that would make Romanians' lives much harder over the next two and a half years.

In 1982 Romania's external debt had been over $11 billion, and an International Monetary Fund team had come to Romania to tell Ceauşescu what he must do to cope with it. Never one to accept outside "interference," Ceauşescu sent the team packing, saying he would take care of the matter himself, and launched a debt reduction program that lowered the debt to some $5 billion by late 1986. Then, in a crash campaign to eliminate the debt entirely by 1989, he called for an increase in exports, including exports of food, and put restrictions on imports so severe that many machines sat idle for lack of foreign-made parts and crop production suffered for lack of imported pesticides. Foreign medicines, even insulin, were in short supply. Ceauşescu decreed that Romania would seek no new foreign credits, and ministries had to get permission from Ceauşescu himself before they could spend over $1,000 in hard currency.

Kirk returned from home leave to a depressed and bleak Bucharest in February 1987. He had a long session with Totu a few days later in which he reviewed Washington's current human rights concerns. He noted that emigration approvals had been very low since MFN renewal the preceding spring and that they would have to come up markedly to fulfill the legal requirement for MFN. The government of Romania had said in the early fall of 1986 that 5,000 Bibles would be printed for the Baptists, but none had yet appeared. Promises of new accommodations for Seventh-Day Adventists in Bucharest and Baptists in Oradea had not materialized. Ion Ruţa was still in jail. Other long-standing concerns remained unsatisfied. Kirk said Whitehead had told him that the U.S. administration needed responses on these matters if it was to recommend another extension of MFN and defend it before Congress.

Totu countered that he had expected Kirk to return with agreement to extend MFN on a multiyear basis, especially as the United States had just restored MFN for Poland without requiring annual renewal. He said Kirk could be confident that emigration would go up. The Adventist and Oradea church issues were "not important," and the delay in printing Bibles was not the Romanian government's fault. (The latter may have been partially true; the Orthodox Church did not want to expedite printing of what it considered heretical literature, the Baptists themselves were divided as to how hard to push the government and the Orthodox Church, and the promised plates and paper were agonizingly slow in coming from the West.) What Romania needed were more high-level American visitors, Totu added, and Kirk should work to this end. It was all very familiar.

In February 1987, Rabbi Arthur Schneier again came to Bucharest and met with Ceauşescu. The rabbi raised a number of human rights problems with the dictator, but to little avail, he told Kirk.

Ceauşescu's next American visitor was Robert Robertson, vice chairman of a newly formed business lobby called American Businesses for International Trade, a group of business executives engaged in trade with Romania who testified in defense of that trade at appropriate congressional hearings and who supported MFN for Romania. Robertson visited Romania several times over the next three years. The Romanians, including Ceauşescu personally, felt Robertson had great influence on Congress and the administration and spared no effort to impress him. During the hour Robertson and Kirk spent with Ceauşescu on March 23,

1987, Robertson told the dictator that the threat to MFN in Congress was greater than in preceding years.

That same day Kirk received instructions from the Department of State to deliver a message from Shultz to Ceauşescu. The latter received Kirk on April 7, without the foreign minister present. The interview began with an oral translation of the secretary's somber written message, which Kirk had brought with him.

Shultz stated, "I am writing to convey to you my deep concern about the prospect for renewal of our Most-Favored-Nation (MFN) tariff relationship." After consulting Congress, the secretary had concluded that "MFN is in serious jeopardy due to widespread concern over matters of fundamental human rights." He cited emigration, the Adventist and Oradea churches, Bibles, and the emigration of Ion Ruţa and stated that "these issues, if unresolved, have the capacity to harm the prospects for renewal of MFN." Noting that he and Ceauşescu had agreed in December 1985 on the desirability of expanding and improving bilateral relations, he closed by saying, "I believe the problems I have cited can be resolved if we approach them in the same spirit."[75]

Ceauşescu, who had probably been hoping for some special communication on world affairs, looked sour as the translation progressed. Kirk then spoke for a few minutes. After reviewing some specifics of the emigration problem, he turned to other human rights matters. He noted that, while the Romanians had made welcome promises on these matters in the summer, the promises remained unfulfilled. Americans, he said, considered problems solved not when decisions were taken but when action was completed, a comment he made because the Romanians were always longer on promises than performance and seemed to think that the mere agreement to do something was enough, even without a follow-through.

Ceauşescu paused for some time before commenting that he was "surprised" by the secretary's letter, which "contradicted" the relations between the two countries. The problems the secretary raised constituted unacceptable interference. They were raised "artificially" and would be settled in conformity with Romanian law. They were not relevant to U.S.-Romanian relations, he said, and MFN should not be a means to interfere in Romania's domestic affairs. Ceauşescu also expressed surprise at the State Department's report on religious affairs in Romania; it had deliberately misinformed the American public about the realities in Romania. He expected ambassadors and embassy personnel to understand these realities, but had the impression they were not being presented in a true light to Washington; the secretary's letter certainly reflected a failure to understand Romanian realities. Romania could live without MFN if this interference was what it brought.

Kirk replied that the United States public and government were concerned about human rights all over the world and that they were a factor in the U.S.-Romanian relationship. It was therefore necessary for the United States to bring these issues to Ceauşescu's attention. The interview terminated without further discussion.

Behind Ceauşescu's complaints about U.S. embassy activities were the Securitate reports he regularly received on U.S. embassy meetings with dissidents in Bucharest and embassy officers' trips to provincial cities to see such persons. As these contacts intensified, Ceauşescu became persuaded that the embassy was focusing too much on human rights rather than on "larger" issues such as world affairs and official Romanian statements. He also considered the State Department human rights report much too critical of Romania.

Despite Ceauşescu's complaints, the various efforts to convey the situation in the United States to the Romanian government did have a positive effect. They enabled Raceanu to get top-level approval for a program of action he drew up to improve U.S.-Romanian relations, the state of which troubled him deeply. There had been no Romanian reaction to Whitehead's November 1986 proposals. The government was not allocating hard currency for use by ministries and others for exchanges and other activities in the United States. Romania's image in the United States was growing steadily worse, and there was real doubt over renewal of MFN. The "political" GSP decision attested to the seriousness of the situation.

Raceanu initially proposed that the Romanians hold an in-depth internal discussion at the top ministerial level on relations with the United States. Maria Groza told him a few days later that Totu "was not too interested" but had agreed to have the Americas directorate submit a program for improvement of U.S.-Romanian relations.

The program the directorate submitted covered a number of fields. It called for invitations to several U.S. officials to visit Romania, including Deputy Secretary Whitehead, Counselor Edward Derwinski, and Assistant Secretary Rozanne Ridgway, and advocated intensified consultations on international matters. It recommended sending a parliamentary delegation to the United States and inviting members of Congress and key congressional staff personnel to come to Romania. It called for renewed efforts to persuade the United States to agree to a cabinet level meeting on trade, to grant more licenses for export of technology to Romania, and to cooperate with Romanian firms in foreign markets. It stressed the importance of obtaining MFN renewal and called for resolving a number of family reunification cases in the immediate future to help achieve this.

The plan also recommended moving to fulfill Romania's part of the cultural exchange program by sending a number of Romanian scholars to the United States, mounting a photographic exhibit there, and having Romanian historians participate in the fall meeting of the American Society for Romanian Studies. It suggested that the government invite several prestigious American journalists to visit Romania and send a number of Romanian journalists to the United States. It called for a delegation of religious leaders to go to the United States and for expediting the printing of 5,000 Bibles for the Baptists. Finally, it advocated filling the vacancies at the Romanian embassy in Washington and commercial office in New York with qualified people (the embassy in Washington had an authorized complement of eleven positions, but only four were filled at the time) and asked for release of the foreign exchange needed to do all this.

In the spring of 1987 Ceauşescu gave his oral blessing to the plan and passed it on to the Political Executive Committee for decision. The committee approved it virtually without discussion after Totu (untruthfully) asserted that he had drawn it up "on Ceauşescu's instruction," a ploy top Romanian officials often used when they wanted to head off any opposition to their proposals. The committee's action made it possible for the Foreign Ministry to obtain the foreign exchange needed to fund the proposed delegations and exhibits and resulted in forward movement on emigration and Bible printing.

This plan is interesting as an example of what the ministry's experts on the United States thought they could ask for in order to reverse the slide in U.S.-Romanian relations. The Americas directorate had taken a similar initiative at a time of crisis in U.S.-Romanian relations in 1983, and Ceauşescu had approved several of their proposals. Much of the 1987 program was the familiar Romanian refrain: high-level meetings, parliamentary exchanges, export licenses, and so on. The United States had already rebuffed these ideas many times.

The proposals for inviting journalists to visit Romania, sending Romanian religious leaders, academics, and cultural exhibits to the United States, taking action on printing Bibles, and increasing emigration permissions had merit, but they were of limited value. Prestigious U.S. journalists certainly would not come to Romania if they were subject to the usual Romanian restrictions on their activities; and even if they were free to interview whom they wanted, these journalists would probably write highly critical stories. The idea of sending Romanian academics and exhibits to the United States was good, but it was at best a small step with largely intangible, long-term benefits. Sending a religious delegation could be somewhat helpful, though such delegations had been sent before, and what they said was largely discounted in the United States. Favorable action on printing Bibles and family reunification cases, on the other hand, would have a significant impact on the immediate problem of MFN renewal.

The program probably represented the maximum the Romanian government would have been prepared to do in the late 1980s to improve its relations with the United States. It was one that could have helped U.S.-Romanian relations materially in the late 1970s and early 1980s, when Romania enjoyed a basically favorable reputation in the United States. It could have been of some benefit in the mid-1980s, when Romania's foreign policy was still appreciated. The world scene was changing, however.

As the second half of the eighties wore on, Romania's foreign policies looked less and less unique, its internal policies more and more retrogressive, and its admirable independence more like contemptible isolation. Preservation of a special relationship with the United States had therefore become more difficult. The Americas directorate's program proved adequate in 1987 to save MFN, though not to put relations on a new footing; by 1988 such a program would have been too little to save MFN; and by 1989 it would have taken a fundamental change in the Romanian regime to halt the continuing deterioration in relations.

Ceauşescu did not realize how much the situation was changing; perhaps he could not have been expected to know. He approved the ministry's suggested program, convinced that it would be sufficient to restore the "special relationship" with the United States. When it did not, he became angry and blamed his subordinates, Hungarian machinations, or Reagan's ideological anticommunism. He pinned his hopes on his own effectiveness in talking to Americans, then sent special envoys to explain the true situation directly to Reagan, and, finally, anticipated change from the incoming Bush presidency. By the time that last hope was dashed, he was already outraged and threatened by what was happening in the communist world. Before he had time to think about the United States, he was swept aside by the forces of reform and convicted by a military court on December 25, 1989, of "crimes against the people." That was his personal tragedy, and his deserved fate.

The most prominent American visitors to Romania in this period were Senators Sam Nunn of Georgia and John Warner of Virginia, who came to Bucharest on April 15, 1987. The visit of these two leading congressional figures on arms control, one of whom, Senator Nunn, was then prominently mentioned as a possible presidential candidate, was a great feather in Romania's cap. The Romanians gave them maximum official and press attention. Together with Kirk they saw the ministers of defense and foreign affairs and spent two hours with Ceauşescu.

The main burden of their discussions was arms control, with Ceauşescu again departing from Soviet positions on a number of points. He called for immediate withdrawal of all short-range missiles from Europe, said there had never been any justification for sending Soviet troops into Czechoslovakia, and stated that the Soviet troop presence in Poland and Hungary "was no longer necessary." He criticized the Soviet presence in Afghanistan and the Vietnamese military occupation of Kampuchea.

Ceauşescu repeated his advocacy of unilateral 5 percent reductions in military budgets, equipment, and manpower, noting that Romania had already reduced its troops and equipment by 5 percent and its defense budget by 10 percent. He claimed great popular support in Romania for this proposal, on which he had organized a popular referendum in November 1986.

This referendum had in fact been the occasion for some of the more absurd statistics ever put out by the Romanian government. The regime asserted that out of 16 million registered voters all but 224 had voted in the referendum and that *no one* had voted against the proposal. The referendum was also open to those between the ages of 14 and 18. Of the more than 1.5 million persons in this category, the regime claimed that only 4 had failed to vote, with none voting against. It was simply a further sign of Ceauşescu's self-delusion that his subordinates felt he would accept such absurd figures from them and that he could believe these figures would do other than make him a laughingstock in Romania and abroad.[76]

In their conversations with Nunn and Warner, Ceauşescu and Totu had a major new problem, namely, that the Soviet Union under Gorbachev was moving on internal reform, while Romania was not. Both took the line that Moscow's internal policies were its own affair and that they wished the Soviets success in carrying out a restructuring that Romania had completed 20 years before. Ceauşescu based the latter, somewhat breathtaking assertion on his introduction in the late 1960s of worker "ownership" of factories and the holding of mass meetings that could "express the people's views directly to the leadership." As Kirk noted to the senators afterwards, these meetings were merely adulation sessions for Ceauşescu. The Securitate orchestrated them very carefully—to the point where the poems and songs at the Romanian national holiday festivities held in the main Bucharest soccer stadium, for example, were prerecorded, so that there would be no slip and no chance for an unexpected comment. The 500-man band, the poets, and the singers merely mouthed their parts or pretended to play their instruments; they did not actually make a sound. This did not seem to bother Ceauşescu and certainly did not prevent him and Totu from citing these kinds of meetings as examples of true democracy.

While the principal focus of the Nunn-Warner discussion was on arms control, the two senators also raised human rights issues with both Totu and Ceauşescu, noting that U.S. concern over these questions was genuine and was affecting the prospects for MFN renewal. Totu replied that Romania objected to the "spectacle" of annual MFN renewal, while Ceauşescu focused on the point that Romania could compete with the United States on human rights any time. The extensive Romanian media coverage of the meeting made no mention of this part of the discussion, however, focusing instead on international issues and the visit's demonstration of Ceauşescu's role as an independent world statesman.[77]

Thomas Simons, deputy assistant secretary of state for European affairs responsible for the Soviet Union and Eastern Europe, arrived in Bucharest on April 16, fresh from accompanying Secretary Shultz on a visit to Moscow. Simons briefed Totu at length on the U.S.-Soviet talks on arms control, and Totu reported to Ceauşescu in detail on Simons's remarks. The Romanians particularly valued this kind of briefing as the Americans gave them more detail on U.S.-Soviet arms talks than did the Soviets. Simons then moved on to bilateral concerns, but Totu relayed little of this to Ceauşescu.

Simons held a much longer session on bilateral matters with Groza. More and more members of Congress and representatives of different American organizations, institutes, and foundations, he noted, were pressing the administration and especially the Department of State about serious violations of human and religious rights in Romania. These groups presented specific and documented cases and asked the administration to suspend MFN in retaliation. Members of Congress in growing numbers were starting to link MFN with human rights in general, not just with emigration, Simons told Groza. Romanian failure to address the human rights concerns could thus lead to loss of MFN, and the overall trade law pending before Congress could be a vehicle for this.

Groza responded with the usual arguments about "interference" and "misinformation" based on "ill-intentioned" sources, while at the same time promising to look into the specific cases Simons had raised. She then expressed considerable concern about the expression of what she called Hungarian irredentist sentiments in the United States, which her government took as a threat to Romania's territorial integrity. The Romanian government had been particularly alarmed by a letter to Shultz signed by 234 members of the House of Representatives calling for better treatment of the Hungarian minority, a letter it considered to be the work of Hungarian irredentists and their congressional supporters.[78]

Groza merely referred in general to hearings and resolutions in Congress calling for better treatment of the Hungarian minority and to demonstrations in New York and Washington. She asked that the Department of State issue a formal statement condemning such activities. Simons reiterated U.S. support of its treaty obligations, including those covering Romania's territorial integrity, but expressed U.S. concern about the treatment of the Hungarian minority within Romania, including their limited access to Hungarian-language schooling, maintenance of their cultural and ethnic traditions, and the 1983 arrests of three ethnic Hungarian activists.

Groza briefed Totu fully on her conversation with Simons. Totu in turn sent a written report to Ceaușescu, but gave instructions that the report gloss over Simons's complaints about human and religious rights in Romania and public opinion in the United States and focus instead on the fact that Simons had raised the Hungarian minority question. This was a deliberate provocation on Totu's part. The Hungarian question was a highly sensitive subject for Ceaușescu, as it was for almost all Romanians. It had been no accident that Ceaușescu queried Shultz about U.S. respect for borders during their meeting in December 1985.

The United States had received another warning on the sensitivity of the Hungarian issue in August 1986. At that time Ilie Șimon, a member of the Foreign Ministry's U.S. department, said to his American colleagues, "This subject [Hungarians] will kill you. We can talk about Bibles all day, but not about Hungarians. Top Romanian officials will react the same way." Șimon's comment was especially meaningful as he was married to

Ceaușescu's niece and thus occasionally visited with the First Family. Knowing of this sensitivity, Totu was trying to convince Ceaușescu that the U.S. government was interested in stirring up the Hungarian question.

U.S. officials realized that the subject of Romania's Hungarian minority was a sensitive issue, but given the frozen international relations of the Cold War, they did not consider border revisions in Eastern Europe a live question. They thought Romanian protestations were a smoke screen to deflect American criticism of their treatment of the Hungarian minority, a debating ploy that could be dismissed with a phrase. It seems, however, that the Romanians had persuaded themselves there was a real danger the United States might back Hungarian territorial claims because of the sinister influence of the Hungarian lobby in the United States.

Indeed, the supposed influence of this lobby was one factor persuading the Romanian government that the United States might be initiating an "anti-Romanian" policy. Totu revealed his own paranoia on this point during an interview he gave from prison in September 1991, after the revolution that threw out Ceaușescu. He said, "Irrespective of what one may say, it was clear that the events which took place in Timișoara [the incident in December 1989 that triggered the revolution] were premeditated and organized by hostile Hungarian elements from Hungary and the United States, together with other circles hostile to Romania."[79]

The day after Deputy Assistant Secretary Simons met with Totu and Groza there was a bizarre incident arising from another failure of communication between the two governments; it was a fairly typical misunderstanding of the nature of the Romanian system on the part of an American congressman. Representative Gary Ackerman of New York had told Ambassador Gavrilescu in Washington that House Majority Leader Jim Wright of Texas would lead a large congressional delegation to Romania if he could be assured that a number of Romanians from a list Ackerman would present would be allowed to leave the country with the delegation. He said Wright would bring a special U.S. military plane for the purpose. The success of such a mission would make a very favorable impression on the majority leader and Congress as a whole at a time when Romania badly needed congressional support.

The ministry forwarded the Romanian ambassador's report of this proposal to Ceaușescu, who said he would welcome a visit by Wright and would receive the delegation himself. He said that he could not agree to a number of Romanians leaving with the delegation, but that as a sign of goodwill the Romanian government would approve the emigration of several of the individuals on the congressman's list and permit them to leave shortly after the delegation's departure.

When the ministry conveyed this response to Kirk, he expressed surprise and said Ackerman had told the Department of State that a senior Romanian embassy official had twice informed Ackerman by telephone, once when he was actually in Wright's office, that the Romanian side accepted his entire proposal, including the provision that the Romanians would leave on Representative Wright's plane. The ministry told Kirk that theirs was the official Romanian position, and the United States should disregard what the Romanian embassy had allegedly said.

The ministry queried the Romanian embassy in Washington immediately after the meeting with Kirk. Gavrilescu replied that neither he nor his subordinates had given any assurances to Ackerman. It developed later, however, that the ambassador was mistaken. The senior Securitate officer at the Romanian embassy, Deputy Chief of Mission Dan Dumitru, had talked with Ackerman and communicated with his Securitate superiors in Bucharest about the proposal without his ambassador's knowledge. He had then received authority from the Securitate in Bucharest to tell Ackerman that his proposal was acceptable and had done so. The Securitate in Bucharest had felt that Ceaușescu was so interested in demonstrating his good relations with leading U.S. congressmen that he would agree to the proposition and had therefore instructed their man in Washington to accede without checking with Ceaușescu.

It would in fact have been very unlike Ceaușescu to agree to a proposition of this kind. He always asserted that he was "independent" and did not give in to "pressure." When he made concessions, he made them as unobtrusively as he could and usually considerably after the concession was requested. He certainly would not want a group of Romanians to go out on Representative Wright's plane and land in the United States with major media attention highlighting Ceaușescu's "concession" and his restrictive emigration and human rights policies. The Securitate showed real political obtuseness in assuming that Ceaușescu would accede, but they probably were so tempted by the favor they believed they would gain with Ceaușescu by procuring a visit from Wright that they failed to think through the price Ceaușescu would have to pay in media terms. The whole incident was typical of the growing and disruptive role of the Securitate in Romanian foreign policy.

Despite the U.S. embassy's telegram to Washington reporting the Foreign Ministry's description of Ceaușescu's position, Ackerman came to Bucharest in mid-April in an effort to preserve his "deal." He spent five hours with Groza before asking Kirk to tell Wright's staff that the trip was off. Ackerman did obtain a promise from the Romanian government that it would give quick and sympathetic consideration to the cases on his list, which the Romanians did. Most of the persons on Ackerman's list received emigration permission within ten days, and all but a few had permission by the end of July. This represented unusually rapid and forthcoming action by Romanian standards, but the whole affair ended as a net loss for the Romanian government. The Romanians' failure to live up to the promises their embassy had made to Ackerman, which he had relayed to Wright, left a bad taste, while the later granting of emigration permissions strengthened the impression in Congress that the Romanian government would yield to pressure.

▼ ▼ ▼

The eleventh session of the U.S.-Romanian intergovernmental Joint Economic Commission met in Romania later in April 1987. This body had been set up at the time of Ceauşescu's visit to the United States in 1973, with the U.S. secretary of commerce and the Romanian minister of foreign trade as co-chairmen. It was supposed to meet annually and had done so for a number of years. The U.S. side had grown quite fatigued with these meetings; they had accomplished very little in helping smooth trade relations in recent years. But the Romanians valued them highly as symbols of their special relationship with the United States. At U.S. insistence, however, the meeting in Washington in 1986 was at the deputy secretary/deputy minister level, instead of at the cabinet level.

The Romanians pressed throughout 1986 and 1987 for a "regular" meeting at cabinet level. The United States resisted because of the lack of usefulness of the meetings, because it did not like the image of a cabinet officer going to Bucharest, and because Commerce Secretary Baldrige was busy and had already visited Bucharest three times since assuming office in 1981. The United States finally agreed to hold a meeting, but with the stipulation that Deputy Secretary of Commerce Clarence Brown would represent the United States. The Romanians continued for some time to push for Baldrige to come but finally settled for Brown.

Brown was actually in a position to be quite helpful to the Romanians, for he had been a congressman for 18 years before joining Commerce. If the Romanians could persuade him of the case for MFN, he would be a powerful advocate with his former congressional colleagues, as U.S. embassy officers pointed out to their Romanian contacts. When Brown came, the Romanians made a real effort to impress him with the beauty and achievements of their country.

In his initial conversation with Totu, Brown made it clear that he was going to deal with human rights concerns as well as with trade matters. He drew on his long congressional experience to tell the minister how important these issues were to favorable congressional action on MFN. Totu rebutted Brown's presentation in his usual blunt fashion and complained about the withdrawal of GSP. He said that Romania could have understood if GSP had been withdrawn for technical reasons, for example because Romania's economic development had reached the point where it no longer qualified for special concessions, but the United States had openly stated it was withholding GSP for political reasons. This Romania could not accept as it was interference in internal affairs and an attempt to impose U.S. standards on independent Romania.

While to some extent making a debating point, Totu was probably accurate in his contention that Romania could have accepted withdrawal of GSP on technical grounds, especially if put in terms of Romania's economic progress. The U.S. side had thought of presenting the case in this fashion and discussed this possibility during Kirk's consultations in the State Department in May 1986. The United States decided not to do this because it was in fact the worker rights provision of the law that had triggered the withdrawal and to try and explain it in other terms would have been misleading. In addition, Romania's economic situation had grown worse, not better, in the preceding years, and so one could hardly speak honestly of economic progress.

Ceauşescu spent an hour and a half with Brown and Kirk. Brown—doubtless to Ceauşescu's disappointment—went through the regular list of U.S. human rights concerns in addition to trade matters. Ceauşescu countered along familiar lines. He stated that annual MFN renewal was "abnormal" and complained about U.S. quotas and licensing practices, which he said were preventing a major expansion of U.S.-Romanian trade. He did hint to Brown that Ion Ruţa might be freed and allowed to join his wife in the United States once he had served one-third of his sentence for "embezzlement" and paid back the money he had allegedly stolen. He then asked Brown to urge more members of Congress to come to Romania.

This suggestion, which was becoming a favorite theme of Ceauşescu's, reflected how out of touch he was with American perceptions and Romanian realities. The pitiable situation of the Romanian population left virtually every American visitor to Romania with a sick feeling in the pit of the stomach and a new appreciation of the absurd dimensions of

Ceaușescu's personality cult. Such visits did sometimes persuade Americans that MFN was desirable, but only as a means of bringing deliverance to the 2,000 to 3,000 Romanians permitted to emigrate each year and of resolving a few human and religious rights cases. This was hardly the image Ceaușescu wanted to promote, and yet he continued almost to the end of his rule to believe that if Americans would come to Romania they would applaud what he was doing for the country.

One reason for Ceaușescu's misapprehension was, as noted before, his subordinates' determined effort to keep bad news away from him. This was evidenced once again when the two sides were working out the agreed conclusions, in the form of a protocol, of the April 1987 Joint Economic Commission meeting. The Romanians strongly resisted U.S. efforts to include the fact that the U.S. participants had expressed concern about human rights and religious freedom in Romania. When the Americans insisted, Ilie Vaduva, who as minister of foreign trade was leading the Romanian delegation, called Raceanu to his office to ask him to intervene. "Please understand," he told Raceanu, "I cannot go to 'the comrade' [Ceaușescu] with a text from a joint intergovernmental economic commission which refers to 'religious problems.' Please help! Talk the Americans into giving up the idea of including human rights in the protocol."

Vaduva, like his ministerial colleagues, wanted desperately to hide from Ceaușescu the fact that his foreign interlocutors had raised "sensitive" questions that might irritate the dictator and reflect badly on the minister. He did not care if the problems were serious ones or significant in U.S.-Romanian relations. He just wanted to be sure the Americans' complaints did not reach Ceaușescu's ears. The two sides finally agreed to a phrase that referred merely to their mutual interest in human rights issues.

Ceaușescu and his government came abruptly face to face with some American realities, however, when the House of Representatives voted 232 to 183, on April 30, 1987, to add to the overall trade bill then before Congress an amendment suspending MFN for Romania for six months and requiring the president to report to Congress every 60 days on the human rights situation in Romania.[80] The very next morning, May 1, a Romanian holiday, State Secretary Aurel Duma summoned Raceanu to the Foreign Ministry and told him to be ready to accompany Totu, who was then with Ceaușescu, to a meeting with Kirk.

Duma handed Raceanu a copy of a Securitate report to Ceauşescu about the vote, with excerpts from the congressional discussion before the vote. When Raceanu read the memo, he realized that the Securitate had based their report on Radio Free Europe (RFE) and Voice of America broadcasts he himself had heard that morning. These broadcasts were by far Romanians' best sources of information on world events and, in the case of RFE, on Romania as well. Most government officials, along with the rest of the population, listened to them regularly, but Raceanu was amused to see them as the basis for a Securitate report to the president of the country.

Totu told Raceanu later that day that Ceauşescu believed the House vote had resulted from the anti-Romanian actions of "hostile circles" in the United States, including Hungarian irredentists, and that the vote was possible because the U.S. administration did not oppose it strongly enough. Totu attributed this circumstance to Reagan's personal anti-communism. According to Totu, Ceauşescu was still convinced that MFN would be renewed because it was in the U.S. interest to support Romania's independent policy. This time, however, Ceauşescu had decided not to yield to U.S. pressure, but to take the initiative. He had therefore instructed Totu to take a firm position with Kirk and had even outlined the points Totu was to make to the U.S. ambassador. Ceauşescu had also indicated that it might be useful to have a talk with the United States at the highest level in Washington to clarify the positions of the two parties. He had asked Totu to think about this idea.

In his May 1 meeting with Kirk, Totu made three basic points.First, he characterized the House vote as an act organized by circles hostile to Romania, an act of "pressure," and "interference" in Romania's internal affairs. He then stated that if MFN suspension became law, Romania would stop all departures to the United States and cancel all departure approvals already given. Finally, he noted that the Romanian government wished to continue to develop conditions conducive to good relations between the two countries. When Kirk asked if the ban on departures would apply solely to persons wishing to emigrate to the United States, Totu, to Raceanu's as well as Kirk's surprise, said it would apply to all travel to the United States, including temporary visits. Totu added that Romania would not let itself "be threatened by the U.S. Congress."

Kirk observed that the U.S. administration had opposed the amendment to the trade bill and continued to do so. Furthermore, the bill was not yet through both houses of Congress. He recalled that Ceauşescu had often said that the United States and Romania could have good relations without MFN. Totu responded, "We will never accept that the United States decides what happens here. Please tell that to Secretary Shultz." U.S.-Romanian relations would be degraded in the event MFN lapsed, he said, and discussions between the two countries would be on a different basis thereafter. The responsibility for this would lie on the U.S. side. Totu probably added these latter points on his own initiative, as he did not mention them when he told Raceanu what Ceauşescu had instructed him to say.

Even in a regime as tightly controlled as Ceauşescu's, the language and tone used by the person delivering the message depended on that individual's convictions and personality. Totu often took an arrogant, assertive position with foreigners in order to intimidate his interlocutors, as well as to impress the Securitate personnel reviewing the recording of his remarks. Totu particularly liked to be in the position of lecturing the United States and the U.S. ambassador. His personal comments frequently went beyond the instructions he had received from Ceauşescu. In this case they ill accorded with Ceauşescu's tentative thought about sending a high-level envoy to the United States, let alone with the point about Romania's desire to promote conditions that would develop good relations between the two countries. If Ştefan Andrei had been foreign minister, he would have spoken in more measured tones, would have been more moderate than his chief. Vaduva would simply have repeated what he was told without giving it any intentional spin. Totu spoke more harshly than Ceauşescu.

In such cases, the individual receiving the message is left to guess how much of it is personal and how much is dictated from above. In a relaxed and democratic government junior officials sometimes tip off their diplomatic colleagues when their bosses exceed their instructions. In Ceauşescu's Romania this happened very seldom, and certainly not on anything as important as this demarche. In this case the embassy report surmised that Totu was probably reflecting Ceauşescu's position in saying that emigration would cease, but it did not credit Totu's assertion that all travel to the United States would stop. A minimum of official travel was in Romania's interest, and the embassy felt it would continue. The embassy did not comment on Totu's other assertions, except to say that any Romanian responsiveness on human rights cases would probably cease in the event MFN suspension became law.

The House vote had seriously troubled Ceauşescu, and, as he had hinted to Totu, he soon decided to send a special envoy to President Reagan. He felt that communication at the presidential level would make it clear that the problems between the two governments were the product of lesser officials and misinformed individuals. He still believed that Reagan wanted to continue the special relationship with Romania and would take measures to do so if Ceauşescu alerted him to the problem. Ceauşescu doubtless also had in mind that Reagan's receipt of his personal envoy would in itself have the advantage of publicly demonstrating the special relationship between the two leaders and thereby refute those who said this relationship was slipping away.

Thus on May 6 Foreign Minister Totu told U.S. chargé Henry Clarke that Ceauşescu proposed to send a "state delegation" to Washington to discuss the full range of U.S.-Romanian relations. Manea Manescu, vice president of the Council of State and member of the Political Executive Committee, would head the delegation as Ceauşescu's "personal representative." Ceauşescu asked that Reagan receive Manescu, who would have a message from him for the president. He also requested that Vice President Bush and Secretary Shultz receive Manescu. The Romanians wanted Manescu to go to the United States prior to the end of May (before Reagan's June 3 finding on MFN would go to Congress), but, if that were not possible, to do so in June (before congressional review of the president's finding and before the current MFN term expired at midnight on July 2–3).

The choice of Manescu was a mark of the importance Ceauşescu attached to this mission. As vice president of the Council of State, Manescu was second only to Ceauşescu in protocol terms. He had been a full member of the party's ruling Political Executive Committee for many years and had served in effect as Romania's prime minister in the 1970s. He had fallen very ill in the late 1970s and was no longer as active in policymaking as he had once been; but he was still close to Ceauşescu and was trusted to carry out instructions to the letter. Reagan had received Manescu as Ceauşescu's personal envoy once before, in September 1984, and Ceauşescu fully expected him to do so again.

When the embassy's report on the proposed Manescu mission arrived in Washington, Kirk was there on consultation and participated in the extensive discussions on how best to respond. On one side was the idea that Ceauşescu liked to do business directly with his opposite numbers; if he was going to make a major shift in policy to meet U.S. concerns, this was how he would do it. It was certainly true that a major shift in Ceauşescu's policy seemed most unlikely, but the United States doubted that Ceauşescu would send Manescu completely empty-handed. The specific concessions the United States was demanding from Ceauşescu seemed small enough that he could grant them without much damage, and the desire to give Manescu something meaningful to say might provide the stimulus for Ceauşescu to make them. While Kirk and, as far as he knew, most of the other U.S. officials dealing with the case did not appreciate how senior Manescu was, at least in protocol terms, they knew Ceauşescu attached great importance to any presidential envoy.

Another consideration was that the way the Romanian (and sometimes the United States) government worked, a visit by someone like Manescu would in itself provide a deadline for completion of projects long languishing in the bureaucracy. Officials are always scratching around for agreements for their leaders to sign when they meet, and often a special envoy can jar matters loose. Thus some pending matters might be cleared up even if Manescu brought nothing really special. Finally, to refuse Ceauşescu's request would be insulting and could lead to a further stiffening on his part. Did the United States want, in refusing this gesture, to assume the responsibility for a new deterioration of relations, with all the consequences that could have for its ability to influence human rights and emigration in Romania?

On the other hand, Reagan's receiving Ceauşescu's envoy would run counter to the U.S. desire to distance itself from Ceauşescu's objectionable regime. It would arouse criticism at home and in some quarters abroad. The Romanian government would doubtless portray it as a sign that all was well between the two countries. Nor was there any certainty that Manescu would bring anything meaningful. Previous high-level meetings, including those of Shultz and Whitehead with Ceauşescu himself, had produced no real changes in Ceauşescu's policies, and there was no sign he was weakening in his resolve to continue his hard-line course. Finally, the president and vice president seldom took time to receive an envoy from a small country, especially from a nation with which relations were strained.

The State Department's first reaction was to find out if Manescu would have anything special to say. The embassy in Bucharest tried several times to learn this, through informal as well as formal inquiries. The answer was always the same—Manescu would discuss the full range of U.S.-Romanian relations and the prospects for their future development, with no indication of what specifics he would raise. In fact, to the best of the Foreign Ministry's knowledge, Manescu was not going to bring any new proposals or have anything new to say. He was merely going to repeat well-known Romanian positions on human rights and religious freedom and to stress noninterference and Romanian independence. This would be similar to his conduct during his 1984 visit to the United States as Ceauşescu's special envoy, when he had spent most of his meeting with Reagan praising Ceauşescu.

If the United States had known how little Manescu would have to say, it would simply have declared his visit not convenient. Because the United States thought Manescu might be bringing something meaningful with him, however, Kirk and the State Department's European Bureau charted a middle course: They would not recommend that the president or vice president see Manescu, but they would ask Secretary Shultz to do so. This in itself was a major concession to the Romanians. Although Ceauşescu would not like the idea that Reagan himself was not receiving his envoy, he should be prepared to send Manescu or a somewhat lower-level substitute to talk to the secretary of state if he really had something to tell the U.S. side. Shultz agreed to receive Manescu, and Shultz's office proposed that the meeting take place at 3:00 P.M. on May 29.

The Bureau of European Affairs informed Ambassador Gavrilescu on May 13 that meetings for Manescu with the president and vice president would "not be possible due to the press of other scheduled events," but that Shultz would receive Manescu on May 29. The department's reporting telegram stated that the Romanian ambassador "did not take the news too well." He said that Ceauşescu would be disappointed and noted that the Romanian president had received a number of U.S. officials over the years. The bureau emphasized to the ambassador that the secretary of state was making himself available and pointed out that last-minute delegations were no substitute for action on long-standing U.S. concerns.

When the U.S. embassy in Bucharest for its part conveyed the decision to Americas director Ion Beşteliu on May 14, he replied with some force that Reagan certainly should receive a special envoy with a message from Ceauşescu. Totu was furious when he heard of the U.S. response and urged Ceauşescu to hold out for Manescu's being received by Reagan. Ceauşescu agreed, and the Romanians told the United States in Bucharest and Washington that they declined the meeting with Shultz and would await appointments for Manescu with the president and vice president once their schedules were more free. Manescu was a special envoy of the president himself, and Ceauşescu had received many American visitors. (The Americas directorate drew up a long list of these meetings—some 30 officials since 1978 and over 80 meetings with Americans in all—and contrasted them with the fact that Reagan had received only two Romanian envoys in the six years of his presidency.) Furthermore, the Romanians said, the issues that Ceauşescu wished to raise required that Manescu be received by Reagan. The Romanian government would therefore await a response from the United States about an appointment for Manescu with the president "sometime this year." To the U.S. observation that there had earlier seemed to be some urgency to the visit, the Romanians replied that the content of the message was more important than its timing.

The Romanian position, particularly the reference to "some time this year," seemed to the U.S. embassy and the State Department to confirm the suspicion that the Romanians had nothing to say. They therefore told the Romanians that they did not expect the president's and vice president's schedules to lighten up in the foreseeable future. To leave a way for the Romanians to pass any genuine message, however, they added that the United States would be glad to receive Ceauşescu's message in a letter through diplomatic channels. Ceauşescu's office instructed the Foreign Ministry not to act on this proposal, and the ministry never saw any sign of a written message, not even one for Manescu to take. No Manescu visit ever took place, even though Romanian officials continued for months to press for the visit and to deplore Reagan's refusal to receive Ceauşescu's personal envoy.

Raceanu considered this U.S. refusal as the de facto end of the "special relationship" between the two countries and a signal that the U.S. administration was no longer willing to give the public appearance of close relations with the oppressive and unpopular Ceauşescu regime. As it turned out, however, the U.S. administration was preparing to recommend MFN for another year, in spite of congressional reservations.

▼ 7 ▼

Back from the Brink
1987

In May 1987 the U.S. administration once again faced a decision on extending most-favored-nation status to Romania for another year, a decision made more difficult by the pending legislation, passed by the House on April 30 as a Trade Act amendment, that would suspend MFN for Romania for six months. The argument within the administration turned on the humanitarian effect of denying MFN. Totu's statement of May 1 that there would be no emigration from Romania to the United States if MFN were denied seemed to show clearly how the Romanians would react to a denial by Congress, even over administration objections.

Kirk, who had returned to Washington to participate in establishing the U.S position, agreed with most of his State colleagues that a denial of MFN initiated by the administration would provoke an even more serious reaction, one that would seriously disadvantage those dissidents and religious groups whose cause the United States had supported. The conclusion was that the 2,000 to 3,000 people who were able to emigrate to the United States thanks to MFN and the marginal human rights benefits derived within Romania were worth the disadvantages of renewing MFN for another year. That was the recommendation the bureau sent to Shultz and that he passed to the White House.

Upon Kirk's return to Bucharest in mid-May, he found that Olimpia Solomonescu had replaced Maria Groza as deputy foreign minister with responsibility for the Western Hemisphere and cultural and press affairs. Groza's departure was a loss for the United States. Beyond being a pleasant and charming interlocutor, she had tried, within the limits of her rank and power, to work for the resolution of problems raised by the United States. She was continually pressing within the Romanian government for emigration approval for those on the lists of family reunification cases presented by the United States, and she argued hard for positive action on U.S. proposals for cultural exchanges.

This, together with the popularity she enjoyed among Americans and other Westerners, had in fact earned her the enmity of a number of leading officials of the Ceauşescu government over the previous two or three years. She had learned, she once told Raceanu, that Emil Bobu—a Ceauşescu confidant, member of the Political Executive Committee's inner leadership bureau, and arguably the most powerful Romanian after the two Ceauşescus—had sought to persuade Elena Ceauşescu in the fall of 1986 that Groza should be removed. Bobu had pointed out that Groza at 70 was past the retirement age of 62 and, furthermore, that her nephew Radu Filipescu, an electronics engineer, had been arrested in May 1983 for distributing leaflets critical of the Ceauşescu regime. (Filipescu had been released from prison in April 1986 and resumed his antiregime activity.)

Groza benefited, on the other hand, from Ceauşescu's desire to associate his regime with that of her father, Petru Groza, head of Romania's first communist-front government in 1945 and president of Romania until 1958. Ceauşescu sought to link himself with the Groza name rather than that of Gheorghe Gheorghiu-Dej, Ceauşescu's immediate predecessor, whose rule had been marked by a number of harsh measures against the population and several purge trials. Ceauşescu liked to portray himself as "humanizing" the system set up by Gheorghiu-Dej and wished to downplay the fact that he rose to power as Gheorghiu-Dej's protégé.

Groza's replacement, Olimpia Solomonescu, came to the ministry from the Central Committee International Relations Department, where she had been deputy head from 1984 to 1987. As a pediatrician, she had practiced in the oil town of Ploeşti for almost 25 years before transferring to Bucharest in 1977 as state secretary (the number three position) in the Ministry of Health. Shortly thereafter, Bucharest had suffered a severe earthquake with much loss of life, and Solomonescu occasionally spoke with feeling of the days and nights she spent at the Health Ministry arranging help for the victims. She left the Health Ministry to become ambassador to Senegal in 1980, returning to Bucharest in 1983 to join the Central Committee apparatus. A compassionate, friendly person with a desire to please everyone, Solomonescu was intelligent and well-educated but lacked Groza's grace and knowledge of world affairs. In her late fifties by the time she came to the Foreign Ministry in 1987, she moved into quiet retirement after the 1989 revolution.

Kirk commented to the State Department following his first session with Solomonescu that she was pleasant, well-informed, and potentially an effective link between the two countries. In the event, she proved too timid and too worried about her own position to be of much help. While always appearing sympathetic and willing to solve problems, she seldom delivered concrete results and in actual fact did little or nothing to push her superiors or the bureaucracy below them to accommodate U.S. concerns.

Her primary aim was to look good in the eyes of her superiors, whom she saw as wanting their subordinates to take a firm line in meetings with U.S. officials. She therefore had the reports of her meetings with Americans emphasize, in detail, that she had reiterated a standard, uncompromising Romanian line. She also directed that the reports mention only briefly what the Americans had said and in a way that gave minimum offense to the report's Romanian readers. This contrasted with Groza's practice, which was to have her remarks summarized briefly and to devote most of the report to what the Americans had said.

Raceanu believes that Groza's handling of a report relating to the daughter and son-in-law of Ion Pacepa, the head of the Romanian Foreign Intelligence Service who defected to the United States in 1978, was the incident that precipitated her downfall. Pacepa had been an intimate of the Ceauşescu family. His defection frightened and enraged the Ceauşescus and led to a major purge of the entire security apparatus. His very name was anathema to the dictator and his wife. Pacepa's daughter and son-in-law, Dana and Radu Damaceanu, remained in Romania, and Pacepa, who was naturally concerned about their welfare, wanted them to emigrate to the United States.

The basic U.S. government guideline in such instances was to avoid making an issue of individual cases unless the individual in question made known a desire for such action. Raising individuals' cases with the Romanian authorities could and often did lead to harsher measures against them, at least until the Romanian government decided to make concessions to the United States on the case. The U.S. government was therefore not prepared to expose individuals to such risks unless it knew they were prepared to take them.

The embassy and the department were convinced that Ceauşescu would never let the Damaceanus emigrate. Ceauşescu had categorically refused to allow the emigration of the family of a less prominent defector, Napoleon Fodor, who had been the Romanian commercial counselor in New York, in spite of letters from President Reagan, ex-President

Nixon (for whom Ceauşescu felt particular admiration), and a host of congressmen and senators, and despite direct appeals from a number of Americans in their meetings with Ceauşescu himself. Ceauşescu had put much more personal trust in Pacepa and felt Pacepa's "betrayal" even more keenly.

U.S. officials believed that raising the case might well worsen the Damaceanus' personal situation, especially as they both still had jobs, as well as an apartment in Bucharest near the U.S. embassy. It therefore seemed imperative to get the couple's consent before raising their case in a major way. The Romanian authorities would know, however, if the embassy tried to communicate with the Damaceanus, and that in itself might lead to reprisals against them. The embassy argued that the United States should leave the initiative to the Damaceanus: If they wanted U.S. government intervention, they should be able to get that message, however informally, to the embassy.

The department, under increasing pressure in Washington to do something about the case, finally instructed the embassy in early 1987 to send Mrs. Damaceanu a routine consular telegram inviting her to the embassy to discuss her possible emigration to the United States. If she was able to come to the embassy, the plan was to ascertain her desires about U.S. government representations on her behalf and to give her a letter from her father. The embassy received no reply to its telegram; it sent a second and a third telegram, both of which also went unanswered. (The Romanian authorities may well have intercepted the telegrams at the post office or at the Damaceanu apartment house.)

On April 27, after obtaining authorization from the Department of State, Diana Henshaw, the U.S. consul general in Bucharest, made a phone call to the Damaceanu residence from a pay phone on the street to avoid having the call blocked by the Securitate monitors of the embassy's outgoing calls. When Dana Damaceanu answered the phone, the consul general told her that her father was well and interested in her welfare, then asked if she had taken any steps toward emigration. Mrs. Damaceanu responded that she was in good health and had submitted a memorandum to the Romanian authorities saying that she wanted to emigrate. She had not filed a formal emigration application, she said, in part because she had not heard anything about her father in ten years and did not know his situation. In fact, her father had tried to reach her many times without success, and Radio Free Europe broadcasts to Romania had included several reports on his activities; but the Damaceanus were apparently cut off from such sources of news. In response to a question from Henshaw, Mrs. Damaceanu said she would like to emigrate but wanted to do it correctly and did not want to cause problems for anyone. She noted that the law prohibited contact with foreigners, and she would need permission to have such contact.

Henshaw wanted to talk to Dana Damaceanu where the conversation would not be monitored by the Romanian authorities and where she could give Mrs. Damaceanu the letter from her father, or at least tell her about it. Henshaw therefore suggested that they meet on the street. Mrs. Damaceanu rejected this but finally agreed that the consul general could come to her apartment at 9:00 A.M. the following morning. When Henshaw showed up the next morning, the apartment was surrounded by plainclothesmen and uniformed security officials, some of whom were stationed just outside the building gate. Henshaw did not try to force her way in but returned to the embassy for instructions.

The embassy reported these developments to the department with the comment that the Romanian authorities had since set up a round-the-clock Securitate presence outside the Damaceanu apartment house. The embassy said it felt another attempt to enter the building would be unsuccessful and would probably lead to the Damaceanus' eviction and transfer to another, unknown location. It recommended against making such an attempt and received no response from the department.

Congressional interest in the fate of the Damaceanus continued. In late April 1987 the Romanian embassy in Washington reported to Bucharest that it had received many letters on the case from members of Congress. Among these was a copy of a letter signed by over 100 members of the House, threatening an anti-MFN campaign if the Damaceanus were not allowed to emigrate. The original of this letter had been sent to Ceauşescu in the international mail.

The embassy's report on this letter came to Maria Groza, acting that week as head of the consular department in the absence of State Secretary Aurel Duma. The report did not mention that the Damaceanus were Pacepa's daughter and son-in-law, and Groza herself did not make the connection. She directed that the telegram be distributed in the normal manner to the directorates interested in emigration matters, including the Interior Ministry's directorate for visas and passports.

When the telegram was distributed, it caused a sensation in the Romanian bureaucracy. The word that the U.S. Congress was intervening in the case of Pacepa's daughter and son-in-law spread through the ministries like wildfire. This provoked a very harsh reaction from Securitate chief Tudor Postelnicu. He telephoned Groza and accused her of spreading information hostile to the regime and playing the Americans' game—as she "always did," he asserted.

Raceanu was in Groza's office when she received Postelnicu's call. Groza pleaded that she had only given the telegram the normal distribution for emigration matters and had not made the connection with Pacepa. Her arguments had no apparent effect, for Postelnicu continued to rant and rave on the telephone. When he finally hung up, Groza, ashen and with trembling hands, ordered the communications service to retrieve all copies of the message.

One reason for the extent of Postelnicu's rage was that Ceauşescu, while agreeing to resolve a number of controversial family reunification cases, had categorically rejected all appeals on the Fodor and Pacepa families, no matter from whom they came, and had given instructions that there was to be no publicity about these cases. The Foreign Ministry had therefore adopted the practice of not even forwarding to Ceauşescu's office any material or appeals it received on these two cases. Groza had violated the rule of silence.

It was one or two days after Postelnicu's call to Groza that Foreign Minister Totu told Groza she should retire in a few days. Although there is no way to prove the contention, in Raceanu's opinion it was the Damaceanu incident, together with Groza's advocacy of some concessions to the United States and the favor shown her by foreigners, that precipitated Groza's sudden retirement.

The affair shows in any case how careful even high officials had to be in a regime such as Ceauşescu's. One had to judge every move in terms of its possible effect on the fears and prejudices of superiors. Normal procedures and sharing of information took second place. This incident also shows how determined Ceauşescu's advisers were to keep unpleasant news quiet. They not only wanted to hide from Ceauşescu what the U.S. Congress was doing; they did not want even the Foreign Ministry staff to know. This atmosphere made it difficult for the ministry, indeed the whole Romanian government, to perform effectively. It also made it difficult for foreigners to do business with the Romanians and to predict, or even to understand, Romanian reactions to information or suggestions.

In this as in other matters, the Ceauşescu regime was increasingly out of step with the movement toward reform in the communist world. This was particularly apparent when Gorbachev visited Romania in late May 1987.

The Romanians set the tone by initially denying entry to several Western correspondents coming to cover the event, including Kenneth Banta of *Time* and Jackson Diehl of the *Washington Post*. They held fast to their refusal to admit some correspondents, despite repeated embassy and State Department efforts to point out that the Romanians were thereby offending publications widely read in the United States and other Western countries. The Romanians claimed that these correspondents, along with many others, had written slanderous things about Romania. They said their country was open to correspondents of goodwill who would write positively about the country. U.S. arguments that denying visas to correspondents was sure to get the Romanians bad publicity had no effect.

The contrast between Gorbachev and Ceauşescu was in stark relief throughout the Gorbachev visit. The Soviet leader, while not commenting on internal conditions in Romania, lost no chance to plug his reformist line. He was publicly critical of phenomena in his own country that all his listeners knew were worse in Romania. His description of the ways he was battling these deficiencies—*glasnost,* measures to reduce nepotism, respect for the cultural integrity of minorities—were just the opposite of what Ceauşescu was doing in Romania. The Romanian people got the point.

The government, for its part, did the best it could to redress the balance. The crowds who greeted Gorbachev and with whom he mingled were made up of carefully chosen, trusted individuals. Their applause was loud and long for Ceauşescu and short and sparse for Gorbachev. The authorities filled stores along Gorbachev's route with merchandise and food that the people of Bucharest had not seen for years. As soon as Gorbachev and the accompanying Romanian escort had passed by, there were struggles between the crowd trying to get in to buy the goods and the police trying to protect the precious merchandise, which they planned to collect and transfer to another location along Gorbachev's route.

The whole visit pointed up a new aspect of Ceauşescu's "independence" from the Soviet Union, namely that it was increasingly one of "independence" from Gorbachev's reforms rather than from his foreign policies, which were gradually coming into alignment with Ceauşescu's previously daring deviations. Thus Gorbachev was moving toward pulling out of Afghanistan, entering into semidiplomatic relations with Israel, and reducing arms expenditures, all positions that had long characterized Ceauşescu's apostasy.

On June 2 President Reagan forwarded to Congress his decision to extend MFN to Romania for another year. The accompanying White House statement said the decision had been "exceptionally difficult" and had been addressed at the "highest levels" of the administration. It noted that the president shared the concerns of the public and Congress about violations of basic human rights in Romania and that he was "disappointed at the Romanian government's very limited response to our numerous expressions of concern." He added that MFN had nevertheless stimulated emigration and enabled the United States to have an impact on Romania's human rights practices and to help strengthen the conditions for religious observance. He had therefore decided that MFN should be renewed as long as it enabled the United States to help substantial numbers of people. He had instructed Shultz "to pursue our human rights dialogue with Romania with renewed vigor."[81]

The Romanian leadership greeted Reagan's action with satisfaction, despite the president's critical language. It surmised that the U.S. decision sprang in part from the firm line taken by Totu in his May 1 talk with Kirk, when he said withdrawal of MFN would lead to a total cessation of emigration. After Reagan's announcement, Totu in fact counseled his subordinates to take a tough approach to the United States on grounds that MFN renewal showed that the Americans were much more receptive when the Romanians spoke to them from a position of strength.

Ceaușescu decided, however, to do more than talk tough to head off congressional action to deny MFN. He was particularly concerned at the possibility the Senate would amend its version of the trade bill, the Omnibus Trade and Competitive Act of 1987, to suspend Romanian MFN for six months as the House had done. He therefore directed a broad campaign to persuade Congress to support MFN. One result was some movement on the issues the United States had been raising. Thus the Baptists told the U.S. embassy on June 8 that printing of 4,000 more Bibles was actually under way. Ion Ruța was released from prison on June 4 and left Romania to join his wife in the United States on June 22.

Emigration approvals continued at the relatively high rate in effect since the beginning of 1987, and more promises were made about church buildings to replace those demolished in urban reconstruction. Three ethnic Hungarian dissidents in Transylvania who had been in prison since 1983—Erno Borbely, Laszlo Buzas, and Bela Pall—received their liberty. A delegation of religious leaders went to Washington to plead the

Romanian case, and the Romanian Jewish choir finally made its trip to sing in the Capitol. The Foreign Ministry, "on behalf of" Ceauşescu, proposed creation of a U.S.-Romanian parliamentary committee to encourage exchanges and visits between the two legislatures.

In mid-June Bud Ogden and Robert Robertson, leaders of American Businesses for International Trade, visited Romania. Their group had previously testified in favor of MFN for Romania, and the Romanians urged them to redouble their efforts in this regard. The Romanians also used a U.S. public relations firm to plead their case. In a May 1991 article, Weston Kosova cited data furnished in 1987 under the Foreign Agents Registration Act showing that the firm of Van Kloberg & Associates received several thousand dollars from the Romanian government in compensation for their claim to have "placed" articles on Romania in papers such as the *Journal of Commerce,* the *Washington Times,* and *Newsday,* and with the Associated Press and station WJLA-TV in Washington.[82]

All this activity—making a few concessions, lobbying, hiring a public relations firm—represented a Romanian attempt to play the game the U.S. way. It showed that the House vote, not to mention repeated American visitors, had convinced the Romanian government of the need for some action. Although it was late, halfhearted, and inexpert, it was clearly an effort. The Romanians thought it had helped persuade the U.S. administration to extend MFN; but its failure to dissuade the House from voting to suspend MFN discouraged Ceauşescu from pursuing the route of concessions further, despite the continued urging of American visitors he respected. He would not admit the basic problem even to himself, namely, that the rosy picture he was trying to paint of Romania's internal situation was false. Gestures could still help, but the time was fast approaching when nothing short of a fundamental change in Ceauşescu's policies could save the "special relationship" with the United States.

In mid-June of 1987, as part of Romania's effort to present its case to the United States, Deputy Foreign Minister Solomonescu made her first visit to Washington. The object was not only to have Solomonescu plead Romania's case but also to enable her to familiarize herself with the situation in Washington and report on it to Bucharest. The Department of State arranged a number of important meetings for Solomonescu, including sessions with Whitehead (who was acting secretary of state at the time) and Assistant Secretary Ridgway, and had Deputy Assistant Secretary Simons host a luncheon for her.

The basic U.S. message remained the same: Romania's image was deteriorating, the administration's decision to renew MFN had been a difficult one, and MFN was in real jeopardy in Congress. The progress on emigration and Bibles and the release of Ruţa were good, but more was needed. The Romanian government's harsh economic policies were also becoming an issue. Whitehead emphasized that U.S. human rights concerns were deep and widely felt, not just the hobbyhorse of a few ill-intentioned people. Ridgway said it would be very difficult for her to defend the administration's MFN decision before Congress; the only way it could be done was on the basis of progress on human rights. Simons noted that MFN was "in deep trouble" in Congress.

Solomonescu for her part stressed that the Romanians wanted Reagan to receive Ceauşescu's envoy, Manea Manescu, and pushed Ceauşescu's new idea of a U.S.-Romanian parliamentary committee. She gave Whitehead a letter from Totu to Shultz asserting that Yasir Arafat, who had recently visited Bucharest, had made significant new concessions on possible PLO-Israeli talks that the United States should pursue. She did not refute the specific U.S. complaints on human rights matters but rather tried to portray U.S.-Romanian relations as good. She did, however, complain that some in the U.S. administration were "taking sides" in the Romanian-Hungarian dispute and that the State Department's human rights report contained "misinformation".

Whitehead said the United States would study Totu's letter and the proposal for a joint parliamentary committee, as well as the question of the Manescu visit; but what was needed was Romanian action on matters of U.S. concern. The administration's whole message to Solomonescu was downbeat, pessimistic, and cautionary about the prospects for MFN in Congress.

Solomonescu's reports to Bucharest, however, gave precisely the opposite picture. They recounted her own points in detail but made little reference to the U.S. counterarguments or the specific human rights matters the U.S. side had raised. Her reports were in fact so slanted that they gave the impression there had been a change in the U.S. attitude, with the United States becoming much more receptive to the Romanian position. The reports concluded there was a prospect that President Reagan might agree to receive Manescu, and even made it appear that Romanian ambassador Nicolae Gavrilescu enjoyed widespread prestige and credibility in the United States.

Following the trip, Raceanu asked Americas section head Ion Beşteliu, who had accompanied Solomonescu, to explain these surprising reports. Why, for example, had Beşteliu written that Gavrilescu was so effective, when he knew perfectly well he was not? Beşteliu said Solomonescu had ordered him to write the reports in that manner because she knew they would go to Ceauşescu, and she did not want to offend him by giving him bad news about the Romanian ambassador and other matters. She thus had Beşteliu frame the whole report for its effect on her standing with Ceauşescu by stressing how effective her presentation had been and omitting any mention of the principal difficulties in the conversations.

It is not that unusual for participants in discussions to show themselves to advantage in their reports (Secretary of State Christian Herter once told Kirk he had never read a memorandum of conversation in which the drafter came out second best); but it is a disservice to the readers if the reporting officers distort the basic nature of the discussion. The temptation to do this is greatest in an authoritarian regime. In the eyes of the timid it becomes a virtual necessity. As dictators thereby get more and more out of touch with reality, it becomes harder and harder to give them bad news and still be in favor; but staying in favor with the dictator is the key to getting a promotion, or even holding onto one's job.

Senior U.S. officials knew the Romanian embassy in Washington often failed to report accurately on what U.S. officials said to them. The department therefore normally sent a detailed report on the talk to the U.S. embassy in Bucharest and usually, though not in this case, asked the embassy to relay the account to the Foreign Ministry. In any case, relaying the department's account to the ministry would not have assured that the information would reach the top in an accurate manner. Even if Solomonescu, or Groza before her, had sent an accurate report to the foreign minister, neither Totu nor his predecessor Vaduva would forward any report to Ceauşescu that they did not think he would like.

Though the embassy and the State Department did not realize how far the withholding of information from Ceauşescu went, they suspected there was some distortion in the reports he received and considered this an important reason for having senior U.S. officials and private-sector Americans convey U.S. concerns directly to the dictator. Such meetings were necessarily infrequent, however; and as Ceauşescu's reputation worsened, the U.S. government became increasingly reluctant to grant him the prestige of meeting with a senior U.S. official. The distorted Foreign Ministry reporting to Ceauşescu thus became a growing obstacle to accurate communication between the two governments.

One thing the Romanian bureaucracy could *not* hide from Ceauşescu was the Senate vote on June 26, 1987, to amend the pending Omnibus Trade Act to suspend MFN for Romania for six months.[83] This vote, which paralleled the April 30 action by the House on its version of the trade bill, meant that the final version of the bill would almost certainly include suspension. The vote caused great irritation and concern in Bucharest, especially as the Romanians had concluded, on the basis of their efforts following the House vote and the reports of the Solomonescu visit, that the Senate would not follow the House's example.

Ambassador Gavrilescu paid the price for this misinformation. Immediately after the Senate vote, Ceauşescu ordered him home. The Romanian government's public reaction was relatively moderate, however, and there was no repetition of Totu's intemperate blast at Kirk following the House vote. Raceanu later learned that, right after the vote and without informing the Foreign Ministry, Ceauşescu had ordered the Securitate to do all they could through lobbyists, the U.S. press, and known friends of MFN to obtain a reversal of the Senate vote. Ceauşescu evidently wanted a relatively restrained Romanian reaction to the Senate vote in the meantime.

Ceauşescu did, however, order the Foreign Ministry to prepare a public statement. This was released on June 27 in the name of Agerpres, the official news agency. The "authorized statement," headlined "An Act Hostile to Romania," declared that the Senate's move was "in total contradiction to the interests of the development of Romanian-American relations" and that the full responsibility for its consequences would rest on those who had voted for it. The statement expressed "surprise" that some senators used the debate on the motion to "slander" Romania and to denigrate the efforts of the Romanian government and people.[84]

On July 21 the Senate passed its version of the trade bill, and it looked as if Romania would lose MFN as soon as the House and Senate reached an agreed version of the bill.[85] This took some of the steam out of that summer's congressional attention to the president's June 3 extension of MFN, though the House Foreign Affairs Subcommittee on Europe and the Middle East did hold hearings on the subject on July 30.

The sole administration witness, Assistant Secretary for European Affairs Ridgway, defended MFN extension on the grounds that it had "enabled us to help substantial numbers of people." She noted that there were valid and "not unimportant" economic and foreign policy arguments in favor of maintaining MFN, but "for the president the humanitarian considerations were most compelling." She also opposed suspending MFN under the pending trade bill, on the grounds that it amounted to termination and that it extended the criteria of the Jackson-Vanik amendment beyond emigration to human rights in general, something that could affect the president's management of relations with a number of other communist countries.[86]

While there was much testimony against MFN for Romania at the hearing, those favoring suspension had their eyes on the overall trade bill, and neither the House nor the Senate took action on the president's extension of MFN. This fact, and the subsequent failure of the House and Senate to agree on a trade bill, meant that Romania would enjoy MFN through July 2, 1988. Before that date, however, the Romanians themselves had renounced MFN "under conditions of Jackson-Vanik."

▼8▼

Pressures Hit the Danger Point
1987

Various U.S. representatives continued to relay American concerns on human rights to Romanian officials in Bucharest and Washington during the summer of 1987, but the pro forma nature of the MFN congressional hearings and growing doubts that the omnibus trade bill would pass made the Romanian government even less responsive than usual. This was particularly evident during the August 29–September 1 visit to Romania by representatives of the joint U.S. executive-legislative Commission on Security and Cooperation in Europe. Led by Representative Steny Hoyer of Maryland, the delegation included Representative Bill Richardson of New Mexico, Senator Frank Lautenberg of New Jersey, Assistant Secretary of State for Humanitarian Affairs Richard Schifter, and the commission staff director, Ambassador Samuel Wise. In their meetings with Totu and Ceauşescu, the delegation raised the usual human rights issues, including Bibles, church buildings, emigration, cultural and scientific exchanges, the situation of the Hungarian minority, and the Fodor case.

Ceauşescu reacted in his usual way, but Totu was belligerent, insisting that Romania was not obliged to respond to U.S. approaches on human rights. He had not, for his part, mentioned internal U.S. problems such as Iran-Contra, he noted. Romania welcomed all visitors but would not allow "inspection tours." He was surprised that the delegation, and Americans in general, lent their ears to "unauthorized sources" and people outside the law instead of relying on the facts and positions presented by Romanian officials. If Romania lost MFN, he said, it would only accept subsequent renewal without conditions and on a permanent basis. The impression he left on the congressional delegation did not contribute to congressional support for MFN.

The Hoyer delegation met with leading religious figures, visited churches, and made a short tour of the countryside. Kirk held a reception for the delegation on August 31, but the Romanian authorities again actively discouraged attendance by cultural and religious figures. One invitee who did come was Liviu Bota, a Romanian diplomat who was director of the U.N. Institute for Disarmament Research in Geneva. His story was revealing.

Following the late 1985 defection of Alexandru Gheorghiu, second in command at their embassy in Washington, the Romanians had adopted a policy of requiring virtually every diplomat who had served abroad for more than four or five years to return home for a period of a few years. Bota had been abroad a number of years in one capacity or another, and many people coveted his well-paid U.N. job in Geneva. His Romanian government superiors had therefore decided to replace him, but they suspected he might not want to come home. They had therefore recalled him to Bucharest "on consultation" in 1985 "for only one day" to discuss a "disarmament-related matter."

Once Bota was in Bucharest, the authorities pressed him to write a letter of resignation to the United Nations. He declined, saying he wanted to present his resignation in person in Geneva. The Romanian authorities refused to let Bota return to Geneva, fearing he would remain there. When U.N. representatives inquired about his status, Romanian officials claimed he could not travel because he had had a "heart attack." U.N. Secretary General Javier Pérez de Cuéllar, suspecting that Bota was being held against his will, said he would accept Bota's "resignation" only if he presented it in person in Geneva or New York. The case became more and more of an issue in subsequent months, and many countries joined the United States and the United Nations in pressing for Bota's release.

The Romanian government then began to allege, first privately and then publicly in a speech at the United Nations by Ambassador Teodor Marinescu that Bota had been a spy. The Romanians hinted privately to Deputy Secretary John Whitehead, during the latter's visit to Bucharest in November 1986, that Bota had been working for the Soviet Union. They finally let Bota leave Romania in early 1988, but by that time the case had further damaged Romania's reputation.

If the Romanians used a tough line on the Hoyer delegation, they tried out "sweet reasonableness" on Morton Abramowitz, director of the State Department's Bureau of Intelligence and Research, who visited Romania in late September 1987. The Securitate was particularly interested in the Abramowitz visit, convinced as it was that State's Intelligence Bureau was an arm of the CIA and that its members were CIA officers disguised as State Department employees. Believing that the CIA had great power in Washington, the Securitate was most anxious to learn the motives behind Abramowitz's visit. Aurel Duma, a member of the cabinet as minister state secretary of foreign affairs and the most senior Foreign Ministry link with the Securitate, involved himself directly in preparations for the visit and attended Kirk's dinner for Abramowitz even though he was much senior to Abramowitz in rank.

The atmosphere at the dinner was as relaxed as it could be, what with all concerned suspecting that their words and actions were being picked up by watchful servants and Securitate microphones. The embassy had to procure servants through the Foreign Ministry Office for Service to the Diplomatic Corps or obtain that office's approval before hiring its own recruits. While many of these servants worked hard and apparently loyally, they all had to report to the Securitate, and many were Securitate employees. Kirk noticed, for example, that a big cheer would go up from their quarters when the Securitate soccer team, highly unpopular with most Romanians, scored a goal.

After dinner Duma moved to a corner with Abramowitz and engaged him in close conversation, with Raceanu acting as interpreter. Enjoying his Remy Martin cognac and his cigar, Duma explained Romania's point of view in an amiable and relaxed fashion, avoiding the hackneyed communist phrases and lecturing tone he customarily employed with visiting foreigners. Raceanu found it a relative pleasure to serve as interpreter for this conversation after so many sessions of unrelieved communist jargon from Duma.

The following day Duma told Raceanu he had concluded that Abramowitz had come to "take soundings" from the Romanians on the situation in the Soviet Union and to determine how far the Romanians were prepared to compromise on internal human rights questions. Duma hoped Abramowitz left realizing that the Romanians were not going to change their internal policies but would "show understanding" for some of the problems of particular interest to the United States, though only in certain cases and then not under pressure. There was no need to prepare a memorandum on the conversation with Abramowitz, Duma said, as he had already informed "the proper people."

Duma's summation constituted a good exposition of the essential Romanian position: no abandonment of the basic line, but some concessions if these did not appear too obviously a result of American pressure. This was approximately what the U.S. side in fact believed fundamental Romanian policy to be, although it could never be sure.

The embassy was quite intrigued that Duma, who was well connected in the Securitate and the president's office and who usually took a very tough line, had adopted a fairly amiable tone with Abramowitz, even though what he had said was largely along the usual Romanian government lines. Duma's attitude seemed particularly significant, coming after the House and Senate votes and Totu's outburst to the Hoyer group. It was certainly at variance with Totu's approach. This confirmed the embassy's opinion that the Romanian government still wanted good relations with the United States and that Totu was not only a bad influence on Romanian policy toward the United States but also an unsatisfactory channel for passing information to the Romanian government.

An incident connected with the annual Bucharest International Trade Fair in mid-October 1987 showed how far the cult of personality had gone and its effect on even minor aspects of U.S.-Romanian relations. The United States was the only Western country to have an individual national pavilion at the fair, and it was Ceauşescu's custom to stop at the U.S. pavilion during his walking tour of the fair. When he visited the pavilion with his wife, Elena, that October, the two paused in front of a Monsanto display, which included a videotape on the company's products. When the Monsanto representatives started to tell the Ceauşescus about the virtues of one of the products, an agricultural pesticide, Elena Ceauşescu interrupted to say, "Natural means are much better; chemicals destroy the environment." The following night the Monsanto videotape and TV monitor were stolen from the exhibit despite the tight Romanian government security around the fair.

The embassy protested to the Foreign Ministry about the theft. In following up on the protest, Raceanu learned that the Securitate, hearing the First Family's disapproval of the pesticide and realizing that thousands of Romanians would see the tape that included it over the next few days, decided to "remove" the tape and the monitor. Needless to say, the embassy never got a satisfactory response to its inquiries, although it several times pointed out that a theft in an area so tightly controlled by the police was not likely to make U.S. firms feel welcome or encourage them to do business with Romania.

The fair coincided with the appointment of former foreign minister Ştefan Andrei as deputy prime minister responsible for foreign trade. This brought Andrei back into the sphere of U.S.-Romanian relations. Kirk saw him several times that October: first in the company of Assistant Secretary of Commerce Louis Laun, who had come over for the fair and for the annual meeting of U.S. and Romanian businesspeople; then with the U.S. businesspeople who had come for the meeting; and finally when seated next to him at a long Romanian luncheon for the business representatives.

Andrei asked Kirk to send him copies of *Time* and *Newsweek* and a book or two on management, an approach so different from what Kirk had heard from other leading Romanians that he could scarcely believe his ears. Andrei noted that he had direct access to Ceauşescu and promised to use this to get answers on American concerns and questions.

He demonstrated this ability almost at once by finding out and passing on to Kirk the fact that Romania was not ready to conclude an agreement to purchase Boeing airliners that had been the subject of inconclusive negotiations for many months. While the news was hardly welcome, at least it let Kirk and Boeing know where they stood at the time, thus considerably reducing their frustration level.

Andrei adhered closely to the party line on human rights and other political issues, however. He told Kirk and Assistant Secretary Laun that the United States should not insist that other countries follow U.S. ways. He averred that issues such as Vietnam and China, where Romania's views coincided with those of the United States rather than those of the Soviet Union, were more important than Bibles, Fodor, and trade disputes. Despite Andrei's caution on political points, Kirk commented to Washington that Andrei's new job brought a relatively powerful player back into U.S.-Romanian relations, one who seemed to have the desire and ability to solve problems.

Andrei's engagement was a positive sign, but it was immediately followed by several negative developments. The first was a Romanian assertion that the United States government was going back on its promises not to exploit publicly the defection of General Ion Mihai Pacepa, former head of the Securitate foreign intelligence. The Romanians complained that the U.S. government had recently given permission to Pacepa to publish a book highly critical of the Ceauşescu family and to hold press conferences on the subject.[87]

Raceanu learned from Andrei, Totu, and his contacts in the Securitate that Ceauşescu had been deeply upset at the prospect of publication of

Pacepa's book, fearing it would reveal unflattering personal details about him and his family. Ceauşescu wanted to prevent publication of the book or at least limit the publicity it received and prevent any word of its contents from reaching Romania. He therefore wanted assurances that the Voice of America and Radio Free Europe would not feature the book in their broadcasts to Romania.

Ceauşescu ordered the Foreign Ministry to discuss the book with the U.S. embassy in Bucharest in the strictest confidence. The ministry decided that State Secretary Duma would deal directly with Kirk on the subject, using briefing material provided by the Securitate rather than the Foreign Ministry. Raceanu would serve as interpreter and note-taker. There would be two copies of the record of the meeting: one for Ceauşescu and one for the new Securitate chief, Iulian Vlad, successor to Postelnicu, who had become interior minister. Duma instructed Raceanu to tell no one about the content of the meetings. If Raceanu's superiors asked about them, he was to say Duma had been discussing the Middle East with Kirk. Duma said the Securitate members handling the case were under similar restrictions.

Duma summoned Kirk on October 19, 1987, and complained that Pacepa's public activities violated U.S. government assurances given at the time of Pacepa's defection in 1978 that the U.S. government would not "exploit" the defection and would "prevent" public revelation by Pacepa of any information that could harm bilateral relations. Duma asked for confirmation that the United States would honor its earlier assurances, specifically citing assurances conveyed by State Department Counselor Matthew Nimetz during a visit to Bucharest in early September 1978.

Kirk said the U.S. government had no authority to prevent a private individual from writing a book or holding a press conference. Duma countered that it was impossible to believe that anyone could hold a press conference in the United States without the authorization of the U.S. authorities. Kirk, unsure where to start the civics lecture, gave a brief description of freedom of speech and the press, but Duma repeated he found it "impossible to believe" that he was wrong.

Both Kirk and Raceanu think Duma really believed that the U.S. government had the power to stop any individual from holding a press conference or publishing a book. Indeed, most of the Romanian hierarchy, including Ceauşescu, were convinced that the U.S. government could, if it wished, control what individuals or the media said in the United States. This was a serious complication to intergovernmental relations, for it meant that the Romanians thought that any statements in any press conference, even those of private individuals, enjoyed the acquiescence, if not the tacit support, of the U.S. government.

A few days after Kirk reported to Washington on his conversation with Duma, the State Department replied that U.S. officials had told the Romanians in 1978 that the U.S. government would "continue to do our utmost to assure that publicity on the Pacepa case is avoided completely, or kept to a bare minimum," but the department stated that this referred only to the initial period immediately after Pacepa's defection. The department instructed Kirk to inform the Romanians of this and to add that, although the U.S. government itself would not attempt to exploit the Pacepa case, Pacepa, as a resident of the United States, had the right to express himself freely. When Kirk conveyed this to Duma on November 3, noting that freedom of expression was guaranteed under the U.S. Constitution, Duma said that he knew of cases where constitutional guarantees had been ignored to prevent offensive statements and dismissed Kirk's assertion that the United States government could not do this. When pressed for examples, Duma merely said he would rather not go into them. Duma seemed convinced that the U.S. government could, if it wished, ignore the U.S. Constitution, just as the Romanian government could ignore the Romanian constitution.

Duma summoned Kirk again on the Pacepa case on November 19, this time to claim that Radio Free Europe broadcasts of excerpts from Pacepa's book violated the U.S. government's pledge that it would not publicly exploit the Pacepa case. Kirk replied on December 8 that the U.S. government had not and would not publicly exploit the Pacepa case and that Radio Free Europe was not a U.S. government agency. Although Congress funded RFE, the system operated under the guidance of an independent federal board of nine members appointed for three-year terms by the president. Its mission was to provide uncensored news, and it had to use "its own judgment" in deciding what coverage to give Pacepa's book. Duma retorted that the U.S. response was unacceptable. As Congress funded Radio Free Europe and the president appointed its board, the Romanian government expected the U.S. government to use its authority to prevent further broadcasts about Pacepa on RFE. It did nothing of the sort, of course, and the broadcasts continued.

Duma told Raceanu after this meeting that "the situation would have been totally different if Nixon had been president," thus confirming Raceanu's conviction that the Romanian hierarchy, despite years of dealing with the United States, had no conception of how American society really functioned. Like Duma, they were accustomed to operating in a centralized and dictatorial society and thus truly believed that the Pacepa book could never have appeared without the support of the U.S. government. The hard-liners used this as "proof" that the administration had allied itself with circles in the U.S. hostile to Romania, that the United States was seeking to undermine the Ceauşescu regime, and that U.S. human rights demands were a means to this end.

Late October 1987 brought another incident to trouble U.S.-Romanian relations, one that again illustrated Elena Ceauşescu's power. The U.S.-Romanian cultural agreement provided for a major U.S. film industry exhibit be shown in three Romanian cities in 1987. The exhibit, "American Film—Today and Tomorrow," had appeared in Timişoara, a major provincial capital, in September. It had come to Bucharest in October and was scheduled to go on to Craiova, another provincial capital, in November. The exhibit was excellent, not overtly political but clearly designed to show the vitality and freedom of American cultural life. It had several features designed specifically to appeal to Romanians, including special exhibits on Johnny Weissmuller (who played Tarzan) and Edward G. Robinson, both of whom were born in Romania. Visitors to the exhibit received tickets to see two or three first-run American films at a local theater.

The exhibit was wildly popular. Some 86,000 visitors had entered the exhibit in Timişoara, and nearly 160,000 attended in Bucharest (these numbers were extraordinary, even though some individuals may have entered more than once). Its scheduled run in Bucharest was extended by a day, until November 1, at the last-minute request of the Romanian cultural authorities.

On the morning of Saturday, October 31, however, the U.S. exhibit personnel arrived to find the doors locked and a crude sign saying, "For technical reasons the exhibit is closed." They also noticed that the banners advertising the exhibit were missing. Their immediate inquiries brought the response from Romanian officials that electrical problems had cropped up, causing the night watchman to turn off the electricity, and an investigation into the problem was under way. Other officials said that a high wind had blown all the banners down.

The embassy public affairs officer finally reached the head of the international relations section of the Romanian Council for Culture and Socialist Education, which was handling the exhibit. This official, Vasile Lazar, said that the council needed the exhibit facility in connection with preparations for several upcoming national events, including countrywide local elections, the celebration of the fortieth anniversary of the proclamation of the Romanian republic, and a national Communist Party conference scheduled for early December. The same upcoming events would prevent the exhibit from appearing in Craiova in November. The embassy officer noted that this was the third different explanation he had received that day, that all these events had already been scheduled for weeks or months, and that they had not prevented the Romanian authorities from asking that the exhibit be prolonged in Bucharest or from making all the necessary preparations for opening it in Craiova in a few days. He said he could not accept the explanation and must assume that there was something else behind the Romanian action. The exhibit closing, he concluded, was a major negative development in the cultural exchange program.

In its report to Washington the embassy speculated that Ceauşescu may have been offended by the long lines outside the exhibit, which was on one route to his office. The police outside the exhibit had been very nervous about these lines whenever Ceauşescu was scheduled to pass by. They had tried various techniques to hide them without great success; the most resourceful officer had simply instructed the people to face the street and wave at Ceauşescu as he passed, drawing a wave of acknowledgment in return.

Kirk raised the issue with Duma when the latter received him on November 3 in connection with the Pacepa affair. Kirk characterized the closing as a major negative development. He said he could not credit the official explanations, especially as there had been so many of them. He trusted the exhibit would be able to open in Craiova as scheduled. In an effort to frighten Duma, he characterized the closure as an action "at variance with the desire of your government at an even higher level for good relations."

It turns out that the "even higher level" was in fact responsible for the closure. Vasile Lazar, the above-mentioned head of the international relations section of the council for culture, had summoned Raceanu and Ion Beşteliu urgently the afternoon before the exhibit was closed. He told them that Elena Ceauşescu had summoned Suzana Gadea, the president of the council for culture, earlier that day and said it was an outrage that the Americans were making propaganda in the middle of the Romanian capital. She ordered Gadea to take measures that very day to close the exhibit and said she did not want to see the banners advertising it when she went home from the office. She also demanded cancellation of the Craiova showing. When the council head told Lazar of Mrs. Ceauşescu's directive, Lazar pointed out that the exhibit had only two more days to run in Bucharest and that it was there as part of the agreed cultural exchange program. His boss nevertheless insisted that Elena Ceauşescu's command be followed to the letter, and that is what was done. The whole incident was a further demonstration of Elena Ceauşescu's power and her negative influence on relations with the United States.

Subsequent developments in Romania confirmed the impression that the Ceauşescus were tightening the screws both to guard against any infection from Gorbachev's liberalization and to pay off their foreign debt. Food was very hard to get and required hours of standing in line. A November 1987 decree ordered a 30 percent reduction in "nonproductive" consumption of gas and electricity. As a result, a single 40-watt bulb was considered the proper light for a one-room apartment. The decree outlawed electric heaters and set escalating charges for any residential consumption of electricity exceeding that required to run one appliance in addition to the single 40-watt bulb.[88]

Gas pressure was low to nonexistent and heating inadequate. Government offices were cold, and Kirk kept a heavy sweater in the office to wear under his suit when he went to call on a minister. Visits to lower officials' offices often required an overcoat. The national symphony orchestra played in gloves with the fingers cut out, and the audience kept their hats and coats on. The actress in a boudoir scene at a play Kirk attended wore a turtleneck sweater under her negligee, somewhat spoiling the dramatic effect of the love scene but keeping her from catching pneumonia. The streets were mostly dark, except where "urban reconstruction" proceeded under night lights.

This reconstruction took a terrible human toll. Residents would receive notice that their house or apartment would be demolished as part of the reconstruction program. Nothing might happen for weeks or months, and then they would be given 24 hours or less to move out before the demolition began.

The overall mood in Romania in the fall of 1987 was one of dreary misery and apprehension about the coming winter. Simultaneously, the government was preparing a big show of support for Ceauşescu in the November 15 local elections and at the party conference scheduled for the following month. The announced election results gave the official candidates almost 99 percent of the votes and were touted as another demonstration of popular enthusiasm for the regime.[89]

A dramatic incident in Braşov, a midsized town some 100 miles north of Bucharest, marred the election celebration for Ceauşescu. Workers in Braşov, as in many other cities, were deeply dissatisfied with their situation. Those at the Red Flag truck factory and a nearby agricultural machinery factory were particularly angry at recent 80 percent deductions from their pay for underfulfillment of the factory's production plan. Some of them saw election day, when groups of people would be parading through town, as an opportunity to show their displeasure.

The morning of that day, November 15, about 200 workers started to move toward the center of town, shouting antiregime sentiments. More and more townsfolk joined them, and several thousand people chanting anti-Ceauşescu slogans finally reached the central square. They forced open the party headquarters building, broke windows, and burned election materials, including photos of Ceauşescu. They located the party food store and threw the contents, including goods such as salami and cheese that had not been in the markets for weeks, out to the crowd. They attacked the city hall, tossing documents and furniture into the street. Both buildings were trashed.

There was no significant police presence in the demonstration area for several hours. The authorities apparently had thought at first that the march was just another election day parade; when they belatedly realized what was happening, they delayed any reaction in order to call Bucharest for instructions and assistance. Partly for this reason, the crowd dissipated much of its energy before the police, assisted by Securitate and military forces, arrived on the scene at midday and dispersed the crowd relatively peaceably by 2:00 P.M.[90]

Such activity may not sound like much compared with the dramatic events of 1989 throughout Eastern Europe, but nothing like it had happened for several years in Ceauşescu's Romania, where only the occasional shouts of a single individual in a city street or the circulation of a single poem constituted the usual extent of public dissidence. It electrified the nation, especially after Western radio stations beamed accounts of the event back into Romania. The government's immediate reaction was to establish a strong police presence in Braşov and isolate the city. For two or three days, they forbade trains to stop at Braşov and required persons not living in the city to obtain special permission to drive there. Meanwhile the authorities moved quickly to repair the physical damage, put a few more goods into the food stores, and provide a little more gas for heating. One Braşov family said that the night after the riot they had hot water in their fifth-floor apartment for the first time in a year.

After the December 1989 revolution, it came out that the Securitate had videotaped the whole demonstration from a nearby rooftop and later used this film to identify participants for interrogation and arrest. Approximately 400 persons were arrested and some 60 brought to Bucharest, tried, and sentenced to various terms of imprisonment for "hooliganism." Their sentences prohibited them from returning to Braşov for five years after completing their prison terms. Virtually all returned to Braşov after the 1989 revolution, however, and formed a "November 15" association.[91] In November 1987 there were reports that several demonstrators had been tortured and some irradiated in jail so they would die a slow, painful, but natural-appearing death. True or not, this type of rumor and the regime's actions subdued the population. Many foreign observers felt—mistakenly as it turned out—that the Braşov events would become a rallying point for the emergence of an organized opposition to the regime.

Some prominent individuals did speak out, however. Doina Cornea and Radu Filipescu gave interviews critical of the regime to French television. They were arrested shortly afterward and spent the next two years in and out of confinement or house arrest because of their persistent criticism of the regime, occasionally to the foreign media. Cornea was named to the postrevolutionary Council of the National Salvation Front, but soon left it. Her continuing public statements against what she considered an effort to institute an "enlightened" communist regime in Romania earned her the enmity of post-Ceauşescu governments and a certain amount of harassment by the state security services.

Another who spoke out was Silviu Brucan, a senior Romanian Marxist. Brucan contrived to send a statement out of Romania to Radio Free Europe shortly after the Braşov events, calling them a "watershed" and stating that "the cup of privation is full and the working class no longer accepts being treated like an obedient servant." He said the regime faced a choice of either mass repression or meeting the workers' grievances, and he expressed his concern that it would choose repression.[92] A few days after RFE broadcast his statement, Brucan came to a dinner at Kirk's residence. Several of the other Romanian guests quietly told Brucan how much they admired him, but none offered to sign onto his statement. To do so would have been to open themselves to the retaliation that all felt sure Brucan would soon receive.

Brucan was a controversial figure. One of the few early members of the Romanian Communist Party still alive in the 1980s, he remained a convinced Marxist and made it clear he maintained his faith even after the events of 1989. As deputy chief editor of the official Romanian Communist Party newspaper, *Scinteia,* from 1944 to 1956, he had pursued a very tough, even Stalinist line, for example writing articles calling for the death penalty for those who opposed the communist takeover in Romania after World War II.[93] Brucan was Romanian minister to the United States from 1956 to 1958 (Romania did not have an ambassador in Washington until 1964) and went from there to New York as ambassador to the United Nations until 1962. Upon his return to Bucharest, he reportedly rejected appointment as director for international organizations at the Romanian Foreign Ministry, as he wanted to be named a deputy foreign minister. When the opposition of Foreign Minister Corneliu Manescu made this impossible, Brucan became vice chairman of the State Council for Radio and Television, a post he held from 1962 to 1967. For several years thereafter he served as professor of Marxism at Bucharest University, though he lacked a university diploma.

By the time Kirk came to Bucharest in 1985, Brucan was a grizzled, white-haired, feisty "old codger," busily stating his views to the diplomatic colony and writing books about how to improve the socialist system. The very fact these writings were not panegyrics to Ceauşescu's Romania and even pointed out flaws in contemporary socialism or communism (though without specific reference to Romania) set them apart from most other Romanian works coming out at that time. Yet Brucan continued to enjoy a number of special privileges. He had a nice villa in the area reserved for high party functionaries, could attend parties at foreign embassies virtually at will, and was able to travel to the West. When Ştefan Andrei was foreign minister, he told Raceanu that Ceauşescu had given him authority, which he regularly exercised, to approve foreign travel for Brucan without checking with Ceauşescu or the Securitate. When Ilie Vaduva succeeded Andrei, he declined to take responsibility for authorizing Brucan's travel and had the ministry pass the word to Brucan that he had to apply to the Securitate for travel approval like any other Romanian citizen. Even after this Brucan was able to obtain permission to travel and publish abroad.

Brucan's intellectual position was nonconforming but Marxist. It appears that Ceauşescu was able to tolerate Brucan's writing and lecturing and perhaps even to welcome it as proof of Ceauşescu's "liberality"— as long as Brucan refrained from direct criticism of the situation in Romania or of Ceauşescu himself. This was a price Brucan had been willing to pay in return for the privileges he received. His November 15, 1987, statement to RFE violated this understanding.

A few days after the broadcast, the authorities curtailed Brucan's access to foreigners and even placed him under brief house arrest in early 1988. This restriction was eased shortly thereafter, however, simultaneously with his renewed cooperation with the authorities in passing messages to the United States embassy (discussed in chapter 9). For the next year Brucan was again able to travel abroad and to be a frequent guest at Kirk's residence and that of Michael Parmly, the embassy political counselor, with whom Brucan had many long talks about U.S.-Romanian relations, the state of the world, and socialism in Romania. After the 1989 revolution, Brucan took great delight in showing visitors photos of himself entering and leaving Parmly's residence, photos taken from Brucan's Securitate file, which Brucan obtained somewhat mysteriously in the days after the revolution.

The U.S. embassy under Kirk was interested in Brucan because of his service in the United States, because he was one of very few persons in Romania to voice any public criticism of conditions in the country, and because he had interesting insights into Romanian developments that he was able and willing to share with the embassy. The embassy acknowledged Brucan's past as a tough Stalinist, that he was still receiving special privileges from Ceauşescu, and that he was certainly a Marxist, not a democrat. This latter became very apparent after the 1989 revolution, when Brucan was briefly an important figure as a member of the executive bureau of the council of the ruling National Salvation Front and chairman of the Front's commission on foreign policy. Soon, though, his intolerant, even authoritarian behavior and statements led to his early return to private life. In November 1987, however, Brucan had shown commendable bravery in speaking out, and ostentatious official U.S. interest in him could help protect him against the Securitate and give heart to other possible dissidents.

Yet another irritant marred U.S.-Romanian relations at the beginning of 1988. Representatives Frank Wolf of Virginia and Christopher Smith of New Jersey asked to visit Romania in early January, as did Senator Arlen Specter of Pennsylvania. Smith and Wolf were among the leading congressional critics of Ceauşescu and opponents of MFN for Romania, while Specter had not been a particularly vociferous critic and had voted in favor of MFN. The Romanians therefore approached the two visits very differently.

Party Secretary for International Affairs Ion Stoian and Interior Minister Tudor Postelnicu in fact argued in favor of "postponing" the Wolf-Smith visit. They mentioned the congressmen's long-standing opposition to MFN and cited press reports that Wolf had met with Reagan in November 1987 and urged him to issue an executive order suspending MFN for Romania.[94] They argued that there was no urgency about receiving persons with such views and said that the Romanian government could tell the Department of State that Romanian officials were so busy with activities connected with the beginning of the new year that they would not have time to meet with Wolf and Smith.

Officials of the Romanian parliament, however, wanted as many parliamentary exchanges as possible to build up their rubber-stamp legislature's prestige and to accommodate Ceauşescu's desire that all Romanian institutions play a prominent role on the international scene. They advocated letting the congressmen come but denying them the customary interview with Ceauşescu. The Foreign Ministry confined itself to pointing out the inconsistency in refusing Wolf and Smith on grounds Romanian officials were "too busy" while accepting Specter's visit at the same time. At Stoian's insistence, the matter was discussed with Ceauşescu, who accepted the parliament's recommendation with the proviso that officials should take an "intransigent" tone with Wolf and Smith.

The Specter and Wolf-Smith delegations arrived in Romania virtually simultaneously in the first days of January 1988 but were handled separately by the Romanians. Specter for his part had relatively amiable conversations with Nicolae Giosan, chairman of Romania's parliament, with Totu, and with Ceauşescu himself. While much of the Ceauşescu conversation was on international affairs, Specter expressed his strong concern over human rights, emigration, and free speech. Ceauşescu said the United States was the only country systematically interfering in Romania's internal affairs. He was not prepared to submit to an examination of Romania's domestic affairs by Congress and would prefer to renounce MFN if the practice continued. His advisers had indeed already counseled him to give up MFN, but he had decided to continue it "on his own responsibility." In retrospect this was an early indication of the direction Ceauşescu's actual thinking was taking, but the U.S. side at the time saw it as more of Ceauşescu's usual bluster.

The Wolf-Smith visit was a completely different story. It started off with a meeting, not with Giosan, but with Marin Ivaşcu, vice chairman of parliament and head of the Romanian group in the Inter-Parliamentary Union, a body bringing together parliamentarians from all over the world.

Smith suggested that, since Romania said it had nothing to hide about its internal situation, it should invite nongovernmental organizations such as Amnesty International and Helsinki Watch to visit and prepare independent reports on the country. Ivaşcu's rejoinder was to criticize Amnesty International for "exaggerations and distortions" about Romania and to surmise that it was unlikely the Romanian government would permit either Amnesty or Helsinki Watch to conduct an investigation in Romania. During this meeting the congressmen said they were too tired to attend the parliamentary dinner in their honor that evening, despite their previous acceptance of the invitation. Romanians attach great importance to such hospitality, and they considered this refusal very impolite.

The congressmen used part of their free evening hours to attempt to visit Dana Damaceanu, the daughter of Securitate defector Pacepa. As they walked toward her apartment building in the company of a U.S. consular officer, militia and plainclothesmen moved to block their access and asked for their identification. The embassy officer said they were from the American embassy and wanted to visit someone in the building. A plainclothesman said that they must arrange any such visit through the Foreign Ministry. The congressmen then said they wanted to deliver a book to Mrs. Damaceanu, making it clear that they were doing this on their own initiative and that Mrs. Damaceanu had not asked them to come. As the police still would not let them through, they identified themselves as visiting U.S. congressmen who wanted to speak to Mrs. Damaceanu. When the plainclothesman again said the Foreign Ministry must arrange any such meeting, the American group left the area.

The next morning Totu received the two congressmen. Before the meeting he had told Raceanu that their "nocturnal escapade" had revealed the real purpose of their trip, adding, "The Americans exaggerate our naiveté if they think by sending a congressman they can stop us from preventing contact with Pacepa's family. We all know that Wolf is a CIA man." This allegation about Wolf was false, but Romanian internal documents had identified Wolf as a CIA man as early as 1985, perhaps because Wolf's congressional district is in northern Virginia, the locale of CIA headquarters. Wolf's effort to contact Pacepa's daughter reinforced the Romanian leadership's conviction about his CIA connection.

The congressmen's refusal to attend the parliamentary dinner and their attempt to contact Damaceanu deeply annoyed Totu, who had opposed their visit in the first place. He adopted an aggressive attitude from the very beginning of his talk with them. He said he could not understand why Congress opposed MFN for Romania on the basis of rumors and untrue allegations about the internal situation in the country. He reacted heatedly when Smith suggested that Romania should invite nongovernmental organizations such as Amnesty International and Helsinki Watch to come and have a look if it had nothing to hide. "You do not know Romania very well," Totu chided, and launched into a discourse about Romania's independence and its resentment of any interference in its internal affairs from whatever quarter. The U.S. Congress spent its time talking about thieves and fascists whom Romania had rightly condemned. Congress might have its doubts about what was really happening in Romania, but Romania had no such doubts and did not need any nongovernmental organizations to come and investigate. Romania knew all it needed to know about its internal affairs. Totu then signaled that he considered the meeting finished.

The congressmen nevertheless attempted to explain their concerns about the specific human rights issues in Romania that had caused them to oppose MFN and to want to come to Romania to see for themselves. Totu interrupted angrily, saying that the Romanian government and he personally knew the position of the two men very well. The government had invited them as guests, not as intelligence agents. Why had they turned down the parliamentary dinner "to do other things"? Congressman Wolf rejoined that he had come with an open mind and was insulted by the accusation that his mind was closed.

Totu then launched another diatribe on independence and MFN, saying Romania's agreement to MFN with the Jackson-Vanik amendment was a favor granted by Romania. Anyone who believed they could get their way by pressuring Romania was absolutely wrong. Romania had lived without MFN and could do so again. If MFN were lost, Romania would accept its renewal only on an unconditional and permanent basis. Without MFN, Congress would have no right to hold hearings on Romania's human rights performance. "You can be sure that we will [hold such hearings]," Smith rejoined, and at that the meeting broke off abruptly.

Totu ordered Solomonescu and Raceanu to send an immediate report of the meeting to the Romanian embassy in Washington along with instructions that the embassy should discourage future visits of this type. He added, "We don't have anything to say to people who come just to root around in the garbage of our society."

These developments at the turn of 1988, together with Romania's increasingly unsavory reputation and its isolation from the reforms within the communist camp, set the stage for the next dramatic event in U.S.-Romanian relations, the Romanian renunciation of MFN under the conditions of the Jackson-Vanik amendment.

▼9▼

Rupture
1988

In early 1988 Deputy Secretary John Whitehead made another trip
to Eastern Europe. The basic purpose of the journey, as the
Department of State described it, was to review the progress in relations since his November 1986 visit, to examine ways to move
ahead, and, where appropriate, to give momentum to ongoing projects
or the resolution of current issues. The Department of State cast the trip
as a whole in positive terms; relations with Eastern Europe had improved
with the winds of reform blowing from Moscow, and the United States
hoped they would continue to improve as reform strengthened. In
Romania, however, the deputy secretary's emphasis was clearly going to
be on "resolving current issues" rather than on "giving momentum to
ongoing projects," and his message was going to be a somber one.

The first problem there arose in connection with Whitehead's instructions to all U.S. embassies on his itinerary that he would like to meet private citizens as well as officials and to travel outside the capital, if time
permitted. As Whitehead was to be in Romania only a little over 24 hours,
it was agreed that travel outside the capital was not feasible. But the
Foreign Ministry argued that time was also too short, and Whitehead's
schedule too crowded, to permit a reception for nonofficials.

The embassy nevertheless included in the program it presented to the
ministry a reception at Kirk's residence for nonofficial Romanians at the
end of the first day of the visit, February 5. This aroused grave suspicions
in the Romanian government. The Securitate was convinced, correctly,
that the embassy would want to invite the religious and dissident figures
with whom Kirk and other embassy officers had been in contact over the
previous months and whom the Romanian government desired to keep
away from Whitehead. At the Securitate's request, the Foreign Ministry

again asked the embassy to cancel the reception on the grounds of lack of time. When the embassy refused, the ministry asked that the embassy include Romanian officials as well, saying that not to do so would be an affront to the Romanian government. The embassy agreed to invite Ion Beşteliu and Raceanu.

Faced with the U.S. refusal to cancel the reception, the Romanian government took steps to prevent nonauthorized invitees from attending. Romanian regulations stipulated that invitations sent by foreigners to Romanians employed in ministries and such institutions as universities, research institutes, churches, and writers' unions must be addressed to the protocol department of the invitees' institutions. These protocol departments then forwarded the invitations to the Foreign Ministry, which, in consultation with the Securitate, decided who should go and whether the protocol departments should even forward the invitations to the addressees.

In this case the Foreign Ministry and Securitate instructed the protocol departments not to forward the invitations to certain invitees and to tell most of the others not to attend. The Securitate knew, however, that the embassy usually sent invitations to invitees' homes as well as to their offices, and the Romanian government feared that some invitees might receive invitations at home, accept them, and try to attend. The Securitate therefore set up a series of roadblocks and security cordons around Kirk's residence to prevent unauthorized guests from attending. Raceanu and Beşteliu, whom Totu allowed to attend the reception for 20 minutes, had to submit their Foreign Ministry credentials and embassy invitations for verification three times at checkpoints on the way to Kirk's residence.

Despite these restrictions, seven nonofficial Romanians did attend. One was Liviu Bota, the Romanian U.N. employee long held in Romania against his will, whom Ceauşescu would, a few days later, decide to allow to leave the country. Another was Nelu Prodan, a brave lawyer and active Protestant, who spent much of his time defending the accused in human rights cases. Embassy officers brought these two men to Kirk's residence in a U.S. vehicle with diplomatic license plates. They parked the car just outside the residence and walked toward the house together. The police stopped the group, saying that the two Romanians must go to the militia station, and the embassy officers insisted upon accompanying them. At the station the militia questioned the two Romanians as to why they were attending the reception but then allowed them to proceed to Kirk's residence.

Another dissident who succeeded in attending was the historian Dinu Giurescu, also about to receive emigration permission, who later said that he had produced his identity papers and invitation at several roadblocks but had passed through them without difficulty. (Giurescu emigrated to the United States in late 1988 but returned to Romania after the 1989 revolution to teach the true history of communism in Romania to a new generation of university students.) Razvan Teodorescu, an art historian who often attended diplomatic functions, also came. As he was a cautious individual and was not a dissident, it is unlikely that he would have attended without Securitate permission. (After the 1989 revolution, Teodorescu became head of Romanian television and was roundly criticized by the Romanian opposition for its broadcasts firmly supporting the postrevolutionary Iliescu government. He left his television job in late 1992.)

Another person who attended the Whitehead reception was former prime minister Ion Gheorghe Maurer, with whom the embassy had not had much contact. Raceanu was surprised when the Securitate told him shortly before the reception that an embassy officer had gone to Maurer's house to invite the former prime minister and that Maurer was planning to attend, despite the fact that Ceauşescu's office had asked him to stay away. To the best of Raceanu's knowledge, as confirmed to the Romanian media by former officials after Ceauşescu's downfall in 1989, Maurer had an agreement with Ceauşescu that he could continue to enjoy numerous privileges on condition that he be demonstrably loyal to Ceauşescu, and he had in fact often publicly expressed his support for the dictator. Maurer had officially nominated Ceauşescu in March 1965 to be first secretary of the Romanian Communist Party and was the only person allowed to call him by his nickname, "Nicule," in public.[95] Raceanu considered Maurer's attendance at this reception to have been a significant break with the past and a personal signal that Ceauşescu was losing support among his former colleagues. The U.S. embassy had initiated contact with Maurer only a few weeks before at the suggestion of the French embassy, which had long been in occasional contact with him. U.S. officials were pleased when Maurer appeared but failed to realize the full significance of his attendance.

The morning after the reception Deputy Assistant Secretary Thomas Simons, accompanied by embassy political counselor Michael Parmly, tried to visit Silviu Brucan's house, but the police stopped their car a block away and explicitly refused to let them call upon Brucan, even though he was no longer under official house arrest. Aurel Duma told Raceanu later that morning about the U.S. attempt to visit Brucan, whose non-attendance at the reception the authorities had systematically ensured. The effort had surprised and irritated the Romanian authorities, especially because it involved a member of Whitehead's party and took place during his visit, leading the Romanians to surmise correctly that Whitehead had given the attempt his blessing. The hard-liners in the Romanian government later cited the attempt as proof that the Americans aimed to destabilize the Ceauşescu regime and should therefore be kept at a distance.

The sixth and seventh nongovernmental Romanians who attended the Whitehead reception were a midlevel official of the Patriarchate international relations department, whose presence was doubtless agreed with the Securitate, and Emil Şechter, the acting head of the Jewish community. Şechter had sent his regrets, but Chief Rabbi Moses Rosen, then in Israel, instructed him by telephone to attend despite the government's injunction. Şechter's attendance was a courageous act, although the fact that the rabbi's instruction came over the open telephone line certainly meant that the Securitate knew Şechter was only following Rosen's orders.

Ironically, all this difficulty about the reception, the failure of most of the guests to show up, and the obvious Securitate presence around Kirk's residence were far more damaging than anything these relatively moderate dissidents might have said. The whole affair greatly annoyed the deputy secretary and confirmed in personal and vivid terms all he had heard about Romania's being a police state. Whitehead indeed cited these events prominently in his press conference at the end of the visit and in later discussions in Washington.[96]

At the beginning of Whitehead's visit the regime had warned the embassy that "Arab and Palestinian students" were going to hold an anti-American demonstration and that the embassy should therefore agree to accept special security and to close the consulate. This sounded bizarre to the Americans. There had been no demonstrations in Bucharest for years other than the periodic rallies in support of Ceauşescu, not surprising in that no one expected Ceauşescu to allow his people to get the idea they could take to the streets. Thus the embassy was convinced that any demonstration that might occur would be at the direction and under the control of the government. That was reassuring in one sense, but it also meant that the police "protection" of the embassy would be under the control of those organizing the demonstrators. The embassy therefore braced for trouble on receiving the ministry's warning. It did not close the consulate, but the Romanian police blocked public access to it. When no visible demonstration had occurred as the morning of February 5 wore on, the embassy successfully importuned the Foreign Ministry to permit customary access to the U.S. installations once again.

The Romanian government did not drop its pretense, however. The official press agency, Agerpres, tried throughout the morning to get any Western correspondents in town to attend "meetings" of Arab students, but neither correspondents nor embassy officers ever found these alleged "meetings." Nevertheless, that evening the official television news reported a demonstration and showed a group of young Arabs at an unidentified location, and the Romanian press on February 6 carried reports of protest meetings. It also asserted that the Arab students had addressed a letter to Whitehead, and a day or two later the ministry gave the embassy such a letter.[97]

The real story was as follows. The Securitate had over the years often proposed organizing a demonstration outside the U.S. embassy or consulate in retaliation for demonstrations outside Romanian installations in the United States. The most common suggestion was that Romanians to whom the United States had denied immigration permission should be the ones to demonstrate, as this would show that it was not only the Romanian government that was hindering movement of people from Romania to the United States. The Securitate also used this logic in proposing a demonstration during Whitehead's visit, but their primary argument in favor of a demonstration was that it would provide an excuse to seal off the U.S. embassy and consulate "on security grounds" and thus prevent any Romanian dissidents from entering to talk to Whitehead.

The Securitate and the Foreign Ministry reached agreement that a demonstration should take place, but the ministry wanted to minimize the possibility that the United States would assert that the Romanian government had organized the demonstration as an insult to Whitehead. The ministry and Securitate therefore advanced the idea of having a demonstration by "foreign students," then claiming that the Romanian government could not deny their right to express their feelings about U.S. policy in the Middle East.

Ceaușescu approved the demonstration plan, but then the Romanians had second thoughts. They were nervous about the possible consequences of allowing a demonstration on the streets of Bucharest, and they could not be sure just what the Arab students might do. They therefore decided not to hold an actual demonstration but rather to keep the notion of a demonstration alive as a pretext for sealing off the American installations, at least while Whitehead was inside the embassy the morning of February 5. Thus they did not cancel their warning to the United

States and directed that the February 5 evening TV news broadcast pictures of a fake "demonstration."

To return to the main business of the day, Deputy Secretary Whitehead's first appointments, following his 9:45 A.M. arrival on February 5 and an immediate briefing at the embassy, were meetings with Deputy Foreign Minister Olimpia Solomonescu and then Ioan Totu. Whitehead, accompanied as usual by Kirk in all his meetings, minced no words with his Romanian interlocutors, telling both officials that MFN renewal would be difficult. There was strong opposition to renewal in Congress, in the administration, and even within the State Department itself, he said, noting that it was too early for any decisions to have been made but that he foresaw a less than even chance for renewal in 1988. He said he would deliver a letter from Reagan to Ceaușescu on that very subject.

Whitehead then stated that while the general view in the United States was that Romania had the worst human rights record in Eastern Europe or the Soviet Union, it was not impossible to save MFN if the Romanians took steps in certain areas. He listed ten specific steps in his talk with Solomonescu: more emigration (there had been no new emigration approvals since October); more Protestant Bibles (none had been printed since the first 5,000); problems with church buildings for the Baptists in Oradea and the Seventh-Day Adventists in Bucharest; resolution of some individual hardship cases; better treatment of minorities, particularly Hungarians (the deputy secretary emphasized that the United States was not advocating a change in borders); removing obstacles to the forwarding of food packages from donors in the United States; tempering the economic plight of the population; correcting the imbalance in favor of Romania in trade with the United States; allowing him to meet Brucan; and compensating for the closure of American exhibits in Romania.

Solomonescu responded to some of Whitehead's specific points. The Baptists, she said, had only recently requested that more Bibles be printed, and the question would be resolved (in fact, no more were printed during the remainder of Ceaușescu's rule). Permission for the Adventists to purchase a new church was forthcoming (the purchase of one building by the Adventists was in fact approved eight months later). The authorization for the Oradea Baptists to remain in their present, enlarged church had "closed" that case. Romania had fulfilled its promises on emigration (indeed, despite the troubling absence of emigration approvals since October 1987, 2,670 Romanians had emigrated to the United States in 1987, a 33 percent increase over 1986).[98] She expressed "surprise" that the deputy secretary wanted to see someone like Brucan.

Whitehead then went over the same ground in a more general fashion with Totu, who listened to Whitehead's presentation with relative good humor. Totu then launched into his customary lecture on the Romanian version of human rights and noninterference in internal affairs. Romania wanted good relations with the United States but would not sacrifice its independence to preserve MFN, he insisted. MFN was only part of the U.S.-Romanian relationship; he would work to keep other ties with the United States if MFN were lost. He and Solomonescu both said they would welcome a visit from Shultz or Reagan in 1988. Whitehead called this unlikely. Totu asserted his surprise at the U.S. decision to withdraw GSP from Romania in early 1987 and at the congressional votes later that year adding MFN suspension to the trade bills. It seemed to him that activists in the United States were trying to change Romanian independence into dependence. In rebuttal Whitehead noted that the United States was not interfering in internal affairs, but it did choose its friends, and it chose them from among those who respected human rights.

Whitehead's meeting with President Ceauşescu came next and lasted three hours. After the initial greetings, Whitehead presented Reagan's letter, dated January 26, 1988, and Ceauşescu's interpreter translated it aloud for his boss. Reagan observed that there was rising concern in the United States, including in Congress, about continuing problems with respect to human rights in Romania. Emigration was a positive note, but its effects were clouded by a growing list of restrictions in other areas, particularly religious freedom, treatment of minorities, economic conditions, and political expression. "Without substantial improvements in the next three months," wrote Reagan, "it will be very difficult for me to decide on renewed extension of MFN for Romania this spring, much less for Congress to accept a positive recommendation." He noted that economic and human rights conditions in Romania would always be important to the U.S.-Romanian relationship. He urged Ceauşescu to do his utmost to clear away the difficulties cited in the letter "so that we can resume the work of building broader and deeper relations between our countries."[99]

Ceauşescu displayed anger, disgust, and dissatisfaction as his interpreter read the letter. He seemed during the next half hour of discussion to be ruminating over its contents before launching into a 70-minute counterattack in the last part of the meeting.

Whitehead expanded on the letter. There was a serious possibility, he said, that the president or Congress would not approve continuation of MFN for Romania. The State Department would collect the facts and present them clearly, but he could not predict the final outcome. There were a number of American leaders who felt that the treatment of Romanian citizens by their own government was not in accord with Americans' feelings as to how human beings should be treated. The United States did not interfere in other countries' affairs, but it did choose its own friends, and human rights affected this choice. His objective and that of the U.S. government was to improve relations between Romania and the United States. The United States respected Romania's independence and was eager to preserve and continue the U.S.-Romanian relationship.

Ceauşescu allowed a long pause before responding. He seemed to be thinking out loud at first but then became more assertive. The contents of President Reagan's letter and Whitehead's remarks betrayed a "surprising misunderstanding of Romanian realities on the part of the U.S. administration." Indeed, the administration seemed to understand less and less about Romania as time went on. Some Americans came to Romania with preconceptions. He regretted that he had overruled his advisers and allowed two such individuals to visit a short while before (an obvious reference to Representatives Smith and Wolf). He then said he was surprised that Reagan had referred to economic difficulties in Romania. Romania, Ceauşescu asserted, was one of the few countries that had been able to increase its people's income each year. He did not know where President Reagan could have gotten such false information about Romania's economic situation.

Kirk practically choked as he heard this comment. Every remotely objective observer of the Romanian scene was horrified by the pathetic economic conditions of the population and the decline in their standard of living from year to year. Ceauşescu's best line of defense, one that other Romanian officials often used, would have been that economic sacrifices were necessary to pay off the foreign debt but that things would improve after that was done. Another possibility for Ceauşescu would have been to say that Romania was building an industrial base, and improvement in consumption would come later. But to assert that living conditions were getting better from year to year simply boggled the mind. It did not seem possible that even as prejudiced and isolated a dictator as Ceauşescu could believe what he had just said, and yet he returned to the point more than once, apparently in genuine disbelief that Reagan would have raised a subject for which Romania presented such a success story.

The published Romanian government statistics certainly painted a rosy picture of the economy, but the United States had assumed that Ceauşescu had other, more accurate, figures available to him. Furthermore, Ceauşescu's observation of life in the streets, however limited, not to speak of his own government's decrees restricting energy use and rationing food, should, it seemed to the United States, have given Ceauşescu some idea of the Romanian people's suffering and made him realize that it was not even a good debating tactic to boast of their well-being.

Ceauşescu's statements in the meeting and the way he made them gave the distinct impression, however, that to a large extent he actually believed what he was saying and was not just putting on a good face for his visitor. This was also Raceanu's impression, and Ceauşescu's conduct at his trial in December 1989 bears this out. When his interrogators asked him, "Why did you so ruin the country? Why did you export everything? Why did you make the peasants starve?" he replied, "I made sure that the peasants received 200 kilograms of wheat per person, not just per family. It is a lie that I made the people starve. A lie, a lie to my face. . . . I made sure that every village had its schools, hospitals, and doctors. I did everything to create a decent and rich life for the people in the country, as in no other country in the world."[100]

The explanation for Ceauşescu's ignorance must be found in the information he received, the way he lived, and the kind of people with whom he surrounded himself as the years went on. The falsification of economic figures started at the bottom, where factory and farm managers reported good results to get bonuses or avoid penalties. The distortion continued as figures went up the line, with each intermediate official painting the picture a little brighter. By the time the figures reached Ceauşescu, they were hopelessly inaccurate. When Ceauşescu visited markets, apartment complexes, farms, or factories, they were cleaned up, painted, and well stocked in advance. The streets he drove down, while not immaculate, were kept in better shape than most others, and people along the way were encouraged to cheer or wave as he went by. Television and radio broadcasts described nothing but fertile fields, humming machines, and happy people. Ceauşescu's associates lost no opportunity to praise him and the success of his policies. There was no one to say that the emperor had no clothes.

Ceauşescu's next comment to Whitehead raised many eyebrows in Washington. Romania, he said, had reached such a level of development that it could even produce nuclear weapons if it wished to do so. He repeated this phraseology several times during the next few months, sometimes adding that Romania had no desire to produce such weapons. The comment was greatly troubling to the U.S. government, despite Ceauşescu's disclaimers of any desire to conduct a nuclear weapons program. The United States began to wonder if the increasingly isolated and perhaps desperate dictator might indeed be planning to construct nuclear weapons. The United States and its European allies, as well as Moscow and Ceauşescu's East European neighbors, would be appalled if Ceauşescu had nuclear weapons at his disposal.

The problems and delays plaguing Romania's single nuclear power station construction project suggested that it would be very difficult for Romania to build a nuclear weapon, however, and would require a lot of money and a lot of foreign help. Following Ceauşescu's remark, U.S. intelligence gave high priority to finding any hard evidence that Romania was engaged in a nuclear weapons program, but nothing turned up. It seems likely that Ceauşescu was merely boasting, but his comment certainly got the U.S. government's attention. While this may have been all Ceauşescu wanted, his statement heightened the U.S. impression that he was becoming increasingly erratic and more harmful than helpful on the world scene.

Ceauşescu then told Whitehead he was "even more surprised" by what President Reagan's letter said about national minorities in Romania. He said that he considered this a "hostile, unfriendly, and anti-Romanian reference" and asserted that this was the first time since 1918 (when Romania regained Transylvania from Hungary) that a U.S. president had made such comments. Ceauşescu came back to this theme several times during the meeting, indicating that this part of the letter had annoyed him the most.

Ceauşescu refuted Reagan's other points in familiar terms, saying that emigration was against basic Romanian philosophy and traditions, as Romanians were proud that their people had stayed in this land for thousands of years. Furthermore, he wanted no religious denominations in Romania that were "agents for foreign countries," presumably a reference to some of the Protestant denominations whose welfare the United States had raised. In saying this, he probably revealed his most serious reservation about these denominations, namely, that they had sources of support other than the Romanian government and were therefore not so much under his control as was the Romanian Orthodox Church. He seemed to have more fear of foreign influence than he did of religion per se, probably doubting that religion could compete with the socialist ideology he espoused.

Ceauşescu then launched into an attack on the U.S. embassy in Bucharest, saying that it should get its information from officials, not from malcontents. He said the embassy or Kirk personally should have asked the government what had happened in Braşov in mid-November instead of talking to troublemakers and sending "embassy agents" to Braşov to talk to everyone except the local authorities. In truth, the embassy had asked many Romanians about what had happened in Braşov, including a number of high Romanian officials. It had also sent embassy officers to visit the scene and ask people about the events. This was normal procedure for any active diplomatic mission, but it ill accorded with Ceauşescu's view that a foreign embassy should be simply another channel for his official propaganda. It was indicative of his warped concept of correct diplomatic practice that he considered the embassy's actions so out of place as to criticize them to the deputy secretary.

Ceauşescu admitted that there were some individuals in Romania who sought to cause mischief. He noted that the U.S. embassy had put some people he characterized as "scum" on its guest list for Kirk's reception for Whitehead later that day. He regretted that the embassy thought it advisable to organize its reception in such a way. Evidently to show how out of step these mischief makers were, Ceauşescu said that he often talked to workers and that they had no complaints. On the contrary, they applauded him when they saw him. They did this because they approved his policies and would not have applauded him if they did not like what he was doing. They applauded him because he promoted the interests of the country, not because his name was Ceauşescu. Furthermore, parliament would reject his ideas if they were against Romania's interests.

Once again during this meeting the brashness—or was it naiveté—of the man was breathtaking. It was well known that the local authorities who assembled workers at the factories Ceauşescu was to visit screened out any possible troublemakers. Securitate members were sprinkled throughout the crowd, which also knew that many among them would report to the Securitate on the proceedings. While waiting for the president, the crowd would rehearse the chants and shouts to be made on his arrival, the little speech of welcome by a designated worker or foreman, and the presentation of flowers by young children. As the time for Ceauşescu's arrival neared, the police invariably grew more and more nervous, eyeing the crowd and making last-minute adjustments. One slip-up could cost them their jobs, and they knew it. When Ceauşescu finally came, workers and police alike went through their roles with apprehension and breathed a deep sigh of relief when he left.

Embassy staff members had witnessed such scenes many times. Everyone in Romania knew how the game was played. Was it really possible that Ceauşescu believed that the stage-managed enthusiasm was genuine? Kirk concluded from Ceauşescu's manner when speaking to Whitehead that the Romanian president really believed that he had a great deal of popular support and had convinced himself he was doing the right thing for his country. These convictions were among the factors that made him so stubborn and so unreasonable.

Noting next that Whitehead had said MFN was in jeopardy in the United States, Ceauşescu asserted that he in fact did not want MFN under the conditions mentioned in the president's letter. If President Reagan recommended the extension of MFN under conditions additional to the emigration provisions in the Jackson-Vanik amendment, Ceauşescu would recommend that his parliament reject it. The United States would then be responsible for the consequences. In retrospect, this ploy appears to have foreshadowed Ceauşescu's renunciation of MFN the next day, except that by that time he was rejecting even Jackson-Vanik and demanding MFN without any conditions whatsoever. Because U.S. officials had heard Ceauşescu and others say on other occasions that Romania could live without MFN, they gave no special significance to Ceauşescu's remark to Whitehead. Neither did Ceauşescu's interpreter, Gheorghe Petricu, when he briefed Raceanu on the conversation shortly thereafter.

Whitehead and Ceauşescu then turned briefly to international affairs, normally Ceauşescu's favorite subject. On this occasion, however, he most uncharacteristically broke off the discussion to return to Reagan's comments about Romania's economic difficulties. Perhaps Reagan was referring to economic problems in the Third World or to the U.S. deficit, Ceauşescu speculated, adding that he really did not understand the reference and reiterating his interest in further developing U.S.-Romanian relations. Noting that he had tried to prevent demonstrations—some justified—against various aspects of U.S. policies, he pointedly avoided any reference to the "demonstration" earlier that day.

When Ceauşescu had finished his long monologue, Whitehead said that he was disappointed that Ceauşescu had "rejected my president's letter." He had not rejected the letter, Ceauşescu replied, only parts of it. Whitehead then asked if Ceauşescu was rejecting MFN, and Ceauşescu explained that he was rejecting only those conditions that lay outside of Jackson-Vanik. Continuation of MFN would be possible only if it did not involve unacceptable conditions or recommendations on matters such as religion, the Romanian economy, and especially national minorities.

Whitehead rejoined that the United States felt that the two sides should be able to discuss everything. To this Ceauşescu replied that he did not want to hear things that constituted interference in internal affairs or comments about nationalities in Romania.

As the discussion was coming to its close, Whitehead said he was not sure where the two countries were headed. There had been great improvement in U.S. relations with Eastern Europe and the Soviet Union, but he did not see such improvement in relations with Romania. Ceauşescu opined that the problem was America's insistence on linking MFN to "conditions" and its "interference in Romania's domestic affairs." Before 1975 there had been no MFN and no problems to discuss, but now some people in the U.S. administration were not happy with Romania's policy of independence. Whitehead denied this. The meeting closed with Whitehead saying "we both have much to think about" and with cautious mutual pledges to work together to improve relations.

Whitehead and Kirk then went on to Kirk's reception for nonofficial Romanians, arriving about an hour late because of the length of the meeting with Ceauşescu. Whitehead had a chance to speak briefly with each of the guests, to state that he had raised human rights and religious questions in his talk with Ceauşescu, and to assure them that the United States continued its interest in such matters.

Totu hosted the official Romanian dinner for Whitehead the same evening, February 5. Totu gave no indication that he thought any dramatic developments were imminent, and Raceanu is convinced that he had no inkling of what was to come the next day. Raceanu and Beşteliu for their part agreed after the dinner that the day had not gone too badly, in fact had turned out pretty well.

Whitehead's schedule on February 6 started with a meeting with Deputy Prime Minister Ştefan Andrei that focused largely on bilateral economic and commercial issues. Andrei spoke at some length about Romania's history of independence and, contrary to his usual custom, avoided answering Whitehead's questions about concrete problems. Raceanu noted that Andrei did not display his usual verve, indeed seemed anxious to get the meeting over as soon as possible. Time was indeed pressing hard, as the Romanians had just asked Whitehead to come to a second meeting with Totu before leaving Bucharest later that morning. Andrei's attitude nevertheless surprised Raceanu, as Andrei had made a determined effort to ensure that he met with Whitehead during the visit. Raceanu thought that Andrei's apparent hesitancy might stem from the presence of the Foreign Ministry's chief of protocol, Petre Moisa, who had been included at the insistence of Securitate head Vlad, Andrei told Raceanu, "probably to watch me."

When the interview ended, Andrei asked Raceanu to stay behind for a moment. Holding Raceanu by the shoulders and looking him in the eye, Andrei quietly said that Totu was shortly going to inform Whitehead that Romania was renouncing MFN. The news hit Raceanu like a thunderbolt. At first he thought he had misunderstood, or that Andrei was joking. In fact he even asked Andrei if it was a joke. When Andrei said "No, I'm not joking," a cold shiver went down Raceanu's spine. "What happened? When was the decision taken?" he asked in a half-whisper. "This morning," said Andrei. "Now hurry up, or you'll be late for the Totu meeting." As Raceanu drove to the Foreign Ministry, he wondered what could have happened overnight to bring about this development so different from the friendly atmosphere of the dinner.

When Raceanu joined the Whitehead-Totu meeting, the preliminary greetings were just concluding. Totu then told Whitehead that he had a message for President Reagan from President Ceauşescu. He proceeded to list five points, reading from notes he had taken in a small notebook: (1) Romania was in favor of developing political and economic relations with the United States without any conditions, including those of the Jackson-Vanik amendment. Romania favored conclusion of a long-term commercial agreement and of agreements on industrial cooperation on GATT principles, with no other conditions. (2) Romania was no longer interested in maintaining MFN tied to the Jackson-Vanik amendment. Romania would only accept MFN without any conditions whatsoever. (3) The United States should stop all activity connected with MFN status for Romania, including discussion of compliance with Jackson-Vanik or any other conditions. MFN for Romania should no longer be debated. (4) A letter from Ceauşescu to Reagan would follow confirming what Totu was telling Whitehead. (5) Matters regarding emigration from Romania for purposes of family reunification would be resolved separately.

Whitehead, after asking Totu to repeat his points slowly so that the U.S. side could transmit them accurately, said that every government had the right to make its own decisions. He asked when the unilateral Romanian renunciation would be effective, and Totu responded, "Today!" At this the experts on both sides of the table began whispered conversations with their chiefs. The U.S. side proceeded to point out that the legal form of

Romania's decision should be negotiated between the two countries, as stipulated by their 1975 trade agreement.

This discomfited Totu, now caught between Ceauşescu's instructions to renounce MFN with Jackson-Vanik "immediately" and the legal provisions of Romania's trade agreement. After a moment's thought, he suggested that the two sides consider that Romania had renounced MFN effective that moment and that the experts subsequently work out the details connected with that decision. Whitehead accepted this. He and Totu agreed that the two sides would discuss the question of a public announcement later, keeping the Romanian decision confidential for the time being. They also agreed that the Romanian decision did not change their mutual desire to continue trade between the two countries and to preserve the other aspects of the relationship.

Whitehead proceeded straight from this meeting to the airport, where he held a brief press conference. After reviewing his program and thanking his hosts, he struck a somber note. "I was disappointed at not being able to convey successfully to President Ceauşescu the deep feelings that my country has about human rights and the importance of individual freedoms. He seemed to resent my mention of these subjects, which are very important to Americans." Whitehead observed that this reaction contrasted with the "positive response" he found to such concerns in other East European countries. He also noted that human rights problems in Romania had been evident to him during his short visit. At Kirk's reception he had met Liviu Bota, who, Whitehead said, had been prevented for two years from leaving Romania to return to his job as director of the U.N. disarmament institute in Geneva. Whitehead also noted that the police had discouraged or prevented a number of other invited guests from attending.

The first journalist to question Whitehead suggested that the stress on meeting nonofficial Romanians did not correspond to the principle of non-interference and that he doubted Ceauşescu had sought to meet unofficial Americans when visiting the United States in 1973 and 1975. Whitehead responded that Ceauşescu would have been quite free to do so, and as a matter of fact the U.S. government would have been delighted had such meetings taken place. He then discussed at some length the difference in the openness of the two societies.[101] Raceanu later asked the Romanian questioner, a friend of his, why he had posed such a stupid question, giving Whitehead a perfect opening. The journalist confessed that the party secretariat had instructed him to do so. The succeeding questions at the conference were mostly designed to elicit praise for Ceauşescu's international views and policies, and Whitehead successfully avoided them.

As Totu had indicated, Ceauşescu sent Reagan a follow-up letter on his decision. The letter, dated February 12, 1988, first noted that Romania had always acted in conformity with the U.S.-Romanian trade agreement of 1975. Although opposing Jackson-Vanik from the beginning, it had permitted emigration for family reunification and other justified reasons.

Ceauşescu's letter then expressed surprise that Reagan had raised "so-called" economic, humanitarian, religious, and other problems in Romania. These were domestic issues, which should not be the subject of discussion between the two countries. The United States had domestic problems too, but the Romanian government considered these matters for the United States to resolve. The Romanian economy had been growing at 5 to 6 percent a year for the past five years, he asserted, while difficulties in the U.S. economy were having a serious effect on international economic relations. He was particularly surprised, he wrote, that Reagan had raised the subject of nationalities. "Only former Horthyites, nationalists, and Hungarian irredentists speak of the so-called nationality problem in Romania, thereby calling into question the current borders and seeking the revision of international treaties."

After a lecture on international law and Romanian independence, Ceauşescu came to the point on MFN: "We have decided to reject extension of this clause [MFN] under the conditions set forth by the Jackson-Vanik amendment. It is our view that approval of this clause should be based on the existing trade agreement, renouncing any preconditions." He proposed discussions between representatives of the two governments to "discuss the modalities of developing economic relations between our countries, in accordance with the provisions of the current trade agreement and renouncing any preconditions." He concluded with the statement that it was in the interest of both peoples to do everything to develop relations between the two countries.[102]

MFN was the key symbol of Romania's "special relationship" with the United States, a relationship Ceauşescu valued highly as a public sign of his international acceptability and stature. Very few on either the U.S. or the Romanian side really believed he would give it up. Raceanu's contacts in the Securitate subsequently told him they, too, had no inkling of possible renunciation before the Whitehead visit. While Ceauşescu had clearly signaled in his discussion with Whitehead on February 5 that he did not want MFN under the conditions mentioned in Reagan's letter, he had also implied acceptance, not rejection, of the provisions of the Jackson-Vanik amendment linking MFN to progress on freedom of emigration. The very next day, however, he rejected Jackson-Vanik itself.

It appeared, therefore, that Ceauşescu had reached his decision between the Whitehead interview and the following morning. There is additional evidence for this. None of the briefing material for Ceauşescu contained a discussion of the possibility of renouncing MFN, much less a recommendation to do so. Neither Ceauşescu nor anyone else had ordered a study in preparation for the Whitehead visit of the effects of such a renunciation on U.S.-Romanian trade. The last such study dated back to 1983, when a Romanian "education tax" on emigrants had threatened MFN (discussed in chapter 1). Nor had Ceauşescu ordered any research on the procedural and legal modalities of such a renunciation.

Raceanu learned later from Ceauşescu's interpreter, Gheorghe Petricu, that Ceauşescu had had a "long and open" discussion with his wife immediately after his meeting with Whitehead. It was well known that Ceauşescu's wife had long favored distancing the United States and Romania and that she felt the United States was trying, for ideological reasons, to recruit enemies of the regime and in general destabilize it by any means possible. The critical comments about Romania by members of Congress and administration spokespersons in recent years had confirmed and heightened her suspicions. She was believed to have argued previously for renunciation of MFN to deprive the United States of an excuse to interfere in Romania's internal affairs and to put an end to U.S. governmental criticism of Romania's internal situation. It seems likely that she would have advanced these arguments once again with Ceauşescu at any long talk with him directly after his meeting with Whitehead.

There were a number of reasons Ceauşescu would have been especially susceptible to such arguments at that point. U.S. criticism of Romania had become increasingly severe as political conditions in Romania deteriorated at the same time they were liberalizing dramatically in many other parts of Eastern Europe and in the Soviet Union. Other recent developments, such as the publication of General Pacepa's revelations, the play the American short-wave radio stations gave the book, U.S. attempts to contact Pacepa's daughter, U.S. insistence on going ahead with the embassy reception for unofficial Romanians during the Whitehead visit, and Maurer's appearance at the reception, had all concerned and angered the Ceauşescus.

Most important, Whitehead had brought a confidential letter from President Reagan himself that referred critically to many aspects of

Ceauşescu's internal policies. Ceauşescu put great stock in communications between heads of state. He could discount unpleasant statements and letters from lesser officials, even secretaries of state, as not really representing the views of their chiefs. Indeed, heads of state were the only people who, in Ceauşescu's view, could talk to him as equals. Thus when Reagan voiced a number of criticisms of Romania's internal affairs in a personal and confidential letter and even raised the minorities question, Ceauşescu was deeply annoyed and worried. He had begun to suspect that Reagan, unlike his predecessors in office, was committed to the destruction of communism on ideological grounds and in fact wanted to overthrow the Ceauşescu regime, not to live with it. The Reagan letter seems to have served to increase this suspicion.

Finally, Reagan's letter and Whitehead himself had indicated that the U.S. Congress or even the administration might take MFN away from Romania in 1988. The 1987 congressional votes to amend the trade bill to "suspend" MFN had been a sign of congressional sentiment, and then Reagan had written that he was not even sure he would recommend MFN to Congress in the first place. For the United States, especially the executive branch, to take MFN away from Romania would be much more humiliating to Ceauşescu than for Romania itself to renounce MFN. If it appeared likely the United States would take MFN away, it would make more sense from Ceauşescu's point of view to preempt the U.S. action.

Whatever Ceauşescu's precise motivations, he clearly made the decision himself, presumably in consultation with his wife, but to the surprise of his other collaborators. That he took the decision the evening of February 5 is further suggested by the fact that, as Ceauşescu's interpreter told Raceanu, there had been much activity in Ceauşescu's personal secretariat that evening, with staff officers going back and forth to Ceauşescu's residence until after midnight. Early the next morning Ceauşescu convened a number of his top advisers and told them he planned unilaterally to renounce MFN under conditions of Jackson-Vanik. He instructed Totu to inform Whitehead about the decision and dictated the five points that Totu read during his meeting with Whitehead.

Subsequent events suggested that Ceauşescu, in renouncing MFN "under conditions of Jackson-Vanik," did not necessarily think he was going to lose MFN and in any case soon convinced himself that Reagan would in the last analysis grant MFN without the Jackson-Vanik conditions. In this Ceauşescu betrayed a total misunderstanding of the political climate vis-à-vis Romania in the United States, not to mention the legal and constitutional restrictions on the U.S. president.

Ceauşescu had often said that the United States "needed" Romania as a thorn in the Soviet side and that U.S. business was keenly interested in trade with Romania. By his renunciation of MFN with Jackson-Vanik, he seemed to be trying to create a situation in which the United States, not Romania, would seek to preserve MFN. Renunciation also showed that he would not yield to pressure from any quarter, West or East. The latter motive, although probably not the principal one, was the main theme of the Foreign Ministry's briefing of other nations once the Romanian action became public.

The Romanians' efforts to implement Ceauşescu's strategy and the U.S. attempt to persuade them that their action had killed MFN for the foreseeable future formed the central themes of the next phase in U.S.-Romanian relations.

▼10▼

Dialogue of the Deaf
1988

Differences in the U.S. and Romanian views as to what exactly Ceauşescu had done by renouncing most-favored-nation status under conditions of Jackson-Vanik became apparent soon after he made his decision. On February 19, 1988, Deputy Foreign Minister Olimpia Solomonescu gave Kirk a copy of Ceauşescu's February 12 letter to Reagan on the matter and discussed the next steps. Reflecting the Romanian desire for intergovernmental discussions on according MFN or the equivalent without conditions, Solomonescu stressed the importance of keeping the Romanian renunciation confidential. Somewhat illogically, she also said that the United States should cease public discussion of Romanian internal affairs in the MFN context. She urged the United States to inform Romania soon of a date to begin discussion of a commercial agreement between the two countries.

Kirk, on the other hand, reflecting the U.S. belief that the forthcoming discussions were simply to focus on the modalities of terminating MFN, not finding some way to preserve it, said the United States would soon be in touch about setting up a meeting to work out the implementation of the Romanian decision to renounce MFN. He stated that confidentiality was acceptable for the moment but that American businessmen and the Congress would shortly need to know what the Romanians had done.

The next day, February 20, Kirk received instructions from Washington that enabled him to respond in detail to the Romanian suggestions. Accordingly, he informed Solomonescu that it was Washington's understanding that Romania did not want the United States to proceed with the annual renewal process for MFN and that Romania wanted consultations under Article XII of the trade agreement, which provided for such consultations when one or the other party was unable to carry out its oblig-ations under the agreement.[103] Kirk said the United States accepted both these points. He suggested late March as the date for the consul-tations and noted they could consider whether to "suspend" or "termi-nate" MFN and how to minimize the disruption of trade consequent upon the Romanian decision. He added that the United States could not keep the Romanian decision secret indefinitely; it intended to inform U.S. businesspeople and the Congress and make a public statement. The Department of State also authorized Kirk to add, if it seemed necessary, that President Reagan was legally barred from extending MFN to Romania unless Romania accepted Jackson-Vanik. Kirk saw that it was certainly necessary to say this and did so.

On February 24 Solomonescu told Kirk that the Romanians wanted prior consultation on the text of any public statement the United States would make; how the United States handled the publicity would show how interested the United States was in good future relations with Romania. She said the Romanians opposed releasing the Reagan and Ceauşescu letters and wanted the forthcoming consultations to cover broad issues between the two countries. The next day, February 25, Kirk informed Solomonescu that the United States agreed not to pub-licize the presidential letters but had to make a public statement soon. U.S. businessmen and the Congress were asking what the situation was, and it was in the interests of Romania as well as the United States to inform them promptly.

That same day, Kirk relayed to Solomonescu a draft text of the U.S. public statement. The draft noted that Romania had decided to renounce renewal of MFN and that the U.S. administration therefore would not exercise its waiver authority under the Jackson-Vanik amendment. It stated that this meant that all Romanian products arriving in U.S. ports after July 2, 1988, would be subject to higher, non-MFN duties and that Romania would no longer be eligible for U.S. government–supported export credits through programs such as the Commodity Credit Corporation and the Export-Import Bank. The statement welcomed and reciprocated the Romanian government's expressed desire to work for better relations, to maintain a broad range of contacts, and to pro-mote trade. It also welcomed the Romanian government's statement that it would continue to allow emigration for family reunification purposes without regard to the economic ties between the two countries. It emphasized the importance of this latter point in light of the "continu-ing intense concern showed by the administration, the Congress, and the

American public with human rights in Romania," adding that "this concern will continue to be a central part of the U.S.-Romanian dialogue."

The Romanians requested two or three changes in the U.S. text. The only substantive change was to indicate that Romania had renounced MFN "under conditions of Jackson-Vanik," to reflect their desire to leave the way open for a renewal of MFN without Jackson-Vanik. As the change would more accurately reflect the action the Romanians had taken, the United States agreed to amend the text. The next day, February 26, shortly after Kirk so informed Solomonescu, the Department of State issued the statement.[104]

On February 27, Solomonescu handed Kirk the text of the statement she said the Romanians would release in two or three hours. The statement was longer and more contentious than the U.S. text, as Kirk immediately pointed out to Solomonescu. It began by stating how Romania had worked for good economic and trade relations with the United States under the provisions of the General Agreement on Tariffs and Trade (GATT) and the U.S.-Romanian trade agreement of 1975. Since the United States had conditioned MFN on a number of political demands, Romania had told the United States it no longer accepted renewal of MFN under conditions of Jackson-Vanik. It called for a meeting between representatives of the two governments as soon as possible to discuss how to develop trade and economic cooperation in the future. In conclusion, it expressed the conviction that the United States would show a "constructive spirit" that would make it possible to find ways to remove obstacles to U.S.-Romanian relations. In giving Kirk the text, Solomonescu took the occasion to stress again that the Romanians wanted the consultations to cover broad issues, not just technical details.[105]

The Romanian announcement was the product of intensive consultations within the Romanian government over many days. Immediately after sending his letter to President Reagan on February 12, Ceauşescu instructed the Foreign Ministry to start work on the text of a public statement on MFN renunciation. He said that this statement should make clear that the Romanian action was due entirely to the position of the United States and that the U.S. stand contradicted the norms of international commerce (under GATT) and the bilateral understandings between the two countries.

The basis for Ceauşescu's argument was that Article 1 of the 1975 trade agreement between the United States and Romania stipulated that the two countries extended MFN to each other in accordance with the GATT agreement, which provided that all GATT members would extend such tariff privileges to each other.[106] GATT made no mention of conditioning this upon progress on emigration or anything else. The United States, in ratifying GATT, had made a reservation under Article XXXV providing for "non-application" of the agreement where member countries had not "entered into tariff negotiations with each other." This covered the fact that the United States was not in a position to extend MFN automatically to all GATT members because extension of MFN was the prerogative of Congress, not of the executive branch, and had to be carried out in accordance with U.S. legislation.[107]

When Romania became a member of GATT in November 1971, the United States invoked Article XXXV to avoid automatic extension of MFN to Romania, which as a nonmarket economy was not eligible to receive MFN under then existing U.S. law.[108] In 1975, with the passage of the Trade Act of 1974 and the Jackson-Vanik amendment, Romania and other nonmarket economies that denied freedom of emigration became eligible for MFN status if, and only if, the president found that waiving the prohibition would "substantially promote" the objectives of freedom of emigration and had "received assurances" that the emigration practices of the country in question would henceforth lead to substantial achievement of free emigration.[109] Acknowledgment of this U.S. reservation gradually disappeared from Romanian governmental statements and also began to disappear from the consciousness of the Romanian leaders, so that many of them actually began to believe that GATT legally entitled Romania to unconditional MFN from the United States. By this interpretation, U.S. action conditioning MFN on emigration was a violation of its GATT obligations.

Furthermore, when Romania first obtained MFN status in 1975, it had given only oral assurances that it would abide by its 1973 pledge to "contribute to the solution of humanitarian problems on the basis of mutual confidence and good will." Although both sides at the time recognized that this was a commitment to facilitate emigration in conformity with the Jackson-Vanik amendment, no written agreement said so. The Romanians used these technicalities as the basis for their 1988 contention that conditioning MFN on the Jackson-Vanik amendment was a unilateral act by the United States, not an agreement between the two countries, and that it in fact "violated" their agreements.

Since Ceauşescu had instructed the Foreign Ministry to use an aggressive, accusatory tone toward the United States, the first drafts the ministry prepared contained a number of contentious debating points and charges against the United States drawn from earlier declarations approved by Ceauşescu. As Deputy Foreign Minister Aurel Duma took each successive draft to Ceauşescu, however, the dictator ordered him to moderate the tone and to include language indicating both a desire on the part of the Romanian government to continue collaboration with the United States and a wish to explore with the United States what would be the best means to this end. He also wanted the statement to express confidence that the United States would respond in a "constructive" manner. It appeared to Raceanu, as Duma brought the successive changes back from Ceauşescu, that the dictator was having second thoughts about his angry decision and looking for ways to preserve his relationship with the United States.

As soon as the United States told the Foreign Ministry that it was about to put out its announcement, Duma proposed to Ceauşescu that the Romanian side anticipate this with its own statement. Ceauşescu refused, saying it was better that the Americans go first and that the Romanian statement appear as a response to it. After seeing the U.S. text, Ceauşescu ordered inclusion in the Romanian statement of a phrase regretting that the United States had come out with its statement before holding the consultations the Romanians had proposed.

The timing and text of the Romanian announcement left the public in some confusion as to whether it was Romania or the United States that had renounced MFN. This was no accident. The Romanian government had designed its statement to reflect its position that it was the United States that had closed the door on MFN because it was not willing to hold talks about preserving MFN without Jackson-Vanik. The Romanians tried to portray Jackson-Vanik and the associated debates on human rights as obstacles to U.S.-Romanian friendship that the Romanians had now removed, thus setting the stage for a new and more harmonious relationship. They had proposed talks to discuss setting up this new relationship, they noted, and it was therefore now up to the United States to respond positively.

The position of the United States, on the other hand, was that, as MFN was impossible without Jackson-Vanik, MFN had been terminated by Romanian renunciation of MFN with Jackson-Vanik, and thus Romania alone was responsible for the consequences of that renunciation for U.S.-Romanian trade and U.S.-Romanian relations in general.

The Romanians now decided to use Silviu Brucan, the former Romanian minister to the United States and occasional critic of the Ceauşescu regime, as a channel to present their views to the United States. In the early days of March 1988, Brucan reappeared from house arrest and approached a British diplomat, an American businessman, and finally Michael Parmly, the U.S. embassy political counselor, with essentially the same basic message: Ceauşescu wanted to discuss preservation of MFN or its equivalent with the United States and was willing to offer in return for MFN a firm commitment to keep emigration at current levels and to maintain his independent foreign policy. He could not, however, change his internal political or economic policies, as to do so "would mean the end of his regime." Brucan said the United States had "misread" Ceauşescu's signals and had made a mistake with its "hasty" announcement on MFN, which had "disappointed" Ceauşescu. According to this message, Ceauşescu recognized that he had lost the battle in Congress and now wanted an executive-to-executive agreement that would not require congressional involvement. He was ready to send Ştefan Andrei to Washington to discuss the whole question.

While some of the rhetoric surrounding these points sounded more like Brucan than Ceauşescu, the embassy concluded that the message came from Ceauşescu. The evidence for this was manifold. It would be like the Romanians to use an indirect channel for such a seemingly frank message and to use Brucan, in whom the United States had shown such an interest, as the messenger. Brucan's sudden emergence from house arrest into this kind of diplomatic activity could not have occurred without government permission. Indeed, only Ceauşescu could have granted it, given Brucan's stature, history, and the attention foreign governments and media paid to him.

Brucan's initial meeting, with the British diplomat, had been arranged at a public restaurant. The two men were followed and were required to sit at a particular table. The maître d'hôtel refused their request to move, despite the fact that many tables were empty. Though it was broad daylight, the waiter placed a heavy metal candlestick on their table and even lit the candle once they sat down. The candlestick was clearly a microphone. It was obvious the Romanian government was carefully monitoring the conversation and wanted all concerned to know that. In addition, Brucan, for what it was worth, told the U.S. political counselor at the latter's house on March 6 that his comments were "authoritative" from "someone directly involved in the affair."

Raceanu, who first learned of Brucan's activity on behalf of MFN when collaborating with Kirk on this book, is convinced that Brucan was acting on behalf of Ceauşescu. He notes that what Brucan said in all these conversations was in agreement with the Romanian government's position and that Brucan could not have come out of house arrest without

Securitate approval and Ceauşescu's specific authorization. He also points out that after these demarches and presumably as a reward, Brucan once again was able to have contact with foreigners and even to travel abroad, a rare privilege for a Romanian.

Several days later, the U.S. embassy passed the word back to Brucan, through the same channels, that neither U.S. law nor the political atmosphere in Washington suggested any possibility that the United States would accord MFN or its equivalent to Romania. The embassy also stated that, if the Romanian government made the same approach through official channels, the U.S. response would be that the United States was prepared to discuss how to continue economic relations with Romania in the post-MFN period, but that an MFN-type relationship would be possible only if Romania changed a great deal.

The State Department tried to drive home the U.S. point of view with an instruction to Kirk to "clarify" for the Romanians what the United States had in mind in the consultations both sides had agreed to hold under Article XII of the trade agreement. Romania could not have MFN without Jackson-Vanik. The consultations were to agree on the mechanics of the transition to a post-MFN trade relationship. The United States sought to preserve a commercial relationship with Romania and viewed minimizing the impact of the loss of MFN on trade as one purpose of the consultations. Given the nature of the consultations, the Office of the U.S. Trade Representative would chair the U.S. side. Kirk presented all this to Solomonescu, who expressed her disappointment and said that the Romanian side still hoped for a more general political discussion at a later date.

While all this jockeying was going on, the United States was watching for concrete signs on the ground as to how relations between the two countries would develop in the post-renunciation era. The signs were mixed, but troubling overall. A good development was that Liviu Bota was given permission to leave Romania on February 11. Bota was the Romanian U.N. official whom Whitehead had met during his February visit and whose detention in Romania he had criticized in his February 6 press conference. The reason the government allowed Bota to leave may well have been because his case had become a general international embarrassment for Ceauşescu, not just a U.S.-Romanian issue, but the gesture was encouraging. On the other hand, Ion Puiu, a dissident political figure with whom the embassy had been in contact for some time, was imprisoned on February 12 and charged with treason. He was released on March 2 but remained under Securitate surveillance. When the prominent American Jewish leader Alfred Moses visited Romania on March 1 and 2, he was denied his usual appointments with high Romanian officials. Totu not only refused to receive Moses, but instructed Beşteliu and Raceanu that if the American raised MFN during his meeting with them, they should simply ignore the question.

Several embassy contacts showed new reluctance to meet with embassy officers, but the embassy felt this might be due to their own caution in the wake of the MFN announcements and not to any governmental directive. On the other hand, the government hand showed clearly when, during a trip Kirk made in mid-March to Iaşi, a provincial capital some 200 miles north of Bucharest, *all* the county and city officials were "too busy" to receive him. The Orthodox bishop, who had agreed to meet Kirk, was "urgently" called out of town, and his subordinates said they had never heard about the appointment. Two well-known Orthodox churches, fixtures on every tour, were closed, in fact locked up tight, when Kirk and his party went to see them.

Kirk had made an appointment to visit the local Roman Catholic seminary, another showpiece of Ceauşescu's religious tolerance, but this was canceled before Kirk's departure from Bucharest. The Catholic bishop in Bucharest had a subordinate quietly tell Mrs. Kirk after mass at the Bucharest Catholic cathedral that the seminary could not officially receive Kirk but that he would much appreciate it if Kirk would go to the seminary. He said the authorities in Iaşi had told the senior clergy to attend a meeting out of town the day Kirk would be there, but a junior priest would meet Kirk at the seminary and show him one or two of the rooms. This would make the point that the seminary could receive the ambassador in spite of the "advice" given it not to do so. Kirk did visit the seminary and spent about ten minutes there in the company of a very nervous young priest.

During a meeting with Totu in Kirk's absence, Henry Clarke, Kirk's deputy, complained about the treatment being accorded Kirk. Totu reacted angrily. He said U.S. embassy trips outside the capital had assumed the character of inspection tours. The embassy was serving as a representative of American churches and posing as an "inspector" in Romania. It should be promoting good relations but had instead contributed materially to their deterioration. Totu made it clear once again that he wanted foreign embassies in Bucharest to become an instrument of Romanian propaganda, confining their contacts to officials and duly reporting whatever these officials told them about the situation in Romania without making any attempt to verify its accuracy.

The Romanian government took other measures to cut off U.S. embassy access to nonofficial sources. The Department of Religious Affairs summoned the heads of religious denominations in Romania on March 24 to tell them not to agree to appointments with Americans and to refuse to see any Americans who arrived unannounced. The Romanians canceled a previously scheduled appointment for Kirk with the minister of justice, and all embassy officers had trouble obtaining appointments with anyone outside the Foreign Ministry. These measures did not seem to the American side to accord with the Romanian efforts to get the United States to agree to talks to restore MFN, and the restrictions were in fact relaxed some weeks later.

There was considerable byplay within the Romanian government behind its tightening and then relaxing restrictions on the embassy. There was general agreement among the Romanian leadership that it was important to show the United States the price it would pay if MFN was lost. As the Americans seemed to attach so much importance to having access to various levels of Romanian society, in and out of Bucharest, it appeared to the Romanians that a good way to show that loss of MFN would hurt was to limit such access. One group, led by Elena Ceauşescu and Totu, argued that these restrictions should remain until the United States granted unconditional MFN. The other group felt that the restrictions should be imposed to show the United States what it stood to lose if it failed to grant MFN or the equivalent but should be dropped after a brief period to show that Romania in fact wanted good relations. It was the second approach—which accorded more closely with Ceauşescu's belief that he could still get MFN—that won the day, thus accounting for the on-again, off-again restrictions on the embassy.

This same thinking led the Romanians to continue their efforts to appear useful to the United States on international matters. Yasir Arafat visited Bucharest on March 22, 1988, and Totu himself informed the U.S. embassy two days later that Ceauşescu was convinced, on the basis of his conversations with Arafat, that conditions were favorable for progress on peace in the Middle East. Totu said the Romanians would be willing to receive a high-level official from Washington to discuss this question or to send an envoy from Ceauşescu himself to the United States to do so. Kirk responded on April 5 that the Bureau of Near Eastern Affairs at the State Department would be glad to receive such an envoy, but the Romanians replied on April 29 that it was "too late" for such a visit. They had obviously wanted a high-profile trip and forgot their "important" message once they learned that the United States would only receive the envoy at the bureau level.

The question of the prospective talks with the United States on the technical aspects of MFN renunciation was the subject of much discussion within the Romanian government during this period. It was clear that Ceauşescu still hoped to hold a high-level discussion with the United States to find a way to obtain "MFN or the equivalent" for Romania, preferably before Romania's MFN tariff privileges expired at midnight on July 2–3. The Romanians were prepared to agree to the U.S. proposal for technical talks in the meantime, but their principal aim in those discussions would be to lay the groundwork for the later, broader talks.

Heading the Romanian delegation was not a desirable assignment in the eyes of the more sophisticated members of the Romanian bureaucracy. They sensed they would not be able to bring back a U.S. agreement to broader talks such as Ceauşescu desired, and they did not in any case want to be personally associated with what would be seen in Bucharest as tantamount to the demise of MFN. Given that a high official from the Office of the U.S. Trade Representative would head the U.S. delegation at the talks, the appropriate Romanian delegation leader would have been the deputy minister of foreign trade responsible for the United States, Nicolae Andrei. He and others argued, however, that the delegation's principal mission—to secure agreement on broader talks— was more political than economic, so the delegation leader should be from the Foreign Ministry.

State Secretary Duma, the logical choice in that ministry, wanted no part of the operation. He persuaded Ceauşescu that Solomonescu, as the senior Foreign Ministry official responsible for U.S. affairs, should head the delegation. Solomonescu, who was a much less experienced, less sophisticated bureaucrat than the others, was thrilled at the "honor" of representing Romania. When she told Raceanu that he was to accompany her, she said with great pride that Ceauşescu himself had picked her. The U.S. embassy thought that Solomonescu was a curious choice, given her overall ignorance of trade and legal matters. They believed, however, that she and her associates from the Foreign and Trade ministries could accomplish the relatively simple technical job the United States envisaged.

The Romanians instructed the members of their delegation to seek a suspension, not a termination, of MFN as of midnight on July 2–3 and to reach agreement on measures to avoid or compensate for the increase in U.S. tariffs that would follow. As Solomonescu and Beşteliu later told Raceanu, Ceauşescu himself—in a meeting with First Deputy Prime Minister Gheorghe Oprea, Deputy Prime Minister Ştefan Andrei, Ioan Totu, Ilie Vaduva, Iulian Vlad, Olimpia Solomonescu, and Ion Beşteliu on March 27—said that the team was to make it clear that Romania had undertaken no formal obligation on emigration at the time it received MFN. It had merely said Romania was ready to settle "humanitarian problems on the basis of mutual confidence and good will," which it had done and would continue to do. The delegation should encourage American companies doing business with Romania to lobby Congress and the administration to renew MFN and should press them, if they were not successful before July 3, to absorb to the degree possible any additional tariff that would result from the lapse of MFN. Solomonescu and Beşteliu both told Raceanu that they felt Ceauşescu was convinced that the Reagan administration, despite its rapprochement with Gorbachev, would want to support a Warsaw Pact country with an independent attitude toward Moscow and that "something would work out" on MFN before July 3.

Ceauşescu also told the delegation to explain that Romanian citizens enjoyed many basic human rights and to complain that the U.S. administration and the Congress encouraged activities in the United States hostile toward Romania. The basic message was to be that Romania wanted good relations with the United States and was prepared to work to that end, but it was not ready to make any concessions on internal economic or human rights questions.

Solomonescu's discussions in Washington on handling the mechanics of MFN went well, with both sides agreeing quickly on "suspension" of the portion of Article I of the bilateral trade agreement that covered MFN, leaving the rest of the agreement intact. The Romanians, however, sought a number of trade concessions to "compensate" for the higher duties. The U.S. side took the position that any possibility that the United States would compensate Romania for its decision to renounce MFN was extremely limited, although the United States would study the Romanian proposals.

Solomonescu's principal discussion at the State Department was with Assistant Secretary for European Affairs Rozanne Ridgway. Solomonescu stressed her government's desire for a second, more senior round of talks and for an early meeting of the cabinet-level U.S.-Romanian Joint Economic Commission. She mentioned only briefly, and then in softened form, the Romanian criticism of U.S. behavior contained in her instructions. Ridgway responded that the United States wanted good relations with Romania but that this would depend in large measure on Romania's actions on matters such as human rights and emigration, matters the United States still considered a very important part of the bilateral relationship. She expressed official U.S. concern over the limitations on U.S. embassy access to nonofficials and cancellation or limitation of American exhibits and exchange programs.

Solomonescu also met with John Whitehead. During their brief talk he welcomed the fact that the two sides were "suspending," not terminating, MFN, as the United States wanted more trade and investment with Romania. He noted that human rights in Romania were, however, still a matter of prime U.S. concern.

Solomonescu's March 30 meeting with the National Security Council staff member responsible for the Soviet Union and Eastern Europe provided an illustrative example of how a bureaucracy does or does not work in a regime like Ceauşescu's. The NSC staffer raised the case of Romanian opera singer Leontina Vaduva, who had a contract to sing the lead in *Manon* at the Houston opera very shortly. She had been scheduled to begin rehearsals there on March 28, but the Romanian authorities had withdrawn her passport the day before she was to leave Bucharest. As Vice President Bush, whose hometown was Houston, was personally interested in the case, the NSC staffer asked Solomonescu to use her good offices to resolve the problem. Solomonescu was not familiar with the matter, she said, but she was sure it was a "misunderstanding" and would communicate with Bucharest about it that very afternoon.

After the interview, however, she told Raceanu that the singer was probably a relative of then Foreign Trade Minister Ilie Vaduva (it turned out she was not) and that it was Elena Ceauşescu who decided such cases. Solomonescu therefore preferred not to intervene in the case from Washington, but would look into it once she returned to Bucharest. This meant in effect she would do nothing, for by that time it would be too late for Leontina Vaduva to make her scheduled appearance.

Solomonescu was very anxious to show her own performance on this important trip in the best possible light to her superiors in Bucharest. She therefore instructed Raceanu and the other drafters of the telegraphic reports to incorporate in the comments they attributed to her the full text of her instructions, including those harsh and critical words that she had downplayed or even omitted. She counted on this to deflect any criticism in Bucharest that she had not been tough enough on the United States. She also wanted to make it appear that she had achieved the objectives set out for her and insisted that the reports indicate that the United States had shown interest in a follow-up dialogue, thereby implying that the United States might agree to the Romanian proposal for a high-level meeting, despite Raceanu's protest to her that the State Department and the NSC had shown no such willingness.

At the insistence of Ion Chioveanu, head of the Americas directorate in the Ministry of Foreign Trade, and Teodor Ripan, head of the Romanian commercial office in New York, Solomonescu also had the final summary report put the most favorable possible light on the U.S. comments that it was prepared to "study" the Romanian requests for commercial concessions to compensate partially for the loss of MFN. Even more serious, this report, which she delivered in Bucharest, omitted virtually any reference to the U.S. comments about human rights. The net impression was not that the U.S. side had been tough, but that the case for renewal was not yet lost.

Totu presented the summary report to Ceauşescu on the day of the delegation's return, April 4, and Ceauşescu informed the party's Political Executive Committee that same day that the delegation had fulfilled its mandate. Solomonescu's prestige and influence within the bureaucracy increased notably as a result, even though subsequent events showed her reports to have been much too optimistic.

Solomonescu's reports reinforced the belief of Ceauşescu and his associates that the United States put so much value on the Romanian relationship that it would find a way to preserve MFN or its equivalent, probably before July 3, and that it would take measures to compensate for at least some of the extra duties levied on Romanian exports if MFN expired before the new arrangement took effect. It certainly appears that Ceauşescu believed Reagan could give him MFN if he wanted to do so. One evidence of this mistaken belief was that Ceauşescu long withheld approval of the text of the technical agreement suspending MFN, even though it had been worked out during the Solomonescu trip and the U.S. embassy had presented a final text to the ministry on April 6.

Other evidence was in Ceauşescu's remarks to a large group of Americans involved in trade with Romania whom the Romanian government had invited to Bucharest in early May to discuss U.S.-Romanian trade opportunities and MFN. A principal Romanian purpose in arranging the visit was to interest these business representatives in the opportunities for trade if MFN were preserved and to persuade them to lobby the U.S. government and Congress for its continuance. The party was led by Robert Robertson, vice president of Occidental Petroleum and American Businesses for International Trade, the previously mentioned group interested in promoting trade with Romania. The Romanian authorities also wanted to show Romanian and international public opinion that American businesspeople engaged in trade with Romania were not happy with the possibility of losing MFN, and that the whole situation was created by U.S. insistence on issues that, in Romanian opinion, had nothing to do with trade and economic cooperation.

That Ceausescu met with this group on May 4 accompanied by Manea Manescu (vice president of the Council of State), Gheorghe Oprea (first deputy prime minister), Ştefan Andrei (deputy prime minister), Barbu Petrescu (mayor of Bucharest), and several members of the cabinet was evidence of the group's importance to the Romanian authorities. Ceauşescu emphasized to the visitors that the text of the agreement on Romania's MFN termination had not yet been signed and that there was still a possibility of transforming it into an agreement that would maintain, not suspend, MFN and do so without imposing Jackson-Vanik conditions. He noted that there were still two months before July 3 in which to accomplish this and asked the business representatives for their support with the U.S. government. That and other portions of the speech seemed truly to reflect Ceauşescu's views at the time, particularly his conviction that he could still have MFN without the Jackson-Vanik conditions.[110]

The Romanians did not limit their campaign to businesspeople. On May 6 Solomonescu told Kirk that the Romanian government was looking for ways other than MFN with Jackson-Vanik to approach the U.S.-Romanian trade relationship and that it would like to send a delegation to Washington to clear up the question before the expiration of MFN in early July. Kirk asked if the purpose of the delegation was to discuss keeping MFN without Jackson-Vanik. He said he thought that the U.S. government had clearly indicated during her visit to Washington that MFN was finished. The two sides had even agreed on the text formalizing the end of MFN. All that remained was to sign it. Solomonescu said the delegation would want to discuss the whole complex of U.S.-Romanian relations. The Romanian government expected that the business representatives who had heard Ceauşescu two days before would be in touch with the U.S. government and that the United States might come up with "other variants" to resolve the MFN problem. Even if it was not possible for Washington to receive a Romanian delegation before the deadline, the Romanian government would like a delegation to go as soon as possible after that time.

Ştefan Andrei, acting in his capacity as deputy prime minister responsible for foreign trade, summoned Kirk three days later to reinforce the government's point. He said that President Ceauşescu would like the secretaries of state and commerce to receive a Romanian envoy with the rank of deputy prime minister before the end of June to discuss bilateral and international matters of mutual interest. He would also like President Reagan to receive the envoy, who would have a letter from Ceauşescu to present to Reagan. Andrei hinted that he himself would be the envoy. Kirk agreed to report what Andrei had said but then proceeded to review some of the current problems in the relationship. He told Andrei about his May 6 conversation with Solomonescu and said he hoped the Romanian government understood that there was no chance of MFN without Jackson-Vanik. Andrei said he realized that the United States could not give MFN without Jackson-Vanik; he added that MFN would not be the focus of the special envoy's trip.

Andrei's May 9 demarche was all the more interesting because it followed a meeting he had had with Raceanu a few days before, when he had asked Raceanu how the Solomonescu trip had gone and what the chances were for MFN renewal. Raceanu reported to Andrei that the technical talks had gone well, but that there was no realistic possibility of retaining MFN. Seeing the astonishment on Andrei's face, Raceanu motioned toward the telephone as a signal that he wanted to tell Andrei something confidential. Andrei took Raceanu to the middle of the room and in a low voice told him that they would not be overheard there.

Raceanu, looking Andrei in the eye, said softly that the Washington trip had convinced him that the United States "wanted nothing more to do with Ceauşescu." "What?" Andrei asked. "The Americans want nothing more to do with 'the comrade'?" "Yes," replied Raceanu. "They cannot stand him any more because of the internal situation in Romania, and I think they are right." Both men fell silent. Andrei gave Raceanu a kiss on the forehead and escorted him to the door. Raceanu has since wondered if he went too far, not in reporting the American attitude but in saying he shared it.

This series of conversations and statements convinces Kirk and Raceanu that Ceauşescu really believed, as he told the American business group, that he could obtain MFN without Jackson-Vanik and also that he might well be able to make the necessary arrangements before July 3.

Furthermore, it appears from Raceanu's conversation with Andrei that even such a relatively sophisticated member of the inner circle as Andrei was sincerely surprised to hear that MFN was gone for good. The optimistic reports the Romanian leaders had been receiving were partly to blame. These reports nurtured their illusions. But the trouble also stemmed from the belief of all of them, except perhaps Andrei, that Reagan, like Ceauşescu, could do anything he wanted. It did not matter if there was a legal obstacle. They felt the American president, like the Romanian one, could ignore the law, or, if necessary, instruct the legislature to change it. The Romanians simply did not understand that the U.S. president is not above the law and that Reagan's power in the United States was much more limited than Ceauşescu's in Romania. They sincerely believed that if Reagan would not grant MFN or the equivalent, it was because he did not wish to do so, not because he was unable to.

On May 18, Kirk told Solomonescu that the United States saw no alternative to suspending MFN, as agreed during her visit. Washington considered the matter settled. Furthermore, the United States would not be seeking ways to "compensate" Romania for higher, post-MFN, tariffs. He also said that in response to Andrei's suggestion the United States was looking into the question of a visit at the level of deputy prime minister, but that it was not likely June would be possible. Solomonescu looked grim. When Kirk went on to raise human rights and emigration, Solomonescu told him that the United States could not expect the same Romanian response to such demarches as under MFN. A written report of Kirk's comments went as usual to Totu; he shared it with the Securitate but forwarded nothing written to Ceauşescu.

Neither Kirk nor Raceanu know if Totu told Ceauşescu orally about the Kirk-Solomonescu meeting. It is doubtful in any case that he reported its full flavor, as further evidence surfaced that Ceauşescu had still not accepted the inevitable. A week after Kirk's conversation with Solomonescu, Silviu Brucan told U.S. political counselor Michael Parmly that Ceauşescu still expected to obtain MFN or its equivalent without Jackson-Vanik. The top Romanian leadership, Brucan said, was confused as to what the U.S. position was and wanted to find out just what the United States would need in return for according MFN. As Brucan himself seemed to understand that MFN was dead, it was clear that the Romanian regime was once again using the former ambassador as a channel to get its message to the United States. Parmly repeated to Brucan that MFN was dead.

A further illustration of Romanian misunderstanding of the U.S. scene was Solomonescu's complaint to Kirk about new congressional hearings concerning Romania, in this case on Romanian refugees in Hungary, and about demonstrations taking place outside Romanian government buildings in the United States. Neither could happen, she asserted, without U.S. government approval. The Romanian government was particularly surprised by the hearings, as Totu had specifically told Whitehead he expected no more hearings on Romania after the renunciation of MFN. Kirk responded that Congress had the right to hold hearings on any subject it wished, and the executive branch supported that right. The people were also free to demonstrate peaceably if they wished.

The Romanians soon received another blow when Reagan informed Congress on June 3 that he was renewing most-favored-nation status for Hungary and China but not for Romania.[111] On June 10 the State Department told the embassy in Bucharest to inform Andrei that it was "too soon" after Romania's MFN decision to try to arrange the appointments he had requested. It would be better to wait and see how developments proceeded on the ground in the post-MFN period. Whitehead, however, would be happy to talk with an envoy after the expiration of MFN. U.S. chargé Henry Clarke conveyed the message to Andrei on June 15. Finally, on June 22, Solomonescu and Kirk signed the agreement suspending MFN at a brief meeting in the Foreign Ministry not reported in the Romanian media. Romania ceased to enjoy most-favored-nation tariff privileges as of midnight, July 2–3, 1988. The MFN era was over.[112]

Meanwhile events in Romania and beyond its borders were making Ceauşescu ever more objectionable in American eyes. The story of the following year is one of continuing deterioration of an already poor relationship.

▾11▾

From Bad to Worse
1988

The year following Romania's loss of most-favored-nation status saw a further deterioration of U.S.-Romanian relations, partly because of the loss of MFN but primarily for two more basic reasons: Ceauşescu's repressive internal policies became increasingly offensive to the United States, while his independent foreign policy was becoming decreasingly important. As Gorbachev adopted many of the "heretical" foreign policy positions long held by Ceauşescu, and as Gorbachev's open acceptance of divergence within the Warsaw Pact made Ceauşescu's independence much less significant, Romanian divergence from the liberalizing developments sweeping through the other members of the Soviet camp became ever more unattractive in American eyes.

The contrast was most striking in internal affairs. Ceauşescu continued to reject moves toward introduction of "capitalist norms" in his country and to criticize them in other nations, including some of his Warsaw Pact allies. In his frantic effort to pay off Romania's foreign debt before the middle of 1989, he turned the economic screws ever tighter on his people. He continued with the "reconstruction" of Romanian towns, especially Bucharest. Building and wrecking crews worked around the clock on the broad "Boulevard of the Victory of Socialism" and the huge "Palace of the People" at its end, tearing down dwellings, churches, and monuments that stood in the way.

When the city authorities notified a family that its dwelling was on the list to be demolished, they promised to provide another alert before the wreckers actually came. Only then would the family learn where its new dwelling would be. A week, a month, or a year later, the family would receive word that demolition would begin shortly, sometimes the next day, and that family members should take their belongings at once to their new abode, the address of which was given only at this point. The residents would remove as many of their possessions as they could from their dwelling before it was demolished and could often be seen still carrying furniture and other possessions out of one side of the building as the bulldozers began razing the other. In some cases the authorities charged families for the service of destroying their dwelling or graciously allowed them to do it themselves at no charge. Foreigners in Bucharest and other areas reported on this process, with further damage to Ceauşescu's international reputation.

Even more horrifying was Ceauşescu's plan to replace Romania's villages with apartment complexes. Although he had alluded to this idea for several years, it was only in March 1988 that he spelled out the program, ordered it to be launched in earnest, and projected its completion by the year 2000. He said it would entail the disappearance of some 7,000 to 8,000 of Romania's 13,000 villages and the transfer of their inhabitants to 5,000 to 6,000 semi-urban centers. This would, he said, free up more land for cultivation and provide more modern, urbanlike living conditions for the rural population.[113] The first such complexes to be built, a few miles from Bucharest, showed what these "modern, urbanlike" living conditions would be. None of the buildings had central heating, and few had indoor plumbing. They were sterile, two- and three-story blocks for four or five families, usually with small muddy areas in between containing new concrete outhouses and sometimes space to keep an animal or two.

While Ceauşescu's program promised a tragedy for all rural dwellers, the Hungarian government made a special point of the program's effect on the ethnic Hungarian villages in Romania and set about awakening the world to its evils. U.S. human rights groups and the U.S. Congress picked up the theme, and "systematization," as Ceauşescu called it, soon became an important subject in official U.S. and other Western discussions with the Romanians. The international outcry helped limit the program's implementation to only a few areas before Ceauşescu's overthrow, although the primary reasons for this fortunate result were the immense resources called for by the plan and foot-dragging by local officials more conscious than Ceauşescu of the disastrous economic and social consequences of the program.

Given the deteriorating conditions of life in Romania and Ceauşescu's plan to push his pet programs ahead at whatever cost, it was not surprising that the Romanian government was reluctant to admit responsible Western journalists, although this refusal resulted in still more bad publicity for the country. Deputy Foreign Minister Traian Pop, acting in July 1988 for Solomonescu (who was on leave), was quite open with U.S. Assistant Secretary of State for Humanitarian Affairs Richard Schifter. Journalists who "distort" and "denigrate" Romanian reality "have no place here," Pop said. Visiting journalists should write about Romania's achievements, not about its problems.

That same month *Time* corespondent Kenneth Banta gained entry to Romania by obtaining a tourist visa at the Bucharest airport, having received no reply to his earlier written request for a correspondent's visa. But the Romanian press agency, Agerpres, refused to arrange any appointments for him with officials, and the Securitate harassed him throughout his stay, confiscating his film on three separate occasions. Upon his departure, the Romanian government's press liaison office nevertheless told him he should write "positive" articles about his stay in Romania and complained to the embassy when he did not. When embassy officers tried to explain to Romanian officials the damage the government was doing to its image by such treatment of journalists and violations of common norms of press freedom, the officials merely repeated their standard line or indicated, by a roll of their eyes, that they understood but could do nothing about it.

The deterioration of Romania's reputation was not limited to the United States. The West European governments, especially the British, French, and Dutch, had generally given human rights violations less prominence in their official discussions with Romanians than had the United States but now began to stress this theme in their talks with the Romanian government and in some of their public comments.

Indeed it was not only the Western nations that were turning away from Ceauşescu. Hungary's relations with Romania, badly strained for a year or more over the treatment of the ethnic Hungarian minority in Transylvania, worsened as Hungary itself moved down the reformist path. Reform of any sort and of any dimension in a communist country was anathema to Ceauşescu, but he was especially outraged that increased freedom of expression in Hungary made it possible for the Hungarian press to criticize his regime and even call for cession of Transylvania to Hungary.

The climax came when a massive demonstration in Budapest on June 27 sounded both themes. This demonstration was in fact an unprecedented event, as never before in Eastern Europe had one member of the Warsaw Pact permitted a demonstration against another. Ceauşescu reacted swiftly. He publicly attacked "Horthyist" (fascist) tendencies in Hungary, described the demonstration as "chauvinistic" and "antisocialist," and ordered the Hungarians to close their consulate at Cluj-Napoca in Transylvania and their cultural center in Bucharest.[114]

The Romanians were having their problems with the Soviets as well. As Gorbachev and Ceauşescu moved in opposite directions in their internal policies, their respective public criticisms of "old thinking" and "deviation from socialism" could be taken, inter alia, as attacks on each other. At the same time, Romania's economy was becoming increasingly dependent on the Soviet Union, which provided virtually all of Romania's natural gas, more than half of its crude oil, and much of its electricity, iron ore, and coking coal. Ceauşescu was nevertheless resisting Gorbachev's efforts to enhance communist-bloc economic integration and promote reformist notions such as unsupervised factory-to-factory contacts. The public statements and communiqué on the visit to Bucharest of Soviet president Andrei Gromyko in mid-May 1988 revealed the deeply differing approaches.[115]

Soviet officials explained their government's basic position to Kirk when he visited Moscow in November 1988. Their new policy of non-interference in Eastern Europe meant that they would not try to pressure Ceauşescu, except by their example; but they left no doubt that they would be delighted if he vanished from the scene.

Romania's growing isolation within Europe showed up dramatically in the CSCE negotiations in Vienna in mid-June of that year, when Romania demanded a major revision in the human rights and emigration provisions of the draft final agreement then gaining consensus among the other powers. On July 1, 1988, the French and German foreign ministers bluntly and publicly criticized the stand Romania had taken in Vienna. That stand was also the first point visiting Assistant Secretary Schifter raised in his discussions at the Romanian Foreign Ministry.

▼ ▼ ▼

Meanwhile, the familiar problems of human rights, emigration, and religious issues continued as sources of bilateral contention. Emigration approvals had dropped markedly since the MFN renunciation at the end of February, and there had been no progress in other human rights areas that had looked promising, such as printing more Bibles or providing church buildings for the Adventists. Kirk found a cooler response than before when he raised these issues at the Foreign Ministry.

The Romanians did arrange an appointment with Chief of Staff of the Romanian Armed Forces Ştefan Guşa for U.S. Vice Admiral Kendall E.

Moranville, commander of the U.S. Sixth Fleet, in connection with the annual visit of U.S. navy ships in June. The United States had decided to go through with the visit, and with the admiral's presence, only after some deliberation. Although the United States did not want to be publicly associated with Ceauşescu, the embassy had argued, it should seek to maintain contact with important elements of the Romanian society and power structure.

The military did not figure prominently in Romanian affairs and was starved for resources. Though it appeared to be under Ceauşescu's total control, in the embassy's view it represented a potential source of opposition. It could in any case become an important element in a post-Ceauşescu era. A military-to-military visit might encourage the Romanian officers to view themselves as professional military personnel, not just as slaves of Ceauşescu. In addition, U.S. naval visits to a Warsaw Pact member were still sufficiently rare to make this one a useful example to the other pact nations and a sign that some autonomy was possible even in the military field.

The Romanian side had also debated the desirability of the visit. The Foreign Ministry had argued successfully that it should proceed on grounds that to cancel such a long-standing tradition would simply lead to a further worsening of U.S.-Romanian relations, which Romania did not want.

The Romanians attempted to send the United States a signal of displeasure, however, through the level of their attendance at the U.S. Independence Day reception on July 4. The Romanian government always exercised tight control over attendance at foreign embassy functions. As noted earlier, the protocol department of every government organization had to submit to the Foreign Ministry lists of staff members who had been invited. The ministry could approve or withhold permission for an individual to attend or suggest attendance by someone else. The Securitate then reviewed the Foreign Ministry's recommendations and made any changes it thought desirable. Then the Foreign Ministry informed the concerned organization about the decision.

For national day receptions—occasions hosted by embassies everywhere on each country's chosen national holiday—Ceauşescu himself decided the level of attendance, based on a recommendation from the Foreign Ministry after review by the Securitate. In the case of the U.S. Fourth of July reception in 1988, Raceanu's department prepared a note for Ceauşescu suggesting attendance at the same levels as in the past. Totu, however, reduced the number of suggested high-level attendees before he forwarded the memo to Ceauşescu. The principal attendee was to be a deputy prime minister, not a vice president of the national council or a first deputy prime minister. Only one minister was to go instead of three or four. Totu said he himself should not attend. Ceauşescu approved Totu's recommendation, and Totu also gave instructions to limit severely the number of other Foreign Ministry officials who went.

All this byplay was unknown to the U.S. embassy, which totally missed the "signal" the Romanians were sending. It reported to Washington merely that a deputy prime minister had come and overall attendance was consistent with preceding years, but that Ceauşescu's message on this U.S. national day was more reserved than previously.

One pleasant surprise at the reception was the attendance of former ambassador to the United States Mircea Maliţa, who had not appeared at an American function for years, despite many invitations. Kirk was in fact astounded when, as he was shaking the hands of the 900 guests, a gentleman he had never seen introduced himself as "Ambassador Maliţa." Kirk could hardly believe that this man whom Kirk and others had invited so often was actually in the embassy garden. Kirk managed a "*Very* glad to see you. I hope we can see you again," to which Maliţa replied "I hope so too." Kirk then motioned to one of the embassy staff to pay special attention to Maliţa. Kirk wondered why the Romanian government, which had kept Maliţa away from the embassy for so long, had permitted him to come at this time of particularly tense relations. It turns out that there was no policy decision involved.

The Ministry of Education had as usual sent to the Foreign Ministry the names of its personnel who had received invitations for the U.S. national day reception, but they were late, sending the list only two days before the party. Maliţa, a professor and therefore under the Education Ministry, was one of the four names on the list. The list came as usual to Raceanu for review. Following Totu's instructions to reduce attendance, Raceanu cut two names but left Maliţa's on the list. The protocol office told Raceanu that, in view of the shortness of time and because they trusted Raceanu, they would send the approved names back to the Ministry of Education without passing them through the Securitate.

Raceanu and Maliţa met totally by chance on a public bus the next day. When Raceanu said he looked forward to seeing Maliţa at the U.S. embassy reception, Maliţa said that he had not received permission to attend. Raceanu countered that Maliţa's name was on the approved list sent to the Ministry of Education. Maliţa went to the ministry's protocol office that afternoon to inquire about the matter. The protocol offi-

cials told him they had no permission for him to attend. When he insisted
that his name had been approved, they agreed to check. Three hours later
they said he could attend and gave him his invitation. But for the late-
ness of the Education Ministry's submission to the Foreign Ministry
and the chance encounter with Raceanu, Maliţa would not have gone to
the embassy and Kirk would never have met him, and the Securitate
enforced its usual prohibition on all subsequent invitations to him.

That the Maliţa attendance at the reception was truly a fluke was shown
by more signs of coolness on both sides of the U.S.-Romanian relationship. Several prominent American Jewish leaders came to Bucharest in
connection with the July 6 celebration of Rabbi Moses Rosen's fortieth
anniversary as chief rabbi. At the anniversary celebration, Kirk read aloud
a letter from President Reagan to Rabbi Rosen. The embassy took steps
to insure that the Voice of America and Radio Free Europe broadcast
the text to Romania, hoping that the Romanians would appreciate the
contrast with the lack of any letter from Reagan on Ceauşescu's seven-
tieth birthday a few months before. This distinction apparently did not
make a major impression, however. Raceanu recalls that Romanians in
and out of government had noted and commented privately on the
absence of any birthday message to Ceauşescu from President Reagan,
but that they did not contrast this with Reagan's message to Rosen,
which attracted little attention.

Kirk summed up the bilateral situation in a telegram to Washington
in mid-July and recommended distancing the United States still further
from the Romanian regime. He suggested that the U.S. government be
somewhat more critical of Romanian policies in public and adopt an even
cooler tone in private. He argued that the United States should show less
attention to Romania's international role, send fewer emissaries to
Bucharest to discuss foreign policy, and hold off on high-level meetings.
He suggested that the basic U.S. line should be that it was Romanian
actions in the human rights field, in international affairs, and on MFN that
had worsened relations. The United States was willing to have better relations, but it was up to the Romanians to take actions to bring this about.

Assistant Secretary of State Schifter took this firm approach when he
visited Bucharest in mid-July. The Romanians had initially hesitated to
agree to his visit. Some officials did not feel it was necessary for Romania
to listen to U.S. complaints about human rights after MFN had ended, and

many ministries were reluctant to arrange appointments for U.S. visitors when this was no longer needed to preserve MFN. Even such a hard-liner as Aurel Duma argued, however, that the government should agree to the visit. He told Raceanu, "Although we know the kind of things Schifter will bring up, we do not have to pay any attention to that," and he pointed out that the Romanians could use the visit to make their own arguments and to demonstrate that the U.S.-Romanian dialogue was continuing.

The Romanians finally agreed to the visit and decided to use it to explain their point of view on two current problems. One was the situation of the Hungarian minority in Romania. The Hungarian issue was very much in the news, and the Romanians feared that the Hungarians were getting the better of them in world opinion. The Romanians decided they would use the Schifter visit to accuse the Hungarians of seeking to slander Romania and even to recover Transylvania. They would urge the United States not to cooperate with these schemes by allowing "irredentist" demonstrations or propaganda by Hungarians in the United States.

The other issue the Romanians wanted to discuss was the case of Dumitru Mazilu, a Romanian diplomat whom the U.N. human rights commission had asked several months earlier to write a report on youth in Romania. The Romanians were convinced that Mazilu's report would not be to their liking, and Raceanu learned that the Securitate had quite illegally opened the diplomatic pouch from the U.N. office in Bucharest to Geneva and found communications from Mazilu that displeased them. The Romanian government therefore forbade Mazilu to return to Geneva or to submit his report there.

When diplomats in Geneva noticed his absence as the weeks went on and requested his return, the Romanians said Mazilu had a heart problem and could not travel. Western embassies in Bucharest, including the U.S. embassy, had stayed in touch with Mazilu, however, and knew he was not ill. The restrictions on his movement soon became an issue in U.N. circles in Geneva and New York.

Kirk and other diplomatic officials in Bucharest mentioned the case to the Romanians several times. The Romanians decided to tell Schifter that Mazilu was a self-important troublemaker, a misfit in society, and even a forger. They hoped thereby to remove his case from the U.S.-Romanian dialogue, but it remained an issue between the two governments until Ceauşescu's fall. (After the revolution in December 1989, Mazilu was briefly the first vice president of the ruling National Salvation Front. He resigned from that position after members of the former *nomenklatura* and the Securitate, unhappy, according to Raceanu's information, with Mazilu's anticommunist position, leaked to the press his connection with the Securitate in the late 1960s.)

In a meeting on July 14 with Deputy Foreign Minister Traian Pop, Schifter took the Romanians to task for their obstructionism in the CSCE negotiations in Vienna. He then went through the whole list of U.S. human rights concerns, including emigration, Mazilu, the Romanian treatment of U.S. journalists, and U.S. embassy access to Romanian officials and nonofficials. Pop gave the standard replies on the issues Schifter raised. He drew on his childhood in Transylvania to explain that Hungarians were happy in Romania and that the minority "problem" was a result of Hungarian government machinations. He went to some lengths to denigrate Mazilu. He cast doubt on the U.S. statements of respect for current frontiers and asked why the U.S. government permitted anti-Romanian activities by Hungary's supporters in America. As usual, the ministry's written report to Ceauşescu on the meeting omitted most of Schifter's complaints on human rights and other matters, saying that the U.S. side had listened carefully to the Romanian arguments.

On August 2, shortly after Kirk returned from consultations in Washington, he thoroughly reviewed U.S.-Romanian relations for Deputy Prime Minister Ştefan Andrei. Kirk relayed the U.S. feeling that there had been a deterioration in U.S.-Romanian relations as a result of Romanian actions on MFN, emigration, human rights, embassy contacts, journalists' trips, and cultural exchanges. He also expressed U.S. concern over the rural systematization program and the economic policies that imposed so much hardship on the Romanian people. He noted that there were new restrictions on access by Romanians to the U.S. Information Service library in Bucharest and on the embassy's access to Romanian religious leaders.

Washington was concerned, Kirk said, that these situations were the result of a deliberate Romanian decision to cool relations, a decision that the increased frequency of Romanian press articles critical of the United States seemed to confirm. The United States continued to respect Romania's independent position on foreign affairs, he added, but positive changes in the attitudes of other Warsaw Pact countries had made Romania's stance relatively less significant. Furthermore, Romania's position in the CSCE negotiations had become a real problem. Kirk concluded by saying that Washington was looking for concrete steps by Romania as a sign that it really did want good relations with the United States.

Andrei, displaying new caution doubtless inspired by the greater tension in U.S.-Romanian relations, excused himself from responding in detail by saying that these were matters for the Foreign Ministry. He went on, however, to state on behalf of President Ceauşescu that Romania did want good relations with the United States. Kirk responded that this was good to hear but recalled the American saying that "actions speak louder than words." The meeting then turned to a relatively businesslike discussion of commercial and trade problems, with Andrei explaining, inter alia, Romania's new conditions for the purchase of Boeing aircraft, conditions that eventually proved unacceptable to the U.S. side.

When reporting the conversation to Washington, the embassy predicted that the details of the talk would reach Ceauşescu, given Andrei's close relationship with him. It recommended deferring action on a high-level Romanian visit while watching for any positive effect Kirk's talk may have had on the problems he had raised.

It turns out that the embassy was probably wrong about Andrei's report. A copy of his written report went to the Foreign Ministry, where Raceanu saw it. It focused largely on the trade portion of the discussion and mentioned in only general terms the human rights issues Kirk had raised. It did not reflect the pessimism of Kirk's comments about the attitude toward Romania in the United States. Andrei may have relayed some of this to Ceauşescu orally, but Raceanu is convinced that Andrei did not tell his boss how downbeat Kirk had been.

Whatever Ceauşescu learned about Kirk's demarche, there was no visible change in Romanian behavior over the next months and thus no U.S. movement on the Romanian suggestion that Washington receive a high-level Romanian envoy. The Romanians for their part showed little interest in a Sense of the Senate resolution on August 10 asking Reagan to tell Ceauşescu that Romania would not get MFN or other trading privileges until it improved its human rights practices and stopped destroying Hungarian villages under the rural systematization plan.[116] The emerging conviction among Romanian officials was that these matters no longer concerned them since the U.S. Congress could no longer vote on MFN for Romania.

There was a sudden flare-up in relations after an incident on August 16. The U.S. embassy's Marine guards, in the course of cleaning house before an inspection by their commanding officer from Frankfurt, inadvertently included in the material they put out for the Romanian trash collectors a few hundred rounds of light weapons ammunition and several cans of Mace, material kept for possible use in the event the embassy was attacked by criminals or demonstrators. The trash collectors, who included Securitate personnel, always screened the trash on the spot before carting it to the dump. Embassy personnel noticed them examining the ammunition and were able to recover most of it, but the Romanians took some away with them.

That very afternoon Totu summoned Kirk to express his "outrage" that the embassy was dumping "weapons" in the garbage. Romanian law, he noted, forbade the importation of arms. The next day he summoned Kirk again. His government had authorized him to state that the embassy stockpiling of arms was a "diversionist" act of a "terrorist" character. He proposed that the embassy give a list of all of its arms to the Romanian government and that a joint Romanian-American team then destroy them. He added that Romania reserved the right to take further measures if the U.S. side did not agree to this proposal.

After consulting the Department of State, the embassy sent a note to the ministry a few days later stating that the material had been thrown out inadvertently. The embassy did not wish to violate Romanian law, but measures to protect embassy property and personnel were within accepted diplomatic procedure, and the embassy intended to continue to exercise that right. Totu then called Kirk in again to reject the note and demand answers to the Romanian charges and proposals, threatening to publicize the matter if the United States did not respond. This did not seem to the United States like a very convincing threat, as publicizing Totu's intemperate remarks would only make him and the Romanian government look ridiculous. The department therefore authorized Kirk to reiterate the previous U.S. position, which he did on September 1. The United States heard nothing more from the Romanians on the matter.

The embassy was quite amused by the importance the foreign minister seemed to attach to a few rounds of ammunition and cans of Mace and ascribed it to his enthusiasm for criticizing the United States in general and the embassy in particular. Raceanu notes, however, that the Securitate had advised the ministry that the arms were clearly in excess of any foreseeable embassy needs, and the Romanian government at first viewed very seriously what it thought was a U.S. program to stockpile arms in the embassy for some unknown purpose. Ceauşescu was informed of the matter and personally instructed Totu what to say to Kirk on both August 16 and 17. More mature reflection on the Romanian side, coupled with the U.S. responses, showed that the matter was not as serious as Romanian officials had first thought, but their initial paranoia pointed up their suspicion of U.S. intentions and the increasingly beleaguered position in which they felt themselves.

Signs of Romania's increasing isolation continued to accumulate through the summer. German foreign minister Hans-Dietrich Genscher sent a letter to Totu in mid-August criticizing rural systematization, which he noted would adversely affect a number of ethnic German villages that had existed in Romania for seven centuries. This letter, which the Germans took pains to publicize, marked a departure from their long-standing low-profile approach to Romania, an approach motivated by the fear that a more aggressive stand would adversely affect the welfare of the roughly 250,000 ethnic Germans still in Romania as well as the emigration of over 15,000 of these each year. The other West European countries were also distancing themselves more publicly from Ceauşescu. In the United States, the House and Senate, citing "deteriorating" human and worker rights in Romania, passed legislation in September 1988 that ended Romania's eligibility for programs of the Overseas Private Investment Corporation.[117]

Evidence continued to accumulate of tensions between Romania and its neighbors as well: with Bulgaria over pollution from Romanian factories on the Danube frontier, with Yugoslavia over water rights, with Poland over trade, and with the Soviet Union over reform. Romania's relations were particularly stormy with Hungary, notwithstanding high-level bilateral meetings to improve them, including a meeting between Ceauşescu and Hungarian party and government leader Karoly Grosz on August 28.

Meanwhile there was increasing evidence of dissidence within Romania itself. Doina Cornea, a brave and persistent critic of the Ceauşescu regime, addressed two open letters to Ceauşescu during the summer on rural systematization, the lack of religious freedom, and the Ceauşescu personality cult. The embassy transmitted the letters to Radio Free Europe, which broadcast them back to Romania. Cornea's continuing critical writings and statements to Western media from her home in Cluj-Napoca were the subject in equal measure of Romanian government wrath and Western attention until the very end of Ceauşescu's rule. Romanian efforts to block attempts by Western ambassadors to maintain contact with her and sometimes to visit her resulted in several nasty incidents, including one where the Securitate manhandled the British ambassador and his wife at the entrance to Cornea's home.

Another brave writer and poet, Ana Blandiana, included in a book for children a story about a cat who was so wonderful that traffic stopped when he drove by and the very trees bowed down as he passed. Children gave him flowers on every possible occasion. He eventually took to wearing a crown. In the concluding episode, a mouse said he considered it a privilege to be eaten by him. The book was on sale for 12 days in September before the censors caught up with the allusions to Ceauşescu's cult of personality; meanwhile all of Romania had a good laugh. Blandiana was sent to a small mountain village, under virtual house arrest.

Romanian officialdom continued to grasp for public signs of American favor. It kept urging the desirability of a high-level visit to Washington and hinting that Ştefan Andrei would be the envoy. It implied that the envoy would not come empty-handed and stated that only such a visit could break the logjam in the relationship.

U.S. officials in Bucharest and Washington had weighed this point carefully ever since the Romanians had first proposed the idea of a high-level envoy, but especially after the Romanians said the envoy would be Andrei. American officials respected Andrei and felt he genuinely wanted better U.S.-Romanian relations. They knew that the way Romania worked, only Ceauşescu could move on points of interest to the United States, but they thought he might use Andrei to convey such concessions. They also considered Andrei the best channel for getting a message back to Ceauşescu short of having an American deliver it directly to the dictator. Thus there were good reasons to permit an Andrei visit. On the other hand, recent high-level meetings seemed to have accomplished nothing beyond reinforcing Romania's contention that it had a close and friendly relationship with the United States. The United States therefore continued to condition any Andrei trip on Romania's taking concrete steps to improve relations in advance.

Although, hypothetically, Andrei would have been a good envoy—the United States had some confidence in him and he would report more accurately than most to Ceauşescu—he had no power of decision. There was no way he could decide on concessions to the United States or even promise that they would be forthcoming. Only Ceauşescu could make such concessions, and he was not prepared to do so. Thus, in Raceanu's judgment, an Andrei trip would have proved as fruitless as had previous high-level contacts.

A similar dilemma for the United States arose in connection with the possibility of a visit to Romania by Deputy Secretary John Whitehead in the first part of October. The Department of State informed Bucharest and other East European embassies in early September that Whitehead was thinking of a trip to all the countries of Eastern Europe in October and that planning should begin. Western countries were staying away from Ceauşescu, however, and no other Western official as high-ranking as Whitehead had visited Romania in 1988.

Kirk therefore sent a message for Whitehead's personal attention urging that he omit Bucharest. Kirk noted, "In Romania, at least, the visit and meeting would be taken as a gesture to Ceauşescu and a boost to his prestige." He pointed out that the Romanians never committed Ceauşescu in advance to a meeting with a visitor other than a chief of state. If Whitehead came, he would be in the position of awaiting Ceauşescu's decision whether to grant him an audience; and "that is not the posture the United States, or the deputy secretary personally, should be in vis-à-vis one of the world's most objectionable dictators."

Kirk also observed that the result of the visit, given the tough message he was sure Whitehead would deliver and the lack of flexibility on the Romanian side, would only worsen relations. He argued that the United States could avoid all this by omitting Bucharest from Whitehead's itinerary, the omission itself indicating clearly what the United States thought of Ceauşescu. If the United States wanted to hold a dialogue at the deputy-secretary level, Kirk argued, it could do so in Washington, where Ceauşescu himself would not be involved.

Whitehead replied that he felt the visit was appropriate "to forestall any misinterpretation about U.S. policy and to convey our strong objections to Ceauşescu's policies at the highest possible level." He wanted to avoid having the United States appear "to be the ones responsible for the deteriorating bilateral relationship" and argued that omitting Bucharest from a trip that included all the other East European capitals would give just such an appearance. He told Kirk, however, to inform the Romanians that he would visit Bucharest only if they would confirm a meeting with Ceauşescu in advance.

When Kirk delivered the message to the Foreign Ministry that Whitehead would visit Bucharest in early October if he could be sure of seeing Ceauşescu, the ministry immediately noted a scheduling problem, because Ceauşescu was slated to visit Moscow and Beijing in October. After checking with Ceauşescu, the ministry told the embassy that although the president was busy during the proposed period, his schedule would be more flexible after October 20. The United States replied that Whitehead's program would make a late

October date impossible, and he would thus have to forgo a visit to Romania on this trip.

Kirk breathed a sigh of relief, as did Totu, who felt that the less Romania had to do with the United States, the better. To Totu's surprise, however, Ceauşescu reviewed the matter again when he heard the U.S. response and instructed the ministry to inform the embassy that Whitehead could come October 10–12 or October 24–28. Upon receiving this information, Kirk asked if it meant that Ceauşescu would receive Whitehead. "That is why he reanalyzed his schedule," was the reply. Whitehead accepted the new Romanian invitation, and the two sides fixed the visit for October 9–10.

Raceanu believes that several factors motivated Ceauşescu's move. One was that a visit from the deputy secretary of state of the United States, coming just after Ceauşescu's trip to Moscow and just before his visit to Beijing, would fit in perfectly with Ceauşescu's desire to appear as a world-class statesman. It would be a real coup de theatre for domestic and world opinion, confirming that the United States, as well as the Soviet Union and China, wished to consult with him. On the other hand, if Bucharest were the only East European capital Whitehead omitted, it would be another clear signal that Ceauşescu's international standing was falling. Furthermore, Ceauşescu had made almost a hobby of relations with the United States, and his pride was such that he was confident he could present Romania's case better than anyone else, with possibly favorable results for U.S.-Romanian relations.

Agreement on the date of Whitehead's visit did not remove the question marks over it, however. The Department of State informed the U.S. embassy that the October 6 press announcement of Whitehead's East European trip noted that in each country Whitehead would "stress the importance which we attach to the protection of human rights" and "meet religious leaders and representatives of a broad cross-section of society." The Foreign Ministry summoned a U.S. embassy representative that very day to say that the ministry was aware of the announcement and did not agree that Whitehead was coming to discuss human rights and meet religious and other nonofficial persons. They assumed that the reference to meeting such persons did not apply to Romania, as the embassy had not asked the Foreign Ministry to set up any such meetings. They also noted that (contrary to protocol and Romanian custom) the Romanian government would not be able to host any official social event for Whitehead. In reporting all this, the embassy recommended that the United States respond that it would not be possible for Whitehead to come unless he had advance assurances that he could meet with nonofficial Romanians.

Whitehead replied the next day that he did not want to appear to be threatening not to visit Bucharest. The embassy should simply tell the Foreign Ministry that it had invited nonofficial persons to meet Whitehead, that Whitehead hoped to make a drive into the country, and that he planned to hold a press conference. It should add that Whitehead did not expect to publicize his meetings with nonofficial persons and that he did not use press conferences to create controversy but to answer questions honestly. The purpose of his trip was to improve relations, not to embarrass the Romanian government. When Kirk conveyed this to Solomonescu on October 8, she made no comment except to say that Whitehead should discuss fundamentals, not details (that is, human rights matters), during his talks in Bucharest. After the meeting Raceanu noted to Kirk as the two walked down the corridor of the ministry, away from the Securitate microphones, that there was no telling what Totu would do next, as he was "furious" at the text of the U.S. press announcement.

Totu would have been yet more furious if he had been aware of Whitehead's answer to a question at his October 6 background briefing for the foreign press in Washington as to why he was going to Romania. He said that the United States desired to improve relations with Romania, though this would be a difficult task. Human rights would be first on his agenda, and he would also discuss emigration, divided families, religious problems, economic deprivation of the Romanian people, rural systematization, and other matters. In a separate, on-the-record comment to a Hungarian journalist, he characterized Romania's policies as "reprehensible."

Whitehead told the Romanian chargé, Dan Dumitru, in a meeting on October 4, that relations were not in good shape. Whitehead said some of his associates thought that the gravity of the situation made a visit to Bucharest untimely, but he had decided to go. He hoped to have a low-key, nonconfrontational visit, but he would want to discuss human rights, trade, and CSCE. The chargé's report to Bucharest emphasized Whitehead's more positive comments and played down his references to the bad state of relations and to his intention to discuss human rights matters. Thus the meeting did not raise additional apprehensions in Bucharest about Whitehead's visit but served rather as one more example of the difficulty of communicating frankly with the Romanian government.

Whitehead arrived in Bucharest a little after 1:00 P.M. on October 9, accompanied by Thomas Simons, a deputy assistant secretary of state for

European affairs, and other officials. He went straight to a luncheon for nonofficial Romanians at Kirk's residence. The Securitate had once more prevented guests from attending; out of six Romanians invited, only one came. Once again it was civil rights lawyer Nelu Prodan, whom an embassy officer brought in his car.

Kirk had arranged a visit after lunch to a monastery about ten miles from Bucharest. As the U.S. party, accompanied by a Romanian government security detail, turned off the main highway toward the monastery, they saw a sign saying the road they had planned to take was barred to foreigners. Kirk consulted with the Romanian security detail, who suggested an alternative route a few miles up the main highway. Kirk was quite surprised, but delighted, at the suggestion. He knew it would take Whitehead right by two villages that the Romanians were in the process of demolishing in connection with the rural systematization program. In fact, the embassy had originally considered using this route for Whitehead but decided it would probably be barred.

Shortly after the caravan turned off the main highway, the Americans saw a sign with the name Vladiceasca. All that remained of the village of Vladiceasca, however, was barren ground, a sidewalk, and gaps in the walk where there had been driveways to houses. A little farther on, the party saw another village, Ciofliceni, in the process of demolition. A few walls were still standing, but most were down. Rubble littered the ground. A bulldozer stood idly in the field on that Sunday afternoon. A middle-aged peasant woman was picking through the remains of what had obviously been her house. It was hard to conceive of a more dramatic picture of the horror that Ceaușescu wanted to perpetrate over the whole of Romania. The entire Whitehead party fell silent for several minutes, looking at each other in virtual disbelief. A bit farther on were the replacements for the villages: poorly constructed, monolithic, three-story apartment houses, looking already like unsightly tenements. The party proceeded without further incident to the monastery, where they had a pleasant visit.

Immediately upon returning to Bucharest, Whitehead met with Totu. Whitehead began by saying that on his first visit in late 1986 he had asked the Romanians if they wanted to improve relations. They had said yes, but had developed no program for doing so by his second visit in February 1988. During the latter visit he had outlined U.S. concerns on human rights, and the Romanians had renounced MFN. Relations had deteriorated further since then. What exactly did the Romanians want?

Totu replied that the Romanians wanted an improvement in relations. They had invited Reagan to visit, but he had not done so. They had proposed sending a presidential envoy to Washington in 1987 and Totu had asked to see Shultz at the United Nations, but no satisfactory answer was received in either instance. After MFN renunciation, they had proposed sending a deputy prime minister to Washington and again had received no answer. The United States had withdrawn GSP and refused to hold Joint Economic Commission meetings at cabinet level. It had used information from foreign sources of bad faith (meaning Hungarians) to criticize Romania.

Totu's list of complaints showed that the Romanians were once again casting relations largely in terms of high-level visits. The United States, however, was focusing on concrete developments on the ground. Whitehead therefore continued the exchange by saying the way to improve relations would be for the two sides to identify areas of agreement and then move on to tackle other, more difficult, areas. Human rights was the most important such issue for the United States, along with emigration. He asked Kirk to explain the current situation. Kirk went at some length through the usual issues of emigration, family reunification, minority rights, rural systematization, economic deprivation, and religious freedom.

Totu said Kirk had spoken from his "traditional position" and that he could not agree with it. As the presentation proceeded, Totu disputed a number of Kirk's points. At one stage in the course of his remarks, Totu said that no villages had been destroyed in the process of rural systematization, a comment particularly striking to the Americans in light of the remains of villages they had seen two hours earlier.

Kirk went on to cover commercial and cultural exchange issues, and Whitehead observed that Romania did not seem to be interested in American investment. Deputy Assistant Secretary Thomas Simons then spoke about U.S. problems with Romanian obstructionism at the CSCE conference in Vienna.

Then Whitehead, noting that Totu had made a number of personal attacks on Kirk, spoke warmly of Kirk's abilities and pointed out that as the U.S. ambassador, Kirk spoke for the president. The Romanians should listen to Kirk more carefully if they wanted to understand U.S. policy. Totu responded with even more attacks on Kirk, which Whitehead also rejected.

Totu then asked Whitehead about the content of the message he was bringing Ceaușescu from Reagan. Whitehead replied that he did not have such a message. This considerably surprised the Romanian side, for Whitehead had brought a letter from Reagan when he visited in February, and the Romanians assumed that he would not have pressed to see

Ceaușescu on this occasion unless he had another special presidential communication to deliver, orally if not in writing. Totu reacted to Whitehead's statement by saying that if Whitehead had no message from Reagan for Ceaușescu, there was no apparent reason for Whitehead to meet the Romanian president. Whitehead said that he wanted to discuss the Middle East and the two countries' relations with the Soviet Union with Ceaușescu, but Totu objected that U.S. relations with the Soviet Union were not Romania's business. There was nothing more to say about Romania's relations with the Soviet Union beyond what was in the joint communiqué issued at the end of Ceaușescu's visit to Moscow earlier that week. As for the Middle East, the United States should after so much time be well aware of Romania's position.

Whitehead rejoined that he had never claimed to have a message from Reagan and would be disappointed and surprised if Ceaușescu did not receive him after having given assurances that he would do so. Whitehead had discussed his trip with Reagan. He was Reagan's principal adviser on East European affairs. If Ceaușescu was truly interested in improving relations with the United States, Whitehead was the person to whom he should talk. Totu said he would inform Ceaușescu of Whitehead's comments, but the Romanian position was as Totu had stated it. After the American party left, Totu told the Romanians that Whitehead had come "with empty hands. 'The comrade' will decide whether to receive him." Solomonescu asked if she should attend Kirk's dinner for Whitehead that evening. "Yes," said Totu. "You go and see what the Americans have to say."

Solomonescu was in fact the most senior Romanian government representative at the dinner. In what was clearly a calculated snub, neither Totu nor Duma, Whitehead's opposite number, attended, and the representative of the Ministry of Commerce was only the head of the Americas directorate there, Ion Chioveanu. Parliamentary vice chairman Marin Ivașcu attended, as did Rabbi Moses Rosen and Professor Mihnea Gheorghiu. Rosen told Kirk later that the government's Department of Religious Affairs had urged him not to go and had told him that the Orthodox, Roman Catholic, and Baptist invitees would not be there. Rosen ignored the department's "advice," but the other religious figures stayed away, even though two of them had sent acceptances before being contacted by Securitate.

After dinner Kirk accompanied the Whitehead party to their rooms in the Intercontinental Hotel. When they started a discussion as to what action to take, Kirk suggested they go to the embassy, as any discussion in the hotel room was certainly being taped and was probably on Securitate video as well. The American visitors, somewhat nonplussed at the thought of being in a Securitate movie, quickly agreed.

At the embassy, Kirk and one or two of Whitehead's party urged Whitehead to leave Bucharest early the next morning without waiting to see if Ceauşescu would receive him. They argued it was undignified and improper for Whitehead, as a very senior U.S. official, to be cooling his heels in Bucharest awaiting the pleasure of a reviled dictator like Ceauşescu, especially in view of Totu's insulting comments earlier. Whitehead disagreed, saying that he had come to deliver a message to Ceauşescu and wanted to do so if at all possible.

Word came to the embassy early next morning not to make any plans for Whitehead after 9:00 A.M., and at that time Ceauşescu received Whitehead and Kirk at Central Committee headquarters. The meeting lasted two and a half hours. Whitehead started out as he had with Totu, saying that during his first visit both sides had said they wanted an improvement in relations. His second visit had been a disappointment, as the United States felt there had been insufficient progress on human rights and Romania had renounced MFN. Now he was not sure where the two countries were headed. The United States had many concerns. There had been very satisfactory progress in U.S. relations with other countries in Eastern Europe. The United States did not want to interfere in internal affairs, but it did have the right to choose its friends. Whitehead then went through the major issues between the two countries, including emigration, printing of Bibles, church destruction, treatment of journalists, exhibits and other cultural exchanges, rural systematization, and the trade imbalance. He asked if Romania wanted better relations; if so, these were things to work on.

Ceauşescu said the U.S. position had changed since earlier Republican administrations. The United States now felt it could interfere in Romania's affairs. The Reagan administration's anticommunist feelings contributed to this, as did the U.S. belief that Romania should be governed by American principles. Romania had not violated human rights, and the economic situation had steadily improved. The U.S. embassy should paint a realistic picture. There were a few insignificant individuals who were not happy, and they were the ones with whom the embassy dealt. He had spoken a few days before with a group of farmers, all of whom had praised rural systematization. Rural systematization had nothing to do with U.S.-Romanian relations in any case. Besides, few cities, Philadelphia, for example, looked the same as they had a hundred years ago.

After countering a few more of Whitehead's points, Ceauşescu said that he had viewed the renunciation of MFN as temporary, in the expectation that the U.S. administration would find a way to grant MFN without conditions. That was why both sides had agreed there would be no publicity about Romania's renunciation of MFN with Jackson-Vanik. The Romanians had respected this agreement, but the United States had not. Ceauşescu had hoped Whitehead would bring ideas about how to restore MFN so that the next administration could take steps to implement them. It was too bad the Reagan administration was responsible for a deterioration of relations rather than an improvement in them.

The discussion then turned to international questions, with Ceauşescu seeming more in tune with Soviet views and more critical of U.S. positions on arms control, the Middle East, and Afghanistan than had sometimes been the case in the past. When asked about the Soviet reform program, he repeated the usual Romanian line that this was an internal Soviet matter, but Romania wished the Soviets well in introducing reforms that Romania had enacted many years before. The meeting ended with Whitehead noting the importance of discussing differences frankly. The United States, he said, had only recently been able to do this with the Soviet Union, and he hoped it could continue to do so with Romania. The meeting concluded by both sides pledging to continue to work for better relations.

It appeared to Kirk that Ceauşescu was in fact reflecting his true feelings when he said he had viewed MFN suspension as temporary and had wanted to avoid publicity to give the United States time to find a way to accord MFN without conditions. He appeared to be speaking equally frankly when he complained about the anticommunist attitude of the Reagan administration and hinted that in the U.S. election year of 1988 he was looking forward to a better attitude from a future, "genuine" Republican administration. It is more difficult to imagine that Ceauşescu could have believed what he said about the progress of the economy, not to mention his assertions that systematization was popular in the countryside and that farmers' praise for it while talking with him proved the point. However, as noted earlier, the information reaching him passed through many filters, and it is possible he had deluded himself into believing that the economic situation was improving and that only a few "insignificant" malcontents failed to favor his policies.

The final item on Whitehead's schedule was a press conference at the embassy, attended by the embassy press officer and a few Romanian correspondents. Whitehead led off by noting that he had come to Romania to move relations forward but had made less progress than he would have liked. In fact relations had moved backward in some areas. He listed a variety of human rights topics that his "thorough and candid" discussion with Ceauşescu had covered and observed that "the sight of whole villages plowed under is hard for Americans to understand." He said his talk with Ceauşescu had covered the importance of exchanges and contacts. It had included a discussion of a number of international questions on which the two countries had much in common. He concluded his opening statement by saying that the task ahead was to identify practical, concrete ways of overcoming disagreements and expanding cooperation between the two governments "where we can." He noted, in answer to questions, his disappointment that the United States had made less progress in relations with Romania in recent years than with the other countries of Eastern Europe or with the Soviet Union.[118]

The October 1988 Whitehead visit represented a net gain for Ceauşescu in Romania and on the world scene but a setback in terms of his relations with the United States. Ceauşescu had met within a month with the leaders of the Soviet Union and China and with the U.S. deputy secretary of state. He could claim to his people and to the world that he was in close touch with the three greatest world powers. At the same time, Whitehead's presentation must have been a shock in light of the information Ceauşescu had received from his subordinates about the U.S. attitude toward Romania. Raceanu believes, in fact, that it was during this Whitehead visit that Ceauşescu concluded definitively that he could not get what he wanted out of the Reagan administration. He still hoped for more from the next administration. Totu was not so sanguine. He told Raceanu and his colleagues, when briefing them on the Ceauşescu conversation, that they should not recommend that Ceauşescu see any more American dignitaries and that they should apply the principle of strict reciprocity to all contacts with the United States.

Whitehead, for his part, told friends and the press on many occasions thereafter that he had been appalled by the internal situation in Romania, particularly by the unforgettable sight of the villages being demolished. That process continued. A few days after the visit Kirk went back along the same road to the monastery he had traveled with Whitehead. All that was left of Ciofliceni was the road sign that had identified it, newly smoothed-over earth, and large tire marks where the trucks and earth-moving machines had been. What had happened there was an omen for villages all over Romania. The villages Whitehead and Kirk had seen were unlucky enough to have been on the road from

Ceauşescu's in-town office to his country residence, and hence among the first to fall under the systematization program. If Ceauşescu had ruled for another decade, much of Romania would have looked the same. In a November 28, 1988, speech to the Central Committee, Ceauşescu reaffirmed his intention to "reshape" the nation's agriculture and declared that systematization represented the "embodiment of a desire for civilized life in the spirit of humanism of our society."[119]

The Whitehead visit marked the virtual end of Romanian attempts to make progress with the Reagan administration, and relations between the two countries further deteriorated thereafter. The Romanians pinned their hopes on better relations with the incoming Bush administration, believing that it would be more "genuinely" Republican and that Bush personally might retain fond memories of Romania from his 1983 visit. They gradually realized, as 1989 progressed, that this was not to be; but their attention was distracted more and more from the United States to the dramatic and, from Ceauşescu's point of view, highly distressing events taking place in Eastern Europe and the Soviet Union.

▼12▼

The Last Act
1989

Events in the weeks following Ceauşescu's October 1988 conversation with Whitehead bore out the conclusion that Ceauşescu had virtually given up on improving relations with what he considered the ideologically anticommunist Reagan administration. In Bucharest and Washington, the Romanians officially protested Whitehead's public criticisms, after leaving Bucharest, of systematization and other Romanian human rights violations, including treatment of the Hungarian minority. They particularly objected to Whitehead's making some of these statements in Hungary, a country with which they had very bad relations.

They also strongly protested the U.S. embassy's continuing contacts with dissidents, accusing by name three junior embassy officers of "recruiting" people to act against the Romanian state. They characterized these officers' activities as "inconsistent with their diplomatic status" and threatened to take "commensurate measures," that is, to expel them, if they did not stop. The embassy rejected the charges, saying that these officers had acted properly in fulfillment of the U.S. desire to stay in contact with a broad spectrum of persons. Contacts with the dissidents continued, and the embassy heard nothing more about the matter.

Romania's obstructionism at the CSCE conference in Vienna continued and indeed threatened to prevent signature of the agreement before the U.S. change in administration. On January 5, 1989, the Romanian delegation, claiming that the draft concluding document contained "provisions not in keeping with the true spirit of the Helsinki Final Act and present-day realities," submitted 17 amendments removing several human rights provisions from the final document. The Romanian initiative triggered a strong reaction from many delegations, including that of the

United States, whose head, Ambassador Warren Zimmerman, characterized it as "absurd and illegal."[120] To make matters worse, Ioan Totu launched a harsh personal attack on U.S. Secretary of State George Shultz in his speech on January 18, 1989, at the conclusion of the conference. Then, when finally signing the agreement, the Romanians made a formal statement that they assumed no commitment to abide by any provisions that they had sought to change.[121]

Ceauşescu further offended U.S. and world opinion by conditioning his support for a global ban on chemical weapons on a similar ban on nuclear weapons, claiming that chemical weapons were appropriate for small nations facing nuclear armed states. His stand was contrary to that of most nations, leaving him in the company only of Libya and other outlaw states. It represented a reversal of his earlier stand in favor of a chemical weapons–free zone in the Balkans and a global chemical weapons ban. Kirk and Raceanu both suspect that his new position reflected his increased isolation and his fear that the United States, the Soviet Union, Hungary, or some other country might seek to attack him. He may have felt that possession of chemical weapons, or at least the claim to have them, might deter such an attack.

Ceauşescu still seemed to nurture the hope that relations with the United States would improve under a new U.S. administration, a hope that the Republican victory in November reinforced. Ceauşescu had often said that the real progress in U.S.-Romanian relations had occurred under Republican presidents Nixon and Ford and that this might happen again under a "real" Republican administration, as distinct from Reagan's ideological one. Furthermore, recalling that then Vice President George Bush had met with him in Romania in 1983, Ceauşescu believed that such an encounter was usually enough to make a visitor "understand" Romania and his policies. Presumably with a view to impressing the future administration, Ceauşescu took a few positive steps after the election on some issues of long-standing concern to the United States: Emigration approvals went up, the Adventists in Bucharest obtained one of the buildings they needed, and human rights lawyer Nelu Prodan received his exit visa and left for the United States. The United States, for its part, continued to resist the idea of high-level exchanges, but suggested that a visit to Washington at the deputy-assistant-secretary level would be appropriate in early spring.

In the meantime Senators Mark Hatfield of Oregon and James McClure of Idaho had informed the State Department in early December that they wanted to visit Romania in the first days of 1989. Kirk urged the Department of State to discourage the trip, arguing that the visit of two such distinguished senators would be a major coup for Ceauşescu, who was fast becoming a world pariah, and might lead him to think that the new administration would indeed be more friendly to him than the old. If the senators persisted in coming, as they did, Kirk recommended that they convey a tough message about continuing U.S. concern for human rights.

Senators Hatfield and McClure arrived in early January and met on January 11 with the chairman of the Romanian parliament, Nicolae Giosan, and with Olimpia Solomonescu at the Foreign Ministry. The Romanian presentations followed familiar lines. The senators, for their part, stated that under the new administration human rights would remain an important part of the U.S. agenda with all countries. They expressed the hope that relations with Romania would be high on the priority list of the new administration, with which the senators had close ties.

Ceauşescu himself did not receive the senators, although he was in town and appeared relatively free. The embassy and Kirk personally had told the ministry that the visit was a unique opportunity for the Romanians to present their case to persons close to the new administration and thus display their goodwill toward the new American team. They noted that for Ceauşescu to refuse to see the senators would, on the other hand, be a break with past precedent and a confirmation that relations would remain strained. In past years Ceauşescu would not have missed any chance to convey his ideas to two such distinguished Americans, even without embassy urging, and would have welcomed the opportunity to play world statesman by receiving them.

The principal reason Totu and other hard-liners had advanced in arguing that Ceauşescu not receive the senators was that the situation in Congress was hopeless and that with MFN gone congressional opinion did not matter for the present. There was thus no need and no use in Ceauşescu's spending time on two senators. Indeed his doing so would simply make the U.S. Congress feel that it still had an important role to play in the U.S.-Romanian relationship. Although Totu knew of the senators' friendship with Bush, Raceanu is aware of no indication that Totu in turn informed Ceauşescu of this relationship and doubts that he ever did so.

Congressman Tom Lantos of California also wanted to come to Romania in January 1989. When the Romanians at the last minute refused to set up any official appointments for him or include visits to ethnic Hungarian areas in his itinerary, he decided to cancel his trip. Lantos then rescheduled his visit, this time as Kirk's "personal guest," and arrived with his wife at the end of March. He was granted no official appointments, and Chief Rabbi Rosen and his wife were the only Romanians who came to Kirk's reception for the couple. The Lantoses were able to travel to the Transylvanian city of Cluj-Napoca in an embassy car accompanied by Kirk's deputy, Henry Clarke, but had to cut their trip short in Transylvania for health reasons.

In late January 1989, the United States and several other Western countries notified the Foreign Ministry that they refused to accept Romania's reservations regarding its obligations under the CSCE agreement it had signed in Vienna. They said they considered the Romanians bound by the document they had all signed and would judge them by that standard. The Romanians in turn rejected the Western position and characterized all criticism as interference.

The Foreign Ministry adopted a similar line in refusing to accept copies of the Department of State's annual human rights report, saying it was "of no interest" to them. Romanian intransigence and growing Western firmness led to unpleasant incidents with a number of Western countries. The Romanians expelled or roughed up several Western correspondents and human rights activists.

Romania's relations deteriorated also with the more liberal members of the Soviet bloc. Romania and Hungary traded all manner of charges, and in late 1988 each expelled a member of the other's embassy staff.[122] Hungary supported a resolution condemning Romania at the U.N. Human Rights Commission in March 1989, while the Soviet Union, Bulgaria, and Ukraine did not vote. This was the first time there had been such a breach in Warsaw Pact solidarity in the human rights field.[123]

Ceauşescu for his part continued to criticize "reformist trends in some socialist countries," saying it was difficult to understand such "backwardness." The extent of his concern became strikingly apparent when in late January he modified his sacred principle of independence by saying each socialist country's freedom to choose its own path presupposed that that country maintained "a clear and logical position vis-à-vis socialist principles."[124] The Soviets, while refraining from direct criticism of Ceauşescu, continued to praise their own reform program in broadcasts to Romania. Soviet ambassador Evgeniy Tyazhelnikov signaled a new willingness to engage publicly in Romanian internal affairs by being the first Soviet ambassador to call on Chief Rabbi Rosen in the 40 years Rosen had been in office.

On March 13, 1989, Radio Free Europe broadcast an "independent manifesto" highly critical of the Ceauşescu regime. It was signed by six leading members of the communist old guard: Gheorghe Apostol, former first secretary of the Romanian Communist Party and ambassador to Argentina and Brazil; Alexandru Birladeanu, former Politburo member and deputy prime minister; former diplomat and party editor Silviu Brucan; Corneliu Manescu, former minister of foreign affairs, one-time president of the U.N. General Assembly, and ambassador to France; Constantin Pirvulescu, cofounder of the Romanian Communist Party, who in November 1979 openly opposed Ceauşescu's reelection as party general secretary; and Grigore Raceanu, Mircea's stepfather, a veteran party member who in 1958 was expelled from the party for opposing the party policy on agriculture and the invasion of Hungary by Soviet troops. The manifesto represented the most significant public statement of opposition to Ceauşescu's regime in years, made all the more weighty by the prominence and previous communist affiliation of its signers and by the fact that it was not just an individual effort but the product of a group able to coordinate among themselves under the nose of the powerful Securitate. It was an instant sensation in Romania and received wide publicity in Western media and government circles as well.

The manifesto asserted that Ceauşescu's policies had discredited socialism, isolated Romania within Europe, and alienated the workers, the very bedrock of socialism. The manifesto criticized a wide range of Ceauşescu's policies for violating international human rights agreements such as the 1975 Helsinki Final Act. Among the policies it specifically criticized were rural systematization, urban reconstruction, the building of the massive "civic center" in Bucharest, compulsory Sunday work, restrictions on contacts with foreigners, and the role of the Securitate. The manifesto called for halting systematization, restoring the constitution, and stopping food exports as first steps "to stop the negative processes . . . besetting our country."[125]

The manifesto had a long history. In early 1988 Gheorghe Apostol first raised with a few selected individuals, including Silviu Brucan, the idea of a group of prominent Romanians issuing some sort of public criticism of the Ceauşescu regime. In late 1988 he spoke more concretely with the eventual signers and persuaded them to join a group effort. He talked, for example, with Grigore Raceanu in the first week of November about joining the effort and in the last week of the same month exchanged views with him on the points the manifesto, or letter, might contain. The signers never met as a group for fear of the Securitate; Apostol coordinated the effort by contacting each individually. He asked Brucan to join the group in late December, following Brucan's return from a trip to the United States, Great Britain, and the Soviet Union.

The pace of activity then slowed because Apostol's wife broke her arm and needed him at home with her; but Mircea Raceanu arranged a meeting between Apostol and the older Raceanu on January 24, 1989, and they met again on January 31. At this point the group had a series of generally agreed points that their statement should contain but had still not decided what form it should take—a letter to Ceauşescu, a declaration, or a manifesto—or what its timing should be. They were thinking of putting it out in the spring, perhaps May, and hoped to obtain a number of additional signatories by that time.

Late on January 31, however, Mircea Raceanu, who knew of their activities, was arrested as an "American spy" (more on this later). The group therefore decided to move quickly for fear the Securitate might learn from their new prisoner about the group's activities (though in the end this fear proved groundless, as Mircea Raceanu never revealed his knowledge of the affair during his interrogation). Apostol, after gathering some additional ideas and suggestions from the eventual signers, gave his notes to Brucan with the request that he refine them, prepare the final version of a manifesto, and pass it to the West. On March 2 Brucan gave a handwritten copy to the U.S. embassy. The embassy forwarded it to Radio Free Europe, and RFE broadcast it on March 13.

After a few days' hesitation, probably due to Ceauşescu's need to recover from the shock of this unprecedented act and decide how to handle its prominent authors, the Romanian government arrested the signers, interrogated them individually, and then released them under a form of house arrest.

The United States immediately and formally protested the treatment of the six. U.S. chargé Henry Clarke told Solomonescu on March 18 that even the meeting at the deputy-assistant-secretary level tentatively set for Washington in April was "on hold" as a result of the treatment of the six and their families and the state of human rights in Romania. If the human rights situation improved, he said, the United States was prepared to resume discussions on a date for the meeting. Solomonescu countered that the six had wanted to destabilize Romania, "which unfortunately you support." The West European countries were also making an issue of the treatment of the six. The French, who had especially close ties to Manescu as a former ambassador to France, even recalled their ambassador for ten days' "consultation" as a sign of their dissatisfaction.

Despite these actions, the Romanian government tightened the restrictions on the six in late March, interrogated them repeatedly and at length, and in early May sent each to a different location, in Bucharest and elsewhere, under tight house arrest, where they remained until Ceauşescu's overthrow in December 1989. Raceanu's stepfather, for instance, was exiled to the village of Cojocna near Cluj-Napoca, where he had been born 83 years earlier.

Meanwhile another dramatic incident was troubling U.S.-Romanian relations. On January 31 the Securitate had stopped Mircea Raceanu and his wife, Maria, on their way to a film showing at Kirk's residence. After interrogating the couple at length, they had incarcerated Raceanu as an "American spy." Immediately thereafter, a team of ten agents from the Securitate conducted a 12-hour search of the family's three-room apartment. They not only refused to show a warrant to Raceanu's wife but took almost everything with them, leaving the apartment virtually empty. The United States learned of Raceanu's arrest shortly thereafter and made low-key inquiries about his fate, judging that too much U.S. interest would merely support the charges against him.

The first public announcement of Raceanu's arrest appeared in the press on March 14. A release from the prosecutor general reported that Raceanu had been arrested "for serious acts of treason" and would be tried and judged in conformity with the law of the land.[126] The government organized meetings all over the country demanding Raceanu's trial and "appropriate" punishment, that is, execution.

One such meeting took place in the Ministry of Foreign Affairs on March 14, 1989. According to the record of that meeting published in a series of articles in *Romania Libera* in late January 1990, all those who took the floor called for the death penalty. They also used the occasion to stress the necessity of defending the great achievements of socialist Romania and its Communist Party under the leadership of President Ceauşescu. Among those speaking were party secretary Ion Stoian, Ioan Totu, Aurel Duma, Olimpia Solomonescu, Ion Beşteliu, international organizations and disarmament head Constantin Ene, and Americas directorate officer (and Ceauşescu relative) Ilie Şimon.[127] Two days later, on March 16, the publicity and meetings stopped as suddenly as they had begun, and

the Raceanu case disappeared from the Romanian press shortly thereafter. Raceanu later learned that Ceauşescu had told his collaborators on
the Political Executive Committee that he had ordered the publicity
stopped because it "would only make Raceanu a hero."

When the anti-Raceanu publicity campaign began, the United States
advised the Romanian government that his execution would be a serious blow to U.S.-Romanian relations.

U.S. officials had no news of Raceanu's fate or that of his family other
than what they learned from a chance encounter on the street that political counselor Michael Parmly had with Maria Raceanu on February 7.
Seeing her on the sidewalk, Parmly stopped his car and got out to speak
to her. In a very brief conversation probably recorded by the long-range
microphones in the hands of the Securitate agents following Mrs.
Raceanu, she quickly confirmed her husband's arrest and told Parmly that
she had been dismissed from her job and that the Securitate had taken
almost everything from the house. She then shouted, for the benefit of
the microphones, "Leave me alone! Leave me alone!"

After the encounter, the Securitate subjected her to a four-hour interrogation, focusing on the purpose of the meeting and what went on
during it. She insisted that it was a chance meeting and that she had
reacted only by asking the embassy to leave her alone.

During the whole period when Raceanu was in prison, his wife and children were very closely surveilled. Two cars were assigned around the clock
in three shifts, with eight Securitate agents in each shift, to watch and follow Mrs. Raceanu everywhere she went. If she spoke with someone on
the street, that person was photographed or videotaped during the conversation. On April 24 she was given a job at the Institute for Public Health
and Hygiene. The same day the institute "hired" a Securitate agent who
sat in the same office, watching what Mrs. Raceanu did and listening to
everything she said. The Securitate tapped the Raceanus' home phone and
turned away all visitors except close relatives. Two agents followed Ioana,
their 20-year-old daughter, who was attending the Academy of Economic
Studies. Even Andrei, their 11-year-old, fifth-grade son, had an agent with
him wherever he went, frightening the children with whom he used to play.
A joke that circulated in Bucharest after the revolution of 1989 was that
Raceanu's family was one of the Securitate's most profitable businesses
during 1989, as it provided employment for 30 agents.

In late March 1989, in an evident effort to open a dialogue with the new
U.S. administration despite the difficulties in the U.S.-Romanian relationship, Ceauşescu invited Rabbi Arthur Schneier to Romania. In their

meeting on March 27, Ceauşescu adopted a relaxed and optimistic mien, Schneier told Kirk. Ceauşescu recalled Bush's 1983 visit to Romania and said he had enjoyed his talk with the then vice president. Ceauşescu also said that he wanted good relations with the Bush administration and that the two countries should put the MFN period behind them. He pointed out that the publicity on Raceanu had not mentioned the country for which Raceanu was spying, implying this was omitted as a favor to the United States (although it was widely "leaked" by the government). Raceanu had betrayed "no real secrets," he said, and another "spy" caught 20 years before was now walking free around Bucharest. This encouraging comment notably lessened U.S. fears for Raceanu's fate.

Despite these hopeful signs, on July 21 a military court, obviously on Ceauşescu's orders, condemned Raceanu to death. An appeals court confirmed the sentence on August 28. In late September, however, according to what Raceanu was told in prison at the time, his sentence was commuted to 20 years' imprisonment.

Raceanu was the last political prisoner released from Bucharest's Rahova prison after Ceauşescu's overthrow. The afternoon of December 22, following Ceauşescu's flight from Bucharest that morning, Colonel Murariu, the acting head of the Securitate's interrogation division, told Raceanu that all the other political prisoners in the jail had been freed, that he had no orders to release Raceanu, but that he would do what he could to make him comfortable. At the same time, authorities at the prison gate were telling Mrs. Raceanu and one of Raceanu's lawyers, who had come to the prison to inquire about his fate, that they knew nothing about it because, they said, he had been sent to the notorious Gherla prison in Cluj. At 7:00 A.M. the next morning, December 23, Romanian radio and television announced on behalf of the newly installed ruling council of the National Salvation Front that "all political prisoners, including Mircea Raceanu, to whom we convey our apology, have been released." Nevertheless, the Securitate, without any explanation, kept him in prison until late that evening, more than 11 hours after the announcement.

In an extraordinary move three and a half years later, on June 24, 1993, the Romanian military prosecutor challenged the validity of Raceanu's release and asked that he be reimprisoned until 2009. The move was doubly curious as Raceanu was by that time living in the United States, but it disturbed many observers of the contemporary Romanian scene. The Romanian press portrayed it as a slap at the United States. The U.S. government made inquiries, and the *New York Times* and other Western media picked up the story.[128] On July 2, President Ion Iliescu's office announced that the president had first learned of the move from the Voice of America, that he had looked into the case, and that the prosecutor general had informed the authorities the initiative was being dropped.[129]

A further irony was that Colonel Gica Popa, the military judge who had sentenced Raceanu to death in July 1989 at Ceauşescu's direction, also presided over Ceauşescu's trial in December 1989. Popa sentenced Ceauşescu and his wife to death for "crimes against the people," rose to the rank of major general after the trial, and committed suicide in March 1990.

In his conversation with Rabbi Schneier on March 27, 1989, Ceauşescu had spoken critically of the six who signed the manifesto, calling them "renegades" who would be subjected to party discipline. He severely criticized the West Europeans for their attitude toward his government and accused them of attempting to recruit Romanians to oppose his regime, the same charge the Foreign Ministry had leveled against the U.S. embassy the preceding November. The term "to recruit" seemed odd to Western ears. Ceauşescu was presumably persuaded that the Romanian people were basically in favor of his policies and that opposition therefore would have to be inspired, or recruited, by outside powers. Apparently he had become convinced that not only the Reagan administration but the West Europeans too were seeking to overthrow him.

His sense of isolation did not stop there; he was certain that Hungary wanted to oust him and take Transylvania from Romania. He was extremely uncomfortable with the reformist tendency infecting most of the socialist camp. His relations with Poland and Czechoslovakia were increasingly strained, and even Bulgarian leader Todor Zhivkov had failed to pay his customary annual visit to Romania in 1988. Indeed, Ceauşescu was assuming a self-defined role as the sole defender of true socialism within the Warsaw Pact. As reform spread in Eastern Europe, he relied increasingly on hard-line allies in Asia. Thus it was clearly no accident that the Romanian press ignored for days the continuing student protests in Beijing in May 1989 but reported approvingly when the Chinese authorities cracked down on the protesters in Tiananmen Square in June.

On April 10 Kirk had a long conversation with Ştefan Andrei at a luncheon the deputy prime minister hosted at the Athenée Palace hotel in Bucharest for a large group of visiting American businesspeople, led once again by Robert Robertson of Occidental Petroleum. Andrei asserted that Romania wanted better relations with the United States and that the best way to achieve them would be through cabinet-level meetings and a trip by a deputy prime minister. When Kirk replied that the United States wanted to see concrete steps on Romania's part before agreeing to any meetings, Andrei asserted that Romania would take such steps, that they had in fact already started with Ceauşescu's comment to Schneier about the Raceanu case, and that additional positive steps would be forthcoming if a meeting were in prospect. He noted that he had a personal stake in U.S.-Romanian relations and that a visit by him would be particularly useful.

Kirk repeated the American concern over human rights and economic deprivation in Romania. He pointed out how increasingly out of step with the rest of the world Romania was and how bad this looked in the United States. Andrei said all that would change because Romania had completed paying off its foreign debt as of April 1, 1989. Romanian history would henceforth be divided into two parts, B.D. and A.D. (before debt and after debt), just as that of the Western world was divided into B.C. and A.D. Romania would be importing more food for its people and more raw materials for industry. Ceauşescu, he said, had already set a specific target for an increase in imports from the United States.

Romania had in fact paid off virtually all of its foreign debt by this time, but at terrible cost to its economy and its people. It had exported large quantities of meat and grain when the Romanian people themselves were desperately short of food. The government cut imports of all kinds—food, medicine, spare parts—to an absolute minimum. The people suffered, and machines, even whole assembly lines, stood idle for want of parts. Ceauşescu received little applause from Western economists or bankers for his debt repayment, as they recognized its cost in economic and human terms. Everyone, including probably Ştefan Andrei, hoped that Ceauşescu would follow a more rational trade policy once the debt was paid, but Romanian economic officials were soon talking of the need to build currency reserves, and imports remained virtually as limited as before until Ceauşescu's overthrow in December 1989.

In a conversation with Robertson and Kirk on April 11, Ceauşescu took a line similar to Andrei's, if less dramatic, on the consequences of completion of debt repayment. He said that Romania wanted good relations with the United States and that trade should go up now that the debt was paid. He claimed he had refrained for months from signing a recommendation imposing higher non-MFN duties on U.S. exports to Romania, and he was going to propose mutual extension of MFN without Jackson-

Vanik to the new administration. The United States should not interfere in Romania's internal affairs.

As for human rights, he went on, it would be wonderful if they were as well guaranteed in the United States as in Romania, where there was no unemployment or homelessness and the population enjoyed free health care, old age support, and equal pay for equal work. The West complained about systematization and the reconstruction of Bucharest, but the Romanian people applauded when new buildings replaced old ones. He visited the construction site twice a week, and no one had complained to him about it. Western allegations of destruction of villages were false, as even Representative Lantos, whom the Romanian government had not hosted because of his anti-Romanian attitude but who had visited Romania as Kirk's guest, had seen when he visited an ethnic Hungarian village listed in Western reports as destroyed.

Kirk's net impression from this conversation was that Ceauşescu, while feeling beleaguered, did not realize how low his regime had sunk in the estimation of the United States and the West. He still seemed to harbor the illusion that Romania's independence from the Soviet Union and value as a trading partner made possible a marked improvement in relations with the United States, even an extension of MFN, without major changes in Romanian internal policy, once the new, less ideological, U.S. president focused on U.S.-Romanian issues. Ceauşescu clearly hoped that the new administration, once it got its feet on the ground, would open the door to high-level contacts leading to better relations; and he thought that pressure on the administration from U.S. businesspeople interested in trade with Romania would materially assist this process.

Ceauşescu was wrong. Kirk went to Washington in mid-April to ascertain just what the new administration's policy toward Romania would be. As expected, he received confirmation that, to the extent the new administration had thought about relations with Romania at all, it was inclined to follow the basic policy of its predecessor. It certainly did not want to embrace Ceauşescu. As before, the U.S. government would try to maintain contact with as many parts of Romanian society as possible while avoiding direct identification with the Ceauşescu government. High-level meetings were out, and Kirk should tell the Romanians that the meeting planned for April at the deputy-assistant-secretary level would itself have to await concrete Romanian steps on human rights issues, including better treatment of the six signers of the March manifesto.

When Kirk delivered this message to Solomonescu on April 25, she replied that he seemed less pessimistic than before his departure for Washington. Somewhat surprised at this unfounded observation, Kirk cautioned her not to underestimate the difficulties Romania faced with the United States. The basic reason for Solomonescu's misguided analysis of Kirk's comments, no doubt reflected in the tenor of her report on the conversation, was probably once again her desire to please her superiors. Realizing that they would pay particular attention to what Kirk brought back from his first direct contact with the new administration, she would thus put the best face on his presentation in her report, just as she had in the case of her trip to Washington the year before.

On the first day of June, Kirk informed Andrei that Romania must take positive steps on issues of concern to the United States if relations with the United States were to improve. Until Romania did so, it would be "difficult to sustain" a substantive dialogue. The Romanian reputation in Washington was so damaged that a "higher-level mission to Washington would likely do little more than reinforce the gulf that currently exists between our two countries." Recent Romanian actions were unhelpful, Kirk added. No Romanian official, for example, had received former under secretary of state David Newsom, who had visited Bucharest during the last week in May as part of a U.S. Information Agency–sponsored trip to several European countries to discuss arms control with governmental and nongovernmental experts. Not only was no senior official available to see Newsom, but the Foreign Ministry had said every single member of the ministry's Americas directorate was too busy to receive him, and not one Foreign Ministry official had come to Kirk's reception for him. The result was that Newsom would go back to the United States and tell his friends, many of whom were still in senior foreign policy positions, that Romania apparently had no interest in good relations with the United States. Kirk then reviewed such other recent problems as the treatment of the six and the difficulties American businesspeople were experiencing.

Kirk emphasized the refusal to see Newsom because it seemed a striking example of growing Romanian obtuseness. Newsom had been a professional diplomat, not an ideologue. Ceauşescu already knew him, as they had met when Newsom visited Romania as under secretary of state in 1980, bringing Ceauşescu a letter from President Jimmy Carter. The very fact Newsom had now come again to Romania at what was a difficult time in the relationship showed that he was more interested and open-minded than many Americans. His visit was an obvious opportunity for the

Romanian government. Newsom would be listened to in Washington just when the Romanians were looking for channels of communication to the new administration. Ceauşescu would surely have received a person like Newsom in earlier days and might well have met with him on this occasion had the Foreign Ministry recommended it, or even informed him about the visit. Totu, who doubtless had given the order that no one in the ministry should receive Newsom, would certainly not have recommended that Ceauşescu see him. Indeed, Totu may not even have informed Ceauşescu that Newsom was coming.

Andrei seemed downcast by his talk with Kirk. He said he had expected Kirk to return from Washington with ideas for advancing commercial relations between the two countries. He thought Kirk was too negative and ruminated that perhaps the new administration had not had time to focus on U.S.-Romanian relations. Romania was ready to discuss trade relations and the question of tariffs "at any level." He remembered Newsom well and would himself have received him if he had been in town during the visit. Andrei's presentation, unusually short and unresponsive, gave the impression—especially his specific reference to "commercial" relations—that he was taking particular care to stay within his own formal competence. He was probably correct in saying that he would have received Newsom, for even at this late stage in Ceauşescu's Romania Andrei probably had that much flexibility. But Andrei was being careful. Raceanu's arrest had shaken up everyone who had been involved in U.S.-Romanian relations, and Raceanu had been close to Andrei for many years. Andrei seemed to Kirk to be speaking for the microphones in the room most of the time, hewing to the strict party line and feeding a possible Ceauşescu illusion that Kirk's stern presentation did not reflect the considered thinking of the new U.S. administration.

Meanwhile Ceauşescu maintained a hard-line stance. Dashing any hope of better living conditions for the population now that the debt was paid, he told a Central Committee plenum on April 12 that the top economic priority was the modernization of industry.[130] The government put additional restrictions on private food sales by collective farmers on April 23. On May 3 it decreed that, in order to conserve energy, hot water in Bucharest would only be available for up to two hours in the morning and three in the evening.

Ceauşescu also made it very clear that he did not like the reforms sweeping the Warsaw Pact states. Speaking on the first day of a June 27–28 plenum of the Romanian Communist Party Central Committee, he said,

"We have always to keep in mind that socialism cannot develop except on the basis of principles of scientific socialism, setting aside inequalities of man over man." Private ownership, he said, is "against the objective laws of nature and social development and is the outcome of violence and armed force." Finally, he spoke out against "de-ideologization in international affairs," which was a favorite theme of Gorbachev's.[131]

Ceaușescu's relations with the West were deteriorating further, not only because of his overall stance but also as a result of Romanian efforts to keep Western diplomats away from dissidents, who were growing—slightly—in number and boldness. On April 3, the Securitate prevented West German ambassador Klaus Terfloth from visiting Corneliu Manescu, one of the six manifesto signers, to deliver a letter from West German Foreign Minister Hans-Dietrich Genscher. On April 5 the West Germans temporarily recalled their ambassador in protest of this action and of Romanian human rights violations. In late April the Romanian police picked up and briefly detained Michael Butler, a second secretary at the U.S. embassy, after he had tried to visit another signer, Constantin Pirvulescu. Dutch ambassador Coen Stork received several warnings from the Romanian government about his frequent contacts with dissidents. A Belgian parliamentarian trying to visit Doina Cornea's house on May 18 was stopped and beaten up by a gang of men. The Romanian government's contention that they were a "bunch of hoodlums" who happened to be present convinced no one. Even the neutral Austrians made a demarche on human rights on May 5.

The Romanians received some further elucidation on the views of the new U.S. administration when Deputy Secretary of State Lawrence Eagleburger received Romanian ambassador Ion Stoichici on June 27. Stoichici started off with the comment that "nothing had changed" since the end of MFN and that Romania wanted good relations with the United States. He urged a deputy prime ministerial visit. Eagleburger, never one to mince words, said that the whole international community felt that human rights had worsened in Romania. In these circumstances there would be no purpose served in administration officials meeting with Andrei. Eastern Europe was in the midst of changes and U.S. attention was shifting to those countries where the chances of change seemed greatest. Romania's internal affairs were its business, but how the United States viewed Romanian policies was for the United States to decide. The Romanian ambassador responded rather frostily, saying that the U.S. view of the Romanian scene was based on distortions of reality.

Totu summoned Kirk on June 30 to express his surprise that Eagleburger had said Romania's image in the United States was colored by developments elsewhere. Totu also rejected the argument that Romania's internal affairs should affect U.S.-Romanian relations. In its report to Washington on the Totu conversation, the embassy speculated that Eagleburger's comments were probably particularly disturbing to the Romanians because they indicated that the new U.S. administration felt as strongly about human rights in Romania as did its predecessor. Raceanu notes that no Romanian foreign minister could summon the U.S. ambassador without Ceauşescu's approval and instructions. Given Totu's reluctance to have anything to do with relations with the United States, it seems even clearer that Ceauşescu had been troubled by Eagleburger's comments and had personally instructed Totu to make these points to Kirk.

Kirk was due to end his tour as U.S. ambassador to Romania on July 5, 1989, and Totu received him on July 3 for ten minutes for a farewell call. The refrain was familiar. Totu said he was sorry he could not speak more positively about what had been "the most negative period" in U.S.-Romanian relations, and Kirk expressed his hope that Romania would take the steps necessary to improve them. Kirk had a meeting with Andrei the same day. Although the Andrei meeting was longer and more cordial than that with Totu, Andrei parroted the official line: Romania wanted better relations and more trade; the United States had not responded to Romanian gestures to improve relations by offering to send envoys to Washington; the United States should not seek to interfere in Romania's internal affairs.

Andrei took a somewhat more objective line when speaking to Kirk in the American embassy garden during Kirk's crowded Fourth of July reception, a time when the Securitate microphones could not be expected to pick up individual conversations. Andrei said that relations were not good, but this downturn would pass, as others had. The important thing was for the United States not to "trouble the waters" by such things as critical public statements in the State Department human rights report or the CSCE forum. This comment, which seemed to reflect more of Andrei's own thinking than what he had said in his office, still revealed a striking unawareness of the extent of Romania's problems in America and the U.S. government's feelings about the Ceauşescu regime.

Ceauşescu spent 40 minutes with Kirk on July 4. Kirk expressed his sincere fondness for the Romanian people and countryside and his regret that relations between the two countries had deteriorated during his three and a half years in Romania. He hoped Romania would take concrete steps that would make possible an improvement in relations. Ceauşescu countered that, as Romania had done nothing to damage relations with the United States, it was not responsible for the deterioration, which he agreed had occurred. He said he failed to understand the change in the U.S. attitude toward Romania and the new U.S. position on revision of frontiers. President Reagan, Ceauşescu asserted, had taken "a very wrong approach" in the later years of his administration. Reagan had apparently concluded that Romania's gestures toward the United States were signs of weakness and had accordingly taken measures to destabilize Romania, a position based on false information about Romania.

Ceauşescu then said that Romania valued its independence. The way to better relations was not through pressure on Romania. The United States should itself take steps to improve relations, or at least cease to support those who wanted to change Romania's borders. Kirk interjected that the United States respected current European frontiers, as George Shultz had personally assured Ceauşescu in 1985. Ceauşescu then noted that he wanted better relations with the United States and hoped that the present difficult period would be brief. He observed in conclusion that all the other Western ambassadors, including those in whose time relations had been difficult, had told him on their departure that they left with a good impression of Romania. Kirk bade him farewell.

Kirk's valedictory telegram to the Department of State said that his final talks with Romanian government leaders had reinforced his belief in the correctness of the U.S. policy of taking a cool attitude toward Romania while expressing a desire for better relations if the Romanians took positive and concrete actions in areas of U.S. concern. He did not expect such actions under Ceauşescu, Kirk added, but thought it important that in the future the Romanian people and their leaders see the United States as being open to this possibility. The United States could show its willingness to respond positively to reform through its actions toward more progressive regimes in Eastern Europe and in the Soviet Union. He urged that the United States promote contacts with as many elements of Romanian society as it could and continue, even increase, its Voice of America and Radio Free Europe broadcasts to Romania. He recommended that the United States make its dislike of the Ceauşescu regime very clear in public statements and avoid high-level meetings, which the Romanians would say foreshadowed a new era in U.S.-Romanian relations. In fact, Kirk concluded, "Any such new era awaits, at the very least, Ceauşescu's passing."

Relations between the two countries over the remaining five months of Ceauşescu's rule followed the lines predicted by Eagleburger in June and Kirk in July. The Romanians continued to push for high-level meetings with the United States, and even for MFN without conditions, but met with absolutely no success. The United States was increasingly focused on the progress of reform elsewhere in Eastern Europe and in the Soviet Union and wanted nothing to do with Ceauşescu's unrepentant regime. Ceauşescu, for his part, continued his own hard-line policies and tried to hold back the flood of reform in the rest of Eastern Europe. The annual summit of the leaders of the Warsaw Pact countries, held that year in Bucharest on July 7–8, provided a typical example. While the leaders of Hungary, Poland, and the Soviet Union were advocating more political and economic reforms, Ceauşescu complained about "disharmony within alliances."[132] As time went on, he became more and more isolated, his stance more and more anachronistic.

The U.S. House and Senate passed resolutions during the summer calling for economic sanctions against Romania, including a boycott of food exports from that country and termination of direct Romanian air services to the United States.[133] The administration, however, did not implement these punitive measures, as it felt they would merely make the Romanian people's pitiable situation worse without affecting Ceauşescu's policies in any positive way.

Andrei's promise of a new era for the Romanian consumer following payment of Romania's foreign debt had indeed come to naught, as Ceauşescu continued to press exports in order to build up exchange reserves and gain resources for his reconstruction and systematization schemes. These made the people suffer even more than before. The economy was devastated, and the country was reduced psychologically and physically to subminimal standards. Prominent intellectuals such as Dan Deşliu, Mircea Dinescu (who once said "God has forgotten Romania"), Alexandru Paleologu, Octavian Paler, and others began openly to criticize the regime's policy. In November writer Dan Petrescu released a public appeal against Ceauşescu's reelection as general secretary of the party at the coming Fourteenth Party Congress.[134]

At the same time, Ceauşescu, living in his own world of grand delusions and unable to understand the extent of the social crisis in Romania and the changes sweeping the rest of Eastern Europe, continued to believe that his people supported his crazy ideas. He reasserted them with vigor during his speech to the Fourteenth Romanian Communist Party Congress in Bucharest on November 20, 1989, and again on November 24, when he promised thousands of participants in a rally celebrating his reelection as general secretary that he would lead Romania to the "golden dream of communism."[135] It was too much for the people to bear!

Eviction of Protestant minister Lászlo Tökés from his church in Timişoara on December 16, 1989, sparked demonstrations against the regime, to which the government initially responded by using force. Ceauşescu nevertheless left for a brief trip to Iran. Returning on December 20, he delivered a televised speech blaming "hooligans in the pay of foreign services," "fascists," and "terrorists" for stirring up unrest in the country.[136] He clearly believed he was still in control—the idea that the communist system had failed and his regime was doomed seems never to have crossed his mind.

To demonstrate his popular support, Ceauşescu convened a large rally in Bucharest on December 21. As he was addressing the crowd and promising more food and fuel for the people, jeers and slogans—"Down with Ceauşescu! Down with communism!"—broke out. Romanian television captured the stunned look on the dictator's face as his speech was drowned out, and the Romanian people knew they had him beaten. He and his wife fled Bucharest the next day in the face of a huge antigovernment demonstration but were captured and imprisoned. Then, on December 25, Nicolae and Elena Ceauşescu were tried and executed.

For Romania and the Romanian people it was the beginning of the end of the worst nightmare in their history.

As for Ceauşescu, he told the court during his December 25 trial that he was ready to submit to a judgment on his rule only by the parliament or the people themselves. The new Romanian authorities, he said, had come to power as a result of a coup d'état organized with the help of foreign agencies.[137] These final words aptly illustrated the misperceptions under which he labored, misperceptions his subordinates had been unwilling to correct.

Ceauşescu's misperceptions contributed to his bad relations with the United States, but so did a number of other factors discussed earlier in this account, many of which arose from the nature of the Ceauşescu regime and the profound differences between the two systems of government. The following chapter reviews the key factors that affected the ability of these two very different, even hostile, regimes to communicate with each other.

▼13▼

Epilogue: Some Lessons

The story of U.S.-Romanian relations during the last years of the 1980s is a somber, even depressing tale, one of steady decline marked by frustration and annoyance on both sides. As reform gained ground in the Soviet Union and Eastern Europe, the Ceauşescu regime became more repellent and less useful to the United States. A deterioration in relations between the United States and Romania was inevitable.

That the two governments were so different also contributed to the problems in their relations. Neither really understood how the other operated. They had contrasting concepts of interstate relations and different ways of conducting them. The authoritarian nature of the Romanian system made it difficult for Romanian diplomats to operate effectively. History shows that problems arise between any widely divergent governments, especially when one is authoritarian and the other democratic. The story of U.S.-Romanian relations during the late 1980s thus provides some lessons for understanding and conducting relations between such states.

One of the foremost problems in U.S.-Romanian relations throughout this period was that the Romanian leadership, Ceauşescu in particular, vastly overestimated the power of the U.S. president and his control over American society. They saw the United States as analogous to Romania, where Ceauşescu could ignore or adjust legal and legislative requirements at will in order to do what he wanted. The Romanian leadership felt that what was true for Ceauşescu surely must be true for a man as prominent as the president of the United States. After all, very little happened in Romania without high-level government approval, that of Ceauşescu himself in an extraordinary number of cases. For example, he authorized any new foreign currency expenditure over $1,000, reviewed the names of scientists and lecturers who were to go abroad on exchanges, and decided the top Romanian attendance at all countries' national day receptions in Bucharest. The Romanians assumed that the U.S. president, who had so many more resources at his disposal, must exert the same kind of detailed direction over American life.

The Romanians therefore saw the U.S. president's encouragement, or at least his acquiescence, behind almost everything that happened in the United States. This led not only to demands that were ridiculous in American eyes, but to serious miscalculations about the U.S. government's position, repeated examples of which appear in the preceding pages.

One important miscalculation was the impression held by the Romanian government and Ceauşescu himself that the U.S. government backed the cession of Transylvania to Hungary. A principal reason for their genuine concern on this issue was that demonstrators outside the Romanian embassy in Washington and the Romanian mission to the United Nations in New York sometimes advocated such a territorial transfer. The Romanian leadership believed that the demonstrators could not have done this if the U.S. government had not agreed with them.

The leadership also felt, to take another example, that General Ion Pacepa, the Securitate defector, could not have published a book in the United States excoriating the Ceauşescus nor held a press conference promoting the book without U.S. government approval or indeed even direct U.S. government support. Similarly, the points Ceauşescu instructed Foreign Minister Ioan Totu to convey to the United States when the Romanians renounced their most-favored-nation status in February 1988 called for the U.S. administration to "stop" the MFN debate in the United States. Deputy Foreign Minister Olimpia Solomonescu told Kirk four months later that the Romanian government was particularly "surprised" that Congress was holding hearings on Romania when Totu had specifically said to John Whitehead that there should be no more such hearings. The hearings, she said, could surely not occur without administration approval.

Another consequence of this overestimation of the U.S. president's power was that the Romanians simply did not believe U.S. officials when they said President Reagan was not legally able to do something the Romanians wanted. An example was the Romanian reaction to the 1987 U.S. withdrawal of the Generalized System of Preferences for

Romania's exports. They viewed it as a specific, directed, and hostile political act by the U.S. administration, even though U.S. officials told them repeatedly, and George Shultz himself wrote Totu, that it was merely the result of a new legal requirement of U.S. trade law on which the administration had no discretion.

The Romanian exaggeration of Reagan's power appeared most dramatically in Ceauşescu's firm belief that Reagan, if he wished, could give Romania MFN without the adhering to the conditions legislated by the Jackson-Vanik amendment. This belief was reflected in the language of Ceauşescu's renunciation of MFN; in his desire to keep this renunciation quiet until his special envoy could work out a new arrangement in Washington; and in his public and private comments on the matter. It was also evident in his statement that the situation would have been different if Nixon had been president and in his attempt to reopen the subject with the Bush administration.

This belief in the omnipotence of the U.S. president forced Ceauşescu and his associates to invent motives other than limitations on presidential power to explain Reagan's failure to do what they wanted. They first stressed that the Reagan administration was "misinformed" about Romanian realities and concluded that if the U.S. government and embassy would rely only on official instead of "malcontent" sources of information U.S. policy would be different. Then they blamed circles "hostile to Romania" that influenced Congress and the administration. They identified these circles variously as ideological anticommunists of the American right wing, human rights and religious organizations, trade unions (particularly the AFL-CIO), and Hungarian irredentists. Finally, Ceauşescu convinced himself that the basic problem was that Reagan's personal anticommunist ideology was leading him to seek to overthrow the Ceauşescu regime.

Then, as U.S.-Soviet relations improved, Ceauşescu became convinced that the two countries were conspiring against him. Interestingly, Ştefan Andrei recalled, during his trial in 1990 and in an article written in 1993, that Ceauşescu carefully noted U.S. White House spokesman Marlin Fitzwater's statement, shortly after the Bush-Gorbachev summit in early December 1989, that Bush had expressed concern to Gorbachev about the situation in Romania. This statement, in Andrei's view, confirmed for Ceauşescu his belief that the United States and the Soviet Union were plotting against him.[138]

However far-fetched to American ears many of these Romanian theories sounded, they strongly influenced Ceauşescu's policy toward the

United States. He seemed increasingly convinced, for example, that the Reagan administration was advancing its human rights demands in order to weaken, or even topple, his regime. This belief made him much more reluctant to grant what Americans saw as only minor human rights concessions. It helps explain his personal alarm when he learned that the U.S. embassy in Bucharest had discarded rounds of ammunition and cans of Mace in the garbage. It was behind the Romanian references to U.S. "recruitment" of Romanians to subvert the government. It constituted a distorted prism through which Ceauşescu and many of his associates viewed U.S. actions.

Such a phenomenon is not exclusive to Romania. Kirk observed the same problem in the thinking of Somali strongman Siad Barre when Kirk was ambassador in Mogadishu in the mid-1970s. Typically, dictators cannot imagine that the U.S. president's freedom of action is less than their own. They view U.S. protestations to the contrary as persiflage to cover hidden motives, and spend much time and energy trying to analyze what these hidden motives are. They usually conclude that the motives are sinister, and they judge U.S. actions in that light.

The Ceauşescu regime also clearly had trouble understanding how the U.S. political process operated and how to exert effective influence within it, but nonetheless made a number of efforts to do so. In some cases, it achieved success from steps it took specifically to advance Romania's cause in the United States. Thus, when the U.S. administration and Congress were debating the annual MFN renewal in 1986 and 1987, the Romanians increased the number of permits for emigration to the United States, released from jail a few dissidents in whom the United States had expressed particular interest, printed Bibles for the Baptists, and spared Jewish buildings slated for demolition under urban reconstruction. These concessions helped Romania gain MFN in each of these years.

In other cases, Romania's relations with the United States benefited tangentially from actions Romania took largely for other reasons. Thus Romania's position as the only Warsaw Pact power to attend the 1984 Olympics in Los Angeles, while largely a consequence of Romania's policy toward the Soviet Union, gained Romania tremendously favorable publicity in the United States. The government's relatively lenient treatment of the Romanian Jewish community and the fact that it allowed Jews to emigrate to Israel, while motivated in large part by Ceauşescu's independence and desire to play the world statesman and by the financial benefits accrued from Israel, convinced the U.S. Jewish community to lobby for MFN for Romania.

It was difficult, however, for the Romanian leadership, working within its own monolithic political environment, to understand the play of forces in the U.S. political system or the role of Congress, the press, and business. The Romanian leaders knew that these sectors were important and sometimes tried the techniques used in democratic societies to influence them. Some of these techniques came naturally to the Romanians and were relatively successful. Others were uncongenial to the Romanians and clumsily employed by them, sometimes doing more harm than good.

The Romanians, for example, encouraged influential Americans from the administration, Congress, and the business community to visit Romania. As a Romanian strong point is hospitality and charm, it was natural to the Romanians to go to great lengths to please visitors, whether allowing U.S. Ambassador to the United Nations Vernon Walters to drive a subway train, delaying a plane for presidential envoy Warren Zimmerman, or arranging top-level appointments for a number of visitors on extremely short notice. From 1978 to 1989, Ceauşescu himself received nearly 100 Americans, in addition to talking with business groups and members of Congress, according to a Romanian Foreign Ministry count. Where there was no fundamental disagreement, the Romanians, wanting to appear responsive to their guests' requests, tended to respond positively, even if they did not mean it.

There was another, less endearing side to this hospitality. The Romanians felt that guests should allow their hosts to schedule and control their activities and thought it improper for guests to do anything outside of the official program. They considered it impolite as well as threatening when Deputy Secretary of State John Whitehead insisted on seeing nonofficial Romanians selected by the U.S. embassy, or when Representatives Frank Wolf and Christopher Smith passed up the parliament's dinner in order to visit defector General Ion Pacepa's daughter. In arranging a program, the Romanians often emphasized entertainment over serious talk, for example taking up a third of Secretary Shultz's six hours in Bucharest with a luncheon at which no meaningful business took place.

The Romanians resented it, furthermore, if their guests criticized Romania after receiving the country's hospitality and often complained officially to Kirk when American visitors spoke ill of Romania after leaving, especially if the visitors had not voiced these same criticisms while in the country. Ceauşescu and Totu finally said they would not accept "inspection trips" by visitors or embassy personnel, a term they appeared to use for visits by travelers who formed and enunciated their own opinions about what they saw instead of merely repeating what officials told them. This problem got worse as Ceauşescu's understanding of conditions in Romania diverged further and further from reality. He then became positively indignant at American "distortions" of conditions as he saw them, while the Americans correctly felt that they were merely stating the obvious, often in muted terms.

American visitors, while appreciative of the attention the Romanians showed them, often saw this hospitality as an obstacle to doing the actual business they had come to accomplish. They sensed themselves constricted by the program their hosts had arranged and longed for a chance to "see for themselves." The visitors felt deceived when nothing came of Romanian promises to "look into" something and saw no reason why they should be less than frank about what they had seen during their visit, even if they had refrained from overt criticism during their trip out of politeness to their hosts.

Some of these issues arose from specifically Romanian circumstances, but some are common to Americans' dealings with many nations. The conflict between the local notion of all-inclusive hospitality and the American desire to have "free time" is one Kirk has often seen. It is exacerbated, of course, in authoritarian societies where the government is accustomed to controlling everything and has much to hide. In many dictatorships, foreigners' visits often hurt, rather than help, a relationship.

Journalists were a particular problem in the Romanian case. The Romanians expected favorable press coverage from journalists they hosted. They wanted these journalists to follow the programs the government had arranged and write only what government officials had told them. They tried to prevent them from visiting places and people the government did not want them to see. When journalists came without a government invitation, the Securitate watched them particularly closely and severely restricted their access to sources in or out of government.

This situation held true throughout most of Ceauşescu's rule, but became markedly worse in the late 1980s. The Romanians harassed, arrested, and expelled journalists from prestigious Western publications such as *Figaro* and *Time*, in the latter case insisting all the while that the correspondent should write "positive" things about his visit. They blacklisted journalists who wrote unflatteringly about Romania and made it difficult for them to reenter the country, as happened to David Binder of the *New York Times* after his interview with Ceauşescu in 1986.

Romanian officialdom considered an interview with Ceauşescu as the ultimate honor for a journalist visiting the country. It could not tolerate the idea that a journalist receiving such an honor could do other than repeat the leader's words, accompanied by adulatory comment. To ensure this, it put conditions on such interviews—written questions and answers, prepublication vetting of the story, publication of the full text— that few major papers would accept.

This problem with journalists is not exclusively Romanian. It is likely to arise wherever there is a dictator, especially one who rules in brutal fashion over a poor country. The issue can be particularly troublesome when such a dictator believes that the U.S. government has great influence, and ultimately control, over the media. What the dictator thus sees as the "refusal" of the U.S. government to stop unfavorable publicity strikes him as a willful political act that he must factor into his assessment of U.S. policy.

The Romanians made repeated efforts to promote their public image within the United States. They sent delegations of religious leaders in ecclesiastical regalia to talk to members of Congress and the administration. They hired a public relations firm, Van Kloberg & Associates, to place favorable articles in the American press. They encouraged businesses trading with Romania to lobby Congress for MFN and gave top-level treatment to Robert Robertson, vice chairman of American Businesses for International Trade, which lobbied for MFN in the late 1980s. They maintained good relations with the American Jewish community, whose work with Congress was of great value to the Romanians.

Romania's other efforts were of little help, however, principally because the Romanian case was such a hard one to defend, except regarding the treatment of Jews. Another reason for the failure of many of these Romanian efforts was that this type of activity did not come naturally to the Ceauşescu regime, and it usually did not invest the resources, talent, and imagination necessary for a full-scale, successful campaign.

This again is a common problem. Although some dictators have been very successful in manipulating the American political scene, others do not understand how to go about it. They resent the resources and political flexibility required.

Romania's diplomats in Washington did not help much in the 1980s. In the late 1960s and 1970s, Romania's able ambassadors in Washington had worked the U.S. scene with great skill. By the mid-1980s, however, their ambassadors were party hacks with neither the ability nor the desire to play the Washington game. They focused on telling Bucharest what it wanted to hear, and on doing nothing that would get them in trouble with the Securitate.

Again, this is all too typical of diplomats from rigid authoritarian regimes. Though there are notable exceptions, most such diplomats would much rather be ineffective than risk charges of disloyalty for wandering from the official line or for taking too active a part in democratic life.

The United States, for its part, pursued its traditional open and democratic approach in dealing with Romania. The U.S. embassy tried to have contacts at many levels of Romanian society, not just with government officials. The United States actively promoted cultural and educational exchanges and complained bitterly as the Romanians reduced these to virtually nil. It pressed the Romanians to allow journalists, representatives of nongovernmental organizations, and members of Congress to enter Romania and travel freely in the country.

All this distressed the Romanian government, which wondered why the U.S. embassy did not confine itself to official contacts and information, rather than poking around the countryside, talking to all kinds of people. There had to be some deeper motive than the expressed one of "getting to know the country and the people." Since the Romanian government was used to being in complete control of events in the country, to have persons out of its control traveling wherever they wanted and talking to whomever they wanted was unsettling. As relations deteriorated and Romanian suspicion of U.S. motives grew, such activities appeared sinister, even threatening to Romanian officials.

This desire to control what goes on and the concomitant unease at freewheeling foreigners is often found in authoritarian regimes, whether leftist, rightist, or traditional, and in some nonauthoritarian regimes as well. American openness, curiosity, and interest in the unofficial and unorthodox are very troubling to many governments. Those who do not understand the American people and their approach look for some "explanation" for this activity. They are all too inclined to see something ominous behind it, the more so because of their often exaggerated notion of America's power and ambition. They see the CIA everywhere. The Romanian Securitate, for example, was certain that the embassy's human rights officers, who kept in contact with dissidents, were CIA employees in search of recruits against the regime, a belief that Ceauşescu himself seemed to hold as well.

This problem, too, is not confined to U.S.-Romanian relations but affects all dealings between open and closed societies. Kirk recalls the efforts of a Dutch ambassador to Somalia to convince Somali dictator Siad Barre that a Dutchman who inadvertently wandered across the Ethiopian-Somali border was only in pursuit of a rare butterfly, and that he had an Israeli map of the area merely because it was the only one available. Although true, the Somalis simply would not believe it. They finally let the naturalist go as a goodwill gesture to a small and friendly country. If that butterfly fancier had been from the United States, Kirk would not have had a chance of persuading the Somalis that he was a simple naturalist.

Americans, whether diplomats, members of Congress, or private individuals, believe they should have the right to pursue any "legitimate" activities all over the world and that to restrict their activities to those applauded by an authoritarian regime is to be derelict in their job, even to betray their heritage. The resultant conflicts often trouble relations between the United States and other countries, especially dictatorial ones.

From the Romanian government's point of view, nothing was more objectionable than the U.S. emphasis on its own conception of human rights. Ceauşescu seemed sincerely to believe that collective rights such as education, employment, and health care were more important than the individual rights the United States was stressing, such as the freedoms of speech, assembly, religion, or the press. Most, though not all, of his collaborators, and clearly Ceauşescu himself, saw no compelling reason why the United States should be concerned about the "rights" of citizens of another country. Why was that the business of the United States? Ceauşescu himself instructed the Foreign Ministry to make this point when criticizing the State Department's human rights report in 1986.

The United States, for its part, considers its conception of human rights to be universally valid and sees it as its duty to help people all over the world secure those rights. This enthusiasm is tempered where other important U.S. interests are at stake, as in the case of China. The utility of Romania's foreign policy independence in the 1960s and 1970s performed a similar function. As this independence became less important to the United States, however, human rights assumed an ever larger role in U.S. policy and public opinion regarding Romania, making Ceauşescu even more suspicious. He continued to believe that the United States needed Romania for geopolitical and economic reasons and could not imagine that the fate of a few dissidents could be more important to the United States than these considerations. He therefore assumed that there must be some other, overridingly important motive behind the "unnatural" U.S. interest in a few "malcontents" and finally became convinced that the United States was working actively to overthrow him.

Ceauşescu's attitude reflects yet another classic problem between the United States and authoritarian regimes. Such regimes cannot fathom why the United States takes up the time of another chief of state with half a dozen prisoners, for example, or an obscure religious sect. Even Ştefan Andrei told Kirk in October 1987 that the United States should talk about issues such as Vietnam, the Middle East, or developed country–developing country economic policy disputes rather than "small affairs" such as human rights. Although more sophisticated dictators around the world understand, at least to some extent, that this is simply the nature of the United States, their less sophisticated peers do not.

U.S.-Romanian relations likewise suffered from the fact that the two governments had different approaches to relations between states. The United States, seeing state-to-state relations as essentially relations between societies, actively promoted free and unstructured exchanges at all levels and in all social sectors. Ceauşescu, viewing interstate relations as essentially relations between governments, and more specifically between top government leaders, believed communications and meetings between chiefs of state were the very substance, as well as the symbol, of interstate relations. It was no happenstance that criticism in a confidential letter from President Reagan convinced Ceauşescu to renounce MFN, or that he hoped to regain it by sending a personal envoy to Reagan.

There were several reasons for Ceauşescu's perception of relations between states. Under the Romanian governmental system, the only person with real power to do anything about most problems, or even say anything meaningful about them, was Ceauşescu himself. If he enunciated a change in policy, his subordinates quickly adopted the new line, but they would never have dared to make concessions or take initiatives themselves. As early as December 1985, the Romanians made it clear that there was little point in Shultz's seeing the Romanian prime minister, as the minister would have nothing to add to what Ceauşescu said. Subsequent U.S. experience in talking with other Romanian ministers, including foreign ministers, bore this out. Though they were bound to echo Ceauşescu's line, they were often incompletely informed about what he had said or done. Thus they were extremely cautious and noncommittal in responding to any new problem and merely repeated standard phrases, especially as they knew the Securitate was checking their conformity with Ceauşescu's words through its microphones in their offices. All meaningful diplomatic exchanges had to be at the top.

U.S. practice, on the other hand, is to handle as many problems as possible at the "working level," and, when top leaders must address a problem, to use preliminary working-level exchanges to explore and clarify the issues that their superiors will discuss. The United States regards this as an essential diplomatic procedure, the key to a successful meeting at the top level.

That is what Shultz had in mind when he proposed to Ceauşescu in 1985 that Ambassador Kirk and State Department Counselor Edward Derwinski work with counterparts in Bucharest and Washington to resolve or refine the human rights issues between the two governments. Ceauşescu betrayed his own distaste for lower-level contacts by naming the foreign minister or his deputy, not some less senior official, as Kirk's interlocutor; but even the foreign minister could not, or would not, do anything but repeat Ceauşescu's latest line. Thus the "informal channel" went nowhere, to the great frustration of the United States. In retrospect, however, it was doomed to fail, given the nature of the Ceauşescu regime.

The Romanian emphasis on contacts at the top level, and with Ceauşescu in particular, had another motive. Such contacts, especially with the United States, were good for Ceauşescu's personal prestige and a sign that Romania's special relationship with the United States was intact. They bolstered Ceauşescu's contention in his relations with his Warsaw Pact allies and the Third World that he had an entree to Washington that could be useful in resolving their problems with the United States. Conversely, holding high-level U.S.-Romanian meetings that bolstered Ceauşescu's prestige was not at all an aim of the United States. By the second half of the 1980s, at least, meetings of top-level U.S. officials with Ceauşescu and his leading associates were positively damaging for U.S. prestige. The United States continued to agree to such meetings, but viewed them as the price it had to pay to get any action out of the Romanians or get any message across to them.

The U.S. government therefore felt it should agree to a high-level meeting only if it appeared that the accomplishments of the meeting would compensate for the disadvantage of holding it. The Romanians, on the other hand, would achieve their principal objective simply by convening the meeting, irrespective of what was said at it. That is why Andrei told Raceanu in September 1985 that he wanted a meeting with Vice President Bush, even if it was only a thirty-second photo session.

The Romanian attitude meant that when the United States did accede to Romanian pressure to hold some high-level meeting, it often turned out that the Romanians had no significant business to transact at it. Thus, as the 1980s wore on, the United States became ever more skeptical about the value of such meetings and ever more reluctant to agree to them. It began to insist on assurances that something it wanted would come out of such a meeting before agreeing to hold it and later demanded that the Romanians take concrete steps on items of U.S. concern before a meeting convened. This attitude frustrated the Romanians and offended Ceaușescu, particularly when it was his "personal envoy" whom the United States refused to receive.

Because the United States is a great power, it is often in the position of conferring prestige on foreign leaders by the very fact of receiving them, while the United States itself seldom gains prestige by doing so. On the other hand, in many autocratic regimes the best and sometimes only way to get things done is through direct contact at the highest level. If the leader in question is distasteful, the same dilemma arises as in dealing with Ceaușescu. In these cases, the best procedure for the United States may well be to demand and collect the price for the meeting in advance, since the other side will achieve its goal by the very fact that the meeting occurs, no matter how inconsequential the discussion at it.

Another problem that arose in U.S.-Romanian relations sprang from differences over the way people relate to one another. The Romanians were much more ready to agree to do something than to actually do it. They felt it natural and polite to give a generally affirmative response to the request of an interlocutor, especially a guest in their country. They promised Kirk dozens of times that they would print Bibles, replace churches, or resolve commercial disputes. This type of affirmative response did not in Romanian eyes constitute a firm commitment to act, only a general willingness to be helpful if circumstances permitted.

Americans meeting this phenomenon for the first time tended to regard such Romanian statements as a commitment and to feel betrayed if action did not follow. Kirk often had to complain to the Romanians about their failure to fulfill commitments to him or to American visitors. In the end, Americans became very cynical about any Romanian promises and tended to insist on delivery of the Romanian part of a bargain before fulfilling the American part. This Romanian practice of saying yes without meaning it occurs in many cultures and is everywhere hard for Americans to handle. They generally prefer to have a definite answer, even if it is negative.

Yet another problem was the Romanian technique of either simply not replying to a request or promising an answer that never came. Kirk recalls Raceanu's pride, and his own gratitude, when Raceanu told him in January 1986 that he had been able to get an answer to Kirk's request to have his own personal chauffeur drive him to a meeting in Budapest. Even though the decision was negative, getting it at least left Kirk just enough time to name another embassy chauffeur, one presumably more trustworthy from the Securitate point of view, to drive the car. And in October 1987 Andrei performed a real service when he said that the Romanians were not ready to conclude a Boeing deal. All too often the Americans were left hanging and impatient with the Romanians' failure to respond—"If the answer is no, why don't they just come out and say it?"

In addition, Romanians are indirect in their approach to most problems, especially sensitive ones, perhaps because they are a Balkan people who have had to deal with stronger neighbors for many centuries. Examples from the 1985–1989 period include their use of a variety of indirect ways to tell the United States that they wanted to send Andrei to discuss MFN after their 1988 renunciation. Thus they had a retired former minister to the United States, Silviu Brucan, convey the message, which he delivered first to a British diplomat, then to an American businessman, and only in the third instance to a U.S. embassy official. It was only two months later that Andrei himself told Kirk officially that Ceauşescu wanted to send a deputy prime minister to talk with Shultz about MFN. Even then Andrei did not say directly that he would be the envoy, but only hinted at the fact.

In this case, the content of the message was simple enough to be understood through an indirect channel, but the United States often missed more subtle signals, such as the nuances of Romanian attendance levels at the U.S. Fourth of July receptions. The Americans, for their part, tended to be more direct, more "undiplomatic," thus sometimes offending their interlocutor or undermining the goal they wanted to achieve. The Romanians would search for the real meaning behind some seemingly direct U.S. action or statement. Thus American praise for Deputy Foreign Minister Maria Groza and suggestions she plead the Romanian cause in the United States, while motivated simply by a feeling that she would do a good job of it, raised the jealousy of her superiors and their suspicion of American motives. This did Groza considerably more harm than good and evidently helped lead to the cancellation of the one trip to North America that she was scheduled to take.

Cultural differences complicate U.S. dealings with many countries. In a hostile relationship the two sides frequently lack the informal relationships that make it possible to understand and clarify these differences. The problem is worse if one party is an authoritarian power whose officials do not have the freedom to discuss differences except in approved, formal fashion. Natural cultural differences can thus be perceived as prevarication, insults, or politically grounded hostility.

In addition to cultural barriers to understanding between the United States and Romania, there were many aspects of the Ceaușescu regime itself that handicapped effective communication with the United States. At the heart of these problems was the dependency for decisions, advancement, even personal safety, on one man, who had to decide even minor issues. Considering that Ceaușescu, however intelligent, was ill-educated, dogmatic, intolerant, and highly suspicious, one can understand the difficulties of any subordinate trying to pursue a rational policy.

This was made worse by Ceaușescu's retaining as senior advisers only those willing to play up to him, to feed his ego, and to avoid offense. Whatever good they wanted to accomplish for their country, they first had to win and keep his favor. Their primary objective was to please and flatter Ceaușescu, and they shaped their reports, recommendations, and decisions accordingly, as the preceding account repeatedly shows—from Foreign Minister Andrei's reporting to Ceaușescu in 1985 that Vice President Bush had asked him to pass greetings to Ceaușescu, even though Bush had done no such thing, to Solomonescu's false report in the spring of 1988 that the MFN issue was not closed, thus reinforcing Ceaușescu's illusion that Reagan could give him MFN without conditions if he so desired.

The rush of Ceaușescu's advisers to give him exaggerated accounts of good news was equaled only by their efforts to avoid giving him bad news. Thus they did not forward to him even the formal, official U.S. requests for release of the Fodor or Pacepa families. They did not give him accurate reports of Romania's ever-deteriorating reputation in the United States or the ever-tougher messages the United States was sending about human rights. This faulty communication within the Romanian government was fundamentally responsible for the inability of the United States to reinforce its direct messages to Ceauşescu by signals through the Romanian bureaucracy.

In this and many other respects, the atmosphere around Ceauşescu was similar to that surrounding an absolute monarch. Ceauşescu's advisers acted like his courtiers, and Elena Ceauşescu was comparable to the powerful wife or mistress of a sovereign. Ceauşescu's courtiers spent most of their time trying to curry favor with the master, flattering him, bringing him good but not bad news, and pleasing his consort. Substance of policy and veracity of information took second place.

Rivals were quick to exploit an individual's mistake—such as Groza's circulating the 1987 House letter asking for emigration of Pacepa's family—to obtain that individual's removal. Every senior official had to weigh every word carefully, for the Securitate reviewed the tapes of their conversations with foreigners to detect any misstep or sign of weakness. The result was that Romanian officials were constantly looking over their shoulders at their colleagues, at the Securitate, and, for the most senior, at Ceauşescu himself.

Given such a work atmosphere, it was only natural that Ceauşescu's advisers and their subordinates hewed strictly to the Ceauşescu line, venturing no personal opinions or speculation. It was imprudent to share any original thoughts with foreigners or even with their own colleagues. This circumstance tended to repel individuals with initiative and creativity and to stultify such qualities in those who originally had them.

The resulting rigidity and lack of imagination in Romanian policy, even on small matters, severely handicapped the conduct of relations. This is a phenomenon commonly observed in rigid dictatorships and indeed is endemic to such regimes. A major complication if relations are basically friendly, it is frequently an insurmountable difficulty if relations are hostile.

The Romanian example also illustrates that Lord Acton's well-known dictum—that "absolute power corrupts absolutely"—applies to both the ruler and the ruler's subordinates. Ceauşescu, like many dictators, acquired a vastly exaggerated sense of his own abilities and successes. His subordinates applauded every idea he proposed and tailored their reports to show all his initiatives as triumphs. There was no check, no second opinion, on his will or even his whims. No one dared tell him that one of his ideas would not work or that one of his policies was not succeeding.

Thus none of his advisers reported to him that the United States would not give him MFN without conditions, even though U.S. officials, members of Congress, and businesspeople had repeatedly made the point painfully clear. None of his associates told him that even as nefarious a policy as rural systematization was disastrous. Ceauşescu repeatedly launched counterproductive policies and then adhered to them, in part because no one objected to them when proposed or told him they were not working once begun. On the contrary, his subordinates organized rallies in Romania and paid for press articles abroad that said these very initiatives were immensely successful, leading Ceauşescu to conclude that the Romanian people and the world approved his bankrupt line.

Foreign interlocutors often observed Ceauşescu's lack of knowledge about his own country, as when the Canadians saw his shock when they told him in 1987 that the first unit of Romania's nuclear power station would be ready, at best, in three or four years, rather than in 13 months as his advisers had been telling him. These same advisers knew they were misleading Ceauşescu, but they criticized the Canadians sharply for telling him the unpalatable truth. American officials, like the Canadians, tried to cut through the web of deceit around Ceauşescu by communicating directly with the dictator, orally or by letter, but the truth was so different from what Ceauşescu had already heard that he usually dismissed it as the product of misinformed or ill-intentioned sources.

It is well known how difficult it is for persons to credit what they do not want to hear. It must have been even more difficult for one so sure of his correctness as Ceauşescu, especially when his subordinates would hurry in to repeat their flattering reports and contradict the bad news just conveyed by the foreigner.

Lack of accurate information is a classic problem of dictatorship. The Romanian example illustrates its effect on policy and the difficulty of breaching the wall of misinformation and prejudice surrounding an autocrat. Indeed the basic theme of the three and a half years covered by this study is the persistent U.S. attempt to make Ceauşescu realize that his reputation in the United States was deteriorating and that the U.S.-Romanian special relationship he valued so highly was doomed unless he took some relatively modest steps on human rights.

Ceauşescu never absorbed this message, and the special relationship ended. The dramatic changes in the Soviet Union and Eastern Europe and their contrast with the situation in Romania would have ended it in any case, but Ceauşescu's opaqueness was a significant factor in speeding its termination. Similar critical misunderstandings have arisen in

U.S. dealings with other hostile nations. Such misunderstandings apparently contributed materially to Iraqi strongman Saddam Hussein's decision to invade Kuwait in 1990.

It is the authors' hope that this study of a failure of communication between the United States and Romania will help alert future policymakers to comparable problems with other countries and provide useful source material for those studying cross-cultural communications and the psychological dimensions of diplomacy.

Appendices

THE WHITE HOUSE
WASHINGTON, DC

December 6, 1985

Dear Mr. President:

I value your messages of recent months and the views you gave to
Ambassador Zimmermann November 22 about my Geneva meeting
with General Secretary Gorbachev and the future course of U.S.-
Soviet relations.

As Ambassador Zimmermann indicated to you, I believe that the
Geneva meeting made an important contribution to putting U.S.-
Soviet relations on a more stable and constructive basis. Holding of
further meetings, as agreed, in Washington and Moscow in 1986
and 1987 will help to focus both sides' attention on the need for
progress on the most difficult outstanding issues—arms control,
regional issues, human rights, and bilateral concerns. In particular,
we hope that the ongoing nuclear and space talks (NST) in Geneva
will lead to deep reductions in strategic and intermediate nuclear
forces to much lower, equal levels in such a way as to strengthen
stability and reduce chances of conflict. The atmosphere at Geneva
was candid and animated, and disagreements were put into clearer
and more constructive focus. The process has a long way to go, and
I will appreciate your advice and impressions in the days ahead.

I want to assure you, as Vice President Bush told your Foreign
Minister on September 30, that we are interested in broadening and
enhancing the U.S.-Romanian relationship. There have been a number of constructive developments: General Vessey's March 1985
visit to Romania created substantial progress in relations between
the U.S. and Romanian Armed Forces, and General Olteanu's
planned visit to the U.S. early next year offers further promise.
Secretary Shultz will visit Bucharest December 15 with a view

toward strengthening our relations through further discussion of bilateral and international issues.

I appreciate your personal role in the resolution of several human rights cases, particularly that of Father Calciu, which were of importance to us. Your government's agreement in June to new, facilitative procedures governing the processing of permanent departures from Romania to the United States was also a positive step, although unfortunately we have not yet reached agreement on the final written form of this understanding. Resolution of the Fodor case, about which I understand and appreciate your views, would have an important positive impact within our political system.

Mr. President, appreciation for Romania's sovereignty is a basic element of U.S. policy toward your country. Despite the differences between our systems, we have managed, over 20 years, to build up an important relationship based on common interests and mutual respect. Bilateral dialogue about human rights has been an important element in seeking to transcend systemic differences and prevent them from impeding progress in our relations. I want to confide in you my own unease about the bilateral stresses which have been created by circumstances resulting in U.S. public and Congressional concerns over human rights issues in Romania. I feel it important that further serious efforts be made to break the momentum of these stresses. An agreement concerning the importation and distribution of Bibles and other religious materials, as well as the easing of certain administrative measures directed against unrecognized religious groups, would be an important step in this direction. Secretary Shultz will be raising those matters in Bucharest.

Secretary Shultz will also be presenting ideas for developing bilateral relations in other areas. Particularly in light of recent terrorist outrages, we would welcome detailed expert-level exchanges with Romanian officials on the suppression of terrorism as well as exchanges of views on other important international questions such as the Middle East. We would plan to continue to exchange views with your government, along lines of Ambassador Zimmermann's visits, on major developments in U.S.-Soviet relations.

With best wishes,

                                        Sincerely,
                                        /S/
                                        Ronald Reagan

His Excellency
Nicolae Ceaușescu
President of the Socialist Republic of Romania
Bucharest

APPENDIX 2

TEXT OF JANUARY 7, 1986, LETTER FROM
PRESIDENT NICOLAE CEAUŞESCU TO PRESIDENT RONALD REAGAN

P 142231Z JAN 86
FM SECSTATE WASHDC
TO AMEMBASSY BUCHAREST PRIORITY

CONFIDENTIAL STATE 012350

SUBJECT: JANUARY 7 CEAUŞESCU LETTER TO THE PRESIDENT

Bucharest, January 7, 1986

Dear Mr. President:

I particularly appreciate the exchange of messages between us regarding various issues in bilateral relations and international affairs. In this context, I welcomed the initiative to inform us, through Ambassador Zimmermann, about the high-level Soviet-American meeting in Geneva. I also welcomed the recent visit of the Secretary of State of the United States of America, George Shultz. I regard all this as an expression of the good relations between our countries, and of our common desire to consolidate those relations and assure the most positive course for them.

As I stressed in meetings with Ambassador Zimmermann as well as with the Secretary of State, George Shultz, I appreciate that the high-level Soviet-American meeting in Geneva was a significant event for the current international situation. It was of great importance, particularly because it led to the establishment of direct contacts and joint decisions regarding the continuation of these contacts and meetings, which open the way to achieving certain concrete, reciprocal, mutually acceptable understandings. However, at present, the fundamental issues of disarmament and prevention of a nuclear war remain practically unresolved, and mankind will appreciate the real value of the high-level Soviet-American meeting only to the extent that concrete accords and real steps are achieved toward these ends.

The fact that production and deployment of new nuclear weapons in Europe and other parts of the world, as well as activities for the militarization of outer space, have continued after Geneva is a reality which cannot but cause concern. If the current situation goes on, if there is no undertaking, by one side as well as the other, of measures and concrete initiatives toward halting the nuclear arm race, it can be said that the Geneva talks will lose their importance, and I would not want that to happen. In my opinion, it would be important that, at least for the duration of the negotiations, nuclear weapons tests be stopped, the production and deployment of new nuclear weapons in Europe be halted, and that activities for the militarization of outer space be renounced. Such initiatives and intermediate measures would be of character demonstrating that the United States of America and the Soviet Union regard with full responsibility and seriousness the problem [of] curbing the arms race, and first of all the nuclear arms race, and of proceeding to disarmament and removing the danger of a nuclear war in which—as the Soviet-American Joint Declaration adopted at Geneva has emphasized—there will be no victor.

Regarding bilateral relations, as you rightly pointed out yourself, an important relationship based on common interest and mutual respect has been constructed between our countries over the last two decades. Recently, however, the development of those relations has been impeded by certain measures and activities undertaken by certain circles in the United States of America. I especially have in mind the pressures being generated in the direction of conditioning the development of Romanian-American economic relations on a series of elements which are in contradiction with the principles and provisions set forth in the joint documents as well as the agreements concluded between our countries, and which can only be interpreted as attempts to interfere in the internal affairs of Romania.

In your letter you indicated that appreciation for Romania's sovereignty is a fundamental element of the policy of the United States of America toward our country. I want to take this opportunity to mention that the independent policy pursued by the Romanian government is not a matter of biding time or expediency ("*politica de conjunctura*"), but has always constituted the fundamental basis of our relations with other countries. In this spirit, Romania has promoted and will continue to promote in its international relations the respect of principles of equality, independence and national sovereignty, noninterference in internal affairs, and mutual advantage.

In fact, the development of Romanian-American relations in the last two decades has been founded precisely on these principles. I should point out that these principles found expression in the joint declarations which I signed, over the last twenty years, with three presidents of the United States of America. I also find these principles in the Romanian-American Trade Agreement, signed in 1975, which remains in force. In the spirit and on the basis of these principles, I believe that all the conditions exist for continued development of Romanian-American relations—and we want to do our utmost in this direction.

In your letter you mentioned some issues related to human rights, which would create a certain tension in the relationship between our two countries. Mr. Shultz developed this idea and referred to the pressure generated by various groups, as well as within the Congress of the United States of America. I affirm to you my profound conviction that such problems cannot exist except to the extent that they are artificially created. I have written to you on other occasions about this problem, about the way in which we understand human rights. We consider that, in Romania, the broadest and most fundamental human rights are assured—the right to work, to a free and dignified life, to full participation in economic and social life in conditions of full equality—thereby assuring the unhampered participation of all citizens in the democratic leadership of our society. We would like those human rights to be fulfilled, in fact, in all countries of the world. I believe that the linking of human rights with the issue of emigration is totally inappropriate. Romania has not encouraged and does not encourage emigration. Of course, in a humanitarian spirit, we have resolved, thus far, numerous family reunification cases. We will also demonstrate understanding in the future regarding valid and justified cases. If there arise certain unclear elements, they should be raised through the usual channels. Recourse to publicity cannot but adversely affect relations between our two countries.

In respect to the understanding reached regarding the procedures for issuance of passports to people within Romania who are leaving permanently for the United States of America, I explained in fuller terms to Mr. George Shultz why I believe that it is not absolutely necessary that it also acquire a written form.

I was surprised, Mr. President, that in your letter you also raised certain points concerning religious freedom in Romania. I do not know what were your sources of information in this regard, but I want to emphasize that, in Romania, the constitution of the country assures the free exercise of activity by the religious denominations, and of the religious practices. No one suffers and no one is subjected to any restriction due to the fact of their belonging to a religious denomination. The denominations publish and print religious publications, including Bibles—and the necessity of importing Bibles from abroad does not exist. The Church itself is opposed (*"insasi biserica se opune"*) to such imports, in that it prefers to print and distribute its own editions. In this context, I would like to tell you that the Romanian state spends hundreds of millions of lei each year for the salaries of priests, as well as for the conservation, restoration, and maintenance of religious monuments. I wanted to tell you these things, Mr. President, in the hope of giving you the possibility of knowing the true situation—although these subjects are strictly internal matters for Romania and we cannot accept, in any form, any interference from abroad in this area.

Romania has always been against terrorism. We have condemned terrorist actions with all firmness, believing that terrorist actions cannot in any way constitute a means of resolving problems, and that they only cause further strains in international relations and poison the international atmosphere. I agree that the competent institutions in our two countries should establish contact in order to discuss this problem in all its aspects.

There are, of course, many international issues in which Romania and the United States of America can actively cooperate, together with other countries and peoples of the world. We believe that political-diplomatic efforts must be intensified to resolve the conflict in the Middle East peacefully, through negotiations, and that a conference should be organized under the aegis of the United Nations in which all interested parties would take part, including the Palestine Liberation Organization as well as the United States of America, the Soviet Union, and other countries which can contribute to a just and lasting solution to the problems which have gathered in that region.

The settlement, through political negotiations, of problems in various regions of the planet, the final renunciation of force and the threat of employing force have, in our view, an essential importance for the normal development of relations between states, and for the improvement of the entire international climate.

I also believe that greater efforts should be made to identify just and equitable solutions in order to eliminate underdevelopment, including the extremely large foreign debts of the developing countries—a problem which constitutes a factor of tension and instability in international life—by establishing a new world economic order based on full equality and equity, by renouncing all protectionist and other measures which impede the normal development of international trade, and by giving mankind broad access to the achievements of science and advanced technology. In my view, the United States of America has a very important role in resolving these problems in the interest of all countries, including the developing countries.

On the whole, Mr. President, I think it necessary that we continue our exchange of views about international issues of mutual interest, including the Soviet-American negotiations as well as, particularly, about ways and possibilities of further developing the Romanian-American relationship which is, we are convinced, in the interest of both countries and peoples, and of the overall cause of detente, cooperation, and peace in the world.

With best wishes.

Sincerely,
Nicolae Ceauşescu

END TEXT.
SHULTZ

APPENDIX 3

TEXT OF JUNE 3, 1986, LETTER FROM
PRESIDENT RONALD REAGAN TO PRESIDENT NICOLAE CEAUŞESCU

0 032226Z JUN 86 ZFF6
FM SECSTATE WASHDC
TO AMEMBASSY BUCHAREST NIACT [NIGHT ACTION] IMMEDIATE

CONFIDENTIAL STATE 174533

SUBJECT: ROMANIAN MFN RENEWAL: PRESIDENTIAL LETTER TO CEAUŞESCU

THE WHITE HOUSE
WASHINGTON, DC

June 3, 1986

Dear Mr. President:

As you know, I am required by American law to forward to Congress
by June 3 of each year a determination concerning continuation of
most-favored-nation (MFN) treatment for Romania. After considerable deliberation, which revealed strong congressional opposition
and reservations within my own administration, I have today signed
a report to the Congress containing my determination to continue
Romanian MFN for 1986–87.

This was a difficult decision for me. It will not be easy for the
administration to defend it in Congress. In my December 6 letter, I
wrote of the heartfelt concerns of large numbers of the American
people regarding observance of religious freedom in Romania. I cannot accept, as you replied in your January 7 letter, that these concerns are artificial or unfounded. I personally share them. At my
request, Secretary Shultz presented to you on December 15 proposals regarding Bibles and treatment of unrecognized religious groups
which we believe are well within your discretionary power to
accommodate. Our representatives have pursued these points in
numerous conversations in Bucharest and Washington.

As I said in my December 6 letter, our interest has not been to
undermine Romanian sovereignty or intervene in Romanian internal affairs, but to uphold the commitments which our two governments have made to address basic human rights issues.

Together with the American Congress and public, I seek to allay
serious concerns which threaten the careful balance in relations

between our two countries. Your government's unwillingness to accommodate these concerns has placed at risk our policy, which benefits Romania substantially. I have decided that, once again, my administration will seek to argue the case for continued Romanian MFN before Congress, recognizing that we are under a severe handicap in doing so, without meaningful steps on the part of your government to address our concerns. However, there is no guarantee that we will be persuasive.

With best wishes.

> Sincerely,
> /S/
> Ronald Reagan

His Excellency Nicolae Ceauşescu
President of the Socialist Republic of Romania
Bucharest

END TEXT.
SHULTZ

APPENDIX 4

TEXT OF JANUARY 23, 1987, MESSAGE FROM
SECRETARY OF STATE GEORGE SHULTZ TO FOREIGN MINISTER IOAN TOTU

O 230016Z JAN 87
FM SECSTATE WASHDC
TO AMEMBASSY BUCHAREST IMMEDIATE

C O N F I D E N T I A L STATE 021238

SUBJECT: MESSAGE FOR FOREIGN MINISTER

Dear Mr. Minister:

I received with great interest Chargé Clarke's report of your comments on the U.S. Government's decision to remove Romania from the list of beneficiaries of the Generalized System of Preferences (GSP) tariff program, and want to take this opportunity to ensure that there is no misunderstanding as to the motivation behind this action and its implications, in our view, for U.S.-Romanian relations.

In 1984, Congress amended the law governing the GSP program, making eligibility for GSP benefits contingent upon a recipient state's actions in affording internationally recognized workers' rights to its workers. As required by the new legislation, we reviewed the status of beneficiaries, and after extended study of available information and consultations with your government, concluded that Romania did not meet the revised GSP criteria.

The action we took in response to a mandate from the Congress does not imply that the U.S. no longer seeks to improve and expand our bilateral relations. On the contrary, I want to reaffirm that my government values its relationship with Romania and stands ready to work cooperatively with you to the fullest extent possible. Deputy Secretary Whitehead's visit to Romania last November was a further indication of our continuing interest, and we are looking at ways of effectively following up on the various matters he discussed there. One positive development is the visit of Ambassador Adams to Bucharest this month for discussions on counterterrorism.

Looking to the future, it is my hope that we will work closely and cooperatively together. With the convening of a new Congress, it is certain that our most-favored-nation (MFN) tariff relationship again will come under close scrutiny. There are a number of outstanding problems, particularly the decline in emigration in 1986, which could place MFN in jeopardy. I would urge that your government focus on these concerns in the months ahead.

With best wishes,

George P. Shultz

END TEXT.
SHULTZ

APPENDIX 5

O 281933Z MARCH 87
FM SECSTATE WASHDC
TO AMEMBASSY BUCHAREST IMMEDIATE

C O N F I D E N T I A L STATE 093007

SUBJECT: MESSAGE TO PRESIDENT CEAUŞESCU

Dear Mr. President:

U.S.-Romanian relations have long been characterized by an open and constructive dialogue that has enabled us to broaden contacts in many areas and resolve a number of difficult problems. In keeping with this tradition, I am writing to convey to you my deep concern about the prospect for renewal of our most-favored-nation (MFN) tariff relationship. As you know, my government believes that this relationship has been beneficial for both our countries and would like to see it continue.

However, after consultations with various members of the U.S. Congress, I must be frank to tell you that MFN is in serious jeopardy due to widespread concern over matters of fundamental human rights.

When Deputy Secretary Whitehead was in Bucharest, he emphasized the importance of emigration to the administration and the Congress. As you know, this issue relates directly to the U.S. legislation which provides for MFN. I well understand your government's position with regard to emigration and appreciate the progress that has been made over the years in cases of family reunification. However, I find it hard to explain the decline of more than 30 percent in emigration to the United States in 1986 as compared to 1975, particularly when there is still a lengthy list of individuals currently eligible for admission to the United States. I hope that approvals for these individuals can be increased substantially in the near future.

Mr. Whitehead and Ambassador Kirk have recently reviewed with Romanian government officials a number of other issues which affect the climate in which MFN is considered in the United States. In particular, they noted the predicament of the Seventh-Day Adventist congregation in Bucharest and the Baptist congregation in Oradea, the printing of Protestant Bibles, and the case of Ioan Ruţa.

I believe that these issues, if unresolved, have the capacity to harm the prospects for renewal of MFN.

During our meeting in December, 1985, we agreed on the desirability of expanding and improving our bilateral relations. In that spirit, we recently have had a constructive consultation concerning our mutual interest in combatting international terrorism, and we welcome the ongoing exchanges between our military leaders. We plan to be in touch with your government in the coming months with proposals for a variety of other consultations. I believe that the problems I have cited can be resolved if we approach them in the same spirit.

Sincerely yours,

George P. Shultz

END TEXT.
SHULTZ

TEXT OF JANUARY 26, 1988, LETTER FROM
PRESIDENT RONALD REAGAN TO PRESIDENT NICOLAE CEAUŞESCU

THE WHITE HOUSE
WASHINGTON, DC

January 26, 1988

Dear Mr. President:

I am pleased you will receive Deputy Secretary of State John Whitehead during his stop in Bucharest. His visit is an important part of the dialogue between our countries. Moreover, it comes at a critical time in our bilateral relations.

There is rising concern in the United States, including the United States Congress, about continuing problems with respect to human rights in Romania. We see your understanding of the seriousness of these problems as the key to success in overcoming them and maintaining the long-standing and mutually beneficial relations between our countries.

It is true that greater numbers of Romanians than ever before have been allowed to emigrate to join family members in the United States, and we recognize the efforts your government has made in this regard. Unfortunately, effects of this effort are clouded by the growing list of restrictions in other areas, particularly in religious freedom, treatment of minorities, economic conditions and political expression. American officials have had numerous discussions about these problems with members of your government.

Precisely because we value our relationship with Romania, we have sought to convey the depth of American concern about these problems. Without substantial improvements in the next three months, it will be very difficult for me to decide on renewed extension of MFN for Romania this spring, much less for Congress to accept a positive recommendation. Moreover, quite apart from the question of MFN, economic and human rights conditions in Romania will always be important to our relationship, and their improvement would serve to strengthen and benefit our bilateral ties.

I have, therefore, asked Deputy Secretary Whitehead to review the situation with you. I urge you to do your utmost to clear away these difficulties so that we can resume the work of building broader and deeper relations between our countries.

Sincerely,

                              /S/
                              Ronald Reagan

His Excellency Nicolae Ceauşescu
President of the Socialist Republic of Romania
Bucharest

TEXT OF FEBRUARY 12, 1988, LETTER FROM
PRESIDENT NICOLAE CEAUŞESCU TO PRESIDENT RONALD REAGAN

DEPARTMENT OF STATE
DIVISION OF LANGUAGE SERVICES
(TRANSLATION)—LS NO 125333 JS/RUMANIAN

Dear Mr. President:

In connection with your letter sent by Deputy Secretary of State
John Whitehead, I wish to acquaint you with the following facts:

Rumania has always acted in conformance with the Rumanian-
American agreement of 1975. Although it has opposed the Jackson-
Vanik Amendment from the outset, Rumania, in the spirit of its
humanitarian policy, has always given exit visas to persons who
have requested them for reunification of their families or for other
justified reasons. You yourself have stated on several occasions,
including in the message you sent me recently, that Rumania has
acted responsibly in satisfying requests for family reunification.

I was surprised that in your message you also referred to some
so-called economic, humanitarian, religious, and other problems in
Rumania. In my discussions with Deputy Secretary of State
Whitehead, I dealt with all these problems in detail, thus I shall
touch upon them only briefly here.

I wish to say first of all that all these problems concern the
domestic policy of our country and cannot under any circumstances
be the subject of discussions between Rumania and the United States.
If we were to discuss them, we would have to point out that the
United States has many economic and social problems, including
that of democracy, with which we do not agree. But we believe that
they are your affair and that it is the responsibility of the U.S.
Government to resolve them.

In regard to economic problems, I should like to mention that in
the international economic conditions of the last few years the
Rumanian economy has continued to develop at an annual rate of
5 to 6 percent. We have ensured a continual growth of the national
revenue and of workers' incomes, as well as a rise in the financial
and spiritual well-being of our entire people. We have eliminated to
a great extent the country's foreign debt, even paying it off in advance. Therefore, on the basis of these facts, we do not understand
where you obtain your information about Rumania's so-called economic problems to which you refer in your letter. One might well

speak, however, of the difficulties in the U.S. economy that have a serious effect upon international economic relations, as well as the economic and financial relations of the United States with other countries, particularly the developing countries. Many political figures, economists, and scientists, as well as institutes specializing in the United States, speak openly about the great deficiencies in the American economy and their effect upon U.S. relations with other countries.

As regards problems of democracy, we have created in Rumania a unique broad-based democratic system that ensures the effective, direct participation of the entire people in the governmental process, a system incomparably superior to many other democratic systems, including that of the United States.

I was particularly surprised that you referred in your letter to the so-called problems of nationalities, which allegedly do not enjoy full rights in Rumania. I think you are well aware that Rumania is a unitary national state in which a limited number of citizens of non-Rumanian nationality have been living alongside the Rumanian population for many centuries. The laws of the country ensure equal rights and obligations: there is no discrimination or restriction of any kind. Only former Horthyists, nationalists, and Hungarian irredentists speak of the so-called nationality problem in Rumania, thereby calling into question the current borders and seeking the revision of international treaties. I believe that you are familiar with the Trianon Peace Treaty—signed by the United States in 1920 —and the Paris Peace Treaty of February 10, 1947, to which the United States is also a signatory. Both treaties recognize the international borders of Rumania.

We want the traditional relations between the United States and Rumania to develop according to the principles of international law —complete equality in rights, respect for independence and national sovereignty, noninterference in internal affairs, and mutual advantage. I think I should emphasize that Rumania strongly adheres to its traditional policy of independence and adamantly rejects any encroachment upon its national independence and sovereignty.

As regards your reference to the difficulties involved in approving the most-favored-nation clause, I should like to inform you that we have decided to reject extension of this clause under the conditions set forth by the Jackson-Vanik Amendment. It is our view that approval of this clause should be based on the existing trade agreement, renouncing any preconditions. In this connection, we propose that representatives of our government and of the U.S. administration discuss the modalities of developing economic relations between our countries, in accordance with the provisions of the current trade agreement and renouncing any preconditions.

We realize that it is in the interest of our peoples that the presidents of the two countries not undertake anything which could impair the traditional relations of friendship between them, but that everything be done to develop these relations and to strengthen cooperation throughout the world in support of a policy of peace and international collaboration.

Sincerely yours,
Nicolae Ceauşescu

His Excellency Ronald Reagan
President of the United States of America

APPENDIX 8

TEXT OF FEBRUARY 26, 1988, DEPARTMENT OF STATE STATEMENT:
"ROMANIA RENOUNCES MFN RENEWAL"

DEPARTMENT STATEMENT, FEB. 26, 1988[1]

The Romanian Government has informed us it has decided to renounce renewal of most-favored-nation (MFN) subject to the terms of the Jackson-Vanik agreement. Therefore, the Administration this year will not exercise the waiver authority under that amendment. The U.S. Government remains firmly committed to the Jackson-Vanik amendment as the law of the land.

Under the Jackson-Vanik amendment, without another annual waiver, Romania's MFN status will expire on July 3, 1988. Therefore, all Romanian products arriving in U.S. ports after July 2, 1988, will be subject to the higher non-MFN duties. In addition, effective July 3, Romania will no longer be eligible for any U.S. Government-supported export credits through such programs as the Commodity Credit Corporation (CCC) or the Export-Import Bank.

Since 1975 Romania has had MFN tariff status under a bilateral commercial agreement, contingent on annual renewal of a waiver provided for by the Jackson-Vanik amendment, Section 402 of the 1974 Trade Act.

We will be consulting with Romanian officials regarding the legal and policy implications for our bilateral commercial agreement of Romania's request. We welcome and reciprocate the Romanian Government's expressed desire to continue to work for better relations, to maintain a broad range of contacts and consultations, and to work to promote trade and economic relations.

The Government of Romania has authoritatively stated to us it will continue to allow emigration for family reunification purposes without relation to economic ties with the United States. We welcome this. It is particularly important because of the continuing intense concern shared by the Administration, the Congress, and the American people with human rights in Romania. This concern will continue to be a central part of the U.S.-Romanian dialogue.

---

[1]Read to news correspondents by State Department deputy spokeswoman Phyllis Oakley; *Department of State Bulletin,* May 1988, p. 43.

APPENDIX 9

TEXT OF FEBRUARY 27, 1988, ROMANIAN AGERPRES
"STATEMENT ON THE ECONOMIC RELATIONS OF THE SOCIALIST REPUBLIC
OF ROMANIA WITH THE UNITED STATES OF AMERICA"

ROMANIA
FBIS-EEU-88-039
29 FEBRUARY 1988

REACTION TO U.S. CRITICISM OF TRADE RELATIONS
AU271520 BUCHAREST
DOMESTIC SERVICE IN ROMANIAN
1400 GMT 27 FEBRUARY 1988

(TEXT) STATEMENT ON THE ECONOMIC RELATIONS OF THE SOCIALIST REPUBLIC
OF ROMANIA WITH THE UNITED STATES OF AMERICA

In connection with the U.S. Government's statement of 26 February
this year on the most-favored-nation status, the Romanian news
agency Agerpres has been empowered to state the following:

The SR of Romania has always made efforts to develop economic
and scientific-technical relations of cooperation with all states, irrespective of social system and without any kind of conditions, on the
basis of the principles of full equality of rights, respect for national
independence and sovereignty, noninterference in domestic affairs,
and mutual advantage in conformity with the unanimously recognized international norms and with the provisions of the General
Agreement on Tariffs and Trade—GATT.

In this spirit, Romania has promoted a policy of expanding and
diversifying its economic and trade relations with the United States
of America as well. These relations have been based on the agreements concluded and the accords signed by the governments of the
two countries. Under an agreement on trade relations between the
SR of Romania and the United States of America concluded on 2 April
1975, Romania and the United States of America granted each other
most-favored-nation status.

Romania has completely fulfilled its obligations under this agreement and has worked to constantly develop relations between the
two countries. Conversely, the United States of America—invoking
the unilaterally adopted Jackson-Vanik Amendment—made the
annual granting of this status contingent upon a number of political
demands, a procedure which is an unacceptable interference in
Romania's domestic affairs and is by no means linked to the trade
relations between Romania and the United States of America.

Moreover, certain hostile circles opposing the development of Romanian-American relations used the annual renewal of this status as a means to slander and interfere in Romania's domestic affairs. Thus, the discussions about the status turned into an impediment in promoting bilateral relations.

The Romanian Government has repeatedly drawn the U.S. Government's attention to the fact that Romania will no longer tolerate such an approach to relations between the two countries, which constitutes a violation of the principles and norms of international relations, of the trade accord, and is at variance with GATT regulations to which both countries are contracting sides.

Taking account of this situation, Romania has informed the U.S. Government that it no longer accepts the renewal of the status subject to the terms of the Jackson-Vanik Amendment and has requested that talks should open on developing economic relations in conformity with the provisions of the existing trade accord by ruling out any kind of conditions.

Before bilateral consultations were held to clarify problems linked to the granting of the most-favored-nation status and to further developing economic relations, the U.S. Government issued a statement on 26 February this year announcing that beginning 3 July this year Romania's most-favored-nation status will expire, that customs duties and tariffs will be increased, and that other economic-financial measures will be adopted in its relations with Romania.

In view of the measures announced by the United States of America, the Romanian Government once again states that it does not wish to have the most-favored-nation status subject to the Jackson-Vanik Amendment and that, in turn, it will examine the problem of applying this status granted to the United States of America, the customs duties and tariffs, and other facilities deriving thereof for U.S. imports to Romania.

The Romanian Government believes that it is necessary for the representatives of the two countrties to meet as soon as possible to discuss ways and means to develop trade exchanges and economic cooperation between the two countries in the future.

The SR of Romania will continue to act to develop Romanian-American economic relations on the basis of the generally recognized principles of international law, equality of rights, and mutual advantage. Romania expresses its conviction that the United States of America will show constructive spirit of cooperation and collaboration that will permit the sides to seek solutions designed to eliminate any kind of obstacles in the road of developing the traditional Romanian-American relations to the benefit of the two countries and peoples, of the cause of peace and international cooperation.

APPENDIX 10

U.S.–Romanian Trade, 1974–1990
in millions of U.S. dollars

Year	U.S. Exports	U.S. Imports	Trade Balance	Total
1974	277.1	130.5	146.6	407.6
1975	189.3	133.0	56.3	322.3
1976	249.0	198.8	50.2	447.8
1977	259.4	233.3	26.1	492.7
1978	317.4	346.6	-29.2	664.0
1979	500.5	329.3	171.2	829.8
1980	720.2	312.2	408.0	1032.4
1981	503.9	611.6	-107.7	1115.5
1982	223.2	370.2	-147.0	593.4
1983	185.7	552.8	-367.1	738.5
1984	246.2	973.6	-727.4	1219.8
1985	206.5	949.7	-743.2	1156.2
1986	251.0	754.0	-503.0	1005.0
1987	193.0	715.0	-522.0	908.0
1988	202.0	681.0	-479.0	883.0
1989	156.0	654.0	-498.0	810.0
1990	369.0	231.0	138.0	600.0

Source: U.S. Department of Commerce, Bureau of the Census, *U.S.–Romanian Trade* (Washington, DC: U.S. Government Printing Office, March 1986); and idem, *Statistical Abstract of the United States: 1991,* 111th ed. (Washington, DC: U.S. Government Printing Office, 1991), p. 808

APPENDIX 11

ROMANIAN EMIGRATION TO THE UNITED STATES, ISRAEL, AND WEST GERMANY DURING THE PERIOD OF MFN, 1975–1988

Year	United States	Israel	West Germany	Total
1975	890	2,000	4,085	6,975
1976	1,021	1,989	2,720	5,730
1977	1,240	1,334	9,237	11,811
1978	1,666	1,140	9,827	12,633
1979	1,552	976	7,957	10,485
1980	2,886	1,061	12,946	16,893
1981	2,352	1,012	8,619	11,983
1982	2,381	1,474	11,546	15,401
1983	3,499	1,331	13,957	18,787
1984	4,545	1,908	14,831	21,284
1985	2,913	1,330	13,071	17,314
1986	1,996	1,282	11,944	15,222
1987	2,670	1,634	12,239	16,543
1988*	730	606	5,961	7,297

Source: The figures represent immigrant visas issued by the respective embassies in Bucharest in the calendar year indicated and reported by the Department of State to the Congress each year.

* U.S. embassy figures for six months until the end of MFN on July 3, 1988.

Notes

CHAPTER 1.
SETTING THE STAGE

1. "Statement of the Position of the Romanian Workers' Party on the Problems of the International Communist Working Class Movement," *Scinteia,* April 26, 1964, p. 1.

2. Agerpres, June 15, 1964; U.S. Senate, Committee on Foreign Relations, *Background Documents on East-West Trade,* 89th Cong., 1st Sess., 1965, p. 280.

3. "Joint Statement on Economic, Industrial, and Technological Cooperation between the United States and Romania," signed by presidents Nicolae Ceauşescu and Richard Nixon, December 5, 1973, *Public Papers of Presidents of the United States: Richard Nixon,* 1973 (Washington, D.C.: U.S. Government Printing Office, 1971–1975), p. 1000.

4. Appendix 10 contains a table showing U.S.-Romanian bilateral trade from 1974 to 1990, compiled by the authors from U.S. Department of Commerce, Bureau of the Census, *U.S.-Romanian Trade* (Washington, D.C.: U.S. Government Printing Office, March 1986), and idem, *Statistical Abstract of the United States: 1991*, 111th Edition (Washington, D.C.: U.S. Government Printing Office, 1991), p. 808.

5. U.S. Senate/U.S. House of Representatives, Committee on Foreign Relations/Committee on Foreign Affairs, *Legislation on Foreign Relations Through 1984,* S.Prt. 99-12, vol. 2 (Washington, D.C.: U.S. Government Printing Office, April 1985), pp. 67–71.

6. "Joint Statement of Principles," signed by Presidents Nicolae Ceauşescu and Richard M. Nixon on December 5, 1973, *Public Papers of Presidents of the United States: Richard Nixon,* 1973, p. 998.

7. See table on U.S.-Romanian trade in Appendix 10.

8. Appendix 11 contains a table showing emigration from Romania to the United States, Israel, and West Germany, 1975–1988, compiled by the

authors from the annual submissions from the President to the Congress "Concerning Extension of Waiver Authority" on MFN for Romania.

9. U.S. House of Representatives, Committee on Ways and Means, Subcommittee on Trade, *Background Material on the Generalized System of Preferences,* 94th Cong., 2nd Sess., 1976, pp. 72–73.

10. Robert L. Hutchings, *Soviet–East European Relations: Consolidation and Conflict, 1968–80* (Madison, Wis.: University of Wisconsin Press, 1983).

11. "Education Repayment Decree No. 402, October 22, 1982," *Scinteia,* November 6, 1982, p. 5.

12. *Public Papers of the Presidents of the United States: Ronald Reagan,* 1983 (Washington, D.C.: U.S. Government Printing Office, 1982–1989), p. 329.

13. Ibid., pp. 817–18.

14. George Bush, "U.S. Policy toward Central and Eastern Europe," Speech in Vienna, Austria, September 21, 1983, *Department of State Bulletin,* November 1983, p. 22.

15. *Public Papers of the Presidents of the United States: Ronald Reagan,* 1984, pp. 769–70.

16. See table in Appendix 10.

17. U.S. House of Representatives, Committee on Ways and Means, *Trade Legislation Enacted into Public Law, 1981 through 1988,* 101st Cong., 1st Sess., 1989, p. 130.

18. "Envoy Questions, Faults Policy," *Washington Post,* May 15, 1985, pp. A1, A28.

19. *Congressional Record,* 99th Cong., 1st Sess., 1985, CXXXI, S9222.

20. U.S. House of Representatives, Committee on Ways and Means, Subcommittee on Trade, *Most-Favored-Nation Status for the Socialist Republic of Romania, the Hungarian People's Republic, and the People's Republic of China,* 99th Cong., 2nd Sess., June 10, 1986, pp. 11ff.

21. U.S. Senate, Committee on Finance, Hearing before the Subcommittee on International Trade, *MFN Status for Hungary, Romania, China, and Afghanistan,* 99th Cong., 1st Sess., 1985, p. 54.

22. U.S. Senate, Committee on Finance, Hearing before the Subcommittee on International Trade, *MFN Status for Romania,* 99th Cong., 2nd Sess., 1986, pp. 200–202.

CHAPTER 2.
THE CAST OF CHARACTERS AND THE FIRST ACT, 1985

23. Decision of the Romanian Supreme Court of April 20, 1992, *Romania Libera,* April 21, 1992, p. 1; Foreign Broadcast Information Service (hereafter FBIS), *Daily Report: East Europe,* 94–059, March 28, 1994, Romania, p. 24.

24. U.S. House of the Representatives, Committee on Ways and Means, Subcommittee on Trade, *Most Favored Nation Status for the Socialist Republic of Romania (1986),* pp. 11ff.

25. *Congressional Record,* 99th Cong., 1st Sess., November 1, 1985, CXXXI, S14684–88.

26. Ibid., S30241–42.

27. *Scinteia,* November 14, 1985, p. 1.

28. Edward Behr, *Kiss the Hand You Cannot Bite: The Rise and Fall of the Ceauşescus* (New York: Villard, 1991), p. 56.

29. Ibid., pp. 119–21.

30. Ibid., p. 121.

31. Ibid., pp. 66–67, 119.

32. Ibid., p. 140.

33. Raceanu's translation of transcript of December 26, 1989, Romanian television transmission of the trial of Nicolae and Elena Ceauşescu, December 25, 1989.

34. For other examples of Elena Ceauşescu's shopping in the United States, see comments by " Mircea Codreanu," actually Mircea Raceanu, in Behr, *Kiss the Hand You Cannot Bite,* pp. 162, 183, 184.

35. Herodotus, *The Persian Wars,* Book IV, 93, trans. by George Rawlinson (New York: Random House, 1942), p. 328.

CHAPTER 3.
SHULTZ TACKLES CEAUŞESCU DIRECTLY, 1985

36. The text of the December 6, 1985, letter from President Ronald Reagan to President Nicolae Ceauşescu is in Appendix 1.

37. George P. Shultz, *Turmoil and Triumph: My Years as Secretary of State* (New York: Charles Scribner's Sons, 1993), p. 693.

38. *Scinteia,* December 16, 1985.

39. *New York Times,* December 16, 1985.

40. *Scinteia,* December 16, 1985.

41. The text of the January 7, 1986, letter from President Nicolae Ceauşescu to President Ronald Reagan is in Appendix 2.

42. Decision of the Romanian Supreme Court of April 20, 1992, *Romania Libera,* April 21, 1992, p. 1; FBIS, *Daily Report: East Europe,* 94–059, March 28, 1994, Romania, p. 24.

43. Interview with S. Andon and G. Roveli, *Romania Libera,* January 26, 1990, pp. 1, 3.

44. Sentence of Romanian Military Court, Bucharest, Romania, February 2, 1990, *Romania Libera,* February 3, 1990, p. 1.

CHAPTER 4.
HUMAN RIGHTS TAKE CENTER STAGE, 1986

45. Dr. Moses Rosen, *Primejdii, Incercari, Miracole* (Dangers, Trials, Miracles) (Bucharest: Publishing House Hasefer, 1991), p. 335.

46. U.S. Department of State, *Country Reports on Human Rights Practices for 1985* (Washington, D.C.: U.S. Government Printing Office, 1986), pp. 1075–87, and *Country Reports on Human Rights Practices for 1986* (Washington, D.C.: U.S. Government Printing Office, 1987), pp. 1012–24.

47. U.S. Senate, Committee on Foreign Relations, Subcommittee on European Affairs, *Romania: Most Favored Nation Status,* Hearing, 99th Cong., 2nd Sess., February 26, 1986, pp. 102–6.

48. Senate Resolution 372, *Congressional Record,* 99th Cong., 2nd Sess., 1986, CXXXIII, S3730–31.

49. *Romania Libera,* January 25, 1990, p. 2.

50. U.S. House of Representatives, Committee on Ways and Means, Subcommittee on Trade, *Most Favored Nation Trading Status for the Socialist Republic of Romania (1986),* p. 191.

51. U.S. Department of State, *Report to Congress on Voting Practices in the United Nations,* June 6, 1986.

52. U.S. Senate, Committee on Foreign Relations, Subcommittee on European Affairs, *Romania: Most Favored Nation Status,* p. 112.

53. *Public Papers of the Presidents of the United States: Ronald Reagan,* 1986, I, p. 713.

54. The text of the June 3, 1986, letter from Ronald Reagan to Nicolae Ceauşescu is in Appendix 3.

55. U.S. House of Representatives, Committee on Ways and Means, Subcommittee on Trade, *Most Favored Nation Status for the Socialist Republic of Romania,* p. 59.

56. U.S. Senate, Committee on Finance, Subcommittee on International Trade, *MFN Status for Romania,* pp. 41ff.

57. *Congressional Record,* 99th Cong., 2nd Sess., 1986, CXXXII, H4973.

CHAPTER 5.
WHITEHEAD TRIES TO MAKE A NEW START, 1986

58. Larry Pressler, *A Visit to Eastern Europe in the Wake of the 27th Party Congress and the Chernobyl Nuclear Accident (Czechoslovakia, Hungary, Yugoslavia and Romania),* Report to the Committee on Foreign Relations, U.S. Senate (Washington, D.C.: Government Printing Office, February 1987), p. 49.

59. Raceanu's translation of tape of December 26, 1989, Romanian television transmission of the December 25, 1989, trial of Nicolae and Elena Ceauşescu.

60. Speech by Nicolae Ceauşescu to the XIVth Congress of the Romanian Communist Party, Agerpres, November 20, 1989; FBIS, *Daily Report: East Europe* 89-224, November 22, 1989, pp. 58–84; *Scinteia,* November 23, 24, 1989.

61. Raceanu's translation of tape of December 26, 1989, Romanian television transmission.

62. *Scinteia,* August 15, 1986.

63. "Report of the Romanian Senate Commission on the Events of December 1989," *Adevarul,* May 11, 1992, p. 3.

64. David Binder, "The Cult of Ceauşescu," *New York Times,* November 30, 1986, VI, pp. 32ff.

65. The U.S. embassy in Bucharest obtained a copy of the decree some months after it was promulgated and summarized it in a confidential telegram to Washington.

66. Shultz, *Turmoil and Triumph,* p. 694.

67. *Expres* (Bucharest) magazine, no. 13, 1991, p. 7; *Time,* May 4, 1992; *Cotidianul,* April 21, 1992; *Tinerama,* April 24–30, 1992, p. 5.

68. A table on U.S.-Romanian trade, 1974–1990, is in Appendix 10.

69. *Scinteia,* November 15, 1986.

CHAPTER 6.
FRICTIONS MOUNT, 1987

70. U.S. House of Representatives, Committee on Ways and Means, *Trade Legislation Enacted into Public Law, 1981 through 1988,* 101st Cong., 1st Sess., 1988, Committee Print, January 27, 1989, p. 130.

71. U.S. House of Representatives, *Communication from the President of the United States: Removal of Romania and Nicaragua and Suspension of*

Paraguay from the List of Generalized System of Preferences Eligible Countries, House Document No. 100-18, January 8, 1987, 100th Cong., 1st Sess., p. 1.

72. Testimony of Joseph Dennin, Assistant Secretary of Commerce for International Economic Policy, Senate Committee on Foreign Relations, Subcommittee on European Affairs, *Hearing,* 99th Cong., 2nd Sess., February 26, 1986, pp. 236–38.

73. The text of the January 23, 1987, letter from Secretary of State George Shultz to Foreign Minister Ioan Totu is in Appendix 4.

74. *Scinteia,* January 31, 1987, and "Ceauşescu Rejects Soviet-Style Reform, Enforces Austerity Policy," *Radio Free Europe Research,* vol. 12, no. 5, Munich, February 6, 1987, pp. 3–6.

75. The text of the March 28, 1987, message from Secretary of State George Shultz to President Nicolae Ceauşescu is in Appendix 5.

76. "Official Communiqué on Referendum Results," Agerpres, November 24, 1986; FBIS, *Daily Report: East Europe* II, November 25, 1986, Romania H1.

77. FBIS, *Daily Report: East Europe,* April 17, 1987, Romania H1.

78. *Congressional Record,* 100th Cong., 1st Sess., 1987, CXXXIII, E936.

79. Interview of Totu by Marilena Tutila, *Romania Mare,* September 27, 1991, pp. 8–9.

80. *Congressional Record,* 100th Cong., 1st Sess., 1987, CXXXIII, H2867-68.

CHAPTER 7.
BACK FROM THE BRINK, 1987

81. *Extension of Waiver Authority under the Trade Act of 1984: Message from the President of the United States, June 2, 1987* (Washington, D.C.: U.S. Government Printing Office, 1987); *Department of State Bulletin,* August, 1987, p. 57.

82. *Washington City Paper,* vol. 11, no. 19, May 10–16, 1991, pp. 26–28.

83. *Congressional Record,* 100th Cong., 1st Sess., 1987, CXXXIII, S8810–11.

84. Agerpres, June 27, 1987; FBIS, *Daily Report: East Europe,* June 29, 1987, p. R1.

85. *Wall Street Journal,* July 22, 1987, pp. 3, 10.

86. U.S. House of Representatives, Committee on Foreign Affairs, Subcommittee on Europe and the Middle East, *United States-Romanian Relations and Most-Favored-Nation Status for Romania,* 100th Cong., 1st Sess., July 30, 1987, pp. 23–25, 49.

CHAPTER 8.
PRESSURES HIT THE DANGER POINT, 1987

87. Ion Mihai Pacepa, *Red Horizons: Chronicles of a Communist Spy Chief* (Washington, DC: Regnery Gateway, 1987).

88. Decree on "Measures to Rationalize Energy Consumption," Agerpres, November 11, 1987; FBIS, *Daily Report: East Europe* 87-218, November 12, 1987, p. 22.

89. "Communiqué of the State Council of Romania Regarding Results of the Election," Agerpres, November 16, 1987; FBIS, *Daily Report: East Europe* 87-221, November 17, 1987, Romania, p. 52.

90. *Eastern European Newsletter,* vol. I, no. 13, November 28, 1987, p. 2.

91. *Lumea Libera,* No. 215, November 14, 1992, pp. 1, 28.

92. Quotations drawn from Embassy Bucharest's translation of Brucan's statement.

93. *Scinteia,* January 3, 1945, and *Scinteia,* nos. 789, 823, and 861, all in the period March–June 1947.

94. *Washington Post,* November 13, 1987, p. A10.

CHAPTER 9.
RUPTURE, 1988

95. *Zig-Zag,* October 2–8, 1990, p. 3.

96. *Department of State Bulletin,* May 1988, p. 55.

97. FBIS, *Daily Report: East Europe* 88-025, February 8, Romania, p. H1.

98. A table showing emigration to the United States, Israel, and West Germany, 1975–1988, is in Appendix 11.

99. The text of the January 26, 1988, letter from President Ronald Reagan to President Nicolae Ceauşescu is in Appendix 6.

100. Raceanu's translation of Romanian television's December 26, 1989, transmission of the trial of Nicolae and Elena Ceauşescu, December 25, 1989.

101. Questions from embassy telegraphic transcript. For similar remarks by Deputy Secretary Whitehead in the United States after his visit, see "John Whitehead: Address before the International Human Rights Forum in New York City on February 26, 1988," in *Department of State Bulletin,* May 1988, pp. 54–55.

102. The text of the State Department's translation of the February 12, 1988, letter from President Nicolae Ceauşescu to President Ronald Reagan is in Appendix 7.

CHAPTER 10.
DIALOGUE OF THE DEAF, 1988

103. Pompiliu Verzariu, Jr., and Jay A. Burgess, *Joint Venture Agreements in Romania: Background for Implementation,* U.S. Department of Commerce, June 1977, pp. 42–49.

104. The text of the February 26, 1988, Department of State statement, "Romania Renounces MFN Renewal," *Department of State Bulletin,* May 1988, p. 43, is in Appendix 8.

105. The text of the February 27, 1988, Romanian Agerpres "Statement on the Economic Relations of the Socialist Republic of Romania with the

United States of America," FBIS, *Daily Report: East Europe* 88-039, February 29, 1988, is in Appendix 9.

106. General Agreement on Tariffs and Trade, signed at Geneva, October 30, 1947; Edmond McGovern, *International Trade Regulation: GATT, the United States, and the European Community* (Exeter, U.K.: Global Field Press, 1986), pp. 543–99.

107. McGovern, *International Trade Regulation,* pp. 543–99.

108. U.S. Department of State, *List of Treaties and Other International Agreements in Force on January 1, 1992,* (Washington, DC: U.S. Government Printing Office, 1992), p. 326.

109. U.S. Senate, U.S. House of Representatives, *Legislation on Foreign Relations through 1984,* pp. 67–71.

110. Speech by President Nicolae Ceauşescu, May 4, 1988 (FBIS, *Daily Report: East Europe,* 88-088, May 6, 1988).

111. *Weekly Compilation of Presidential Documents,* vol. 24, no. 23, June 3, 1988, p. 748.

112. *Weekly Compilation of Presidential Documents,* vol. 24, no. 26, June 28, 1988, pp. 877–78.

CHAPTER 11.
FROM BAD TO WORSE, 1988

113. Dinu C. Giurescu, *The Razing of Romania's Past,* International Preservation Report (New York: World Monuments Fund, 1989), pp. 47–50; and *Ceauşescu Becomes Romania's Planner,* Radio Free Europe Research (Munich), vol. 13, March 31, 1988, pp. 7–9.

114. *Scinteia,* June 29, 1988; see also *Facts on File,* vol. 48, no. 2484, July 1, 1988, p. 482.

115. *Scinteia,* May 14, 1988, p. 1.

116. U.S. Senate, *Legislative Activities Report of the Committee on Foreign Relations, January 6, 1987–October 21, 1988,* 100th Cong., 2nd Sess., 1988, p. 86.

117. U.S. House of Representatives, Report 100-922, *Amending the Foreign Assistance Act of 1961 with Respect to the Activities of OPIC,* 100th Cong., 2nd Sess., 1988, p. 7; U.S. Senate, Report 100-500, *Miscellaneous International Authorization Acts of 1988,* 100th Cong., 2nd Sess., 1988, p. 7.

118. Text from the U.S. Embassy Bucharest telegram transmitting Whitehead press conference transcript, October 10, 1988.

119. "Speech by Nicolae Ceauşescu at the Central Committee of the Romanian Communist Party on November 28, 1988," *Facts on File,* vol. 48, no. 2508, December 16, 1988, p. 937.

CHAPTER 12.
THE LAST ACT, 1989

120. "Romania Balks," *Facts on File,* vol. 49, no. 2513, January 20, 1989, p. 26.

121. "Chronology 1989," *Foreign Affairs,* vol. 69, no. 1, p. 230; *Congressional Record,* 101st Cong., 1st Sess., 1989, CXXXV, E554.

122. On November 19, 1988, the Romanian government expelled Karoly Gyoerfy, a counselor of the Hungarian embassy in Bucharest, on the grounds that he had disseminated leaflets slandering Romania and its leadership. On November 24, the Hungarian authorities retaliated by expelling Pavel Platona, a counselor of the Romanian embassy in Budapest. *Facts on File,* vol. 28, no. 2407, December 9, 1988, p. 919.

123. *Congressional Record,* 101st Cong., 1st Sess., 1989, CXXXV, E780, 1859.

124. *Scinteia,* January 27, 1989.

125. U.S. embassy translation.

126. "Communiqué of the Prosecutor General of the Socialist Republic of Romania," *Scinteia,* March 14, 1989, p. 3.

127. *Romania Libera,* January 21 (p. 2), 25 (p. 2), 26 (p. 2), and 28 (p. 2), 1990.

128. *New York Times,* June 30, 1993, p. A5.

129. *Evenimentul Zile,* July 3, 1993, p. 1.

130. *Facts on File,* vol. 49, no. 2526, April 21, 1989, p. 291.

131. *Filaret Press,* June 29, 1989, p. 6.

132. *Scinteia,* July 8, 1989; and *Facts on File,* vol. 49, no. 2538, July 14, 1989, p. 520.

133. Representatives Tony Hall of Ohio, Christopher Smith of New Jersey, and Frank Wolf of Virginia introduced H.R. 2765 on June 27, 1989, to prohibit the import of wine, cheese, meat, and other agricultural products from Romania (*Congressional Record,* 101st Cong., 1st Sess., 1989, CXXXV, H3257). Senator Claiborne Pell proposed on July 19, 1989, and the Senate later adopted, a Sense of the Senate amendment to the Foreign Relations Authorization Act of 1990, similar in content to the resolution passed by the House (*Congressional Record,* 101st Cong., 1st Sess., 1989, CXXXV, S8215).

134. *Adevarul de Duminica,* February 18, 1990, p. 2

135. FBIS, *Daily Report: East Europe,* 89-224, November 22, 1989, Romania, pp. 58-84; *Facts on File,* vol. 49, no. 2558, December 1, 1989, p. 895.

136. *Scinteia,* December 21, 1989, p. 1; *Facts on File,* vol. 49, no. 2562, December 31, 1989, p. 957.

137. Raceanu's translation of Romanian television transmission of the trial of Nicolae and Elena Ceaușescu, December 25, 1989.

CHAPTER 13.
EPILOGUE: SOME LESSONS

138. "Ştefan Andrei: Last Word," *Europa,* July 1991, 2nd year, no. 33, pp. 6, 7; Ştefan Andrei's article in *Vremea,* May 1, 1993, pp. 1, 2.

Bibliography

A principal source for the material in the foregoing pages is the personal experience of Kirk and/or Raceanu, who participated in most of the activities and meetings described. In addition, Kirk had access, in preparing the manuscript, to the communications the U.S. embassy in Bucharest sent to Washington and other U.S. diplomatic missions, and those the embassy received from them, during the period covered. Even though most of these communications remain classified, the Department of State reviewed the resulting manuscript, determined that it did not damage national security, and therefore interposed no objection to its publication. Another principal source for the material in this book is Raceanu's personal records of his activities as acting deputy director of the Americas directorate at the Romanian Foreign Ministry during the period covered.

In addition, the authors consulted a number of published works. Following is a partial list of the materials consulted. Most had only a few pages on the period focused on in this book, but many included useful background material or analysis.

BOOKS

Amnesty International. *Romania: Human Rights Violations in the Eighties.* London: Amnesty International, 1987.

Bachman, Ronald D. *Romania: A Country Study.* Washington, D.C.: Federal Research Division, Library of Congress, 1989.

Bauman, Michael, ed. *Man and Marxism: Religion and the Communist Retreat.* Hillsdale, Mich.: Hillsdale College Press, 1991.

Behr, Edward. *Kiss the Hand You Cannot Bite: The Rise and Fall of the Ceauşescus.* New York: Villard, 1991.

Brown, Aurel, ed. *The Soviet–East European Relationship in the Gorbachev Era.* Boulder, Col.: Westview Press, 1990.

Brown, J. F. *Eastern Europe and Communist Rule.* Durham, N.C.: Duke University Press, 1988.

Brzezinski, Zbiginew. *The Grand Failure: The Birth and Death of Communism in the Twentieth Century.* New York: Charles Scribner's Sons, 1989.

Byrnes, Robert F. *U.S. Policy toward Eastern Europe and the Soviet Union.* Boulder, Col.: Westview Press, 1989.

Ceauşescu, Nicolae. *An Independent Policy for Peace and Cooperation: A Selection of Speeches.* Edited by Edward J. Van Kloberg, III. Washington, D.C.: Political Science Library, 1987.

———. *Romania on the Way of Building Up the Multilaterally Developed Socialist Society.* 32 volumes. Bucharest: Meridiane, 1970–1989.

Cox, Philip S., ed. *Sources of Human Rights Violations in Romania.* Washington, D.C.: American Foreign Policy Institute, 1986.

Crowther, William E. *The Political Economy of Romanian Socialism.* New York: Praeger, 1988.

Dawisha, Karen. *Eastern Europe, Gorbachev, and Reform: The Great Challenge.* New York: Cambridge University Press, 1990.

De Nevers, Renee. *The Soviet Union and Eastern Europe: The End of an Era.* London: IISS Adelphi Papers No. 249, 1990.

Echikson, William. *Lighting the Night: Revolution in Eastern Europe.* New York: William Morrow & Co., 1990.

Eyal, Jonathan. *The Warsaw Pact and the Balkans: Moscow's Southern Flank.* Basingstoke: Macmillan, 1989.

Fischer, Mary Ellen. *Nicolae Ceauşescu: A Study in Political Leadership.* Boulder, Col.: Lynne Reinner, 1989.

Forsythe, David P. *Human Rights and U.S. Foreign Policy: Congress Reconsidered.* Gainesville, Fla.: University Presses of Florida, 1988.

Frankland, Mark. *The Patriots' Revolution: How Eastern Europe Toppled Communism and Won Its Freedom.* Chicago, Ill.: Ivan R. Dee, 1992.

Funderburk, David B. *Pinstripes and Reds: An American Ambassador Caught between the State Department and the Romanian Communists, 1981–1985.* Washington, D.C.: Selous Foundation, 1987.

Gaddis, John Lewis. *The Long Peace: Inquiries into the History of the Cold War.* New York: Oxford University Press, 1987.

Gati, Charles. *The Bloc That Failed: Soviet–East European Relations in Transition.* Bloomington, Ind.: Indiana University Press, 1990.

Georgescu, Vlad, ed. *Romania, Forty Years (1944–1984).* Washington Papers, no. 115. New York: Praeger, 1985.

Giurescu, Dinu C. *Illustrated History of the Romanian People.* Bucharest: Editura Sport-Turism, 1984.

———. *The Razing of Romania's Past.* New York: World Monuments Fund, 1989.

Glenny, Misha. *The Rebirth of History: Eastern Europe in the Age of Democracy.* London: Penguin, 1990.

Gordon, Lincoln, et al. *Eroding Empire: Western Relations with Eastern Europe.* Washington, D.C.: Brookings Institution, 1988.

Griffith, William E., ed. *Central and Eastern Europe: The Opening Curtain?* Boulder, Col.: Westview Press, 1989.

Gwertzman, Bernard, and Michael T. Kaufman, eds. *The Collapse of Communism.* New York: The New York Times Company, 1991.

Harrington, Joseph F., and Bruce J. Courtney. *Tweaking the Nose of the Russians: Fifty Years of American-Romanian Relations, 1940–90.* Boulder, Col.: East European Monographs, 1991. Distributed by Columbia University Press, New York.

Hitchings, Thomas E., ed. *Facts on File: World News Digest with Index.* New York: Facts on File, Inc., 1983–1989.

Hutchings, Robert L. *Soviet–East European Relations: Consolidation and Conflict, 1968–80.* Madison, Wis.: University of Wisconsin Press, 1983.

Hyland, William G. *The Cold War: Fifty Years of Conflict.* New York: Random House, 1991.

Iorga, Nicolae. *History of Romania: Land, People, and Civilization.* New York: Ames Press, 1964.

Jowitt, Kenneth. *New World Disorder: The Leninist Extinction.* Berkeley: University of California Press, 1992.

———. *Revolutionary Breakthroughs and National Development: The Case of Romania, 1944–65.* Berkeley: University of California Press, 1971.

Kissinger, Henry. *White House Years.* Boston: Little, Brown & Co., 1979.

Kovrig, Bennett. *Of Walls and Bridges: The United States and Eastern Europe.* New York: New York University Press, 1991.

Linden, Ronald H. *Communist States and International Change: Romania and Yugoslavia in Comparative Perspective.* Boston: Allen & Unwin, 1987.

Long, William J. *U. S. Export Control Policy: Executive Autonomy vs. Congressional Reform.* New York: Columbia University Press, 1989.

Mastny, Vojtech. *Helsinki, Human Rights, and European Security: Analysis and Documentation.* Durham, N.C.: Duke University Press, 1986.

McGovern, Edmond. *International Trade Regulation: GATT, the United States, and the European Community.* Exeter, U.K.: Global Field Press, 1986.

Miller, Robert Hopkins. *Inside an Embassy: The Political Role of Diplomats Abroad.* An Institute for the Study of Diplomacy Book. Washington, D.C.: Congressional Quarterly Books, 1992.

Nelson, Daniel N. *Alliance Behavior in the Warsaw Pact.* Boulder, Col.: Westview Press, 1986.

———. *Balkan Imbroglio: Politics and Security in Southeastern Europe.* Boulder, Col.: Westview Press, 1991.

———. *Romanian Politics in the Ceauşescu Era.* New York: Gordon and Breach Science Publishers, 1988.

Newsom, David D., ed. *The Diplomacy of Human Rights.* Washington, D.C.: Institute for the Study of Diplomacy, Georgetown University, and University Press of America, 1986.

Nixon, Richard M. *The Memoirs of Richard Nixon.* Volume 1. New York: Warner Books, 1978.

Otetea, Andrei. *The History of the Romanian People.* New York: Twayne, 1970.

Pacepa, Ion Mihai. *Red Horizons: Chronicles of a Communist Spy Chief.* Washington, D.C.: Regnery Gateway, 1987.

Plowman, Edward E. *From China to El Salvador to Romania: How Religion Is Faring around the World.* Hillsdale, Mich.: Hillsdale College Press, 1991.

Prins, Gwyn, ed. *Spring in Winter: The 1989 Revolutions.* Manchester: Manchester University Press, 1990.

Public Papers of the Presidents of the United States: Richard M. Nixon (1969–1974). 6 volumes. Washington, D.C.: U.S. Government Printing Office, 1971–1975.

Public Papers of the Presidents of the United States: Ronald Reagan, (1981–1987). 12 volumes. Washington, D.C.: U.S. Government Printing Office, 1982–1989.

Quinlan, Paul D. *The United States and Romania: American-Romanian Relations in the Twentieth Century.* Vol. 6. ARA Publications. Los Angeles: American-Romanian Academy of Arts and Sciences, 1988.

Romanian Communist Party. *Directives of the 13th Congress of the Romanian Communist Party on the Economic and Social Development of Romania during the Five Years 1981–1985, and Future Guidelines up to 1990.* Bucharest: Editura Politica, 1979.

Rosen, Dr. Moses. *Primejdii, Incercari, Miracole* (Dangers, Trials, Miracles). Bucharest: Publishing House Hasefer, 1991.

Shafir, Michael. *Romania: Politics, Economics, and Society—Political Stagnation and Simulated Change.* Boulder, Col.: Lynne Rienner, 1985.

Shultz, George P. *Turmoil and Triumph: My Years as Secretary of State.* New York: Charles Scribner's Sons, 1993.

Sloss, Leon, and M. Scott Davis, eds. *Game for High Stakes: Lessons Learned in Negotiating with the Soviet Union.* Cambridge, Mass.: Ballinger, 1986.

Spero, Joan Edelman. *The Politics of International Economic Relations.* 4th ed. New York: St. Martin's Press, 1990.

Starr, Richard F. *Communist Regimes in Eastern Europe.* 5th ed. Stanford, Cal.: Hoover Institution Press, 1988.

———. *East-Central Europe and the USSR.* New York: St. Martin's Press, 1991.

Starr, Richard F., ed. *United States-Eastern European Relations in the 1990s.* New York: Crane Russak, 1989.

Tismaneanu, Vladimir. *The Crisis of Marxist Ideology in Eastern Europe: The Poverty of Utopia.* London: Routledge, 1988.

———. *Reinventing Politics: Eastern Europe from Stalin to Havel.* New York: Free Press, Macmillan, 1992.

Tismaneanu, Vladmir, ed. *Uprooting Leninism, Cultivating Liberty.* New York: Free Press, 1992.

Tismaneanu, Vladimir, and Judith Shapiro, eds. *Debates on the Future of Communism.* New York: St. Martin's Press, 1991.

Vine, Richard D., ed. *Soviet–East European Relations as a Problem for the West.* London: Croom Helm, 1987.

Weiner, Robert. *Romanian Foreign Policy and the United Nations.* New York: Praeger, 1984.

ARTICLES

Fisher, William. "Fighting Change: Romania in the Era of Glasnost." *New Leader* 70 (June 29, 1987): 11–13.

Georgescu, Vlad. "Romania in the 1980s: The Legacy of Dynastic Socialism." *Eastern European Politics and Societies* 2, no. 1 (Winter 1988): 70–93.

Giurescu, Dinu C. "Romania: The Protracted Struggle." *Democracy Bulletin* 2, no. 4 (Winter 1990–1991), 9–10.

Luers, Willam H. "The U.S. and Eastern Europe." *Foreign Affairs* 66, no. 2 (1987): 249–62.

McElwain, Scott. "The United States and Central Europe: Differentiation or Detente?" *East European Quarterly* 21, no. 4 (Winter 1987): 451–68.

Powers, Charles T. "Romania: A Country Slowly Falling Apart." *Human Events* 48 (April 16, 1988): 10–11.

Stevenson, Adlai E., and Alton Frye. "Trading with the Communists." *Foreign Affairs* 68, no. 2 (1989): 53–71.

Whitehead, John C. "The Department of State: Requirements for an Effective Foreign Policy in the 1990s." *Presidential Studies Quarterly* 19, no. 1 (Winter 1989): 11–24.

GOVERNMENT REPORTS AND DOCUMENTS

Administrative Conference of the United States. *Legislative Veto of Agency Rules of the INS vs. Chadha.* Washington, D.C.: U.S. Government Printing Office [hereafter GPO], 1984.

Ceauşescu, Nicolae. *Rapoartul la Congresul al XIII-lea al Partidului Comunist Roman* (Report to the 13th Congress of the Romanian Communist Party). December 1984.

————. *Rapoartul la Congresul al XIV-lea al Partidului Comunist Roman* (Report to the 14th Congress of the Romanian Communist Party). November 1989.

Congressional Record (99th Cong., June–August and October–November, 1985; 99th Cong., February–March and June–August, 1986; 100th Cong., February–April and June–August 1987; 100th Cong., February and June 1988.

Library of Congress, Federal Research Division. *Romania: A Country Study.* July 1989.

Pressler, Larry. *A Visit to Eastern Europe in the Wake of the 27th Party Congress and the Chernobyl Nuclear Accident (Czechoslovakia, Hungary, Yugoslavia and Romania).* Washington, D.C.: GPO, February 1987.

U.S. Commission on Security and Cooperation in Europe. *The State of Human Rights in Romania.* Washington, D.C.: GPO, 1989.

U.S. Congress. *Communication from the President of the United States: Removal of Romania and Nicaragua and Suspension of Paraguay from the List of Generalized System of Preferences Eligible Countries.* Report to the Committee on Ways and Means. 100th Cong., 1st Sess., 1987.

―――. *Communication from the President of the United States: Removal of Romania and Nicaragua and Suspension of Paraguay from the List of Generalized System of Preferences Eligible Countries.* House Document No. 100-18. 100th Cong., 1st Sess., January 8, 1987.

―――. Conference Committee Print. *Summary of the Conference Agreement on H.R. 3: The Omnibus Trade and Competitiveness Act of 1988.* 100th Cong., 2nd Sess., April 19, 1988.

―――. House Committee on Foreign Affairs. *United States-Romanian Relations and Most Favored Nation Status for Romania.* Hearing. 100th Cong., 1st Sess., July 30, 1987.

―――. House Committee on Ways and Means. *Trade Legislation Enacted into Public Law, 1981 through 1988.* 101st Cong., 1st Sess., January 27, 1989.

―――. House of Representatives. *Amending the Foreign Assistance Act of 1961 with Respect to the Activities of OPIC.* Report 100-992. 100th Cong., 2nd Sess., 1988.

―――. *Human Rights in Romania and Its Implications for U.S. Policy and Most Favored Nation Status.* Hearing. 100th Cong., 2nd Sess., June 24, 1987.

―――. Joint Economic Committee. *Slow Growth in the 1980s: Country Studies on Eastern Europe and Yugoslavia.* 99th Cong., 2nd Sess., 1986.

―――. *Legislative Activities Report of the Committee on Foreign Relations, January 6, 1987–October 21, 1988.* 100th Cong., 2nd Sess., 1988.

―――. *MFN Status for Romania.* Hearing. 99th Cong., 2nd Sess., August 1, 1986.

―――. *Miscellaneous International Affairs Authorization Acts of 1988.* 100th Cong., 2nd Sess., 1988. S. Rept. 100-500.

―――. *Most-Favored-Nation Trading Status for the Socialist Republic of Romania, the Hungarian People's Republic, and the People's Republic of China.* Hearing. 99th Cong., 2nd Sess., June 10, 1986.

―――. *Recent Developments in U.S. Human Rights Policy.* Hearings. 100th Cong., 2nd Sess., February 10 and 17, 1988.

―――. *Romania: Most Favored Nation Status.* Hearing. 99th Cong., 2nd Sess., February 26, 1986.

———. Senate. *Comparing Major Trade Bills.* Hearing. 100th Cong., 1st Sess., April 2, 1987.

———. Senate Committee on Finance. Subcommittee on International Trade. *MFN Status for Hungary, Romania, China, and Afghanistan.* Hearing. 99th Cong., 1st Sess., 1985.

———. Senate Committee on Foreign Relations. *Background Documents on East-West Trade.* 89th Cong., 1st Sess., 1965.

———. Subcommittee on European Affairs. *Religious Persecution behind the Iron Curtain.* Hearing. 99th Cong., 1st Sess., November 14, 1985.

———. Subcommittee on International Economic Policy and Trade. *Commercial Lending to the Soviet Bloc.* Hearing. 100th Cong., 1st Sess., November 17, 1987.

———. Subcommittee on Trade. *Background Material on the Generalized System of Preferences.* 94th Cong., 2nd Sess., 1976.

———. *U.S. Goals of Upcoming Consultation with Socialist Republic of Romania.* 97th Cong., 2nd Sess., 1982. S. Rept. 97-552.

———. U.S. Senate/U.S. House of Representatives. Committee on Foreign Relations/Committee on Foreign Affairs. *Legislation on Foreign Relations through 1984.* Vol. II. Joint Committee Print. April 1985.

———. *United States Trade Relations with Eastern Europe and Yugoslavia.* Hearing. 100th Cong., 1st Sess., October 28, 1987.

U.S. Department of Commerce. Bureau of the Census. *Statistical Abstract of the United States: 1991.* 111th ed. Washington. D.C.: GPO, 1991.

———. *U.S.-Romanian Trade.* Washington, D.C.: GPO, March 1986.

U.S. Department of State. *Country Reports on Human Rights Practices for 1984.* Washington, D.C.: GPO, 1985.

———. *Country Reports on Human Rights Practices for 1985.* Washington, D.C.: GPO, February 1986.

———. *Country Reports on Human Rights Practices for 1986.* Washington, D.C.: GPO, February 1987.

———. *Country Reports on Human Rights Practices for 1987.* Washington, D.C.: GPO, February 1988.

———. *Country Reports on Human Rights Practices for 1988.* Washington, D.C.: GPO, February 1989.

———. *Country Reports on Human Rights Practices for 1989.* Washington, D.C.: GPO, February 1990.

———. *Department of State Bulletin.* Washington, D.C.: GPO, 1983–1989.

———. *List of Treaties and Other International Agreements in Force on January 1, 1992.* Washington, D.C.: GPO, 1992.

———. *Report to Congress on Voting Practices in the United Nations.* Washington, D.C.: GPO, June 6, 1986.

Verzariu, Pompiliu, Jr., and Jay A. Burgess. *Joint Venture Agreements in Romania: Background for Implementation.* U.S. Department of Commerce, June 1977.

The Weekly Compilation of Presidential Documents, 1985–1989.

PERIODICALS

The Economist (London), 1985–1989.

Foreign Broadcast Information Service. *Daily Report: East Europe,* 1985–1989.

The New York Times, 1985–1989.

Romania Libera (Free Romania) (daily newspaper), September 1985–December 1989, and April 1992.

Scinteia (The Spark) (daily newspaper), January 1945, and September 1985–December 1989.

The Washington Post, 1985–1989.

Index